DIAL "H" FOR HIT MAN

Death. It's a hell of a way to make a living.

They are perverse. Pitiless. And they all have their price. Driven by simple greed or twisted lust, they shoot, strangle, stab or torch their victims at someone else's order. They are coldhearted killers, and they do it for cold, hard cash.

Now, from the authentic files of *True Detective* magazine, read the chilling true accounts of the most ruthless murders for hire ever reported, committed by HIT MEN like: Michigan's Todd Plamondon, a hustler who killed a john's wife for $5000; Albert Vargas of Los Angeles, who supported a heavy drug habit with murder; and North Carolina's Daniel McMillian, who shot a man six times for a grand total of $900.

WHETHER IT'S A CRIME OF PASSION
OR
A COLD-BLOODED MURDER—
PINNACLE'S GOT THE TRUE STORY!

CRUEL SACRIFICE (884, $4.99)
by Aphrodite Jones

This is a tragic tale of twisted love and insane jealousy, occultism and sadistic ritual killing in small-town America . . . and of the young innocent who paid the ultimate price. One freezing night five teenage girls crowded into a car. By the end of the night, only four of them were alive. One of the most savage crimes in the history of Indiana, the four accused murderers were all girls under the age of eighteen!

BLOOD MONEY (773, $4.99)
by Clifford L. Linedecker

One winter day in Trail Creek, Indiana, seventy-four-year-old Elaine Witte left a Christmas party—and was never heard from again. Local authorities became suspicious when her widowed daughter-in-law, Hilma, and Hilma's two sons gave conflicting stories about her disappearance . . . then fled town. Driven by her insane greed for Witte's social security checks, Hilma had convinced her teenage son to kill his own grandmother with a crossbow, and then he fed her body parts to their dogs!

CONTRACT KILLER (788, $4.99)
by William Hoffman and Lake Headley

He knows where Jimmy Hoffa is buried—and who killed him. He knows who pulled the trigger on Joey Gallo. And now, Donald "Tony the Greek" Frankos—pimp, heroin dealer, loan shark and hit man for the mob—breaks his thirty year oath of silence and tells all. His incredible story reads like a who's who of the Mafia in America. Frankos has killed dozens of people in cold blood for thousands of dollars!

X-RATED (780, $4.99)
by David McCumber

Brothers Jim and Artie Mitchell were the undisputed porn kings of America. Multi-millionaires after such mega-hit flicks as BEHIND THE GREEN DOOR, theirs was a blood bond that survived battles with the mob and the Meese Commission, bitter divorces, and mind-numbing addictions. But their world exploded in tragedy when seemingly mild-mannered Jim gunned down his younger brother in cold blood. This is a riveting tale of a modern day Cain and Abel!

Available wherever paperbacks are sold, or order direct from the Publisher. Send cover price plus 50¢ per copy for mailing and handling to Penguin USA, P.O. Box 999, c/o Dept. 17109, Bergenfield, NJ 07621. Residents of New York and Tennessee must include sales tax. DO NOT SEND CASH.

FROM THE FILES OF TRUE DETECTIVE MAGAZINE

HIT MEN

Edited by ROSE G. MANDELSBERG

PINNACLE BOOKS
WINDSOR PUBLISHING CORP.

*The editor wishes to express
her sincerest thanks and appreciation
to Stan Munro whose tireless research efforts
made this book possible.*

PINNACLE BOOKS are published by

Windsor Publishing Corp.
850 Third Avenue
New York, NY 10022

Copyright © 1981, 1983, 1984, 1985, 1986, 1989, 1990, 1991, 1992, 1993, 1994 by RGH Publishing Corporation. For complete copyright information, see appendix.

All rights reserved. No part of this book may be reproduced in any form or by any means without the prior written consent of the Publisher, excepting brief quotes used in reviews.

If you purchased this book without a cover, you should be aware that this book is stolen property. It was reported as "unsold and destroyed" to the Publisher and neither the Author nor the Publisher has received any payment for this "stripped book."

The P logo Reg U.S. Pat. & TM off. Pinnacle is a trademark of Windsor Publishing Corp.

First Printing: September, 1994

Printed in the United States of America

TABLE OF CONTENTS

CONTENTS

"DIAL 'H' FOR HIT MAN!" by Walt Hecox	7
"FEMME FATALE AND HER BAND OF KILLERS" by Bruce Stockdale	24
"10-G HIT ON PAM!" by Bruce Gibney	51
"KILL ALL THREE AND TORCH THE HOUSE!" by Bill G. Cox	64
"BABY-FACED ANGEL WAS A COLD-BLOODED KILLER!" by Don Lasseter	80
"SENT HER STUD TO SNUFF HER EX!" by Gary C. King	99
"MURDER-FOR-HIRE GOES HAYWIRE: 4 DIE IN VAIN!" by Barbara Geehr	113
"THE HIT MAN STRUCK AT 12 O'CLOCK HIGH" by Michael Litchfield	134
"DIAL-A-DEATH SLAY SCHEMES!" by Terrell Ecker	150
"A TANGLED WEB OF CONTRACT MURDER!" by Olga Kogan	167
"VIXEN'S QUICK-KILL SCHEME" by Bruce Gibney	180
" 'HIT CONTRACT' CLIMAXED THE FAMILY TRAGEDY!" by Bud Ampolsk	193
"SHE TRIED TO KILL FOR HER KID!" by Bill G. Cox	212

"EVIL 'PUPPET MASTER' MADE THE GARDENER DO HIS KILLING!" by John Railey	229
"A LOVE TRIANGLE TRIGGERED THE FREELOADER'S LETHAL SCHEME!" by Gary C. King	242
"THE VICTIM REFUSED TO DIE!" by Tom Basinski	261
"GRISLY CASE OF THE 'GORILLA' HIT MAN" by Walt Hecox	282
"CALIFORNIA'S BIZARRE WEB OF 4-WAY LETHAL SEXCAPADE" by Don Lasseter	299
"A LAWSUIT GOT HIM SHOT IN THE FACE!" by Bruce Gibney	325
"THE COKE DEALER'S BRUTAL HIT MEN" by Bill Kelly	340
"HAVE GUN, WILL MURDER!" by Howard & Mary Stevens	353
"GANGSTER'S MOLL URGED HIT MAN TO KILL" by Philip Westwood	370
"GAY LOVERS' LETHAL PLOT AGAINST SUE ELLEN!" by David Benson	385
"LETHAL COUPLE . . . 3 KNIVES . . . 1 COLD CORPSE!" by Olga Kogan	404
"WHERE THERE'S A WILL, THERE'S A MURDER!" by Jayne Schorn	417
APPENDIX	431

"DIAL 'H' FOR HIT MAN!"

by Walt Hecox

A steady drizzle splashed off the already soaked surface of Correia Road, a sloping levee bank that doubles in brass as a support for the twisting byway and as a sturdy dike that holds White's Slough within its assigned boundaries in California's San Joaquin delta.

It was Saturday morning, a circumstance that may be of even less significance to ranch managers on a rainy day than it is to homicide detectives. Saturday is just another day of the week for each of them with work to be done.

One ranch manager driving a pickup truck saw the small red Toyota parked on the shoulder of the road as he drove west along the top of the delta an hour or so earlier while hurrying to a fence washout created by the eternal rain. At the time, he had noticed that there were no fishermen standing on the riverbank and wondered why, if there were none, the car was parked there.

When the little automobile was still there on his return, the ranch manager stopped to investigate.

The car was empty and, despite the steady drizzle, the passenger window was open. He found a puddle of water stained deep crimson about 10 yards from the parked car. It looked like diluted blood. The manager glanced at the bottom of the delta bank, then plunged down to the water's edge. A man was lying there. He was wearing a plaid shirt, blue jeans, and cowboy boots, hardly the correct costume for a damp day on the delta. His head was stained with blood and he appeared to be quite dead. The manager returned to his pickup, hurried to a telephone, and summoned help. The date was April 10, 1982.

Deputy Sheriff Richard Caccam, on routine patrol for the San Joaquin County Sheriff's Department that morning, was dispatched to the levee road. He checked out the body, saw what seemed to be a bullet wound and another head injury, and immediately requested homicide detectives.

Detective Pete Rosenquist, from the sheriff's homicide detail, left department headquarters in Stockton for the murder site. He spotted patrol cars a couple of hundred feet away on the levee and joined Deputy Caccam. Footprints, tire tracks, and bloodstains would not last long on the gravel and asphalt surface of the road and its shoulder in the rain.

After being briefed on the available facts by Deputy Caccam, the detective descended, scrambling and sliding down the levee embankment, and examined the body. It lay on its right side a foot above the waterline. Although the cold, stormy weather could have been a contributing factor, it appeared to the investigator that the person at the water's edge had not been dead long. There was no sign of decomposition; the corpse seemed to be just emerging from rigor mortis.

Detective Rosenquist could see an apparent bullet wound behind the dead man's right ear and a dark, bulging bruise on his forehead above the left eye. The man's throat had also been slashed, the knife blade leaving a wound that was long and bloody, but not deep enough to be lethal, in the sleuth's estimation.

By the time his examination of the body was over, the storm had advanced to savage proportions. Howling winds tore at the raincoats of patrol officers, Detective Rosenquist, and technicians who arrived to help process the crime scene. Physical evidence, if it ever existed, was washed into White's Slough by torrents of water.

There was no sign of identification on the body. The man was middleaged and completely dressed. To Detective Rosenquist, the bullet wound behind the dead man's right ear indicated an execution-type murder, probably by someone who knew the victim. It had been made by a large-caliber gun. The second injury, on the victim's forehead above the left eye, was a bulging bruise. The investigator decided that it had been made by the same bullet which had entered the back of the victim's head.

He wondered about the red Toyota parked by the road—whether it belonged to the dead man. Certainly, he reflected, it would not be the killer's. Yet he thought it was strange that, if all identification was removed from the body, the dead man's car would have been left at the crime scene. The prober also had reason to wonder just who owned the automobile, if not the killer or his victim.

Other than the body, and possibly the parked car, there was nothing in the way of physical evidence at the crime scene. If there had been footprints, the driving rain had washed them away. No shell casing was found near the body or the automobile. Detective Rosenquist believed that the bloodstained puddle, located on the road 35 feet from the car, indicated the dead man had been shot while standing on top of the levee and dragged to his resting place beside the water. If that were so, the drag marks had been washed away by the driving rain. The storm had become one of major proportions.

Turning his attention to the automobile, the sleuth found a registration certificate indicating that it was the property of a woman named Ramp. Other identification found in the automobile indicated that the owner was old enough to be the dead man's mother.

There was no sign of blood, a struggle, or any kind of violence in the automobile. Aside from having photographs taken of the crime scene and the surrounding area, little else could be accomplished there, a circumstance that made the task there more difficult, particularly in view of the vile weather. With no clues available, the technicians and investigators looked harder for anything they might be missing.

Detective Rosenquist did notice that the passenger window of the Toyota was rolled down. That was strange, he thought, considering the weather. Possibly, he decided, it had been lowered early in the night before the rain started.

Intent on identifying the dead man, and if possible, notifying his relatives of his death, Detective Rosenquist returned to sheriff's headquarters in Stockton. There he asked Identification Department staff to search the files for anyone named Ramp who might answer the murdered man's description. They produced the name Henry Ramp. His physical description—height, weight, approximate age, complexion, and hair coloring—closely matched the dead man's.

Detective Rosenquist decided that he should go to the neighborhood in Stockton where the car's owner lived, find a neighbor who knew her and who might help ease the blow if his suspicions were correct, then go to her house and tell her what had happened. He found a neighbor who knew the woman well and agreed to accompany him.

The Toyota's owner was a woman in late middle age. When Detective Rosenquist entered the house with the neighbor, he noticed that she had a visitor—a woman in her early 30s who sat silently in the room and listened.

Told by the investigator that her car had been found deserted on Correia Road in the San Joaquin delta, the woman responded quickly, "Well, my son had the car last night."

"Can you describe him?" Detective Rosenquist asked.

She described her son and, as she finished, the investigator could see signs of distress on her face.

"You're trying to tell me something," she concluded.

"We've got a body out there," the investigator told her. "From your description of your son, it seems likely he is the man. Even the clothing is the same."

The woman sobbed. Tears streamed down her face. "My God, I can't believe it. I don't know what to do. Oh, my God!" She paused, then looked at the heavyset woman sitting across the room, whose face had been immobile up to that time. "This lady is Henry's wife," the older woman added.

Detective Rosenquist had the feeling that someone had pressed a switch or pulled a string. The heavyset woman's expression changed. A strangled sob emerged from her mouth, then a scream.

"What am I going to do?" she cried as she started to run from the room. As she left, she exclaimed, "All this for seven dollars!"

Detective Rosenquist wondered about the woman's parting remark. He turned a questioning glance at the older woman, who explained, through her sobs, that Henry Ramp had been carrying only seven dollars in his pocket when he'd left the house the previous evening. Apparently the younger woman thought he had been murdered for his money.

Overall, the scene at the Ramp home puzzled the sleuth. There was no point in questioning either woman further. Both were shifting from one stage of hysteria to another and back. He asked for the name of someone who could give him background information on Henry Ramp and was directed to his wife's sister, a woman five years younger than her sister.

Leaving the two women in the care of the neighbor who had gone to the house with him, the prober proceeded to the next step. He was glad he had thought to bring a friend of the family with him.

Fingerprints on file with the state of California taken while he was applying for a position 10 years earlier positively identified the murder victim as Henry Ramp. Now sure of the dead man's identity, Detective Rosenquist drove to Euclid Street in Stockton, where he visited the home of the dead man's sister-in-law and questioned her.

The 29-year-old woman told the detective that Henry Ramp was employed as a correctional officer by the California prison system. He'd worked for seven years at the Duell Vocational Institute, a medium-security prison for men in nearby Tracy. After working there three years, he had been transferred to California's oldest and best-known penal institution for women at Tehachapi, about 250 miles to the south.

"Henry and my sister come up here for vacations," the woman explained. She said the two of them had traveled to Stockton that April so they could observe Easter with their families.

"While they're up here he usually stays with his mother and my sister with our family," the young woman added. Recently, she said, she had been staying with the Ramps in Tehachapi and had traveled north with them.

News that Henry Ramp was a correctional officer for 10 years before his murder would, Detective Rosenquist knew, probably provide an oversupply of murder suspects. During 10 years as what amounts to a prison guard, the dead man must have made enemies. No matter that the past seven of the 10 years had been spent at Tehachapi, or, for that matter, that Duell was not supposed to house the "state's most violent prisoners. There were some really tough women in Tehachapi and some people in Duell the average man wouldn't want to meet on the street at high noon, in bright sunlight, on a crowded street.

An autopsy conducted the morning after the body was found revealed that Henry Ramp had been killed execution style. A bullet entered his head just under the dead man's right ear and stopped just before emerging after breaking the bones in the skull above his left eye after passing through his brain. The bullet was recovered and identified by forensic analysts as a .357 magnum.

Detective Rosenquist and his companions at the San Joaquin County Sheriff's Department, totally lacking physical evidence except for the bullet and the Toyota, sifted through the dead man's friends, family, and acquaintances in Stockton and at the Duell Institute, located just 20 miles away. As they expected, the probers found a lot of former prisoners who had no love for Henry Ramp. But after several weeks, they were no closer to finding the correctional officer's killer than they had been on the day his body was found.

Henry Ramp's wife, after attending his funeral, returned to their home in Tehachapi, promising to provide any help she could to Detective Rosenquist. From time to time, she fed him morsels of information, but nothing he could sink his teeth into. Eventually, though, the break he was waiting for reached the investigator. He studied his information and decided that he had an excellent chance of finding the answers he wanted in Tehachapi.

There were two solid reasons for the detective's trip south.

His journey to the little city near the prison, located in the barren and rugged Tehachapi Mountains near the southern end of the 400-mile-long Sacramento-San Joaquin Valley, was not exactly a shot in the dark. During his investigation the detective had already started to make a detailed study of the murdered man's finances.

The study of the Ramp family's money matters had been the only productive portion of Detective Rosenquist's investigation. Through friends and acquaintances of the dead man, he learned that the couple had prospered through most of the early years of their marriage. Ramp had worked hard, moonlighted when he found it possible, and set every penny aside. His wife also had contributed steadily to the family income.

According to the couple's friends, by the time Henry Ramp was murdered, the couple had been able to pay off the mortgage on the home they had purchased in Tehachapi. Part of the reason for that was because they had realized a considerable profit when they sold a home in the Tracy area. San Francisco Bay area commuters, fleeing from inflated real estate prices in Alameda, Contra Costa, Santa Clara, San Mateo, and Marin County, had begun hopping over the ridge that divides the Livermore Valley from Tracy in the San Joaquin in search of bargain-basement home prices.

Bargain basement on one side of the ridge meant fat profits on the Tracy side for homeowners who, for one reason or another, sold their property. That accounted, in part, for the Ramp's prosperity. And, once again, when they moved south, they had bought at a low price and seen their property appreciate rapidly.

According to Detective Rosenquist's information, all that prosperity was yesterday's news. He heard rumors from the dead man's friends that lately Henry Ramp had been playing the stock market. He had been buying and selling through one of the best-known brokerage houses on the Pacific Coast, but his friends said he had climbed on a financial toboggan and had been sliding steadily downhill.

The second reason that sent the detective south was a telephone call from the Stockton Crime Stopper's program. The call, taken originally by the Stockton Police Department, was turned over to Detective Rosenquist after the city officers heard the nature of the information.

An individual who did not identify himself said he knew a man who believed he had the answers to the Henry Ramp murder. The trouble was, the man would not talk because he was sure that if he did, he, too, would become a victim.

Several days of negotiating followed. Detective Rosenquist eventually set up a lunch meeting with a man who identified himself as Jack Concord.

Concord said that he had three roommates in a Stockton dwelling on Pelem Street, including Al Warren and Bob Maahs.

"You've got to know Maahs if you're going to believe me," Concord said. "He was a windbag, a braggart—if you can call the things he talked about bragging. He talked about having a gig here and a gig there, and those gigs always involved crimes of some sort. All four of us worked for a large department store. That's how we met."

Concord told the detective that Warren got a lot of mail from the little city of Tehachapi, which adjoins the women's prison facility there. One day, Concord reported, a letter postmarked Tehachapi arrived—it contained $1,000 in cash. Concord asked Warren about the money.

Warren explained that the money had been sent to pay for a hit on someone. It was not one he would carry out, he maintained, but its sender actually expected him to do the job.

"I'm not going to do it," he'd added. "I'm just using it as a ruse to get a little extra money from my ex-wife." He indicated that there was no love lost between him and his former wife currently living in Tehachapi.

"This is just another way for me to suck some money out of her," Warren continued. "She wants me to do this hit for her, but I'm not going to do it. I'm just going to keep the money."

Concord said that Warren, as was his habit, wound up going to Lake Tahoe and blowing the money at the gambling tables on the Nevada side of the lake. Later, Maahs found out what Warren had done and became enraged. According to Concord, he told Warren that it was his contract, his hit, and the money had rightfully been his. He added that $25,000 was involved and that it was easy money. He wasn't going to have that kind of opportunity blown away by a two-bit gambler who never won.

Maahs said the money had been sent for the purchase of guns and equipment so the job could be done right.

Concord told the detective that he had listened to Maahs talk and had not believed a word. The man was always "blowing smoke." If a person believed Maahs, the informant told Detective Rosenquist, he was the biggest hit man who ever lived. But, he added, he never meant a word he said.

Eventually, Concord told Detective Rosenquist, Maahs had approached Concord himself and asked him if he would drive the getaway car after the murder.

Concord told the investigator his answer had been, "Get out of here! There ain't going to be no killing and I ain't driving no car."

Maahs didn't give up, Concord said. He approached the fourth man living in the apartment, then a friend of the four roommates. He got the same answer every time: "Let me alone. I ain't driving no car."

Meanwhile, Concord went on, Maahs acquired a .357 revolver. That was not particularly strange, Concord said. Maahs seemed fascinated with weapons and owned several guns.

Maahs eventually changed his story. Concord told Detective Rosenquist that his acquaintance approached another man, told him he was going to rip off some drugs from a peddler during a phony buy that night, and asked him to drive the car.

"Once again, you have to understand the guy he talked to," Concord said to Detective Rosenquist. "He was putting anything he could find up his nose, in his mouth, into his veins — anything. The guy was high on one drug or another all the time."

Concord told the investigator that the fourth man, Joe Walnut, agreed to drive the car. Concord himself had to go to work that night. When he came home, he found Maahs sleeping on the couch. He awakened when Concord entered the room and said, "Hey, we did it tonight, Jack."

Still not believing any of it, Concord told Detective Rosenquist that he said, "Yeah, sure, OK," and went to bed and to sleep. When he awakened, he said, he found Maahs, Warren, and a girlfriend of one of the men all gathered in the kitchen listening to a police radio scanner. They were, Concord said, talking about a murdered man whose body had been found in the delta. Later, he could hear the voices on the scanner talking about going to notify relatives if they could be found. Still later, the police discussed visiting an address on Euclid Street.

Listening to Concord, Detective Rosenquist remembered his own visit to Ramp's mother's house, where Ramp had been staying, and then talking to his wife's sister at another dwelling on Euclid Street.

Still, Concord said, he made no connection between Maahs' bragging and the murder. He took care of some errands that day, went to work in the afternoon, returned to the apartment, and went to bed without talking to anyone. The next thing he knew, Concord woke up when Maahs walked into his room and threw a newspaper on his chest.

The major local page-one story announced that Henry

Ramp had been killed. He read a few lines and learned that the body had been found on Correia Road.

Concord told the investigator that he was lying there, thinking, "My God! They did it, they actually did it," while Maahs stood above him, grinning.

"I was lying there with chills running up and down my spine while he's standing above the bed grinning," Concord said. "It didn't dawn on me they were going to do it, because he was always talking like that, but I realized they actually had."

The informant said there had been several payments to Maahs and mentioned several items he had purchased. After one payment of $6,000, Concord said, Maahs bought an expensive motorcycle and paid cash for it. A few days later, he had purchased an expensive television set and paid cash for that item, too. He named the places where Maahs had bought each.

One hitch turned up in Concord's story: he flatly refused to testify. "I'm not going to court," he said. "There's no way I'm going in there and lay my life on the line."

Checking out the informant's story, Detective Rosenquist discovered that Maahs had paid cash for both a motorcycle and an expensive television set in 1982. The investigator obtained a search warrant for Maahs' living quarters, where several firearms were confiscated. There was no .357 magnum among them. Without witnesses, the district attorney declined to prosecute at the moment and ordered the weapons returned to Maahs.

As other work piled up on the homicide detective's desk, the Henry Ramp murder case lay dormant. But the investigator had not given up his quest for the killer. He remembered, too clearly, the attitude of Ramp's wife when he informed the murder victim's mother about her son's death. She had sat in the room and listened stoically while he told his story. Originally, the detective had thought she was just another neighbor and bystander. Not until the dead man's mother had begun to cry and become hysterical, and he had turned his gaze on her, did she suddenly react, sobbing, screaming, and making her remark—"All this for seven dollars."

Detective Rosenquist remembered thinking that it was as though someone had turned on a switch that triggered the hysterics. That switch, he thought, might have been his eyes. When he looked at Mary Ramp, she seemed to suddenly think that she had to do something, that she should scream, sob, get hysterical.

Whatever spare time he had, the detective invested in delving into Mary Ramp's private affairs. A check of her telephone calls revealed a series of extremely short messages from Tehachapi. All were from Robert Maahs' current address in Stockton.

Detective Rosenquist decided that Maahs must have called Mrs. Ramp's home, telling her to go to a pay phone and call from there to make sure he avoided detection. Further investigation proved that was exactly what the suspect did. Moreover, the telephone calls all coincided to within one or two days with several of Maahs' large purchases.

Digging further into the Ramp family finances, Detective Rosenquist discovered that Ramp had worked double shifts at the southern California prison. That had enabled the couple to pay off their house there free and clear; they were worth in excess of $150,000 in cash and real estate about a year before his death.

At that time, Ramp had become interested in the stock market. Small investments in the beginning were losers, in spite of the fact that Ramp was dealing with one of the coast's best-known brokers. He began to invest more money, eventually taking a mortgage on the house. And he lost a great portion of that money.

Mary Ramp, the investigator learned, was outraged and

determined to do something about the situation. Out of the $150,000 Ramp had available to him, he had lost $130,000 in the market. A lifetime of savings was almost gone after a six-month-long plunge into the stock market.

Searching through the Ramp family's telephone bills, Detective Rosenquist found an Indiana number. He called it. It was an insurance company. Shocked representatives of the company reported that the policy had been just 30 days old when Ramp died. They had refused to honor the policy, then had been forced to pay a penalty for the refusal. That and another $50,000 paid the murder victim's widow almost $100,000. Of that, Detective Rosenquist believed that most of $25,000 went to Robert Maahs.

Still, without witnesses, it was impossible to file charges against Maahs, Mary Ramp or Maria Theresa Fredericks, her sister. Concord had said that letters to Warren from both women had urged him to take part in the murder of Henry Ramp. The younger woman was conspiring with her sister from the beginning, according to the informant. But Concord would not testify.

On one of his trips to Tehachapi, Detective Rosenquist learned that while Mrs. Fredericks had been married three times, she had only been divorced once. Checking with local police he also learned that her second husband, whom she had never divorced before marrying the third, had visited her there and had become involved in a barroom fight. His name on a police report caught the investigator's attention. He decided to see if the man had any information.

The man, Willie Fox, at first refused to talk; then he suggested to the investigator that they go to a place where they could be completely alone. Detective Rosenquist borrowed an interview room in the area police department and listened to a story that would break open the case.

Fox told the detective that he and his wife had done nothing but argue when he traveled to Tehachapi, intending to reconcile their marriage if possible. She had been dating another man and they were disagreeing over her relations with him. During a lull in the wordy battles, he said, she had told him plans were nearing conclusion for the murder of Henry Ramp.

"You're out of your mind!" Fox said he had responded.

Maria Theresa told him that she and her sister, Mary, had already sent $1,000 to Al Warren to do the job.

"I told her she was really crazy. I said Al would just take the thousand dollars and go to Nevada and blow it on the gambling tables. That's all he ever did with all the money he had," Fox said.

When he attended Ramp's funeral and gathered with the family at the house on Euclid Street where Maria Theresa was living, Fox said he found himself sitting opposite his wife.

"She asked me why I was staring at her," Fox recounted.

"You did it, didn't you?" Fox said he replied. "You really did it."

Fox told the detective that his wife had looked away and has never spoken a word to him since.

When Fox said that he would testify, Detective Rosenquist returned to Stockton and told Jack Concord that he had another witness and intended to subpoena Concord's testimony. One by one, he gathered up more witnesses. Al Warren, afraid of Concord's evidence and desperate to make any deal he could, now told about driving to the scene in another car, following Maahs and Ramp, who were riding in the Toyota.

"I never thought he'd do it," Warren declared. "Never once did I think he'd do it. Right until the last minute I thought he would claim it was too wet, too rainy, too late—something!"

Joe Walnut told much the same story. He said that they had driven out to Correia Road, where he fully expected

Maahs to rip some dope off the man riding with him in the Toyota. When Maahs descended from the little car carrying a shotgun and a .357 magnum, Walnut decided that this artillery was a little too heavy to use for a minor dope theft.

"Plans have been changed," he said Maahs told him. "We're going to hit this guy."

"You're crazy!" Walnut told the investigator he said.

"I'm going to hit him!" Walnut said Maahs insisted.

"Well, get on with it," Walnut reported he said. "I never believed for a moment he'd do it. Anyway, there I am out there on the levee with a guy who has two guns and I don't have any. I wasn't in a position to argue."

The next thing he heard, Walnut said, was the roar of the .357 magnum. "Then I knew he had done it." He said that because Ramp, after being shot, moved his hand toward a shirt pocket where he customarily carried a .45-caliber derringer, Maahs slashed Ramp's throat with a buck knife. Later, Walnut said, both the buck knife and the .357 were thrown into White's Slough. Divers, hooks, and magnets could not recover either weapon. One of the divers reported, "The muck is about four feet deep down there."

A warrant was issued. On West Flora Street in Stockton, where he had moved into the home of a young woman, Robert Warren Maahs, 26 at the time, was arrested for the murder of Henry Ramp. On April 20, 1983, exactly one year and 10 days after the murder, Mary Ramp was arrested for her husband's death. Her sister, Maria Theresa Fredericks, was arrested on the same day.

While Maahs awaited trial, Detective Rosenquist learned that he had twice conspired unsuccessfully to have three key witnesses to the Ramp murder killed.

On September 15, 1986, Robert Warren Maahs, who was 29 at the time, was sentenced to 25 years to life in prison for the murder of Henry Ramp. Almost two years later, Mary **Barbara** Ramp, by then 40, and her sister, Maria Theresa

Fredericks, 35, pleaded no contest to charges of the second-degree murder of Henry Ramp. They will serve sentences of 16 years to life in prison for their crime. Al Warren, who turned state's evidence, entered a plea of guilty to voluntary manslaughter, and Joe Walnut, who also testified for the state, pleaded guilty to being an accessory after the fact.

Maahs, Mrs. Ramp, Mrs. Fredericks, and Al Warren are serving their sentences now. Joe Walnut's accessory sentence amounted to the seven months in jail he had served, plus probation.

EDITOR'S NOTE:
Jack Concord, Al Warren, Joe Walnut, and Willie Fox are not the real names of the persons so named in the foregoing story. Fictitious names have been used because there is no reason for public interest in the identities of these persons.

"FEMME FATALE AND HER BAND OF KILLERS"

by Bruce Stockdale

**Baltimore, Md.
May 11, 1989**

"But they that will be rich fall into temptation and a snare and into many foolish and hurtful lusts, which drown men in destruction and perdition."

— 1 Timothy 6:9

On Tuesday, November 12, 1985, at 5:54 p.m., Frank Lee Ross, a 46-year-old auto mechanic, was walking on Gold Street after picking up an auto part at a nearby parts store. Gold Street intersects about 100 feet to the east with busy North Avenue, a major east-west thoroughfare bisecting Baltimore City. It had just gotten dark, but the rush-hour traffic on North Avenue provided plenty of light.

Suddenly, from out of the shadows came a figure. He carried a pistol, approached Frank Ross from the rear, placed the weapon to his head and fired. The victim collapsed on the sidewalk while his attacker made good his getaway through an alley running into Gold Street.

Baltimore City police were stumped by the apparently random, motiveless nature of the killing. After months of fruitless investigation, they reluctantly consigned the case to the inactive roster.

On Monday, October 6, 1986, at 6:59 p.m., acting on a tip phoned in by a person who claimed to have heard shots fired in the vicinity of Clifton Park High School in northeast Baltimore, Officer John Kyle found the body of a black male, subsequently identified as 48-year-old Albert Robinson. He had been shot in the head with a large-caliber handgun. He was dead.

Unable to come up with a suspect for the mysterious slaying, police theorized that the man had been a transient riding a freight train who had come to grief during a drunken altercation with another hobo, had gotten himself shot and thrown off the train. The autopsy had shown a high level of alcohol in the victim's blood at the time of death.

With no leads to follow up on, and no suspect on which to focus, the police had no alternative but to let the case lie dormant, utilizing their resources on cases with a better chance of being solved.

On Friday, March 6, 1987, at 10:15 p.m., police were called to the 2100 block of Aisquith Street on a "shots-fired" report where they found the body of a black woman lying on the sidewalk. She was identified as Helen Wright, a 65-year-old retired domestic with an address on nearby Kennedy Street. She had been shot six times in the back of the head. A bag of Chinese food was found lying next to the woman's body.

Interestingly, this had not been Wright's first encounter with violence. On February 1, 1987, Helen Wright had been shot in the head at point-blank range by an unknown assailant for no apparent reason. She had survived that attack. This time Wright had not been so lucky.

Again, police were mystified by the murder of an apparently harmless retired woman with no known enemies, no criminal record, no involvement in drug trafficking or any other illegal activity.

On Saturday, September 19, 1987, at 4:32 p.m., Bonnie Dodson and her boyfriend, Ronnie Mitchener were awaiting delivery of some cocaine. At 4:25 p.m., a black male presented himself at the northwest Baltimore row house and claimed that he was there to consummate the drug transaction. After making an unsuccessful effort to get Mitchener to leave on the pretext that he was only supposed to deal with Dodson, the man pulled out a pistol and opened fire on them both. Mitchener was killed but Dodson survived.

On Wednesday, October 14, 1987, at 9:14 a.m., Henry Barnes, a 46-year-old furniture salesman, left his home in the 1800 block of a west Baltimore street and got into his car. Suddenly, a black male armed with a sawed-off shotgun approached from the driver's side, put the muzzle of the weapon against the startled man's neck and fired. The pumpkin slug tore through the victim's artery and killed him instantly. The killer made a successful getaway.

On Sunday, March 6, 1988 at 11:30 p.m., Bonnie Dodson, just released from the hospital, went to a relative's house on Division Street in west Baltimore. As she left, she was attacked by a black male who cut her throat from ear to ear with a straight razor and left her for dead. Bonnie Dodson's luck stayed with her, however. She not only lived, she recovered.

On Friday, May 19, 1988, at 10:05 p.m., Bonnie Dodson was sitting on the front steps of a west Baltimore row house on Hollins Street waiting for a relative, Geraldine Parrish, to come out of the house where she was getting something. Suddenly, a black male came out of the house, shot her in the head three times and ran away.

Bonnie Dodson, exhibiting the cat's proverbial nine lives, survived this ordeal, too. With this, she was dubbed by astonished Crimes Against Persons Unit detectives as: "The Unkillable Bonnie Dodson."

As with the previous cases, Bonnie Dodson was unable to provide sleuths with any clues as to who her assailant might be.

As the unsolved killings and brutal assaults continued to pile up, a concerned John J. MacGillivray, commanding officer of the Crimes Against Persons Section of the Baltimore City Police Department (BCPD), decided that the time had come to take extraordinary measures to stop the carnage. The violence was not only wreaking havoc with the section's case closure statistics in homicide cases (80%), but was also hurting the city's image and attempts to promote tourism. MacGillivray decided to organize a special squad to investigate all the apparently random murders which remained unsolved. The squad would be directed in its efforts by 38-year-old Detective Sergeant Gary Childs, a 17-year BCPD veteran with extensive experience in all phases of criminal investigation. In turn, Sergeant Childs appointed the lead investigator assigned to each unsolved killing to comprise the Special Investigative Squad (SIS). Accordingly, Detectives Gary Dunnigan, Richard James, and Michael Crutchfield found themselves combining their resources and skills in an effort to come up with answers to the questions: Who had shot down in cold blood and for no apparent reason Frank Ross, Albert Robinson, Helen Wright and Ronald Mitchener? And who had made three vicious attempts on the life of Bonnie Dodson?

The sleuths' first step was to sit down and familiarize themselves with the material in all the case dossiers with which they were concerned. This done, they sat down together in the homicide unit conference room and brainstormed the cases.

While it was frustrating, the sleuths were able to detect one common thread running through the cases — all the victims were covered by life insurance. And the designated beneficiary in two of the cases was the same person — one

Geraldine Parrish. This didn't really mean she was behind the violence but Sergeant Childs was sufficiently intrigued by this information that he ordered a background check on the woman.

A trip to the fifth floor where Central Records was situated, reflected no record of any prior arrests in Baltimore City for Geraldine Parrish, 53, with an address on Kennedy Street off East North Avenue.

Learning this, Sergeant Childs was pondering the advisability of pursuing this line of inquiry when, on Wednesday, February 24, 1988, at 11:15 a.m., Detective Crutchfield took a telephone call relevant to the Henry Barnes homicide which would ultimately close all the cases vexing the SIS.

The woman, who declined to identify herself, claimed that she had overheard the dead man's wife, Bernadette Barnes, discuss the possibility of taking a contract out on her husband's life with a co-worker by the name of Mary Baxter. This had allegedly taken place at Bernadette Barnes' place of employment, the Baltimore City Department of Social Services' Johnston Square office on Guilford Avenue.

Advised by Detective Crutchfield of this development, Sergeant Childs and Crutchfield wasted no time responding to the Department of Social Services building at 1510 Guilford. It was just 10 minutes away from police headquarters.

Interviews with co-workers of Henry Barnes quickly developed information that Bernadette Barnes had openly stated that she was looking for someone to kill her husband because he was continually harassing her and would not leave her alone. In due course, Mrs. Barnes was able to arrange the hit through Mary Baxter who had put her in touch with a relative by the name of Rodney Jones.

Mary Baxter was picked up and taken downtown to the

homicide unit office for interrogation. She did not seem the conspirator type. She readily agreed to assist police to the fullest possible extent in their quest to bring to justice Henry Barnes' murderer.

She named her distant relative, Rodney Jones, as a participant in the killing. Jones, she said, could be found at the Baltimore City Jail where he was awaiting trial on drug charges. She also agreed to call Bernadette Barnes on the telephone to try to get the now-suspect to make incriminating statements for recording on a police tape recorder.

As Michael Crutchfield played a tape containing sounds of traffic in the background (to give the other party the false impression that the call was being made from an outside pay phone), Mary Baxter talked to Bernadette Barnes at her home.

Explaining that the police had been making inquiries at the Social Services office in reference to the Barnes case and that they seemed to know too much, Baxter asked what she should do.

"They're on a fishing expedition and bluffing," Barnes replied. "Just be cool and pretend you don't know what they're talking about. That's the way I'm going to play it."

Based on the information gleaned from Bernadette Barnes' co-workers, Detective Crutchfield was able to convince Circuit Court Judge John Prevas that probable cause existed to believe Bernadette Barnes had conspired to have her husband killed. He requested that a search of her residence on West Lafayette Street be conducted.

The search warrant authorized by Judge Prevas was executed in the early morning hours of Wednesday, February 1, 1989. It yielded an insurance policy with a face value of $22,000 on the life of Henry Barnes. Bernadette Barnes was the designated beneficiary.

Meanwhile, Detectives Dunnigan and James went to the Baltimore City Jail to interview Rodney Jones, named by Mary Baxter as instrumental in arranging the "hit" on Henry Barnes.

Rodney Jones, true name Rodney Vice, impressed the sleuths as a typical product of the Maryland corrections system. He already owned a five-page rap sheet by the age of 25 which showed priors dating back to 1976 for everything from bicycle theft as a juvenile to armed robbery as an adult.

Typically at first, Rodney Jones denied complicity in the murder of Henry Barnes. But when confronted with the fact that his relative, Mary Baxter, had turned informer, the muscular young man decided to follow suit hoping that by doing so he would get a good deal from prosecutors.

While the lawmen explained that they did not have the authority to commit the state to any deal, they assured Jones that his cooperation would be brought to the attention of prosecutors and the court.

With this, Rodney Jones launched a tale of evil conspiracy and cold-blooded murder that stunned even the most case-hardened lawmen.

He related that over the course of several months in 1987, he had discussed with his relative, Mary Baxter, the possibility of hiring someone to kill Henry Barnes at the behest of Bernadette Barnes.

On Tuesday, October 13, 1987, he, Mary Baxter, and Bernadette Barnes met at his home on Aiken Street in east Baltimore to finalize arrangements for the contract. Barnes supplied Jones with a photograph of her husband, a description of his car, their home address and the time her husband usually left to go to work.

The next day Jones met with the hit man he had recruited for the job, one Edwin Gordon. He gave Gordon the photo and a sawed-off shotgun concealed in a gym bag. Then they drove to the 1800 block of West Lafayette Street and staked out the victim's car. Since Jones had a court date downtown that morning on a probation violation charge, he did not wait for Barnes to come out. About two hours later, Gordon showed up in the courtroom and made a circle with his thumb and forefinger, signaling that the job had been done.

Rodney Jones met with Mary Baxter and Bernadette Barnes. They gave him a $200 payment on the contract with the promise of an additional $3,000 payable when the life insurance money came through. A few weeks later, he got another $950 from Bernadette Barnes who, when advised that Edwin Gordon was pressing him (Jones) for payment of his fee, asked him to meet her at the Social Services office on Guilford Avenue.

This meeting took place on December 10th. At this time, Bernadette Barnes gave Rodney Jones $4,000 with $500 going to Mary Baxter for her help in arranging the contract.

The sleuths were happy with their newly discovered witness, but as experienced criminal investigators they knew well that much more work remained on the case before it would be ready for court. There would have to be corroboration of what Rodney Jones had told them before a conviction would be assured in light of the Maryland accomplice law.

"Why did you give the contract to Edwin Gordon?" asked Detective James.

"He had a reputation for being good at this line of work," Jones replied.

"What reputation? Can't you be more specific?" asked Detective Dunnigan.

"Well, I know for a fact that he killed three people before he killed the Barnes dude. And done his damndest to kill another."

"Who was he doing these contracts for, Jones?" asked Detective James.

"For a woman in my neighborhood by the name of

Geraldine Parrish."

Geraldine Parrish. Geraldine Parrish. The name rang a bell with Gary Dunnigan who remembered that one Geraldine Parrish had held a life insurance policy on Frank Ross, who had been shot down on Gold Street in November of 1985. Parrish had not been followed up as a suspect at the time. They had lacked hard evidence and she had not had a Baltimore City criminal record.

The time had obviously come to put her under a microscope.

Rodney Jones' information on Geraldine Parrish's part in the series of contract killings was largely hearsay. Hoping for harder facts, Detective James asked: "Jones, who do you know that can back up your assertions about Geraldine Parrish?"

Jones thought a minute and replied: "You should talk to Bobbie Roberts. She's related to Parrish. I know Bobbie was involved with her because Edwin Gordon came to my house one night back in '85 lookin' for a piece to do a job. He told me he had come from Bobbie Roberts' house where he had got the contract. I got him a Luger for five hundred bucks."

It had been a productive session at the Baltimore City Jail and Gary Childs was one happy cop when he learned of it. However, he was going to have to talk with Bobbie Roberts before leveling any formal accusations against anyone.

Bobbie Roberts was picked up and brought down to the homicide unit office for questioning. Unlike Mary Baxter, however, she showed herself to be made of stern stuff, adamantly denying any knowledge of or any part in any murder conspiracy. She was released with the admonition to keep herself available for any additional interviews.

With this, Sergeant Childs decided the time had come to get a search warrant for the Parrish residence on Kennedy

Street. This SIS did not yet have sufficient evidence to sustain any formal charges. But all that was necessary to sustain a request for a warrant was a showing of "probable cause."

Childs spent the next several hours composing the affidavit in support of the search warrant. It outlined that evidence pertaining to the murder of Frank Ross might be found at the residence of Geraldine Parrish on Kennedy Street.

The completed affidavit was presented to Circuit Judge John J. Prevas who, applying the probable cause standard, duly authorized the search.

The early morning hours of Friday, July 22, 1988, found the SIS backed by a contingent of Eastern District uniformed officers, "turning up" the brick row house occupied by Geraldine Parrish and a family member.

The sleuths hit pay dirt when they spotted what appeared to be several insurance policies lying in plain view on the top of a bedroom dresser. Sergeant Childs' examination disclosed that the heavyset, 53-year-old woman had taken out life insurance policies on Frank Ross, Bonnie Dodson, Helen Wright, Bobbie Roberts, the family member with whom she shared her house and . . . Albert Robinson, the man found shot to death next to the railroad tracks near Clifton Park High School on October 6, 1986. With this, Geraldine Parrish was arrested and formally charged with first-degree murder and conspiracy in the cases of Frank Ross, Helen Wright and Bonnie Dodson. The case of Albert Robinson was promptly taken out of mothballs and assigned to Detectives Donald Waltemeyer and Corey Belt for investigation.

Based on what Rodney Jones had told the sleuths, warrants were issued for the arrests of Bernadette Barnes and Edwin Gordon for first-degree murder and conspiracy in the death of Harold Barnes. The Barnes woman turned herself in and pleaded not guilty. Gordon was nowhere to be found and the fugitive squad drew the assignment of running him down. They accomplished this task on Friday, July 22, 1988, taking him into custody at his Woodbourne Avenue address. He was charged with first-degree murder and conspiracy and held at the Baltimore City Jail on high bail.

Matters were helped along when an incensed Bobbie Roberts, learning that Geraldine Parrish had taken out an insurance policy on her life without her knowledge, agreed to turn state's evidence in hopes of lenient treatment. Since she was instrumental in the plot against the life of Albert Robinson, she was to prove to be a key witness for the prosecution.

While Assistant State's Attorney Mark Cohen pored over the record in this, the most celebrated and complex case of his career, the SIS was continuing to amass evidence designed to put Geraldine Parrish out of circulation for life.

On Thursday, August 11, 1988, Detectives Belt and Waltemeyer went to New York City where they learned that Geraldine Parrish had been getting public assistance from the New York City Department of Social Services. Then they drove the 25 miles to Plainfield, New Jersey. There, they interviewed a former family member of Geraldine Parrish who stated that he believed she had tried to poison him. Finally, they spoke to a relative of victim Albert Robinson who related that Geraldine Parrish, while the pastor of a storefront church in Plainfield called ironically the "HELPING HANDS OF MERCY," had taken out life insurance on Albert Robinson allegedly to cover burial expenses in case he died. By some strange coincidence, somebody had subsequently shot him, but he had survived this attack. The local police had investigated this crime, but had been unable to solve it.

When Gary Childs reported this to Mark Cohen, the disgusted prosecutor remarked: "Some preacher. She has people whacked for their life insurance at the same time she's ripping off the taxpayers!"

Workhorse of the Baltimore City State's Attorney's Office Violent Crimes Unit, 37-year-old Mark Cohen draws some of the more difficult assignments in the office. While he was confident of a successful prosecution of Geraldine Parrish on the merits of the case, he knew there was always the possibility that she might seek to evade justice with an insanity defense.

This appeared to be a distinct possibility in light of a psychiatric evaluation conducted on Parrish's behalf when the prosecution was still considering going for the death penalty against her. The examining psychiatrist reported that when he examined Parrish on August 11, 1988, "She stated that she was hearing voices which were pulling out her hair, putting her feet in a bucket and 'doing things to me.' "

The psychiatrist concluded: "The evaluation suggests that Ms. (sic) Parrish is acutely psychotic and may have a chronic mental illness. The evaluation further suggests that she is presently not competent, that she is not able to understand the nature or object of the proceedings or to assist in her defense."

With the possibility of a viable insanity defense looming large on the horizon, Mark Cohen obtained a court order transferring Geraldine Parrish to Clifton T. Perkins Hospital for evaluation by state psychiatrists.

Meanwhile, with the help of information provided by now-state's witness Bobbie Roberts, the SIS had been able to come up with the hit man in the Albert Robinson homicide. It was 19-year-old Lionel Robinson, the young man who had telephoned police about hearing shots behind Clifton Park High School. His motives had not been that of a good citizen seeking to report a crime after all. On the contrary, it turned out that Geraldine Parrish, before paying for a hit, always demanded proof positive of the victim's death beforehand, and this was Lionel Robinson's way of providing it.

With Lionel Robinson put behind bars, all the culpable persons in the deaths of Frank Ross, Helen Wright, Ronald Mitchener, Albert Robinson and Henry Barnes stood accounted for. The formidable task of proving guilt beyond a reasonable doubt in a court of law remained to be accomplished.

After extensive consultations with State's Attorney Stuart Simms, Mark Cohen decided not to seek the death penalty against Geraldine Parrish. Death penalty trials were always very chancy propositions in Baltimore City, even more so because the state had no witnesses who had actually seen Geraldine Parrish kill anyone. And it would have been inconsistent to ask for the death penalty in the case against Edwin Gordon since it was not sought against Parrish.

Bernadette Barnes and Edwin Gordon stood trial in Baltimore City Circuit Court in February 1989, for first-degree murder and conspiracy in the death of Henry Barnes. Barnes elected to plead not guilty, but changed her plea to guilty in the middle of the trial when it became obvious that her chances of beating the rap were nil. Gordon was convicted by the jury after a short deliberation. On March 15, 1989, the two stood before Judge Elsbeth Levy Bothe for sentencing.

"I am not sorry about what happened because he put my life through holy hell," the 43-year-old Barnes said in explanation of why she had her husband murdered. "I'm glad that he's gone. I'm glad that he's out of my life."

"This is indeed an extraordinarily strange case," Judge Bothe said knowingly. "It's just a totally incredible situation. I have no feeling but that the court is carrying out the plan that was initiated. I'm doing nothing more than carrying out the contract. First, she paid to have her husband exterminated. Then, she cheerfully agrees to take a life sentence. I am carrying out her wish. She's rid of her husband and she's going to prison."

With this, Judge Bothe imposed a life sentence on Bernadette Barnes. Since Gordon had not pleaded guilty or shown any remorse at all for his crimes, he was sentenced to life imprisonment without the possibility of parole.

Rodney Jones, who had provided the prosecution with evidence needed to make the cases against Barnes and Gordon, was allowed to plead guilty to second-degree murder. He got his reward in the form of a 30-year sentence with parole eligibility in seven years and six months.

The way was now clear for Geraldine Parrish to stand trial when the Clifton T. Perkins staff, who, having had extensive experience with fakers like her, reported her as responsible and competent to stand trial.

Mark Cohen decided to try the Albert Robinson case first against Parrish and co-defendant Lionel Robinson. He felt that it was the strongest case of all. He hoped that once Parrish was convicted in this case, the futility of going to trial on the others would be apparent to her and her attorney and she would therefore plead guilty, thereby sparing everyone the time and expense of trials in the other cases.

The trial in the case of Maryland v. Geraldine Parrish and Lionel Robinson began on Monday, March 27, 1989 in Baltimore City Circuit Court, Judge Elsbeth Levy Bothe again presiding. As the jury of six men and six women were being selected to hear the case, Geraldine Parrish gave a hint of the tactic she was going to use to try to beat the rap—a "crazy" act. She stood up and told Judge Bothe, "Missy, I been sitting for too long."

In his opening statement, Prosecutor Cohen offered the state's version of the October 6, 1986 killing of Albert Robinson, explaining that under Maryland law, Geraldine Parrish was as guilty of first-degree murder as Lionel Robinson "even if she did not pull the trigger."

Describing the victim as a man with a drinking problem, he laid out a scenario in which Albert Robinson was lured to his death by alcohol. He asserted that Geraldine Parrish had organized two trips to New Jersey to kill the victim with the second accomplishing its criminal purpose.

His key witness was Bobbie Roberts who had participated in both trips but who had turned state's evidence in exchange for immunity from prosecution.

Roberts testified that the first trip was in August 1986, when she, Lionel Robinson, and Parrish went to New Jersey to find Albert Robinson. The plan was for her to pose as a woman who had met him in a bar and wanted to continue drinking with him. Parrish had told her that Robinson was a notorious alcoholic who would follow them for a drink.

Arriving, Roberts knocked on Robinson's door and greeted him when he answered. "I said, 'Albert, don't you remember me?" she testified. "He said, 'Yeah, yeah, that's right.' "

He then accepted her offer of a drink and quickly became drunk. Then she led the drunken man to the car but he was so drunk that he did not even recognize Parrish, the storefront preacher who had taken out a life insurance policy on him in 1982.

Parrish slipped a mickey into the liquor Robinson was drinking and they drove around the New Jersey countryside looking for a good place to kill him. Finding a clearing, they took Robinson out of the car and Lionel Robinson shot him. Then they returned to Baltimore only to learn the next day that Robinson had survived the attack.

Wanting that $10,000 to support a heavy drug habit, Parrish decided to return to New Jersey to finish the job. Roberts testified that although they had trouble finding their quarry on the second trip, Parrish eventually spotted him on the street, exclaiming: "There he go! There he go! There's the sucker right there!"

Although it was hard to believe that Robinson had been so befuddled by drink during the first attempt on his life that he didn't even realize someone was trying to kill him, the fact remained that the group had little difficulty luring him into the car. Again, the group drove around looking for a good place to kill Robinson.

Eventually, they pulled off a highway where they decided to shoot him. "I pulled Albert out of the car and he fell down into a ditch," Roberts testified. At this point, just as Lionel Robinson was about to shoot, a state police car approached. Seeing this, she said, "Oh man, we can't get Albert out of the ditch! Oh man, we're going to get locked up!"

But Parrish had the presence of mind to take the gun, conceal it, and explain to a curious state trooper that the drunken man had fallen into a deep ditch while trying to urinate. Asked by the somewhat suspicious trooper if he was in any trouble, Albert Robinson managed to mumble that he was all right. With that the trooper left. The group then headed back to Baltimore, where they again proceeded to look for a good place to kill Albert Robinson.

Roberts told the jury that at first, they were going to kill him near the water off Key Highway, but canceled that plan because people were fishing in the area. The next idea, to kill Robinson in Leakin Park, was vetoed by Parrish who said: "We can't kill him in Leakin Park. People are always killed in Leakin Park. The police are probably there."

Roberts testified that they eventually decided to drop off the two Robinsons near Clifton Park, where the younger Robinson would shoot the older man near the railroad tracks.

Later, Lionel Robinson told Roberts that he led the

drunken victim to the tracks where he shot him. He told her: "I shot him in the eye and everything came out the other side."

Parrish wanted to see the killing reported in the media before she would believe the victim was dead and pay Lionel Robinson, Roberts testified. Therefore Parrish told Lionel to call the police so the body would be discovered promptly. Hence, the calls to the police that led to Lionel Robinson's coming to their attention.

Bobbie Roberts' damning testimony, which jibed with all the corroborating testimony in the case, could not be shaken by Defense Attorneys Robert Durkin and William Purpura. She left the witness stand with her credibility intact.

As the trial progressed and the evidence started to pile up, Mark Cohen was not surprised to see that a desperate Geraldine Parrish had apparently decided to go into her crazy act. Would she be able to get away with it? he wondered.

As the second day of proceedings drew to a close, when Police Agent Theresa Cunningham was testifying, Parrish started to shake uncontrollably, roll back her eyes and foam from the corners of her mouth. As she slumped back into her chair, Judge Bothe dismissed the jurors, then expressed her irritation.

"Mrs. Parrish? Mrs. Parrish, I know you can hear me," the stern no-nonsense judge said. "We're not going to have things like this going on. No one is listening to you."

Agent Cunningham testified that more than an hour after the body of Albert Robinson had been discovered, police were still receiving 911 calls from an anonymous man who wanted to tell them about the body. When the police dispatcher determined that the call had come from a pay phone at North Collington Street and Sinclair Lane, the agent drove to that location and found then 17-year-old

Lionel Robinson.

Prosecutor Mark Cohen saw that it was dawning on Geraldine Parrish that her patently fake attempts to portray insanity were not going anywhere, and if she was to avoid conviction, her only hope was to try to lie her way out of the trouble she was in. Therefore, unlike her co-defendant, Lionel Robinson (who did not share her self-confidence in the ability to prevaricate), she elected to take the witness stand to testify in her own defense.

Parrish told the jury that she did not lure the man to a violent death as charged by the state, and did not get $10,000 in life insurance after his death. She further stated that she did not even remember the repeated attempts to end Albert Robinson's life. She claimed that she did not know how to read or write, or even spell her first name. She had obtained driver's licenses in Maryland and New Jersey only because another woman took the test for her. She also said she could not count.

"So you wouldn't know what comes after the number one?" asked a skeptical Prosecutor Cohen upon cross-examination.

"No, I don't," replied Parrish.

Eyebrows were raised when the jurors heard this and Mark Cohen knew then that Geraldine Parrish had just dealt a crushing blow to her own credibility; indeed, it lay in shreds on the floor of the courtroom.

So when she offered her own version of events, radically different from the prosecution's scenario, it was unlikely that the jurors would believe these.

Parrish told the jurors of a long history of drug abuse — at one point standing before the jury box to display marks that she described as needle tracks. She claimed that other people supplied her with heroin, cocaine, and other drugs and plotted the insurance murder of Albert Robinson without her help. She claimed that a man known to her only as

"Gold Teeth" was living at her Kennedy Avenue home at the time of the Albert Robinson murder, keeping her a prisoner in her own home at gunpoint. A relative had plied her with Valium while Gordon gave her heroin, Parrish said.

With her testimony concluded, the opposing attorneys followed up with emotional closing arguments before a crowded courtroom—arguments that were repeatedly marked by objections from both sides and occasional warnings by Judge Bothe to "just stick to the facts."

In his final statement to the jury, Prosecutor Cohen angrily challenged the defense contention that the state had failed to prove their case beyond a reasonable doubt.

Shouting in a voice that occasionally came close to cracking, Mark Cohen held aloft the insurance policy found in Parrish's home. He asked the jury if it was compatible with common sense that Parrish would take out $10,000 worth of life insurance on a man whose life had no real value from a financial standpoint—without an ulterior purpose.

Speaking of the victim, Cohen said that while Albert Robinson may have been a man with problems, "He didn't deserve to be shot in Clifton Park for ten thousand dollars. He was worth more than ten thousand dollars to his family and he didn't deserve that fate. No one deserves that fate."

With reference to co-defendant, Lionel Robinson, Prosecutor Cohen reviewed the testimony of Police Agent Cunningham relating how the 17-year-old had been identified as the party making the phone calls to the police about shots fired in Clifton Park. This was done, explained Cohen, because Parrish was not going to pay him until the incident was verified by the media.

"He realized that if he (the victim) is not found, then he doesn't get paid," Cohen said, slamming his hand down on the trial table to emphasize his point.

But Defense Attorney Purpura suggested that Geraldine

Parrish had for her entire life been "abused and used, and in fact she is being abused and used in this trial itself."

He went on to say that his client did not have the mental capability to "solicit or conspire or become a killer of Albert Robinson." He described Parrish as a woman with an alcohol and drug problem who served as a self-ordained preacher but was otherwise illiterate. In an apparent reference to his client's stability, he touched the back of her chair and told the jurors: "She is something else . . . you can see it and feel it."

You are so right, Bill Purpura, thought Mark Cohen.

With closing arguments completed, the jurors filed out of the jury box to begin their deliberations, leaving Mark Cohen to sweat out the question: Had Geraldine Parrish's mental incapacity act fooled the jurors into believing she had just been the tool of others, instead of the mastermind of the conspiracy to murder Albert Robinson?

He was heartened by the relatively short time—three hours—that it took the jury to come back with a verdict in the complex, hard-fought case: guilty of all charges against her. They also found co-defendant Lionel Robinson guilty of the same charges. The 19-year-old sat stunned after the verdict against him was announced, his eyes watering as he glared at a back window in the second-floor courtroom.

Judge Bothe polled the jurors and declared the verdict official. Since little was known at that point about the defendants' social histories, Judge Bothe wanted the benefit of presentence investigations before meting out punishment in their cases. This was so ordered and the defendants were remanded to the Baltimore City Jail pending sentencing.

The social investigation into the life of Geraldine Parrish was to provide as much grist for the mill of the criminal justice system as the criminal one. It revealed Geraldine Parrish had been convicted of the unlawful killing of someone on a previous occasion. On May 15, 1972, she had been found guilty of manslaughter in New York City. According to a relative (and verified by official records), Parrish, while working as a prostitute to support her drug habit, killed another prostitute over the affections of their pimp. Apparently regarding this as a matter of not much importance, the New York authorities had let Parrish off with three years of supervised probation. She had also been arrested for assault, possession of a deadly weapon, attended false pretenses, and possession of narcotics, but had never served any time on any of these charges. Other names that Parrish had been arrested under included Geraldine Brown, Geraldine Jones, and Geraldine Rogers.

The court investigator was able to collect evidence, some hearsay, some documentary, that defendant Parrish had been married to a total of nine different men! It was doubtful whether she had bothered with the formality of divorcing the previous husband before marrying the next one. If she hadn't, this would have made her a bigamist as well as a convicted murderess.

For example, it was noted that in January 1988, Parrish, under the name of Roslyn W. Brown, had married Reverend Rayfield Gilliard, a recent widower. Hearsay had it, however, that she had already been married to one of her many roomers in the Kennedy Avenue house. By some strange happenstance, the 77-year-old retired minister died on February 2, 1988, less than a month after the marriage. On July 1, 1988, Parrish married husband number nine and promptly took out two $20,000 insurance policies on his life.

Geraldine Parrish, born Geraldine Brown, was part of the great urban emigration from the rural South that took place in the 1950s. She had run away from home at the age of 15 with little formal education and even fewer skills. She apparently adopted a way of life of surviving by skillfully exploiting the gullibility and weaknesses of others. This fundamentally criminal cast of mind became more serious when Geraldine acquired a heroin habit at the age of 21.

Lionel Robinson also had a record of involvement with the juvenile and criminal justice systems. Technically a juvenile when he murdered Albert Robinson, he had prior arrests for a handgun violation, escape from a juvenile institution and possession of cocaine.

But what goes around comes around.

On Thursday, May 11, 1989, the two convicted murderers stood before Judge Bothe for sentencing.

Geraldine Parrish cried, pleaded and begged for mercy before Judge Bothe handed down her sentence. She blamed the murder on her co-conspirators, her co-defendant, even her relatives.

"Please, Your Honor, have mercy on me. I was just doing what I was told to do. I didn't know no better what to do. If I did, I wouldn't have done this."

Each time she tried to speak, Parrish barely got out the first words of a sentence before starting to cry.

"I didn't do this. I was with them, but I didn't do this," she said, before pleading to be sent to the Patuxent Institution, which she referred to as "the place with the fences on it." Every convicted criminal wants to go to Maryland's unique prison, the Patuxent Institution, because it is a notorious loophole in the criminal justice system and it represents a way to get back on the street in a relatively short time.

However, Parrish's song-and-dance did not sway Judge Bothe, who said that she agreed with Prosecutor Cohen's description of the murder as a cruel, heartless deed done out of greed.

"It was a murder committed for money, a piddling amount of money at that, against a hapless alcoholic," she said.

With this, the judge sentenced Parrish to two concurrent

life sentences plus 20 years with an identical sentence imposed on Lionel Robinson.

But for Mark Cohen, the job that he had undertaken was still only half-done. The books remained to be balanced in the murder cases of Frank Ross, Helen Wright, and Ronald Mitchener; plus the three attempts on the life of Bonnie Dodson.

The wisdom of his legal strategy was to become obvious on Wednesday, May 24, 1989, when Geraldine Parrish and Edwin Gordon appeared in court to plead guilty to all charges lodged against them in the aforementioned cases. As the tall, distinguished-looking prosecutor had hoped, Parrish's defeat in the bitterly fought Albert Robinson case sapped the spirit of the defense. Seeing the futility of further fighting their cases, the two co-defendants decided to get it over with.

Before their pleas could be accepted, however, the law required the submission of a statement of facts by the prosecution to serve as the legal basis for Judge Bothe's decision.

Accordingly, Prosecutor Cohen and his assistant Jack Lesser laid out in horrifying detail before a hushed courtroom the evil done by Geraldine Parrish and her cohort, Edwin Gordon.

On Tuesday, November 12, 1985, Edwin Gordon was visiting Bobbie Roberts at her home on North Collington Street in east Baltimore when Geraldine Parrish arrived and contracted with Gordon for a "hit." Later that evening, Frank Ross was shot and killed by a 9-mm Luger furnished to Gordon by Rodney Jones. Posing as a relative of Frank Ross, Parrish called the hospital to get verification of the victim's death. This done, Parrish counted out $1,500 and gave the same to Gordon. This transaction was witnessed by state's witness Bobbie Roberts.

On Friday, March 6, 1987, Rodney Jones, Edwin Gordon, and Geraldine Parrish met at the home of a relative of

Parrish and planned the contract murder of a roomer at the Kennedy Avenue residence, Helen Wright, a retired domestic. Upon arriving there, Parrish asked Wright to go out for Chinese food. While Jones and Wright were in the living room, Parrish and Gordon went to an upstairs room where Parrish slipped a handgun to Gordon. Jones, Gordon and Wright then went to a Chinese carry-out restaurant and as they walked on the 2100 block of Aisquith Street during the return leg of the trip, Gordon shot Wright several times in the back. Wright collapsed whereupon Gordon shot the woman three more times in the head. After the shooting, Parrish paid Gordon $1,500 for the "hit" while Jones received $500 for his help.

On Saturday, September 19, 1987, Bonnie Dodson and her boyfriend, Ronald Mitchener, were visited by Edwin Gordon under the guise of a drug supplier. Suddenly, Gordon opened fire with a handgun, killing Mitchener and seriously wounding Bonnie Dodson.

On Sunday, March 6, 1988, having just been released from the hospital, Bonnie Dodson was lured to a house in west Baltimore by a relative, Geraldine Parrish. As she left the house, she was attacked with a straight razor by Edwin Gordon who cut her throat. State's witness Rodney Jones was later told by Edwin Gordon that he was the person responsible for the attack.

On Thursday, May 19, 1988, Geraldine Parrish lured Bonnie Dodson to a house on Hollins Street and told her to sit on the steps while she went to get something. As Bonnie Dodson sat on the steps, Edwin Gordon stepped out the front door and shot her three times in the head. Later, while Rodney Jones and Edwin Gordon were inmates together at the Baltimore City Jail, Gordon described this, his third unsuccessful attempt to murder Bonnie Dodson to state's witness Jones.

The motive for the attempted murders, explained Prosecutor Mark Cohen, was the $20,000 each in life insurance policies carried on Bonnie Dodson, Helen Wright and Frank Ross — with Geraldine Parrish beneficiary of them all.

Geraldine Parrish had nothing to say this time as Judge Bothe sentenced her and co-defendant Edwin Gordon to six concurrent life sentences for their crimes. Gordon, of course, was already serving a sentence of life imprisonment without the possibility of parole for Henry Barnes' murder.

Although Geraldine Parrish will technically be eligible for parole in 20 years, as a practical matter she, too, is facing the reality of spending the rest of her life behind bars.

Of course, the demise of the good Reverend Gilliard had not escaped the attention of the homicide unit, either. On Monday, July 25, 1988, Detective Crutchfield interviewed one Donald Jarvis, one of the husbands of Geraldine Parrish and a roomer at the Kennedy Avenue row house. He told the sleuth that when the police had searched the house on July 22, 1988, they had overlooked a safe located in the basement. Geraldine Parrish's last-known husband, Bernard Morris, added that he had asked her several times what was in the safe and she had told him that it was none of his business. She also had told him that she could not open the safe because she had lost the key and could not remember the combination. The safe was described as being the size of a standard three-drawer file cabinet.

Returning to the homicide unit, Detective Crutchfield advised Sergeant Childs of the results of his field interviews with Bernard Morris and Donald Jarvis.

Sergeant Childs sighed and said, "Mike, I've never seen a movie with this many twists and turns in it. Draw up an affidavit for a search of the safe. Maybe that will give us a clue as to what happened to the good reverend."

As it turned out it did, with the search yielding pay dirt in the form of a marriage certificate showing that Roslyn

W. Brown and Rayfield Gilliard were united in holy matrimony in Baltimore, Maryland, on January 18, 1988. Also found in the safe was a death certificate which showed that he had died just 15 days later, on February 1, 1988, with the cause of death listed as "cardiovascular disease." Interestingly, the safe also contained a will dated January 27, 1989, which left an estate comprising $440 a month in social security benefits, some west Baltimore real estate, plus $1,000 in cash. The recipient? None other than his wife, Roslyn W. Brown, a/k/a Geraldine Parrish.

When Gary Childs learned of the results of the search, he immediately got on the phone to Mark Cohen who promptly got a court order for exhumation of the body for autopsy in order to determine whether Rayfield Gilliard had been a victim of the ruthless gang of killers.

But this proved to be easier said than done as Detective Donald Waltemeyer, drawing the assignment of locating the corpse for exhumation, soon discovered.

The first body dug up in December 1988 from Baltimore's Mount Zion Cemetery was actually autopsied before the morgue attendant noticed that the identification tag on the toe was not for Rayfield Gilliard!

When Donald Waltemeyer returned to the cemetery with the wrong body, an embarrassed cemetery manager explained that his records wrongly indicated that the body in question was in Row 83. Reviewing the records, he found that the former Baptist minister actually was in Row 78, Grave 17. In an apologetic manner he said, "At the time of this person's interment, we had some youngsters working here. They did not put the person in the grave they stated they had put him in. It's so hard to get competent help these days, you know."

Several weeks later, Detective Waltemeyer had arranged for the gravediggers to try again. With the benefit of hindsight, he checked the toe tag—and found another person's name on it. Knowing that the M.E.'s office did not have the resources to waste in autopsying the wrong bodies, Sergeant Childs held an urgent conference with the state's attorney's office and it was decided to hold the Gilliard homicide investigation in abeyance.

The body was reburied as the first one had been.

Learning of this bizarre footnote to the sensational Geraldine Parrish case, a *Baltimore Sun* reporter interviewed the owner of the funeral home who had handled the Gilliard funeral arrangements.

"The funeral cost his widow about fifteen hundred dollars," he said. "She buried him as cheap as she could."

Advised by the reporter that the police considered the death suspicious, he added: "I don't know what to believe. Reverend Gilliard told me shortly before his death that he was very much in love with his bride."

With Geraldine Parrish standing convicted of first-degree murder in no less than three cases and sentenced to two life sentences, Maryland authorities have apparently decided that no useful purpose is to be served by pursuing the Gilliard case further. As a result, the whereabouts of his body and the truth concerning his manner of death will forever be a mystery.

Thus ends the story of one of the most ruthless gang of killers ever recorded in the annals of Baltimore criminal jurisprudence.

EDITOR'S NOTE:
Bonnie Dodson, Bobbie Roberts, Mary Baxter, Donald Jarvis, and Bernard Morris are not the real names of the persons so named in the foregoing story. Fictitious names have been used because there is no reason for public interest in the identities of these persons.

"10-G HIT ON PAM!"

by Bruce Gibney

**Boone County, Indiana
October 15, 1985**

Sheriff Ern Hudson predicted, "Sooner or later someone is going to talk. And when they do, we'll be there." Hudson is not only the sheriff, but also the chief investigator of Boone County, Indiana. He is a crimesolver, not a fortune teller.

But on this case, he was as right as any turban-garbed swami. Someone finally did talk — almost five years after the brutal hammer-and-bullet murder of a rural Boone County housewife.

It came too late to save another Indiana woman, found dead while on a sexy frolic in south Florida. But not too late to catch her killer.

Pamela Mason was a lifelong resident of Boone County, and a co-owner of one of its most popular establishments, the Big Red Flea Market.

"Pamela," a friend remarked about the 42-year-old woman, "was the salt of the earth. She was just a great old gal, and just about the last one you'd figure to get mixed up in controversy."

On October 15, 1985, this folksy, pretty woman was found sprawled in her garage, brutally murdered.

Sheriff Hudson, who was in Indianapolis administering a

polygraph exam in another case, was notified shortly after the body was discovered. He double-timed it back to Boone County.

The Mason home was located off North Highway 421. Police cruisers and county vans had already filled the U-shaped driveway when the sheriff arrived. Hudson questioned the officers at the scene and then entered the garage. Inside, it was cool and dark.

Pamela Mason was sprawled in the second bay of the six-bay structure, her head turned awkwardly. Blood trailed from the right side of her head and formed a sticky pool on the cement floor.

After making his inspection, Hudson questioned the detectives and crime technicians. Later he interviewed Pamela's fiancé and a shocked relative of hers.

Slowly a story emerged. At 11:00 a.m., Pamela and her relative had gone to nearby Pittsboro to inspect a house Pamela planned to buy. Afterward, the pair ate lunch at a fast-food restaurant in Lebanon.

The relative said that Pamela then dropped her off at her house and continued on her way back to the farmhouse. According to the relative, Pamela planned on picking up her grandson from the day-care center. Instead, the relative got a call from the day-care center director. "She said [Pamela] had never arrived," the relative told Hudson. "I knew something was wrong."

The relative tried to call Pamela at home. Upon getting no answer, she picked up Pamela's grandson and drove to the family home.

Pamela Mason's car was in the driveway, the relative said, but no one answered the door. She checked the first floor, then called for Pamela's fiancé.

"I came right over," the fiancé told Sheriff Hudson. "I searched the rest of the house. Then I tried the garage."

The garage doors were locked. The fiancé said he used an electronic opener from Pamela's car to raise the door. He went inside . . .

"She was on the floor," the fiancé told Hudson. "There was

so much blood."

The investigation continued into the early evening. Criminalists measured and photographed the body, then made a thorough search of the sprawling garage. The search extended to the farmhouse and the palatial grounds.

The murder was a real shocker. According to the pathologist, Dr. John Olson, the victim had suffered massive bruises on the right side of the head with a hammerlike object. The blow had fractured the victim's skull from her right ear to above the right eye.

"It was a tremendous hit," the pathologist noted.

Then Pamela was shot four times, all at point-blank range. The investigators determined that the murder occurred between 2:30 to 2:45 p.m., when a neighbor saw Pamela standing by a fence at her mailbox, and 3:30 p.m., when her relative pulled into the driveway.

The murder appeared to be coolly professional. Despite an exhaustive search, the investigators found almost nothing that could link the killer to the shooting. From the bullet wounds and other evidence, it appeared that the victim had been lured or forced into the cavernous garage where, in effect, she was executed.

The motive for the gruesome execution was elusive. As the co-owner of the Big Red Flea Market, Pamela often carried a lot of cash. Yet her purse, containing almost $2,000 in cash, was found untouched in the garage near her body.

Pamela had not been sexually assaulted. And there was no indication that she had fought with her assailant.

From the little evidence there was, it appeared that on a warm, Indian summer afternoon, a deranged gunman with murderous lust in his cold heart had happened by the big, rambling farmhouse, spotted Pamela Mason near the mailbox, and then lured—or forced—her into the garage, where he used a hammer and then a pistol to end her life. The gunman then ambled away, leaving a good woman dead, and not a clue to his identity.

It was strange, Sheriff Hudson reasoned. Damn strange.

One person who might clear up the strangeness, the sheriff

hoped, was **Pamela's ex-husband,** 47-year-old John Mason. Deputies had gone to the hulking man's plush apartment at the Big Red Flea Market, but he was not home.

Early in the evening on the day of the murder, John Mason called a relative of his from southern Indiana and learned that the police were looking for him. Mason promised to return home immediately.

On October 16th, John Mason walked into the sheriff's station, looked Ern Hudson in the eye, and said, "You wanted to talk to me?"

Sheriff Hudson pointed him towards a chair. "Maybe you could tell us where you were yesterday morning?" he asked.

Mason nodded.

As the Boone County businessman outlined it, October 15th had been a busy day. In the morning he went to the Boone County State Bank to discuss a business loan with one of the bank officers. In the afternoon, his business done, he hunkered down at a bar on West Wilcox, drinking highballs with his girlfriend. Around six o'clock they ate dinner, then headed to Nashville, Tennessee.

"I didn't hear about Pamela until I called my [relative]," John Mason told Sheriff Hudson. "He told me the cops were looking for me, so I came right back."

Mason said he knew nothing about his wife's murder. Although divorced, he said he still felt close to his wife. "I married that girl when she was fourteen," he said. "I've known her all my life." He declared that he was both saddened and angry by the news of her murder. He told the lawman, "I sure as hell hope you catch who did this."

So did Sheriff Hudson. "John, would you mind taking a polygraph exam?" he asked.

"Heck no!" Mason replied. "I had nothing to do with this—I swear. But if this will help you, I'll do it."

With the interrogation over, Mason left the sheriff's office.

That was not the last to be heard from John Mason. On October 22nd, the gruff businessman hired an Indianapolis private eye to conduct his own investigation into his ex-wife's death. He put up a $100,000 reward for information leading to the arrest of the murderer.

But the one thing Mason didn't do was to take the polygraph exam. He did keep his scheduled appointment, but he told Sheriff Hudson at the last minute that his lawyer had advised against it.

That didn't surprise Hudson. Mason, after all, was the prime suspect in his wife's murder.

"Heck, it all went back to the motive," Hudson would tell a reporter years later. "Who profited from her murder?"

The answer came back—Mason. And it all centered around the breakup of the couple's marriage.

John Mason admitted that he was angry and bitter after his wife left him. He also admitted that he "was none too happy" to learn that Pamela had been secretly seeing another man— an auctioneer at the Big Red Flea Market. That steamed Mason, too, since he himself had hired the man who later ran off with his wife.

Mason was also steamed, Sheriff Hudson learned, because Pamela and her boyfriend planned to open an auction house and enter into direct competition with John Mason. That hurt, too.

But the biggest pain Mason felt involved the sprawling farmhouse. As part of the divorce settlement, Pamela planned to mortgage that house, and use the money to buy another home in Pittsboro. The deal was to be finalized on October 18th—three days after Pamela was brutally murdered.

A hammer blow and four bullets to Pamela Mason's head had changed everything. John Mason now had full title to the farmhouse and to the Big Red Flea Market. It was a cool $300,000 windfall—and all it cost was Pamela's life, a very high price indeed.

That much money made John Mason an instant suspect. And he hadn't helped himself much, either, during the interrogation. During questioning, Mason had burst into tears and stopped several times to regain composure.

But Sheriff Hudson noted about the tears, "He turned them on and off."

Mason denied any involvement in his wife's murder. But at one point in his interrogation, Mason noted cryptically to Sheriff Hudson. "A man who is married as long as I have can do just about anything when his wife divorces him and runs off with another man."

He also reminded Hudson, "Just remember, Ern—a good friend doesn't talk."

Convinced that Mason was behind his wife's murder, Sheriff Hudson plugged ahead, looking for the evidence that would put Mason behind bars.

However, the swap-meet impresario had an ironclad alibi: on the afternoon of the murder, Mason was either at the Boone County State Bank or swilling drinks at a local bar.

Mason had not wielded the hammer and pulled the trigger himself—someone else had done it for him, the sheriff and his sleuths reasoned.

Over the next four months, the investigators searched for the hired gun. They questioned dozens of witnesses. At one point, Sheriff Hudson presented the case before a county grand jury, hoping to force someone to talk. But no one did.

Mason, still a free man, went back to work. The Big Red Flea Market boomed. The money rolled in. The 47-year-old widower maintained a high profile, and held court at his favorite bars, often in the company of a lovely woman.

A frequent date was 43-year-old Ilse Daniels, the owner of a South Meriden Street diner. The two were often seen snuggling and drinking at a bar that was one of Mason's favorite hangouts.

In late November, the lovebirds left for an extended vacation. For lovely Ilse, the sex-and-sun romp lasted less than two weeks. On December 8th, her partly clothed body was found face down in less than a foot of water off a beach at Fort Pierce, Florida.

John Mason and several of his buddies were questioned. Mason appeared devastated. He had reported Ilse missing at 11:00 p.m., after they'd became separated on the beach.

"This is an awful tragedy," he told the police.

Tragedy it was. But was it an accident?

An autopsy showed that Ilse had drowned, but it appeared that she had been forcibly held under the water, because she had received several blows to her head. Then a witness told the police that he had seen a woman struggling with a man in the area.

John Mason claimed he knew nothing about it. When investigators asked him why he'd reported Ilse missing almost six hours after they were last seen together, he replied, "I was looking for her. I was hoping I could find her."

Mason was not charged with any crime. But the Fort Pierce authorities remained suspicious.

So did Sheriff Ern Hudson. Two bodies in just two months. Apparently, tragedy followed John Mason like a black cat.

The sheriff wondered: Did Ilse Daniels know something about Pamela Mason's murder? And was that the reason she had been silenced?

Months passed. John Mason returned to Boone County and got back to business as if nothing had happened. He soon found another girlfriend. That never seemed to be a problem for him.

Taking his favorite seat at his favorite bar, Mason looked right at home. Two tragedies in a row had hardly made a dent in his hearty exterior.

However, at the Boone County Sheriff's Office, Sheriff Hudson, one of Mason's few worries, was hard at work. "I knew that sooner or later someone would talk," he later told a reporter. "And when they did, I wanted to be there."

Someone did talk. And Hudson was there.

For years, David Ralston had heard the rumors. In early 1990, after he'd suffered a heart attack and it looked as though he might not make it, he called Sheriff Hudson.

"You remember Pamela Mason?" he asked the lawman.

Five years had passed. But to Hudson, that awful afternoon in the six-bay garage, captured forever in ugly 8-by-10-inch crime scene photographs, was like yesterday.

"Yes," the sheriff replied.

"I think I can help you solve it," Ralston said. In return, he asked the lawman for a small favor. His son was in jail on a drunk-driving rap. "Do what you can for him," Ralston said, "and I will return the favor."

"Deal," Sheriff Hudson said.

Then Ralston told Hudson that John Mason had contacted a hired hit man to kill his wife Pamela.

Hudson nodded. That was almost common knowledge, as far as he and his sleuths were concerned. "Who is the hit man?" he asked.

Ralston said that he didn't know. What he did know was that Mason had never actually met the hit man, but had contacted him through an intermediary—Bill Grand.

"Grand set it up," Ralston said.

Bill Grand was one of Mason's old buddies. But when the sheriff questioned him about the five-year-old murder, the 39-year-old Grand came clean in a hurry.

"I didn't do it!" he told Sheriff Hudson. "The guy who set it up was Sal Reidy."

That name rang a bell for Hudson. Reidy was a jack-of-all-trades who had lived in an apartment behind the Big Red Flea Market and had run errands for Mason. Like Ralston and Grand, Reidy had already been questioned in the lengthy investigation.

In the preceding year, the sheriff learned, Reidy had dropped out of sight. No one seemed to know where he was.

No one—except Bill Grand. "He moved to Florida," Grand told the detectives. "Orlando."

"Good," Hudson said. "You can show us where."

On April 9, 1990, Sheriff Hudson, Detective Francis Shrock of the Indiana State Police, and Bill Grand piled into an unmarked car and made the 16-hour drive to Orlando, Florida.

Orlando is theme-park heaven, home to Disney World and Epcot Center. The apartment complex the Hoosiers parked in front of on the night of April 10th was a far cry from the Magic Kingdom, however—it was a tacky little joint that threatened to be overrun by palm trees and swamp grass.

Outside the apartment, the lawmen taped a microphone to

Bill Grand's chest and supplied him with the cover story that Mason had become paranoid with fears that one of his friends might go to the police about Pamela Mason's murder.

The story was believable. Ilse Daniels had been murdered off Fort Pierce, and the police suspected that she had been slain so that she could never talk to the authorities.

Bill Grand went up to Reidy's apartment and knocked. The door opened and he walked in.

Outside, crouched by the unmarked car, the investigators monitored the conversation.

With everything going on tape, Grand told Reidy that he had become afraid of Mason. "He's gone completely off his rocker," Grand said. "He thinks everyone is against him. Hell, he shot out my windows."

"That's why I got the hell out of Boone County," Reidy said. "I sure as hell didn't want to end up dead."

Outside, by the parked car, investigators continued to monitor the conversation in secret. After they felt that they had enough on tape, they turned off the recorder and went to the apartment themselves.

Sheriff Hudson was the first lawman through the door.

"What's going on?" Reidy demanded, his eyes growing as big as fried eggs.

Hudson told Reidy how the investigation had him fingered as the middleman in the Pamela Mason contract murder. They showed him the microphone taped to Grand's chest and replayed a portion of the tape.

"You were the middleman," Hudson declared. "We want to know who the hit man was."

Reidy shifted uneasily. He was between a rock and a hard place. The rock was John Mason, his longtime friend, employer, and confidant. The hard place was Sheriff Hudson—and the taped conversation linking Reidy to Pamela Mason's murder.

Reidy chose to face the hard place.

His story began in autumn 1985. Reidy said he operated a gun booth at the Big Red Flea Market and lived in an apartment behind the auction bar. John Mason was his good buddy. They both liked to drink and have a good time. Mason also hired him to do odd jobs—like follow Pamela Mason around and report where she went and whom she saw. It was easy work and he liked the money. A good deal, indeed.

Reidy said that Mason took him aside one day and asked if he knew anyone who did strong-arm stuff.

"I told him I did," Reidy said. "John wanted a shake-up done on this guy who was seeing Pamela. I told him I would see what I could do."

Reidy said he put Mason in touch with a man named John L. Morgan, a hard-drinking 55-year-old tough guy from Alexandria. Reidy said he thought that was it. Then on October 15, 1985, Pamela Mason was murdered.

Did Morgan kill the pretty divorcee?

"I can't really say," Reidy told the sheriff. "Mason never talked about it, and neither did Morgan. But after the murder, Mason gave me a sealed envelope which I took to Morgan. It was about an inch-and-a-half thick, and I would bet my last nickel that it was filled with crisp bills."

Reidy said he later delivered another envelope with $1,000 to Morgan.

After the murder, Reidy continued to see Mason. But it was never quite the same. "He seemed different—real uptight," Reidy said.

Shortly after the murder, Mason got drunk in a bar and, according to witnesses, started dancing and singing about his wife's murder.

Two weeks later, Ilse Daniels drowned in Florida.

Sal Reidy said he didn't know if Mason had murdered Ilse or not. But it was possible—very possible.

That finished the interrogation. Reidy had told the lawmen plenty. But he wasn't through yet.

"You're coming with us," Sheriff Hudson told Reidy.

"Where are we going?" Reidy asked.

If he expected jail, the answer was a surprise.

"Indiana," Hudson replied. "We want you to help us solve the Mason murder."

The Hoosier lawmen returned on Wednesday evening.

Sheriff Hudson and Detective Shrock had gone three days without sleep — and they weren't finished yet.

John Morgan, the Alexandria bar owner and freelance hit man, was holding court at the Center Point Tavern, in Alexandria. Investigators fitted Reidy with a wire and sent him inside, prepped with the same story used on him 16 hours earlier — that John Mason was going crazy over his wife's murder and that Morgan's role in the murder was in danger of being revealed.

"There is no way in hell they can trace that to me!" Morgan told Reidy, even as his confession was secretly being taped.

Next, it was John Mason's turn. The investigators found him at a Lebanon bar, shortly before 2:00 a.m., filling his face with "shooters." Reidy used a "flip-flop" version of the same story, now suggesting that Morgan was the one losing his mind over the crime.

As he was being taped, Mason didn't sound alarmed. "So what?" he asked. "What can they prove?"

Mason had good reason to feel secure. Five years had passed since he'd swaggered out of the sheriff's office. That was a lot of water under the bridge. If the investigators had anything, he figured they would have used it by now.

Mason finished his drink. "Don't worry," he told Reidy. "I ain't going to lose any sleep over this. What is done, is done."

Mason was wrong, though. It wasn't done yet.

With tapes in hand, the investigators had no trouble in getting arrest and search warrants.

John Morgan was first. On the evening of April 11th, a lodge brother called him to say it was important that they meet at a Chevrolet dealership in Alexandria.

The lodge brother was also a cop. When Morgan pulled into the car lot, Sheriff Hudson was there waiting for him. On seeing the sheriff, Morgan dove under the dashboard. Hudson pulled the door open, stuck a gun in Morgan's face and ordered him to freeze.

John Morgan was booked into the county jail, charged with murder.

John Mason was arrested a short time later. "What is this

about, Ern?" he asked Sheriff Hudson when he was brought to the jail. When the sheriff told him, Mason said he wanted to see his lawyer.

Morgan, however, made no fuss. When he was questioned at the police station, the bar owner-hit man simply said, "You got me."

The story Morgan gave, tape-recorded during several interrogation sessions, was a bone-chiller . . .

Morgan related that John Mason first approached him in 1985 to have him rough up Pamela Mason's boyfriend. "He said he didn't like the guy and wanted him hurt," Morgan said.

Morgan said he took the job. But he had little success. "The guy was hard to isolate," he told the detectives. "There were always too many people around. I just couldn't get to him."

Later, he said, he hired two other guys to do the job. But they had only limited success.

Morgan reported back to Mason. He said he figured Mason would blow a fuse. But Mason had other plans. "Forget about him for the time being," Mason said, according to Morgan. "I want you to get Pam."

"How did he want you to do that?" Detective Shrock asked.

"Same way," Morgan answered. "Shoot her." Morgan said the initial contract was $5,000. Later the price went up to $10,000.

On the day of the murder, Morgan said, Mason drove him past his home and pointed out his wife as she was working in the yard. Morgan returned a short time later and told Pamela that her ex-husband had hired him to fix a fence on the property. "We went into the garage and I asked her for a hammer," Morgan said. After she gave him the hammer, he asked for nails.

"When she went to get the nails," Morgan continued, "I went up behind her and hit her on the side of the head with the hammer."

Pamela dropped to the floor, but she wasn't dead.

Morgan said he went out to the car, got his pistol, and returned to the garage.

"She was begging for her life," Morgan said coldly. "So I shot her."

The first bullet went into Pamela's head, but it didn't kill her. Morgan said that she reached up with her arm to stop him, so he shot her again.

"That still didn't do it," Morgan said. So he shot her two more times. The fourth slug finally did it.

Then Morgan got in his car and drove home. About a mile north of Highway 421, he threw away the hammer and pistol he had used on Pamela Mason. Later he went back and retrieved the pistol. "Damn good weapon," he explained.

In October 1990, John Morgan was found guilty of first-degree murder and was sentenced to 110 years in prison.

In September 1991, John Mason went to trial for the murder of his ex-wife Pamela. Judge Jack O'Neil presided and Rebecca McClure prosecuted the case. On October 5th, Mason was found guilty and sentenced to 110 years in prison. In a separate trial, Mason was also found guilty of the attempted murder of Pamela's fiancé and drew a 30-year sentence for that crime.

Five years earlier, John Mason had told Sheriff Hudson, "Remember, Ern, a good friend doesn't talk."

John Mason will spend the rest of his life behind bars, remembering how wrong he was.

EDITOR'S NOTE:
David Ralston, Bill Grand, and Sal Reidy are not the real names of the persons so named in the foregoing story. Fictitious names have been used because there is no reason for public interest in the identities of these persons.

"KILL ALL THREE AND TORCH THE HOUSE!"

by Bill G. Cox

The house fire was raging when firefighters responded to the alarm in a north side residential neighborhood of Abilene, Texas, on the late summer night of Monday, June 11, 1990. Thick smoke roiled into the sky and flames shot from the roof as the fire units pulled up to the 1500 block of Lillius Street at 11:55 p.m.

As the firemen unrolled hoses and began pouring water onto the inferno, police patrol cars and an ambulance arrived, their wailing sirens and rotating red-and-blue emergency lights adding to the dramatic scene.

Even at that late hour, residents in their nightclothes spilled from their homes to gape at the scene. Some neighbors shouted to firemen that three elderly people lived in the house. Firefighters looked through a window of the bedroom at the southwest corner of the white frame home and saw someone lying on the bed. They broke through the window and carried a man outside. Finding some signs of life, the rescuers rushed the man, who was covered with curious wounds, by ambulance to a hospital.

The firemen also discovered a woman in the living room. She was in a recliner in front of a television set that was still on. When the woman was examined on the front lawn, firemen and police officers made a shocking discovery. She had been stabbed and slashed repeatedly! Her wounds were similar to those noted on the man who was taken to the hospital.

The intensity of the roaring flames was centered in the southeast bedroom and an adjoining hallway in the back. It wasn't until the fire was extinguished that the charred body of another man was found in the back bedroom. He, too, had suffered stab wounds, though the badly burned condition of the body made them less apparent.

The victims were identified as 65-year-old Mandell Eugene Summers, his 64-year-old wife, Helen Vern Summers, and Mandell's 60-year-old brother, Billy Mack Summers. The husband and wife were dead when carried from the burning home. The other man, Billy Summers, was pronounced dead on arrival at the hospital.

Homicide detectives who responded to the call were faced with tracking down a vicious killer who had evidently gone from room to room, methodically murdering the three elderly family members.

While firemen were still battling the flames, officers started canvassing the neighborhood for possible witnesses who could throw some light on the fire tragedy that had become a murder mystery.

They located a woman who recalled having seen a car drive out of the alley behind the Summers' home about eleven o'clock or shortly thereafter. She thought it was a yellow or light brown Monte Carlo, but she hadn't gotten a license number. She said there were several men in the car. When detectives searched the grounds behind the victims' house, they found a pair of pantyhose in the alley that they speculated might have been used by one of the killers as a mask. They also observed that the telephone wire outside the house and the screen on the back bedroom window had been out.

For 13 hours, the homicide investigators and crime scene technicians worked at the murder scene, searching for evidence, a weapon, and leads. The detectives were under the supervision of Detective Sergeant Danny Spohn, head of the Crimes Against Persons Unit and a 16-year veteran of the Abilene Police Department. Spohn and his team believed that the killer or killers had gained entry through the back bedroom window.

If it were an intruder bent on burglary loot, the sleuths wondered, why had it been necessary to kill the elderly occupants with such obvious viciousness? Even if the burglar had been accosted by the family members, detectives believed he could have fled the house without the mass slaughter.

But it seemed that the Summerses had been killed, one by one, where the stalking knifer found them and that the intruder had entered with the intent of killing the three occupants. The female victim had obviously been watching television, or had possibly dozed off, when the killer struck. Blood on the chair indicated she had been slain there.

Lieutenant Eddie Haas, a fire department arson investigator, observed that the blaze appeared to have started in the southeast bedroom, where the badly charred body of Mandell Summers was found. Haas and others detected the odor of a combustible fluid with which the killer might have doused the victims and the surfaces around them.

Suspecting that the fire had been set to cover the murders, the sleuths took samples of flooring and carpet from the house. The intense heat of the fire had destroyed windows and burned through the peak of the attic wall at the rear of the home. Haas planned to submit the samples to a private laboratory for analysis to yield more information on the cause of the fire.

When detectives asked neighbors for names of relatives who could be notified of the tragedy, they were told that Mandell and Helen Summers had an adopted son, Gregory Lynn Summers, who lived in Abilene and was associated with his dad in the home improvement business. Neighbors related that Mandell's younger brother, Billy Summers, who was said to be mentally handicapped, had lived with the Summerses for some time. The brothers were frequently seen working together in the yard.

One neighbor remembered that Mandell and Helen had come to her home on Saturday to discuss a paneling project for her house. A close friend of the Summerses told officers that she had visited the couple at home on Monday night, stopping to give them some vegetables from her garden about three hours before the family's deaths. She said the couple was highly respected and well thought of in the community. She admired the way the Summerses had treated Billy Summers, who had moved in after his mother died.

During her visit, the tearful friend said, there had been nothing to hint that such horrible violence would strike later that night. Mandell had talked about plans to retire in the near future.

No sharp instrument that could have inflicted the stab wounds was found in the house or the neighborhood. Though the home showed some signs of having been rifled or searched, it was not yet determined if valuables had been taken.

Neighbors recalled that the Summers residence had been burglarized about a year before by a burglar or burglars who entered while the occupants were asleep. The burglar made off with a large amount of cash and jewelry, the neighbors said. Was it possible that the same intruder had returned again, this time killing the occupants? the investigators wondered.

Gregory Summers, the adopted son, could not be located when officers tried to inform him about the slayings of his relatives. But at 8:00 a.m. the next day, while the detectives were still at the scene, he showed up. Sobbing emotionally, he said he had heard about his parents' and uncle's deaths on a radio newscast. Gregory said he had spent the night at his girlfriend's home, an address that officers looking for him had not known about.

When he regained his composure, Gregory told Sergeant Spohn that there was no reason for burglars to target his parents' home. Mandell Summers was in bad financial shape—in fact had gone bankrupt—the son said. In better times, Gregory said, his father did not have bank accounts but "operated out of his pocket," sometimes carrying as much as $4,000 to $5,000 on him. Maybe someone had heard rumors about Mandell's habit of having big sums of cash in his possession.

Established investigative routine leads detectives, when a murder occurs, to investigate immediate family members. If a wife is murdered, her husband automatically becomes the foremost suspect. Or vice versa. Such are the ways of the human race, experienced sleuths know; the line between love and hate is whisper thin.

Gregory Summers was no exception to this procedure of screening the victims' inner family circle. Detectives heard varying opinions from neighbors and friends about Gregory's relationship with his adoptive parents. Some people said it was a turbulent relationship, and had been ever since Gregory was a child. Others remembered the family as being "close," and described Gregory as "a good old boy."

But the son's emotional display in front of his parents' home on the morning after the murders hadn't struck Sergeant Spohn just right. For one thing, the detective sergeant had noticed that when Gregory was crying the loudest with hands over his eyes, he seemed to be watching through his fingers the effect he was having on the officials. Other investigators had observed this, too.

As the murder probe continued, Spohn told the news media, "It's the most serious crime we've ever had in Abilene, at least in terms of the number of victims."

Veteran officers couldn't remember a previous triple homicide case in this quiet university city. The police department was giving top priority to the shocking massacre that had occurred in a quiet residential neighborhood.

The entire Crimes Against Persons Unit, aided by a specially assigned training officer, was working the murders, with Detectives Roger Berry and Joel Lujan specified as lead investigators.

As Deputy Police Chief Melvin Martin said, "Anytime we have a major homicide like this, we'll devote whatever it takes. Some of the other less serious cases have to wait because we don't have the manpower to do it all."

Patrol units had been unable to locate the Monte Carlo seen leaving the alley, but the search continued throughout the city. And the background investigation on Gregory Summers intensified at Sergeant Spohn's direction.

The adopted son's image regarding his familial relationship was darkening considerably as detectives talked to friends and business associates of the slain parents and uncle. One relative said that Gregory treated his parents "very ugly sometimes" and had been fired by his father several times from the home improvement business. But Mandell had always let him come back, at his wife's urging.

An employee of the elder Summers recalled hearing Gregory threaten his father on more than one occasion during on-the-job disputes. During one exchange, Gregory had shouted at his father, "I'm going to burn your house down with you in it!" the construction worker recalled.

About three years earlier, one family friend told detectives, Gregory Summers had claimed he was kidnapped. When he turned up after his disappearance in a Big Spring, Texas, hospital, the friend had accompanied Mandell and Helen Summers to visit Gregory. When the father accused him of staging the kidnapping, the son turned to him and said, "I can't wait to see you dead!" the witness reported.

An ex-wife of Gregory's told the sleuths that during her marriage, which had been an abusive one, Gregory had mentioned he "would like to kill his father and if his parents died, it [the estate] would all go to him."

The former spouse said that Gregory collected an insurance payment after a blaze at their own home in August 1985. One morning after Gregory left for work, his wife was awakened by a friend shouting that the house was on fire. She, the friend, and five children managed to escape without harm. Gregory later collected $25,000 from an insurance firm for the fire damage, the ex-wife related.

She also remembered that during the marriage, two pickups parked in the drive at Gregory's house had burned. The ex-wife said Gregory had been unsuccessful in collecting insurance claims because of the suspicious nature of the fires.

In view of the information being uncovered, Sergeant Spohn ordered his investigators to bring in Gregory Summers for further questioning.

Asked to verify his whereabouts on the night of the murders, the 32-year-old Summers repeated that he had been with his girlfriend. But he told a different story about how he learned of the deaths. This time he said he had called a friend, who told him about the slayings.

When detectives accompanied Gregory to the girlfriend's residence to question her, he repeatedly interrupted the interview. The young woman declined to answer any questions after that.

The detectives still didn't have evidence to support a charge against Gregory Summers. But they continued to press for it. Considering the neighbor's story about seeing a car with several occupants leave the alley behind the Summerses' home late on the murder night, Spohn and his detectives theorized that more than one person might have been involved in the slayings.

Two days after the murders, Gregory Summers asked the

police department to release property in his parents' home to him so that he could protect it from possible theft. They granted his request, only to learn later that he had sold the valuable tools and other items to a pawnshop for a ridiculously small amount of money. Also, he had immediately filed claims for payment on his parents' insurance policies.

The homicide sleuths punched a hole in Gregory's story that his father didn't have bank accounts at the time of his death and was in severe financial condition. Checking bank records, the sleuths found out that Mandell Summers currently had in excess of $4,300 in a checking account. Also, the estate, including the house, cars, and various insurance policies, totaled about $107,000, a tidy sum indeed for the sole heir, Gregory Summers!

When the report was received from a forensic pathology laboratory in Dallas where autopsies were performed on the three murder victims, it confirmed what the detectives had already thought: All three had been dead from multiple stab wounds before the house fire started.

A few days after the murders, the busy detectives received some totally unexpected information from an informant. The man said that the story of the murders in the local newspaper had prompted him to come forward. Explaining that he had known Gregory Summers since the third grade, the tipster told investigators that Gregory had met him in a local bar in the spring of 1989 and later asked if he was willing to commit mass murder.

"He asked me to kill his parents and his uncle," the informant related. "He offered me fifty thousand dollars from an insurance policy. And he told me there would be jewelry, guns and four or five hundred dollars at the house. He told me that, after the killings, to set the house on fire to cover any evidence."

The man said he quickly refused the offer. Now, a year later, shocked by the heinous crime, the witness contacted police.

The informant's statement left no doubt in the minds of the detectives that Gregory Summers had for a long time been thinking about killing his parents and uncle and burning their house. However, they didn't yet have a case to take to the district attorney's office and seek a murder complaint.

Sergeant Spohn instructed Detectives Berry and Lujan to keep digging and talking to everyone they could find who knew the suspect. The sleuths' perseverance turned up another witness who had visited the Summerses on the day of the murders. The man said that when he entered the house, Mandell Summers was on the phone talking to his son.

From the conversation, the visitor had understood that Mandell was rebuffing his son's demand for money, saying he had given Gregory money on the previous evening and asking what he had done with it. Mandell hung up after saying, "I don't have any more money because I haven't been paid for the job [a current project]."

Other evidence showing that the father was cutting off his financial support to Gregory came to the investigators in the form of handwritten notes. The notes were found by relatives when they were going through the fire-damaged house to salvage any possessions. Mandell Summers had indicated in the notes that he planned to remove Gregory as the executor in the Summerses' wills.

Another note voiced Mandell's intent to shut off utilities at Gregory's house, which Mandell had been paying for under his own name. The phone service had been shut off on June 7th, gas service was to end on June 11th, and water on June 18th.

Another damning piece of information to enhance the growing circumstantial case against Gregory Summers was the old police report on the burglary at the Summerses' house a year before the murders. When the report was pulled from the files, it showed that about $3,000 and a large amount of jewelry had been taken in the break-in. But the most startling part was that fingerprints taken from the sill of the window where the burglar entered had been identified as those of Gregory Summers.

The investigators learned further that Gregory, who had been broke at the time, purchased a touring motorcycle after the burglary. No charge had been filed in the burglary, presumably because of the reluctance of Gregory's adoptive parents to pursue prosecution.

Everything pointed to the troublemaking son as the killer, but the question in the minds of the homicide sleuths was: Did Gregory do it himself or did he have help? Could he have plotted the family murders and hired someone to do it?

The key that unlocked the mass of information that they accumulated during the almost round-the-clock investigation came to the detectives 10 days after the murders. It came in the form of a phone call from an anonymous informant. The caller gave only the names of two men he said might know something about the case before he hung up.

The names were Raymond Gonzales and Paul Flores, who were thought to live in Haskell, a town near Abilene. Losing no time after receiving the tip, the Abilene detectives picked up Gonzales at Haskell. At first, the 19-year-old denied knowing anything about the Summers case. Later, however, he decided to make a voluntary statement.

The statement made by the suspect implicated three other men. Gonzales related that he, Andrew Cantu of Abilene, and Paul Flores of Haskell entered the Summers home on the night of June 11th. The suspect said he saw Cantu stab Mandell Summers with a knife and then set fire to the house. Gonzales also stated that Cantu told him that Gregory Summers was going to pay Cantu $10,000 for killing the Summerses.

Combining this confession with the statement of the witness who told of being offered $50,000 by Gregory Summers a year earlier to commit the murders and burn the house—and the other details gathered from witnesses who had heard Gregory make similar threats—detectives filed an affidavit of probable cause for arrest warrants. The warrants charged Summers and Cantu with capital murder and Gonzales and Flores with burglary of a habitation.

Shortly thereafter, Summers and Flores were taken into custody by the investigators. Cantu apparently had fled the area, the investigators learned. He was thought to be armed with an Uzi submachine pistol and was described as extremely dangerous in the police bulletin relayed to state law enforcement agencies.

Gregory Summers, who denied any knowledge of the slayings, was remanded to the Taylor County Jail in lieu of $2 million bond. Gonzales and Flores were jailed on the burglary charges and their bond was set at $250,000 each. From their statements, detectives believed they had not been intent on murder when they pulled the burglary.

Checking the suspects' backgrounds, the officers learned that Cantu had been released on parole from the state penitentiary in December 1988 after serving about nine months of a five-year sentence for burglary convictions. Cantu knew Mandell Summers from working for him for several months, the detectives discovered.

Flores, also an ex-con, had been freed from prison less than a month before the murders. He had been paroled on May 14th after doing six months of a four-year sentence for unauthorized use of a motor vehicle. There was no record of Gonzales having previously been in trouble with the law.

Flores made a statement to the investigators, giving an account of the murder night, which he would repeat in later trial testimony. Flores claimed that on June 10th, the day before the mass killings, Cantu tried to recruit him, Gonzales, and another man to help with the job.

"Cantu said he was going to have to waste three people," Flores said. "He said an 'adopted son' wanted these people wasted."

According to Flores, Cantu didn't mention the name of the "adopted son."

Flores said that all three men refused to help Cantu kill anyone, but he and Gonzales agreed to take part in the burglary after it was mentioned that a large sum of money might be found in the house. On June 11th, the trio entered a back window after the outside phone wire had been cut by Cantu, said Flores. Flores related that Cantu then went from room to room, stabbing the victims with a knife that he had bought from Flores earlier that day. After the stabbings, the three searched the house for the "big money" that Cantu had spoken of—including $10,000 in a dresser drawer and $23,000 supposedly hidden under a mattress.

Finding no money, the burglars left by the same window. Cantu sprayed a can of charcoal lighter fluid back into the window, over Mandell Summers' body and the interior of the room. Flores said Cantu then ignited the flammable fluid, intending the fire to cover up the murders.

The murder weapon was discarded a couple of blocks from the house as they drove away, Flores said. Later, Cantu disposed of a pair of athletic shoes and a black sweatsuit he was wearing at the time.

As the search continued for Andrew Cantu, investigators worked to tie together the evidence against him. While talking to a resident in the block where the murder knife was reportedly discarded, detectives located the weapon. Children had found the knife earlier, but the resident said it hadn't been connected in anyone's mind to the murders.

Detectives also grilled relatives and associates of Cantu's. Witnesses living at a house where Cantu was also residing recalled that Gregory Summers visited Cantu there twice the day before the murders.

The men talked privately, but one witness said Cantu appeared extremely nervous after Summers left. Another witness told the sleuths that the next night, June 11th, two men, whom he knew only as Raymond and Paul, joined Cantu at the house at about 10:15 p.m. When they left, Cantu remarked that they had to "do a job," the witness said.

Cantu was wearing a pair of borrowed athletic shoes and black sweatpants when he left with the others, the man recalled.

A close woman friend of Cantu's said that when he returned to the house later that night and she inquired where he had been, Cantu told her, "Don't worry about it. I had to take care of business." Later, after she saw news reports of the murders, she had asked Cantu if he did it. Cantu denied any involvement, but told her, "If I didn't keep my mouth shut, I would end up in a plastic bag out on a dirt road."

Detectives also grilled the man who was with Raymond Gonzales and Paul Flores when Cantu had tried to recruit them for the burglary job. He said he had left the group when Cantu mentioned "wasting" three people. But a week after the murders, he encountered Cantu at a local dance and asked if he had done it.

"He said, 'Yeah,' and told me to shut up," the witness said.

Another relative of Cantu's told detectives that the trio had been highly nervous when they came to the relative's house early on June 12th. From their actions, the men apparently had come away from the Summerses' home empty handed in the way of the cash loot, the sleuths deduced. Cantu had even body searched his two accomplices, for what reason the witness didn't know. The investigators believed that Cantu thought the others might have found money and concealed it from him.

Sergeant Spohn and his homicide sleuths got some good news when a fellow lawman, a Taylor County deputy, advised them that he had been trying to serve an arrest warrant on Gregory Summers since the first of the year for his nonpayment of child support owed to an ex-wife. In fact, Gregory was $16,000 in arrears on the support payments but had somehow eluded the contempt of court arrest warrant. Now, Spohn believed, they had the motive for Gregory wanting his parents dead: an urgent need for big funds to avoid going to jail.

On June 26, 1990, less than a week after the arrest of the others charged in the case, the elusive 23-year-old Andrew Cantu was nabbed in Irving, Texas, near Dallas. Acting on a tip supplied by Abilene investigators, Irving detectives and Dallas County deputies nabbed Cantu hiding in the attic of an apartment occupied by a woman friend. No Uzi submachine pistol was found, and he was taken into custody without resistance.

Returned to Abilene for arraignment on the capital murder charge, the suspect denied to reporters that he was involved in the slayings. His bond was set at $1 million.

On May 22, 1991, Cantu went on trial in state district court in Abilene. After a week of testimony, the six-man, six-woman jury deliberated only slightly more than two hours before returning a verdict that found the defendant guilty of capital murder. The same jury would determine punishment — either life imprisonment or death by lethal injection.

Against his attorney's advice, Cantu took the stand in his own defense during the punishment phase. He denied killing the Summerses, maintaining that the real killers were Gonzales and Flores who had testified against him.

Admitting that he made his living by selling cocaine, Cantu testified that he was in Fort Worth trying to buy the drug on the night of the murders. When he returned to Abilene later that night, Gonzales and Flores came to his house. He related that he knew they had slain the Summerses and was angry about it.

"Greg had talked these young people into killing three grown adults," Cantu said. "I did know that it was going to happen, though I didn't stop it. I didn't stop it, but I didn't do it. I don't have a pretty past, but I ain't no murderer."

Cantu said he refused Gregory Summers' offer to kill the family for a large sum of money. "I told him, 'I don't do people.' I told him just because I know people who smoked people, it don't mean I smoked people or approved of it," Cantu said.

The jury deliberated about 70 minutes before mandating the death penalty for Andrew Cantu.

Meanwhile, while Cantu's trial had been underway in Abilene, jury selection began for Gregory Summers' capital murder trial in Denton, Texas, where the case had been moved on a venue change because of the extensive publicity. As he awaited completion of the jury selection, Summers gave a newspaper interview claiming his innocence. He told a reporter *he* was the reason for the murders, but was not responsible for the killing of his family.

Summers claimed that the killer came to the Summerses' home looking for him for revenge because he had cooperated with federal authorities in a drug and stolen vehicle investigation in Houston. When they didn't find him, they killed his parents and uncle, he said. Summers said he acted as an informant for the FBI for about a year. The FBI later declined to comment.

Claiming that he had no reason to kill his parents, the accused mastermind of the murder plot added, "They were my bread and butter. If I ever needed money or anything, my parents were always there."

The prosecution agreed, in a sense, that Gregory indeed was dependent on his parents for financial help. But they cast that need in a different light when testimony began before a jury. The district attorney asserted in his opening statement that Gregory Summers' immediate need for money to keep him from going to jail on the nonpayment of child support was a major reason he hired a contract killer to do the murders.

During final arguments, Prosecutor Miles LeBlanc told the jury that the elderly people were slain because Gregory Summers "made a cold, calculated decision that his parents were worth more to him dead than they were alive. Bill Summers was killed only because he was in the way."

The defense attorney argued. "Why would a person kill the goose that lays the golden egg? That amount of money wouldn't last any time at all."

On August 21, 1991, Gregory Summers was convicted of capital murder by a seven-man, five-woman jury that considered the evidence for only two hours before returning the verdict. The next day, the same jury took only 10 minutes to set his punishment at death.

The verdict was automatically appealed to the Texas Court of Criminal Appeals. Meanwhile, Summers is awaiting execution on death row of the Texas Department of Corrections, as is Andrew Cantu, whose case was also on automatic appeal to the higher court.

In September 1991, Raymond Gonzales and Paul Flores both pleaded guilty to the burglary charges before Judge Billy John Edwards of the 104th State District Court in Abilene. The judge sentenced Gonzales to 20 years and Flores to 30 years in prison. They are both currently serving their terms.

"BABY-FACED ANGEL WAS A COLD-BLOODED KILLER!"

by Don Lasseter

Holy Jim Canyon in Orange County, California, was anything but heavenly on Friday, September 6, 1991. It was hot as hell, and the dead body of a young man lay undiscovered in the rural hills.

While most of the nation enjoyed cooler temperatures that week, the canyon baked under hot blasts of Santa Ana winds, southern California's answer to Switzerland's Foehn and France's Mistral. Blowing from the desert toward the Pacific Ocean, the pressure-heated wind escalated temperatures and, some people swore, sent fevered brains into murderous ventings of heated rage.

Just out of reach of refreshing coastal breezes, the brush-covered terrain, sparsely populated with scattered mobile homes, was one of the last wild outposts in the lower tip of Orange County.

Twisting ravines in the region provided shady hiding places for undocumented immigrants from across the border, 100 miles to the south. One such individual, a day laborer, was trudging with a companion along a dry stream bed on that blistering morning when he was abruptly jolted by the sight of a dead body. The least they could do, the two figured, was make an anonymous call to the police.

Investigator Bob Blackburn and his partner, Mike Wallace, of the Orange County Sheriff's Department (OCSD) were on their way to a meeting in Long Beach when the call came in on their car phone. They flipped a quick U-turn and headed south on the 405 freeway. Shortly after 10:00 a.m., after a hectic 40-mile drive, they turned off Trabuco Canyon Road, bounced nearly two miles along an unpaved track, and stopped near a couple of parked black-and-whites.

Sergeant Rick Starr, OCSD, led them to the discovery, about 60 feet from the dirt road.

Lying face up among cactus, dry shrubs, and rocks, the body of a young man lay sprawled in the dirt. The bent left knee jutted skyward, while the right leg, also bent at the knee, rested easily on the ground. He might have been asleep, but the blood and the heat-accelerated decomposition made it clear that he would never wake up. A hefty rock, 14 inches wide, lay in silent witness near his left shoulder. Dried blood stained the rough surface of the stone.

Fortunately, marauding animals common to the area had wreaked no additional damage to the human remains.

The victim wore a white T-shirt, gray shorts, and white L.A. Gear sports shoes with black stripes. No identification papers were in the pockets. Detectives Blackburn and Wallace guessed that he had been there at least a couple of days.

While waiting for the forensic specialists to arrive, the investigators began preliminary probing.

Both investigators were well experienced for the grim task. Bob Blackburn, at age 36, already had 12 years on the force, five of them with the homicide unit. Before that, he helped originate the position of riding shotgun in the department's new helicopter air support team. Mike Wallace, at 42, had 11 years with the sheriff's department, four of them spent chasing killers. He had recently been paired with Blackburn, and this would be their first case as partners, with Blackburn as lead investigator.

Sergeant Starr pointed to a blue 1980 Toyota Corolla that sat next to the dirt road. He had already checked the registration and processed a Department of Motor Vehicles (DMV) records check. He found that it belonged to Damian Allen McKenna, date of birth October 15, 1971. The records said McKenna was 6 feet tall, weighed 185 pounds, and had brown hair and green eyes. The victim lying on the ground matched the description.

One of the uniformed officers told Blackburn that he responded to a complaint in the area the previous Monday, and the blue Toyota had not been there at the time. At least that was a start in narrowing down the time frames of the victim's death.

When criminalist Liz Thompson and Deputy Coroner Steve Eicherly arrived, Blackburn watched closely as the experts examined the victim. Bloodstains on the victim's head and the adjacent rock suggested an injury of blunt force trauma, but there was no visible bone damage or crushed tissue. The victim's bruised "raccoon eyes," which usually accompany head trauma, seemed to reinforce the possibility that the youth had been bludgeoned to death with the heavy stone. But Detective Blackburn was troubled, feeling instinctively that the rock told only part of the gruesome story. He would have to wait to see if his theory was justified, though, because the advanced decomposition made an on-site determination of other lethal injuries impossible.

The investigators spent the remainder of the morning searching the area and photographing the body.

Back at sheriff's headquarters by mid-afternoon, the investigators fed fingerprints lifted from the corpse to the identification bureau computer and confirmed that the victim was indeed 19-year-old Damian McKenna. Before leaving to notify the victim's family, Blackburn heard from Deputy Coroner Eicherly, and learned that his instincts had been right. X-rays of the victim's head revealed the presence of bullet fragments, with an entry wound above the right ear. Blackburn requested a gunshot residue (GSR) test on the victim's hands. Maybe it had been a suicide. The youth could have fallen against the rock and bled on it after shooting himself. What about the gun? It was possible that the men who made the report had found it and taken it with them.

At 4:15 p.m., Detectives Blackburn and Wallace stood at the front door of the victim's family home in upscale Mission Viejo. A woman answered the door, and the investigators were faced with the hardest part of their jobs. After gently informing the victim's relatives of the tragedy, and waiting for them to regain composure, the investigators asked a few routine questions, then left.

During the three-day Labor Day weekend, Blackburn couldn't get the victim and the circumstances out of his mind. He was positive that this was not a suicide and was anxious to get the investigation underway.

On Tuesday morning, Blackburn attended the autopsy. People unfamiliar with police work often wonder how investigators can watch such proceedings without being sick. Blackburn explains that sheriff's homicide investigators, in their first week of training, are sent every day to watch post-mortems to learn how to focus on the scientific aspects of the examination and try to ignore the horror of it. For most of them, the indoctrination works, but some never quite get the hang of it.

Blackburn had seen too many autopsies by this time to be fazed by them anymore. He could see the bullet wound, but he also thought that he could see some evidence of another possible bullet entry in the back of the head. He asked the technicians to continue checking to verify his suspicion. He also took some photos of the wounds. The GSR tests were inconclusive.

Suicide had not yet been ruled out. On the contrary, the possibility was reinforced when Blackburn learned from Damian McKenna's family that he would sometimes drive up to Holy Jim Canyon when he was depressed or when he just wanted to be alone.

Hoping that something in the blue Toyota might provide a lead, the two investigators drove to the impound facility where forensic specialist T.J. Jurjis and criminalist Liz Thompson had pulled the car into a property bay and were methodically examining every square inch of it. They lifted several latent prints from various surfaces. From the car's interior, they recovered articles of clothing, jumper cables, and a checkbook in the name of McKenna. There was also an assortment of maps of Orange, Los Angeles, and San Diego Counties. Nothing in the car shed any light on the cause of the victim's death or hinted at any possible foul play.

On Thursday, Investigator Blackburn talked again to a family member who recalled that when Damian had left the house on Tuesday night, September 3rd, he had been wearing a diamond stud earring and had carried a gold-plated money clip given to him by his grandfather. Neither item would ever be found.

Interviews the two investigators conducted with some of McKenna's acquaintances revealed nothing useful. The old guideline—that the trail cools off rapidly if no leads are found within the first 48 hours—seemed to be taking effect.

Who would want Damian McKenna dead? There just didn't seem to be a reasonable motive. Was it drug-connected? His family didn't know of any drug-related problems. Damian was a nice young man, they said, whose

20th birthday was just a month away. He was even a father. The child, 10 months old, was in the custody of the mother, Destinni Mardesich.

Lawmen learned that Damian and Destinni, both very attractive young people, had met in November 1989 at school in Mission Viejo. She was 15 and he was 18. They thought it was cute that they shared the same first and last initials. Petite at 5-foot-1, Destinni had an angel face. In another time, she might have been a model for Botticelli, with her green eyes, cupid's-bow mouth, cherubic cheeks, and blonde hair that cascaded past her shoulders. Damian's dark hair, too, was shoulder-length, framing pleasant features that radiated when he flashed his impish smile. They began dating, and within a short time, she realized that she was pregnant. The baby was born on November 24, 1990.

For a while, the couple lived a teenagers-in-love story, with plans for marriage. They lived with his relatives for four months of 1991, and in their own apartment during May. But Damian and Destinni simply weren't ready for the long-term commitment. They quarreled, and she asked him to move out.

Investigator Blackburn learned that Damian had been devastated by what he regarded as rejection. He had never been in trouble before, but he "went off the deep end" and dabbled with drugs to ease his emotional pain.

After the discovery of Damian McKenna's body, Destinni visited his family frequently and expressed her sorrow. She told them how much she loved Damian. The relatives continued to keep Detective Blackburn informed of anything they could remember.

Still curious about the injuries to the victim's head, Blackburn carefully examined the photos taken during the autopsy. He scrutinized one that had been enlarged for him, and found what he had suspected all along. There was a beveled hole in the back of the victim's head, a second bullet entry wound. Pathologists later confirmed it.

Grabbing his partner, Mike Wallace, the two sleuths hurried back to Holy Jim Canyon. They spent hours swinging metal detectors back and forth. They got down on their hands and knees and crawled in the choking dust and heat until they nearly wore holes in the knees of their trousers. Intensive, dedicated effort, combined with a little luck, frequently produces results. The sleuths' intensive work in the canyon paid off in the form of two .22-caliber shell casings that had been well hidden by brush several yards from the body. The luck came on Saturday, December 14th, eight days after Damian McKenna had been found.

While relaxing at home, Blackburn was notified by telephone, at 12:45 p.m., that a deputy sheriff had been interviewing a teenage girl, a runaway, who seemed to have some knowledge related to the McKenna homicide. The teenager had mentioned a girl named Tania who reportedly said that she knew who killed Damian McKenna. The sergeant said that he would keep Blackburn posted.

Four hours later, Blackburn's phone rang again, and he was informed of another break. A youth had checked himself into a hospital "for protection" from someone who might hurt him, and asked to speak to the police. The responding deputy had heard the youth say that someone named Glen had killed McKenna.

While Blackburn was working to verify these stories, another informant walked into the South County Substation in Laguna Niguel. The young man wearing an oversized hat, reported that his name was Tony Gibbs and said he was the boyfriend of Destinni Mardesich and had some important information.

It took Blackburn about 20 minutes, weaving through heavy Sunday afternoon traffic on the San Diego Freeway, to reach the South County Substation where Gibbs, age 19, waited for him.

The nervous youth told Blackburn that he was pretty sure that two guys had killed Damian McKenna. He thought their names were Ryan and Mike.

From having no suspects just a few hours before, the investigator now had three names — Glen, Mike, and Ryan — and was looking for a young woman who might have additional information.

Trying to calm down Tony Gibbs and keep him talking coherently, Blackburn listened to the youth's story. He said that he'd met Destinni two years earlier. They had dated and broken up, and she had started seeing Damian. When Destinni split up with Damian in May, Tony resumed his relationship with her.

"She started telling me stuff about Damian and how he said he was going to shoot her and the baby. She was worried."

Gibbs paused, gulped, and continued. "I told her, 'He ain't gonna do it.'"

Detective Blackburn waited patiently for the young man to get to the point, and tried not to look at the large, floppy-brimmed hat the young man seemed to be hiding under. Gibbs blurted out, "She's been having meetings off and on with this guy named Ryan who did it."

"Do you know where we can find Ryan?"

"No, I'm not sure," Gibbs replied.

"Was anyone else involved?" Blackburn asked.

"Yeah, Jon — don't know his last name."

Blackburn jotted down the name "Jon" as a possible suspect, and crossed off "Mike," which had apparently been a nervous error by the informant.

"When did you first hear about all this?" asked Blackburn.

"She told me about it the night it happened," Gibbs stammered. "She came in and I asked her where she was, and she said, 'I didn't do it.' I asked her, 'Do what?' "

Gulping again, Gibbs quoted Destinni, "I didn't kill Damian."

He had been shocked to hear that anyone had killed Damian. Blackburn wanted more details. Gibbs continued.

"They went out there in Jon's truck. She was in the bed of the pickup, covered with a blanket." Jon owned a brown Toyota pickup, Gibbs said, with a camper shell on the back. The rear window was out, and the hole was big enough for anyone to crawl from the cab to the bed.

"She left about 11:00 p.m. [Tuesday] and said they would be gone a couple of hours. I was pissed 'cause I thought she was out screwing around."

"What happened after they left?"

"I was kind of wondering how it happened," Gibbs continued. "She said Ryan and Jon went over to talk to Damian and got him to go out to Trabuco Canyon to meet them, and they were gonna talk about drugs, or have him hold some drugs for Ryan. Destinni was hiding in the back of the truck." Gibbs said he thought that Destinni had heard some conversation about hurting her or the baby. "That's when they shot him."

"She told you she didn't do it. Who did?"

"Ryan shot him in the back of the head, and then Jon said that Damian was still alive and so they shot him again, and he was still breathing, so I guess they picked up a rock and smashed him over the head with it. They left him lying there and took off."

"Did she tell you specifically who shot him?"

"Ryan. With a twenty-two caliber. I think it was a rifle."

Observing that the youth was still nervous, Blackburn tried to calm him down. Gibbs groaned, "It got real scary. I thought, what is this chick, a black widow or something? Am I next?" He told the investigator how he had been hiding, trying to avoid Destinni and Ryan since then, and that

Ryan had a lot of big knives. "I just think the guy's a lunatic," he exclaimed.

A couple of days earlier, Gibbs stated, Jon had called him to say there were some loose ends to take care of. "The only loose end I know of is me! I haven't been to my house in two days. That's why I'm wearing this stupid hat." Gibbs was doing everything possible to stay out of the path of Destinni, Jon, and Ryan. He was terrified.

The interview with Tony Gibbs had lasted over an hour. Now Detective Blackburn needed confirmation of the young man's statements. Gibbs agreed to call Destinni and allow the officer to tape the conversation. But on two tries, at 6:00 and 6:45, Gibbs only reached Destinni's answering machine. Gibbs agreed to come in the next morning and try again.

On Tuesday morning, at 10:25, Destinni Mardesich answered her telephone and heard the voice of Tony Gibbs.

"Hi, Des," he said. "I'm at a friend's house. . . . I want to talk to you." After a few minutes of chitchat, Gibbs told her. "I'm all stressed out. Everyone's talking about them murdering Damian. . . . I'm worried that I'm next."

Destinni wanted to know what Tony meant by "everyone," and if he had told anyone. When he denied that he had, she told him not to worry, that Ryan and Jon weren't aware of how much he knew.

Trying to pry more specifics from her, Gibbs asked, "What are we gonna do if the police come and talk to you?"

Calmly, Destinni responded, "They already have. It's like I said, I haven't seen [Damian] in four months and I was with you that night. We were home together."

"Well, what if Ryan decides to shoot me with that twenty-two?"

"He doesn't have a gun. That was someone else's. It's been returned to them." Destinni carefully avoided saying whom.

Tony Gibbs went squarely to the heart of the matter. "But why did you have Damian killed? Seriously? Honestly?"

After a slight pause, Destinni spoke. "Because I thought he might do something to me or the baby. You don't understand Damian. He was jealous and had a lot of anger . . . because I loved the baby and he wanted all of me."

"Yeah, but why wouldn't you just have Ryan or Jon just beat the hell out of him . . . like break his kneecaps or something?"

"Tony, I think of that every day, and I wished that's how it was. But it was rash. . . . He said he was going to kill the baby. Even if they would have broke his kneecaps, he still would have had the baby shot."

"What about when the police find out what really happened?"

Confidently, Destinni announced, "They can't. They have no evidence." After a few more exchanges, she added, "Even if they find out the truth, I was here with you. You know what I'm saying? Even if the truth comes out, I was still here. I wasn't in the back of the truck; I was with you, having sex, having dinner, talking, watching TV, whatever. I was here."

Following her denial that she had given Ryan and Jon any reward for what they did, Destinni chatted with Gibbs for a few more minutes, and the conversation ended.

Investigator Blackburn thanked Tony Gibbs for his help, made some suggestions for keeping out of harm's way, and hurried to his next appointment. He walked into a coffee shop at 3:30 p.m., where Tania Barnes waited for him with Investigator Mike Wallace. Tania was the young woman mentioned by the teenage runaway as possibly having some information about who killed Damian.

Tania said that she had been "hanging out" with Ryan Lo, who was 17, for nearly three months. She candidly admitted that she had met him when she went to his house to do some drugs. She said she made the acquaintance of Destinni just three or four weeks before.

Within the past few days, Tania had been at a gathering in Destinni's apartment and overheard some conversation between Ryan and Destinni. "They started saying how it's impossible for the police to find them." Another friend, Jon Freshour, had joined the group, and commented that if the police got too close, they could frame another young man.

After learning the name of the youth they would target as the fall guy, Blackburn asked, "What were they going to do to frame him?"

"They were going to put the gun at his house and put bullets in his car," Tania replied.

Asked if they had said anything about the actual murder, Tania replied, "The only thing I know is that he was shot, I guess, in the back of the head, at point-blank or something, twice."

Tania had been frightened that they would hurt her to keep her from informing, she told Blackburn. Ryan Lo, she said, had told her to be careful not to reveal anything or he would come and get her. "It can always get you killed," Ryan had said, apparently meaning cooperation with police. "Maybe it already has."

Once more, Blackburn arranged for a telephone call to be taped. Tania, sitting at sheriff's headquarters, whispered into the mouthpiece to Ryan Lo, saying that she wanted to know what he meant when he said he would come get her.

"What did you say to the cops?" he demanded.

"All I told them was that you said you were gonna come down to get me . . . that I was scared."

"You really don't get it, do you?" Lo barked. "I could go to jail for the rest of my life. So can Jon and Destinni."

Tania wanted to know if they were angry at her just because she happened to overhear what they said. When Lo said that they were, Tania asked if that included Jon.

"Yes," said Lo. "Jon doesn't do anything without me. Jon's just a pussy [cat]."

Growing more confident in her role, Tania asked, "Did Destinni want him to die? Like, did she ask you?"

"Stay out of it, Tania," Lo warned. "By the way, if this phone is tapped by the cops, I'll — you know — since this is a recording, I can just say that everything I've said so far is a lie and I'm just playing along with the story. There we go. I had to make sure I said that."

Investigator Blackburn smiled and shook his head. Tania remarked to Lo, "That was so stupid."

"No it's not. It's called a legal loophole," Lo retorted.

Following more banter, the conversation concluded with Lo cautioning Tania, "Like I said, turnabout's fair play. You ruin one life, expect to have yours ruined in return."

Tania would be protected from harm, Blackburn assured her as they parted company. He and Wallace sped to the home of the youth who had checked himself into a hospital to seek protection. He was the one whom Lo and Freshour planned to frame if anything went wrong. He had erred, he said, when he named "Glen" as a suspect. There was no Glen. It was Ryan Lo and Jon Freshour. The youth's parents were grateful for the investigator's visit, and promised to be on the lookout for any planted gun or bullets.

Another lead developed on Thursday. Blackburn heard from the county jail that an inmate had some "primo" information about the killing of Damian McKenna that he wished to trade for a reduced sentence. When the informant heard that Blackburn wasn't in the business of making deals, his proposition died.

Late that same night, the watch commander notified Blackburn that Ryan Lo had appeared at the South County Substation angrily asking why the police had been investigating him. People were calling him a murderer, he complained. Lo had agreed to travel to Blackburn's office in Santa Ana on Friday morning for an interview.

Just before midnight, Investigator Wallace returned a call from a pal of Jon Freshour's who said that both of them wanted to come in for an interview on the following morning.

Early Friday morning, September 20th, Blackburn sent his ex-partner, Investigator Bob Russell, to round up Destinni Mardesich and bring her in for a talk. By 9:25 a.m., she faced Blackburn and Wallace in a small interview room, with a video recorder running. Destinni didn't seem alarmed. She told the officers that she had heard from several people that Damian had been looking for her and their child. She was afraid he was following her with the purpose of harming them because he had made threats about taking the baby away from her. During those weeks, she became friendly with Ryan Lo who told her that if she needed assistance, he would meet Damian and threaten him.

Destinni said that she went along that evening to "hear what Damian said about her and any threats." She denied seeing what happened, but she said she heard it all. Asked what she heard, Destinni described two shots, separated by a short amount of time. Then there were "dragging noises." Ryan Lo had told her later, she divulged, that she might have heard him hitting Damian in the head with a rock.

Convinced that Destinni was the brains and the driving force behind the killing, Detective Blackburn arrested her immediately.

Shortly after lunch, Ryan Lo sat in the same interview room. Cocky and confident, wearing a black baseball cap, Lo tried to verbally fence with Blackburn. When the defiant youth leaned back in his chair and put both feet on the table, Blackburn stood up and told him to stop acting like a "punk kid." Lo looked startled, and put his feet on the floor. Blackburn later speculated that Lo had rarely been confronted with authority, and perhaps respected, or needed it. Lo, too, was arrested on the spot.

Jonathan Freshour failed to show up for an interview. A patrol deputy drove by his residence, and by coincidence, saw him leave the house with two buddies. The deputy stopped to talk to them and discovered that all three were carrying illegal knives. The deputy hauled the trio in for possession of deadly weapons.

When Freshour was brought to Blackburn for questioning, the investigator wanted to try an experiment. With the videocamera aimed through a one-way mirror, all three suspects, Lo, Mardesich and Freshour, were placed in the interview room together. At first, the trio laughed and whispered. Lo, apparently aware of the camcorder immediately, resumed his cocky display. Holding the lip of a soft drink can between his teeth, he tilted his head back to drink it.

Joking and laughing about having posed for arrest photos, the angelic-looking Destinni snorted, "They even took a picture of my ass."

Ryan Lo smirked toward the camera and put his feet back on the table. Destinni wondered aloud if she would be raped in jail.

Jon Freshour commented, "It's the end of the world as we know it," then swaggered toward the mirror and said, "Wave to the pretty camera. They hope we'll say something stupid."

Ryan Lo stood up, stepped to the mirror, blocked the camera's view with his hands, then pulled a sliding chalkboard in front of it. Freshour's voice could be heard saying, "You shouldn't have done that, dude."

Detective Blackburn had seen enough. All three suspects were held in custody. Freshour served nine days for the weapons charge and was released, while Lo and Mardesich were held on suspicion of murder.

Within a few days after the arrests, Blackburn was able to confiscate the murder weapon from a man who had let Lo borrow it. It was a black .22-caliber Charter Arms survival rifle, the barrel and body of which could be easily disassembled and stored in the hollow stock. Ballistics tests proved that the casing Blackburn and Wallace had found in Holy Jim Canyon were fired from the rifle.

Another important witness came forward on September 20th. Phil Spangler had been arrested with Freshour on the weapons charge. After conferring with his lawyer, Spangler agreed to talk to the investigators and tell what he knew about the murder.

Spangler, Lo, Freshour, and another young man had been friends for several years. They often hung out together at a local pool hall. They were known as the "Four Horsemen," Spangler told Investigator Blackburn. "Jon is Famine, I'm Pestilence, Ryan is Death," he said. The fourth member was "War."

Answering Blackburn's questions, Spangler described how on the night of the murder, Lo called him over to Mardesich's apartment to baby-sit. Lo, Freshour, and Mardesich wanted Spangler to watch the baby while they were out searching for Damian. He saw the survival rifle and told the investigator that he had been with Freshour and Lo four days before the killing when they borrowed the gun. Spangler admitted that before the trio left the apartment, there was talk of luring Damian to the canyon for a dope deal and killing him.

While they were gone, Spangler was lonesome, so he called the fourth buddy, "War," and asked him to come over.

Shortly after midnight, Mardesich, Lo, and Freshour returned and openly talked about "taking care" of Damian. Lo commented, "He won't be bothering Destinni anymore." Alibis were discussed, and everyone agreed on the cover story.

After hearing Phil Spangler's account, Blackburn located the "fourth horseman," who confirmed what his buddy had said.

Another young woman who had been at the apartment that night turned up. She told the investigator that Destinni said, "I'm going to get them to take care of him [Damian] because I can get them to do anything for me."

One more witness, a longtime friend of Lo's, added some details. A week after the murder, Lo had revealed to him that, "We capped him." Both Lo and Freshour seemed to want credit for the shooting, the young man said. They had described to him how the gun had jammed before the shooting, how Damian crumpled when the bullets struck him but was still "gasping," so they went back and "dropped a rock on him."

The witness quoted Freshour as saying he "never had a rush like it before."

With the mounting evidence, the case was turned over to Deputy District Attorney Ron Cafferty of the Orange County D.A.'s office. Cafferty brought murder charges against all three defendants. The only problem was that Jonathan Freshour was missing. He remained missing for over three months, until March 6, 1992, when he was stopped by the Utah State Highway Patrol on the California warrant. His car was searched, and the officers found a canister of gunpowder and two pipe bombs inside a suitcase.

Freshour had accumulated quite a record during his absence in Joseph County, Indiana. There were two counts of grand theft auto and two counts of armed robbery. The charges were dropped in deference to the California murder indictment.

The Orange County district attorney decided that all three defendants would stand trial as adults, even though they were teenagers at the time of the murder.

Their respective defense attorneys agreed to trials without juries before the distinguished Superior Court Judge Donald A. McCartin. Famous for his caustic sense of humor and offbeat style, McCartin had sent nine men to death row in as many years. The upcoming trials would be his last before retirement, and the defense counsels hoped that he would go out with leniency toward their clients.

In his opening statement at the beginning of the joint trial for Lo and Mardesich, on Monday, December 7, 1992, Prosecutor Ron Cafferty pointed to Destinni, and said, "She looks like the golden-haired angel off the top of a Christmas tree. She's probably very diabolical and full of ice water."

Cafferty added, "The depravity of it all is just amazing. You're talking about middle-class, south Orange County kids."

On December 7, 1992, after hearing testimony from witnesses and reviewing the evidence, Judge McCartin found Ryan Lo and Destinni Mardesich guilty of first-degree murder. Four months later, on April 19, 1993, they stood before him to be sentenced. He faced the tough decision of sending them to state prison as adults, or turning them over to the California Youth Authority as juveniles, which would allow both of them to be released, with clean records, at the age of 25.

Saying that he was "not thrilled with" his own decision, McCartin opted for the latter, which stunned Prosecutor Cafferty and many observers. Most agreed that Lo was certainly the triggerman, and many thought that Mardesich was the agitator. Few would dispute that Judge McCartin had been quite lenient.

Jonathan Freshour was found guilty of second-degree murder, but in a twist of odd jurisprudence, received a more severe penalty. Because he was over 18 at the time of the murder, he was not eligible for juvenile treatment. Freshour was sent to state prison to serve from 15 years to life.

Investigator Blackburn, who is extremely selective about granting interviews to the news media, spoke on camera to a television network team. The subject of the program was the need for more consistent and tougher penalties in the juvenile justice system.

Blackburn spoke as an expert in favor of the proposition that many teenage killers should be held responsible for their crimes. They should, he said, be punished appropriately.

EDITOR'S NOTE:
Tony Gibbs, Tania Barnes, and Phil Spangler are not the real names of the persons so named in the foregoing story. Fictitious names have been used because there is no reason for public interest in the identities of these persons.

"SENT HER STUD TO SNUFF HER EX!"

by Gary C. King

Thursday, September 11, 1986, started out as a quiet morning on the Willamette River near the town of St. Paul in northern Marion County, Oregon. The ongoing dredging of the river had begun early and would continue throughout most of the day. Underwater deposits of sand, silt, and rocks were being removed to maintain water-channel depth for safe and easy navigation.

Operated by a company out of Wilsonville, a city near Portland, the dredge was essentially a power shovel mounted on a floating hull. After the dredge loosened material on the river bottom with a rotary cutter, a bucket retrieved the sludge and dumped it into a scow.

The operation was going well until shortly after 5:00 a.m., when something that sounded like firecrackers began "popping" from the riverbank. Puffs of smoke rose slowly from the area where the sounds seemed be coming from. The workers soon realized it wasn't firecrackers they'd heard. They watched in horror as one of the dredge operators fell down, crying out in apparently intense pain. Blood stained his shirt, mushrooming outward from the small entry hole. The workers realized as they watched their co-worker writhing in agony on deck that someone was shooting at them!

The workers took cover wherever they could. Someone

used the dredge's two-way radio to notify the authorities and ask for assistance for the injured worker. Within minutes, the riverbank was crawling with Marion County sheriff's deputies in search of the gunman. Unfortunately, the shooter had already fled.

The worker was promptly treated by paramedics and then transported to a local hospital. The wounds were serious but not life threatening. Although the dredge operators were relieved that their co-worker would survive, everyone, including the victim, was puzzled over what the motive for the early-morning attack could have been. Sheriff's detectives were also baffled, and had no clues to the motive or the gunman's identity. With little to go on, a report of the incident was filed. The case would remain open, but there was little that investigators could do unless new evidence surfaced.

Five days later, on Tuesday, September 16th, 30-year-old William Maurer got up shortly after 4:00 a.m., his usual time on workdays, and prepared to get ready for his job on the dredge. He dressed, had coffee and a light breakfast, then whispered goodbye to his 26-year-old live-in companion, Candice Hill. She stirred, mumbled something back to him, and fell back to sleep. William, still a little jumpy from the previous week's shooting attack on one of his co-workers, pulled on a light jacket, never even thinking that the intended victim had been him! He probably never noticed the car that had passed by his house that morning, as it had on previous mornings recently, and he probably never saw the men getting out of it.

William Maurer had taken barely three steps down the sidewalk past the side of his house when the shots rang out. It all happened so fast that Maurer likely never had time to figure out he'd been shot. He reached for his neck, then went down on the ground next to the sidewalk.

Maurer's companion, Candice, was awakened by the

sounds of the gunshots. Startled, she recalled the shooting at Maurer's place of employment the previous week. She quickly pulled on a robe and went outside to investigate. Candice soon found Maurer. He was lying in a pool of blood that was getting larger with each passing second. As Candice stared in horror at Maurer, something told her that he was beyond help. But even though he appeared to be either dead or near death, she realized that she had to summon help immediately. It wasn't until Candice turned to run back inside the house that she saw the handgun lying alongside Maurer's body.

Had he committed suicide? she wondered. And if he had, why had he done it right there at the side of the house? It was all too much for her to absorb at that instant, and none of it seemed to make any sense. Candice called 911 and asked for medical and police assistance.

Paramedics and a team of road deputies from the Clackamas County Sheriff's Department arrived a short time later at Maurer's home, located in the 33000 block of South Meridian Road in rural Clackamas County near the hamlet of Woodburn. A deputy medical examiner confirmed that Maurer was dead, then released the paramedics. Seeing the apparent gunshot wound to the neck and observing the handgun next to Maurer's body, the officials present concurred that William Maurer had apparently committed suicide. They reported their findings to Sergeant Sam Metzger at the sheriff's office.

Metzger, now retired, called Detective John Turner at home. Turner, who had just gotten out of bed and was getting ready for work, was still bleary-eyed.

"I want you to run down to south county and take a look at a suicide," Metzger told Turner. "It looks like a suicide, but I just want you to go down and take a look at it. We've got a twenty-two lying alongside the body, and everything looks pretty cut and dried."

Turner assured Metzger that he would stop by and assess the situation on his way into headquarters. Driving all the way from his home on the Clackamas River near Eagle Creek, Turner arrived at Maurer's pale-green, shingle-sided house with brown trim about an hour later. The house, he noted, adjoined an azalea and fruit tree nursery, and was about four miles south of the community of Whiskey Hill, approximately halfway between Woodburn and Whiskey Hill.

When Detective Turner arrived at the scene, he was briefed by the road deputies and the medical examiner. He walked up beside the house to where Maurer's body was lying, just outside the back door, as the medical examiner and the deputies continued to talk. As was his custom, Turner stood back and took in the "big picture." As naturally as he breathed, he began analyzing the situation.

"Have you guys touched the body?" Turner asked the deputies when they had finished talking.

"No, we haven't," responded one of the deputies. "We wanted to wait until you got here."

"Has anyone checked the gun to see if it has been fired?" asked Turner. Again, their response was "No." Turner, known for his "gut hunches," had a bad feeling about William Maurer's death. Something, his gut told him, other than a suicide had occurred there.

When Turner and the deputies checked the gun, they discovered that no rounds had been fired from it. That, Turner pointed out, meant that they were dealing with a homicide, not a suicide. Someone, he reasoned, had shot Maurer as he was leaving his house for work. As Turner continued to inspect what was now considered the scene of an apparent murder, he spotted two small indentations in the side of the house Maurer and Candice shared.

"Did you guys see these bullet holes?" Turner asked as he pointed to the indentations. Again, the road deputies hadn't noticed. Turner got on the phone and explained to Sergeant Metzger that they had a homicide and that he needed help. Metzger sent sheriff's department criminalist John Gilliland and Detective Mark White to assist Turner with the investigation.

When Turner and White began asking questions, they learned that Candice Hill was not Maurer's wife. He had separated from his wife, they were told, and divorce proceedings were pending in Clackamas County Circuit Court. Maurer's wife, Tamara Lynn Maurer, lived just up the road a bit on Oregon Highway 211. William Maurer had moved into the three-bedroom house along with his two young children in January, the detectives learned.

A neighbor who owned the house that Maurer had been renting stopped by that afternoon to put away agricultural equipment. He was shocked, as was most of the community, when he learned what had happened.

"He was from Molalla," said the neighbor, providing what little background information he knew about Maurer. Shortly after Maurer and his children moved into the rental house, said the neighbor, they began attending a Methodist church nearby. Maurer's children attended a school in Whiskey Hill. The neighbor explained that Maurer had worked as a dredge operator for a Wilsonville company and appeared to be a truly decent man. Maurer had been a good tenant and was known to be a devoted father to his two children. The detectives made notes of the information, particularly the employment details, which they intended to check out later.

In the meantime, Detectives Turner and White learned that Maurer and Tamara were married on March 7, 1979. However, after their separation on October 15, 1985, both Maurer and Tamara filed petitions in Clackamas County Circuit Court a month later seeking the dissolution of their marriage. Since there was a dispute over the custody of their children and their home, a domestic relations trial had been scheduled for August 26, 1986. But for reasons that weren't clear, the trial had been postponed and rescheduled for January 29, 1987.

As they pored over court documents, the detectives learned that Maurer had requested a restraining order against his wife. He charged in the request that Tamara had slapped him, punched him, and, in divorce legalese, "had placed him in immediate fear of serious bodily injury." On November 26, 1985, Circuit Judge Sid Brockley granted Maurer's restraining order, which prohibited Tamara from "molesting, interfering with or menacing William Gordon Maurer" in any way.

The following day, November 27th, Maurer filed an affidavit with the court alleging that Tamara had "cleaned out our cash deposits and life insurance loan values. She also mortgaged our home without my knowledge or consent and got sixteen thousand dollars," Maurer wrote. "Our home is no longer free and clear."

The bitter divorce disputes continued in much the same manner over the next several months, Detectives Turner and White learned, with each party accusing the other of wrongdoing. However, it appeared that Maurer was winning the battle.

For example, according to the court records that Turner and White were studying, Circuit Judge Howard J. Blanding awarded Maurer temporary custody of his two sons on May 22, 1986. Later, court documents showed, Tamara failed to abide by court orders that she provide a complete accounting of her financial matters, particularly the mortgage on the family home. She was held in contempt of court, and she failed to appear on July 24th for a subsequent court hearing. At the time of Maurer's death, the family home was in foreclosure.

Since spouses and former spouses are always a good

starting point in a homicide investigation—all the more so in cases involving bitter divorce proceedings—Turner and White decided that a visit with Tamara Maurer, 27, was in order. When they arrived at her home on the evening of Maurer's death, they were met by Tamara and a young man.

The young man was introduced to the lawmen as Tamara's friend, Jon Patrick Thompson, 18. While Detective White interviewed Tamara, Turner took Thompson outside to his car to talk to him. Turner soon suspected that Thompson was more than a mere friend of Tamara's. Turner believed that he was her boyfriend, that they were intimate, and that he lived with her. It was conjecture at that point, but Turner's feelings were based on one of his astonishingly reliable gut hunches. Turner couldn't help but wonder what Tamara, an attractive young woman, saw in Thompson, a wiry kid with kinky hair and Dumbo ears who didn't seem too swift. Turner decided that love must be blind.

Turner didn't get much out of Thompson during the initial interview. Based on the scant statements Thompson made, Turner was led to believe that Thompson had been in bed with Tamara at the time of Maurer's death. However, when White came out following his interview with Tamara, the detectives noted distinct discrepancies in the stories they had been told. Aside from giving each other an alibi, Tamara and Thompson hadn't kept their stories straight. That fact alone gave both detectives a bad feeling about the case and cast a lot of suspicion on the couple. But since they had given each other an alibi, the discrepancies, by themselves, weren't enough to warrant holding either of them in connection with Maurer's death. Under those circumstances, the detectives simply wouldn't be able to place either Thompson or Tamara at the scene and, as such, wouldn't be able to arrest them. Frustrated, Turner and

White left.

Meanwhile, Dr. Karen Gunson, deputy state medical examiner, performed a definitive autopsy on Maurer's body. There were no surprises, however. Maurer had died from a bullet that passed through his neck and severed his spinal cord. Gunson said the bullet probably killed him instantly.

When word about Maurer's death, particularly the manner of his death, began circulating throughout the community, people naturally began to talk. As the detectives questioned more and more people, they heard over and over that Maurer's death involved more than a simple crime of passion. The more people they interviewed, the more they heard that Jon Thompson, and possibly Tamara Maurer, had hired somebody to bump William Maurer off. A "for hire," or contract, killing—aggravated murder, in other words—is an offense punishable by death.

Turner and White decided to turn up the heat on Tamara and Thompson. The sleuths confronted them with some of the details that they had learned, particularly that people were saying Thompson had hired a hit man to kill Maurer. The two detectives interviewed Thompson and Tamara again and again over several days, trying to shake their stories loose and get an incriminating statement from them. But it was all to no avail. They just couldn't get enough to make an arrest.

In the meantime, Detectives Turner and White continued to interview people claiming that Thompson had hired a hit man to kill Maurer. After obtaining several such statements, they began focusing on a possible other suspect. The information they had suggested that Barry Lynn Larson, a 30-year-old Canby resident, was the triggerman. Armed with probable cause, Turner and White arrested Larson on suspicion of murder at 6:45 p.m. on Thursday, September 19th, at his home in the 400 block of South Knott Street.

Following Larson's arrest, the detectives finally felt that they had enough probable cause to arrest Thompson, too. But when they went to execute the warrant at Tamara's home and other places Thompson was known to frequent, they discovered, much to their dismay, that he had fled.

It took most of that same night before the detectives had any clues to Thompson's whereabouts. Backtracking Thompson's movements of the previous 24 hours all over Clackamas County, Turner and White finally found out that the fugitive teen had fled to Washington State. They put out an APB detailing the warrant for his arrest and advised Washington authorities that they believed Thompson had friends there.

It was during the early-morning hours of Friday, September 20th, when a Lewis County Sheriff's Department deputy on routine patrol near the town of Chehalis, Washington, some 120 miles north of Clackamas County, produced the next break in the case. Just before 2:00 a.m., the deputy spotted a male hitchhiker on Interstate 5, right outside the Chehalis city limits. An inexplicable case of instinct, as much as anything else, prompted the deputy to pull over and question the young man. When he did, he could clearly see the young man's face, which he recognized from the APB that had been issued only hours before. He took the young man into custody, and confirmed his identity as Jon Patrick Thompson at the Lewis County Jail a few minutes later.

Detectives Turner and White were exhausted when the call came in from Lewis County. Turner had arrived home at 1:00 a.m. after putting in a long, grueling day. He hadn't even had time to go to bed when he found himself getting dressed to hit the road again. This time, however, he had a nearly two-hour drive ahead of him, a drive that both he and White were too tired to make. As a result, they agreed to meet each other at headquarters, where they decided it would be prudent to pick up a reserve deputy to do the driving for them.

Both Turner and White catnapped during the drive to Lewis County. When they arrived, they rousted Jon Thompson out of his jail cell and took him into an interrogation room. After reading him his Miranda rights and obtaining his signature on the Miranda card, signifying that he understood his rights, they began the questioning. Much to their surprise, Thompson decided it was time to talk.

Before long, Thompson admitted that he and Tamara Maurer were lovers. They had been sleeping with each other for some time, and eventually Thompson began living with her. At one point, according to Thompson's confession, Tamara began talking about wanting her husband dead. He had caused her a lot of problems in court, and she feared losing her children to him. She was willing to pay someone to get rid of him for her. Eventually, said Thompson, they found Barry Larson, and he agreed to be the triggerman.

In chilling detail, Thompson described how they set up the killing. From information supplied by Tamara, Thompson and Larson knew where Maurer was living. They knew what time he normally left for work, and they drove over to his house a couple of mornings prior to the killing just so they could be certain. Moments after Maurer walked out the back door, said Thompson, Barry Larson got him in his sights and shot him with a Marlin .22 semiautomatic rifle.

When Detectives Turner and White returned to Clackamas County with Thompson, who had waived extradition, they interviewed Barry Larson again in an attempt to rattle him. The sleuths presented certain details of Thompson's confession that implicated Larson, figuring they could anger him and get him to finger both Thompson and Tamara in retaliation. Larson, however, denied everything, claiming, just as he had done at the time of his arrest, that he had nothing to do with William Maurer's murder.

It wasn't until Turner and White made inquiries at Maurer's workplace that the shooting incident of September 11th in which the other dredge worker had been injured, came up. When they heard the details of the early-morning shooting from the Marion County Sheriff's Department, Turner and White became convinced that William Maurer had been the intended target. Apparently, the would-be assassin had muffed it and shot the wrong man! As a result, the detectives reasoned, the killers had to try again. Unfortunately, they had been successful on their next attempt.

Turner and White next returned to Tamara Maurer's home, located in the 86000 block of South Oregon Highway 211, to try and shake her story loose. When they explained how Thompson had confessed to being her lover and had arranged for Larson to kill Maurer, Tamara became visibly upset. Nonetheless, she denied everything that Thompson had told them. But Detectives Turner and White never gave up. They grilled her even harder.

Tamara continued to deny involvement in her estranged husband's murder, but there were inconsistencies in her statements as she changed her story a couple of times. Turner, angry, got right in her face at one point, nearly nose to nose, and told her that none of what she was telling them made any sense.

"I told her that Thompson has told us one thing, and now she's telling us another," Turner later recalled. "I told her that there's got to be a middle ground someplace. She was living with him, she knew what she was doing. I told her that she couldn't tell me that she was lying in bed with Thompson, asleep, when he got up at 2:00 a.m. to get out there and bump this guy off at 4:00 a.m. It didn't make any sense, her sleeping that sound." The sleuth bore in.

Detective Turner's relentless questioning and badgering

finally caused Tamara to start crying. Turner, sensing that she had seen the handwriting on the wall, so to speak, didn't let up. He turned the tape recorder back on, and she gave him an entirely different statement from the ones she had made before. Her statement, however, wasn't sufficiently incriminating for Turner to make an arrest—yet.

Meanwhile, in order to make an airtight case against their suspects, Turner and White still needed to find the murder weapon. They knew they were looking for a .22-caliber semiautomatic rifle, but they didn't know where to find it. After filing affidavits for search warrants, the detectives searched for the rifle at the suspects' homes and other locations where they might have hidden it. However, the rifle was nowhere to be found.

Frustrated, the detectives returned to Jon Thompson and Barry Larson. After considering the seriousness of the charges he was facing, Larson, stopping short of making a complete confession, agreed to cooperate. He told the sleuths that he knew where the gun was and directed them to a creek a couple of miles from Tamara Maurer's house.

A Clackamas County Sheriff's Department diving team focused their search in Butte Creek, near the Meridian Road Bridge in the rural community of Monitor. A short time later, the diving team located the rifle in about five feet of water directly beneath the bridge.

As they continued backtracking and putting their case together, Detectives Turner and White traced the rifle to the original purchaser who, in turn, linked it to Barry Larson. Larson, they learned, had recently bought the weapon from the original purchaser.

A firearms examination was subsequently conducted on the rifle, in which bullets fired from the rifle were compared to slugs found at the crime scene. However, results of the examination were not publicly revealed.

Nonetheless, both Thompson and Larson were formally

charged with aggravated murder in connection with William Maurer's death. Neither entered a plea at their arraignment on Monday, September 22nd. As a result, Clackamas County District Court Judge Robert L. Mills ordered Thompson and Larson to return the following Monday for a preliminary hearing. Following the preliminary hearing, both were bound over for trial and both were ordered held without bail.

Lee S. Wagner, a deputy district attorney, said the prosecutor was leaning toward seeking the death penalty if Thompson and Larson were convicted in the murder-for-hire case.

"We are proceeding at this time as a capital case against Thompson and Larson," said D.A. Wagner.

Meanwhile, after conferring with the district attorney's office, Detectives Turner and White decided it was time to bring charges against Tamara Maurer and arrest her for soliciting her husband's murder. Armed with an aggravated murder arrest warrant, the two detectives showed up at her home a few days later. To their surprise, however, she wasn't there. The house was nearly empty, and they subsequently learned that she had fled the state.

It wasn't until January 27, 1987, though, that the sleuths learned that Tamara was in California. By questioning all of her known relatives and acquaintances, the detectives eventually traced her to a Redding hotel. Upon learning the new information, Turner and White put out an APB for her arrest and left immediately for California.

Turner and White spent much of the next day, January 28th, sitting in their car staking out the hotel where Tamara was believed to be staying. While they were sitting across the street from the hotel, unbeknownst to them, police officers in nearby Chico had picked up Tamara on the murder arrest warrant. Turner and White were notified of the arrest a short time later, and Tamara was eventually brought back to Oregon to face the charges against her. She pleaded innocent to the charges.

In the meantime, facing possible death penalties, Jon Thompson and Barry Larson worked out a plea-bargain arrangement with the district attorney's office through their attorneys. In return for life prison sentences, both agreed to plead guilty to murder and to testify against Tamara Maurer at her trial.

On Thursday, July 2, 1987, Alfred J. French III, a Clackamas County deputy district attorney, outlined his case during opening statements to the seven-man, five-woman jury. French said he would prove that Tamara Maurer had solicited and agreed to pay Barry Larson $10,000 to kill her estranged husband. French said he would show that Tamara had initiated the murder-for-hire plan and was actively involved with her boyfriend, Jon Thompson, in soliciting Larson to commit the murder. French told the jurors that he planned to call at least 35 witnesses, including Thompson and Larson, to testify.

However, after the jury visited the scene of the crime, the home where Tamara had lived with Thompson, and the dredging operation site on the Willamette River where the worker mistaken for William Maurer had been shot, Tamara, fearing the death penalty, stood up in court and pleaded guilty. She decided to work out an agreement similar to Thompson's and Larson's with the district attorney's office.

Tamara Maurer, like Jon Thompson and Barry Larson, is serving a life sentence at an Oregon correctional facility.

EDITOR'S NOTE:
Candice Hill is not the real name of the person so named in the foregoing story. A fictitious name has been used because there is no reason for public interest in the identity of this person.

"MURDER-FOR-HIRE GOES HAYWIRE: 4 DIE IN VAIN!"

by Barbara Geehr

Floral City, Florida
August 3, 1990

When the middle-aged woman returned to her home on the evening of Friday, August 3, 1990, and found her front door locked, she immediately sensed that something was wrong. Like most people living in Floral City, a rural Citrus County community near central Florida's Gulf Coast, she never locked her doors. Despite its growth, the march of progress, and an increase in crime, Floral City was still the kind of place where friends and neighbors felt free to drop in unexpectedly. To them, a locked door would mean the same thing as a sign reading, "Not Welcome."

As soon as she unlocked the door and entered the hallway, the woman's sense of something being wrong turned to certainty. The light in the bathroom, which was usually off, was now on. The television set in the living room, which was usually on, was now off. And her carpenter friend, Roger Wilson, who always slept on the living room couch when he visited on weekends, was nowhere to be seen.

"Roger?" she called out. "Roger, where are you?"

The homeowner, an attractive woman in her mid-50s, had moved into this house, which was situated on the main highway running through town, five years earlier. It was her first independent step following the bitter end to a stormy 28-year marriage, which had produced three sons, now all adults. She'd planned to channel the frustrations and the anger lingering from the divorce into renovating the pleasant old place, but somehow she'd never been able to get started.

Things were different now. Jerry Lee Clark, the 54-year-old man she would be marrying as soon as the financial settlement on her divorce came through, had recently given up his home in Weekie Wachee and moved in with her. Practically the first thing he'd done was to set the renovation project into motion. Presently, he had already finished stuccoing the outside of the house and had begun a "facelift" inside. Roger Wilson, a 36-year-old friend, regularly came in from Weekie Wachee on weekends to help.

The worried woman continued onto the foyer where, after snapping on the light, she found Roger Wilson. Shock coursed through her as she stared at him, stretched out on the floor, with a bullet wound in his head. She whirled and ran to the bedroom to awaken Jerry, her husband-to-be. But he wasn't in the bed. The bed hadn't been slept in. Jerry was lying face down on the floor, with his head badly beaten and his throat slashed. Beside him lay the still form of a neighbor—47-year-old Robert Hemingway, an employee at a car-parts shop nearby. He, too, had bruises on his head and a slashed throat.

Struggling against the near panic she felt, the shaking woman managed to pick up the telephone on the table next to the bed and call the Citrus County Sheriff's Office in nearby Inverness. Patrol officers responded to the scene within minutes. Sheriff Charles Dean and a team of his investigators followed.

HIT MEN

While the deputies put a barricade of yellow tape around the property to seal it off as a crime scene, Sheriff Dean and his investigators checked through the house to make sure that the three men's killer—or killers—were not still lurking there. In the process, the officers found a fourth body. The victim was stuffed into the walk-in closet of the bedroom. Like Clark and Hemingway, the fourth man had been badly beaten in the head, and his throat had been slashed. The distraught woman identified the last victim as 45-year-old Lawrence Johnson, the owner of the neighboring car-parts shop.

"I knew I shouldn't have left the house this afternoon," the homeowner told Sheriff Dean as she tried to calm down. "But I had to get my ailing mother to the hospital and settled in—and I had to run so many errands. Everything took so much longer than it would have, and because I figured Jerry and Roger would have already eaten, I stopped and had dinner out. That's what made me late getting home. When I found my front door locked, I sensed right away that something was terribly wrong—not only because of the door being locked, but also because I had let a stranger into the house and had left him there when I headed out."

"Perhaps you'd better tell me about that," Sheriff Dean said.

The homeowner told the lawman that sometime around the middle of the previous month, a man in his mid-20s had come to her house, asking for water for an overheated car. "His appearance made me feel a little uncomfortable," she said. "He looked—well, for want of a better word—scraggly. He had a mustache and a beard and was wearing one of those sleeveless denim jackets.

"Anyway, I gave him the water and thought that was the end of it," she said. "But a week later, he came back. This time, he brought some beer, which, he said, was to show his appreciation for my previous help. During the short time we talked, he naturally observed the renovations going on inside the house. He told me his name was John, that he was a carpenter, that he needed work and would like to help. I told him Jerry Clark, my husband-to-be, was in charge of the renovations and the person he would have to talk to. When the stranger left, he said he would stop again soon to talk with Jerry."

"Did he?" Sheriff Dean asked.

"Yes," the homeowner replied. "He came back this afternoon, just as I was leaving to drive my mother to the hospital. He said he was stopping by to find out if he could help with the carpentry work. I told him Jerry was inside with a friend who was already helping him, but to go ahead and talk to Jerry anyway. I realize now that was a big mistake."

"Why do you say that?" the sheriff asked the woman.

"Well, as he turned to go inside, his jacket sort of opened, and I saw a knife and some other small object wrapped in a cloth stuck inside his belt," she answered. "I told myself they had to be carpentry tools of some kind. Still, I felt uneasy. His car — an old green Blazer — was parked outside the house. So before I got into my own car and drove away, I took down the tag number. I was surprised to see the tag was a Putnam County temporary one." The woman took a slip of paper out of her purse and turned it over to the sheriff.

"I believe we'd better take you into protective custody," Sheriff Dean advised. "That way, we'll know you're safe. You, rather than the four men, may have been the intended victim."

During the initial autopsies the following morning, the medical examiner determined the cause of death of each of the four men. Roger Wilson had been killed by a bullet fired from a 9-millimeter pistol and was probably the first of the four men to die, the M.E. said. Clark, Hemingway and Johnson died from the multiple blows to the head and the slashed throats. "A piece of heavy pipe may have been the murder weapon in these instances," the pathologist told the sleuths. "It would be difficult to determine the order in which these three victims were killed," he added, "because all of the killings probably took place within a time frame of an hour and a half."

A blood-spatter expert agreed with the medical examiner's findings, adding that Wilson, Clark and Hemingway had been killed at the spots where their bodies were found. As for Johnson, the last victim, the expert said that he had been dragged, face down in his own blood, through the house and then hidden in the bedroom walk-in closet.

"Concerning the nature of the blows to the heads of Clark, Hemingway, and Johnson," the blood expert continued, "the low height from which they were delivered indicates the men, in each instance, were lying face down on the floor, with the assailant leaning over them and striking them many times."

Through a series of neighborhood interviews they conducted on Saturday morning, the Citrus County investigators learned that three different individuals had seen a 1977 green Blazer parked on the road in front of the murder house for "a couple of hours" during the late afternoon through the early evening of the previous day. One of these witnesses, a woman living in clear view of the house, said, "I'm always concerned whenever I see a strange automobile of any kind parked anywhere near my home. I keep close watch on it until it leaves. That Blazer was parked in front of [her neighbor's] place from late afternoon until six or six-thirty in the evening."

Had she ever seen the Blazer there before? The female neighbor replied that she had. "Two other times in the past couple of weeks," she said. "But it wasn't there long either of those times. This time, it stood there for a couple of hours or more."

Two male neighbors also told the sleuths that they'd noticed the Blazer in front of the house on the previous afternoon. "This is a closely knit neighborhood," one of the witnesses said. "We're always on the lookout for strangers and strange cars."

The other neighbor commented, "We can't understand how these killings happened right on our own doorstep without one of us knowing what was going on!"

Meanwhile, the investigators who were checking the temporary license tag on the green Blazer learned that the tag had been issued to International Auto Sales, a used-car dealership located some 75 miles away in Melrose, a city in Putnam County. A dealership employee, questioned by telephone by Sheriff Dean, disclosed that the tag had been assigned to a man named John C. Barrett, the company's part-time mechanic who had only recently purchased the vehicle there.

The employee said that Barrett hadn't been seen in three or four days. He described the mechanic as being 25 years old, 5 feet 10 inches tall, weighing about 150 pounds, and having light-brown or dirty-blond hair. "He also has a very noticeable chipped tooth, and there's a Mickey Mouse tattoo on his left arm."

The Melrose witness was able to furnish the lawman with the address of Barrett's residence, a double-wide mobile home in the western part of the county, where the part-time employee lived with his common-law wife Patsy and five children. He described Patsy as 25 years old, 5 feet 4 inches tall, and weighing somewhere between 160 and 185 pounds. "She drives a 1980 brown Pontiac Firebird," the telephone witness explained.

The most surprising bit of information the sheriff obtained from the dealership employee was that the co-owners of International Auto Sales were Dorsey Sanders

III, the oldest of three sons born to the woman who owned the home in which the murders were committed, and Scott Allen Burnside, an in-law.

Citrus County investigators put out a BOLO (Be On Look-Out alert) on the green Blazer and on John Barrett. On Monday morning, a tip came in from an anonymous caller who said that Barrett, his common-law wife, Patsy, and their five children had been seen at a shopping center in Starke, Florida, on the day before.

Also on Monday, the investigators began an extensive background check on the used-car dealership's part-time mechanic. From his recent application for a gun permit, they learned that Barrett served in the U.S. Army from May 1983 to September 1985, was self-employed as a home improvement contractor from 1985 to 1989, and worked as a security guard until January 1990. During this last nine-month stint, he was also taking courses at Career City College, in Gainesville. In June 1990, he was hired by the Veterans' Administration to cut grass. That was a summer job, scheduled to end in early October. It was during this time, according to the gun permit application, that Barrett became employed as a part-time mechanic at International Auto Sales.

The investigators, in checking Barrett's employment record from his latest job to his earliest, learned that an employee at International Auto Sales had seen him drilling a pipe to make "what appeared to be a silencer. It was one day when I was out doing some work at the ranch belonging to Sanders's [relative]," the employee explained. "I had to go into the tool room in the barn to pick up something, and that's how I happened to see Barrett drilling on the pipe."

The investigators learned from the personnel director at the Veterans' Administration Center that Barrett quit his summer job there at the beginning of August after complaining of being ill. "That was the last we saw of him," the personnel director said. "Actually, he is still considered a hospital employee, because the summer job doesn't end until October 5th," the director pointed out.

At Career Center College, where Barrett was taking courses while employed as a security guard, the investigators obtained information of more immediate interest. The suspect's instructor in a security specialist's course described the program as including instruction in firearms safety, marksmanship, and the use of a PR-24 police baton. "The course is intended to qualify students to apply for licenses as armed security guards," said the instructor, a former Metro-Dade police officer.

The ex-lawman also told the sleuths that a short time after completing the course in July, Barrett returned to speak with him. "John was very upset," the instructor recalled. "He said his wife had been assaulted by three or four men, and he wanted to get even with them. He asked me for any help I could give him in constructing a silencer. I pointed out that suppressors are illegal, so I couldn't help him."

The investigators, not considering it necessary to delve further into Barrett's work history, decided to check if he had a police record. In a call to Captain Cliff Miller, the sheriff of Putnam County where Barrett had lived and worked, the probers learned that the suspect had no criminal record, but he had reported a couple of burglaries at his mobile home in October and December 1988 and November 1989.

As for the reported sighting of Barrett, his common-law wife, and the children at the shopping mall in Starke two days earlier, Captain Miller suggested, "If that's true, it means Barrett and his family are headed north. He has relatives in Ohio."

Because Barrett's abandoned mobile home was located

in Putnam County, the Citrus County investigators had to join forces with Putnam officers to search it. Putnam Sheriff Miller obtained the necessary warrant and, early on Tuesday morning, August 7th, a search team, comprising investigators from both counties, descended upon the mobile home.

The investigators found the tan double-wide dwelling in the West Lake section of the county to be one of several mobile homes set up along a dirt road. Dominating the litter-strewn front yard was a white 1977 Mercury Cougar, its hood propped open, its ashtrays overflowing and its rear seat piled up with empty beer cans. Near the entrance to the home, a swing set seemed to be patiently awaiting the return of children. Inside, a stuffed bear rested quietly on the floor next to an overturned mattress, and the nose of a toy pistol was sticking out from under a pile of cheerleader pompoms.

The chaotic state of the interior and the fact that the air conditioner had been left running were clear signs of the Barretts' hurried departure. Out of the chaos, the investigators took into evidence a bloodstained towel, numerous miscellaneous items, and several martial arts supplies. Then, after cordoning off the property with yellow plastic police tape, they began a search for additional evidence in the wooded area surrounding the mobile home.

The sleuths went only 25 feet into the woods before spotting a 1977 Blazer bearing the temporary tag number jotted down by the Floral City woman whose home had been turned into a charnel house. The investigators passed it on to Sheriff Dean. However, the Blazer was no longer green. In an apparent effort to conceal it, it had been repainted.

"Quite obviously," Citrus County Sheriff Dean said when his sleuths informed him of their findings, "Barrett and his family are on the run in a vehicle other than the Blazer. Let's get the tag number on Patsy's Pontiac Firebird and put a BOLO out on that. Also obtain four arrest warrants charging John C. Barrett with first-degree murder—one for the murder of Roger Wilson, one for the murder of Jerry Clark, one for the murder of Robert Hemingway, and one for the murder of Lawrence Johnson. In the meantime, I'm going to talk to the press."

At a gathering of reporters from area print and electronic media at the Citrus County Sheriff's Office late that afternoon, Dean named 25-year-old John C. Barrett as a prime suspect in the killing of the four men in the Floral City woman's home on Friday, August 3rd. "Barrett is known to have been at the . . . home at the time of the murders, as well as two times during the two weeks prior to the murders," the lawman said.

"We have not yet determined a motive for the killings and do not believe Barrett knew any of the four victims," the sheriff continued. "However, we do think the murders became necessary somehow as part of a definite plan.

"Concerning the method used in the killings," the sheriff went on, "there were multiple causes of death which we do not wish to reveal until after the suspect has been taken into custody. I will tell you, however, that the four men were systematically killed, and that the time between the first killing and the last was probably not more than an hour and a half.

"We have issued BOLOs on Barrett, who, we believe, is presently traveling in a brown 1980 Pontiac Firebird with his common-law wife and children. They were reportedly seen at a shopping mall in Starke two days ago."

In closing the news conference, Sheriff Dean warned, "We believe Barrett may be armed with a nine-millimeter pistol and should be considered dangerous. He is not only skilled in the use of weapons but also, probably, in the martial arts. No citizen should attempt to approach him, nor should any law enforcement officer attempt to take him without plenty of backup.

"Other than that, we no longer consider [the Floral City woman] in danger. She was released from protective custody this afternoon."

Melrose residents learned through the news stories that John Barrett, who had lived in the area since 1988, was being hunted in the killing of four men in Citrus County. Some were shocked. Others were worried that he might return. A bartender who had served Barrett many times said, "John seemed like a nice person to me. We never had any problem with him. Everybody around here knows him, and now they're all concerned for their safety."

A neighbor who lived a short distance down the road from Barrett's former mobile home said, "The couple seemed like an ordinary couple with a bunch of kids to me. I don't know what it is about that double-wide trailer they were living in. People who move in there seem to come and go."

The manager of a convenience store where Barrett had worked for a short time said, "John was weird. I picked up bad vibes from him. He said he was studying to be a marshal, and he knew a lot about guns. But he was pleasant with the customers, and he loved his kids. He and his wife regularly bought gas, cigarettes, beer, and groceries here. He also rented videos here. Most of them were for the kids.

Meanwhile, lab tests on the towels taken into evidence during the search of Barrett's mobile home showed that the blood and hair strands matched Roger Wilson's. Some of the blood also matched Jerry Clark's and John Barrett's.

On Wednesday morning, August 8, 1990, Citrus Sheriff Dean received the tip he was hoping for. Richard Holzberger, the sheriff of Butler County, Ohio, phoned from Hamilton, the county seat, to advise that he had received an anonymous tip about the Barretts on Tuesday. According to the information, John Barrett and his family had spent Monday night with relatives of Barrett's in a rural community near Hamilton. "I don't know when they arrived in this area," Sheriff Holzberger said, "just that they were at the relatives' home on Monday night."

The Butler County sheriff explained that his office knew John Barrett well. Not only had the suspect lived in the area until 1988, but warrants against him in two felony cases were also outstanding against him. "One is on seven hundred dollars worth of videotapes he allegedly stole. The other is for the theft of a television set, two video cassette recorders, and a dryer with a total value of nearly two thousand seven hundred dollars."

When Sheriff Dean asked where Barrett was at the moment, Sheriff Holzberger answered, "Hiding out in a cornfield where he is supposed to stay until he is picked up by one of his relatives at six o'clock Friday morning. He is then supposed to be taken to Detroit. I was told he has a survival kit with him, plenty of water, and a duffle bag packed with clothes. He also has a knife."

Sheriff Dean wanted to know where that cornfield was located.

"In Warren County," Holzberger replied. "I'm in the process right now of arranging a helicopter search of the cornfield."

Dean said he would immediately arrange to have his key investigators on the Barrett case flown to Hamilton. "They will be carrying arrest warrants on both John Barrett and his common-law wife," he said.

It was well into the evening by the time the two helicopters and law enforcement officers from five Ohio police agencies ended what proved to be a futile eight-and-a-half-hour search of the Warren County cornfield and the Florida investigators arrived in Hamilton. The Citrus County investigators' first order of business was to accompany the Hamilton County team to the home of John Barrett's relatives. They found Barrett's common-law wife, Patsy, and the children still there.

Patsy readily admitted knowing about the Floral City murders. "John told me he had to kill four men and needed to get out of town," she told the investigators. "He wanted me and the kids to go with him, but was afraid of being spotted in his Blazer. I told him we could go in my Pontiac. After he hid the Blazer in the woods next to our trailer, we piled the kids into my car, and all of us left town together."

The Citrus County sleuths arrested Patsy on the Florida warrants, charging her as an accessory after the fact in each of the four murders, and booked her into the Butler County Jail in Hamilton.

During the questioning of Barrett's relatives concerning the murder suspect's whereabouts, one of his kinfolk confirmed that Barrett had left the cornfield and was now in Hamilton at the home of a longtime friend. The investigators rushed to the given address. They found Barrett there, unarmed, drunk and sleeping on a couch in the living room. At half past three o'clock in the pre-dawn hours of Thursday, August 19, 1990, they arrested him without incident on the Florida warrants charging him with four counts of first-degree murder and the Ohio warrants charging him with two felony thefts.

According to statements by Barrett's friend, who had known the suspect off and on since 1980, Barrett arrived at his house unexpectedly on Wednesday morning, saying he was on vacation. "I was going fishing with a couple other guys in the afternoon, so I invited John to come along," the friend said.

"The four of us drank two cases of beer during the fishing expedition and, after sunset, went onto a bar. After we were there forty-five minutes or so, John told me he'd got himself into a lot of trouble he couldn't get himself out of. When I asked him what he meant, he answered, 'I'm riding a whirlwind. I killed four people in Citrus County, Florida.'

"I asked him if he shot them, and he said, 'No. I hit them in the head with a hammer and a pipe.' I didn't know if he was telling the truth. He's always had a tendency to exaggerate if he thinks it makes a good story."

The friend continued. "John and me left the other two guys at that bar and went onto another bar. We stayed there drinking until it closed. We then came back here to my place, and John holed up on the couch for the night."

Later on Thursday morning, Barrett waived extradition, and a Butler County common pleas judge approved returning him to Citrus County, Florida, to face the murder charges against him there.

Also on Thursday, Barrett, now shackled in leg irons, made a first appearance before a municipal judge on the Butler County felony theft charges. Asked if he understood those charges, he answered that he did. The magistrate ordered him held without bond and set a preliminary hearing on the Butler County charges for August 17th. He acknowledged, however, that by that date, Barrett would undoubtedly be back in Florida. "I have no problem with that," the judge commented. "The importance of the Florida charges far outweighs that of the Ohio charges."

Butler County Sheriff Holzberger now telephoned Citrus County Sheriff Dean to apprise him of the latest developments. Dean said he would call a press conference to announce the capture and arrest of both Barrett and his common-law wife. "And I'll question Barrett when he gets back here and is sober," he added.

Later on Friday, Barrett's common-law wife waived extradition. On Saturday, she was returned to Florida, entered into the Citrus County Jail in Inverness and, at first appearance, ordered held without bond.

Meanwhile, Citrus Sheriff Dean had held his press conference and announced the capture of John Barrett and his common-law wife in Butler County, Ohio. A news service reporter, seeking a reaction from someone who knew Barrett, went to International Auto Sales, where Scott Burnside, the co-owner of the business, readily gave an interview.

Burnside described Barrett as someone who had worked for the company as "an informal employee" and who had purchased a 1977 Blazer there. He also told the reporter he was "as surprised as anyone" to learn that Barrett might have committed the Floral City murders. "He didn't seem violent. He didn't seem like a Charles Manson or a Ted Bundy," Burnside said. "He was just a regular guy who drank beer and told jokes."

On the heels of the extensive publicity following Barrett's capture, Donald Williams, a relative of Barrett's who lived near Barrett's former dwelling in Melrose, came forward to tell Sheriff Dean about a brutal plot that had backfired and left those four men dead in Floral City.

Williams related that the Floral City woman and her former husband had been involved in property settlement disputes since their divorce five years earlier. "A hearing on her final appeal—which demanded property, assets, and cash totaling a half-million dollars—was scheduled for August 8th, and it was likely she would win," Williams said. "If she did, her former husband would be broke. Young Dorsey, who figured to inherit his father's fortune, would have nothing to inherit; and he and Scott Burnside would probably lose their used-car business."

"I get the picture," the sheriff said.

"Obviously, not any one of these three people wanted to see her grab the brass ring on the merry-go-round," Williams continued, "and they apparently figured the only way to prevent it was to do away with her. Young Sanders and Burnside hired John Barrett to do the job."

"How do you know that?" the sheriff inquired.

"Because John called me at my home in late July and asked me if I wanted to make some money," Williams answered. "When I went over to his trailer to find out what he was talking about, he told me the plan would be worked out shortly and we could collect at least six thousand apiece for the job. He said he was going to drive to Floral City a couple of times beforehand to check things out."

Williams admitted he had ridden to Floral City with Barrett two times. "During those drives, John explained I didn't have to take part in the actual killing . . . he just wanted me to drive the car. I thought about it a lot but finally backed out. I told John I couldn't be part of a murder."

Sheriff Dean wanted to know how the appeal on the divorce settlement, which had been scheduled for August 8th, turned out for the Floral City woman, Dorsey Sanders's mother.

"She won," Williams replied.

After Williams left, Sheriff Dean ran a background check on the informant. As far as he could find out, Williams had never been charged with any crime.

On Monday, August 13, 1990, the Citrus County investigators, with the necessary cooperation from the Putnam County Sheriff's Office, served search warrants at International Auto Sales in Melrose and at the ranch owned by the Floral City woman's former husband, where Barrett had reportedly been seen drilling a pipe for "what appeared to be a silencer."

From the used-car dealership, they took into evidence receipt books, telephone records, license tag receipts, a map of central Florida, a sample of metal shavings, and miscellaneous other items.

The list of items taken at the ranch included a box of 9-mm ammunition, some items commonly used to make a silencer, a tool-and-die set, metal shavings, a metal pipe, and some steel wool. Miscellaneous correspondence and documents were also confiscated.

While the searches were being carried out in Putnam County, the Citrus County investigators were questioning Barrett's common-law wife, Patsy, at the county jail in Inverness. Patsy told them that when Barrett returned to their home after the killings, she went with him to International Auto Sales, where John Barrett told young Dorsey Sanders and Scott Burnside that everything had gone wrong, and he had killed four men, but he had not killed Sanders's mother.

"John returned the nine-millimeter gun and the hatchet-type hammer Burnside had supplied as murder weapons and promised to get rid of after the mission was accomplished," Patsy said. "Burnside became very upset. He told John to get rid of his Blazer, burn his clothes, and get out of town. He gave John three hundred dollars to flee."

By Tuesday morning, August 14th, the investigators had obtained warrants charging both Dorsey Sanders III and Scott Allen Burnside with four counts of first-degree murder in the slayings of Roger Wilson, Jerry Clark, Robert Hemingway, and Lawrence Johnson. Expecting to serve the warrants and to take the two men into custody at their place of business, Citrus County sleuths teamed up with Putnam County investigators and went to International Auto Sales. They found the used-car dealership closed and its owners gone.

The investigators then proceeded to young Sanders's residence, a converted transport trailer on his father's 700-acre ranch. Sanders was not there. The ranch itself was deserted. At Burnside's residence, the same thing happened. The co-owner of International Auto Sales was not at home, and no one would admit to any knowledge of his whereabouts.

That evening, Dorsey Sanders III surprised everyone when he walked into the Putnam County Sheriff's Office. "I heard you were looking for me," he said. He was promptly arrested on the warrant charging him with the first-degree murders of the four men at his mother's home in Floral City on August 3, 1990. At first appearance the following morning, the judge ordered him held without bond.

The search for Burnside got underway with investigators issuing BOLOs on the suspect and his automobile and with distributing throughout five counties "wanted" fliers bearing his photo. The probers' inquiries brought a response from a Putnam County Department of Corrections probation officer, with information that Burnside was on probation for a 1981 felony conviction. That conviction was for the sale or purchase of hallucinogens and heroin. "Burnside has served only nine years of a seventeen-year probation sentence," the officer said.

With John Barrett in jail in Butler County, Ohio, Dorsey Sanders in jail in Putnam County, Florida, and Scott Burnside on the run, the residents of Melrose, where all three men had lived and where International Auto Sales had been closed, could only shake their heads in disbelief.

Barrett, having now agreed to extradition, was transferred to the Citrus County Jail, where he was held without bond. On Wednesday, September 5, 1990, a Citrus County grand jury indicted him on four counts of first-degree murder in the slayings of Wilson, Clark, Hemingway, and Johnson.

On Monday, October 16th, a sealed indictment against Dorsey Sanders III was opened in the Fifth Judicial Circuit Court. It charged the used-car dealer with criminal solicitation to commit murder in the first degree, four counts of first-degree murder, and accessory after the fact to murder in the first degree. His trial was set for

June 17, 1991, at the Citrus County Courthouse in Inverness.

Sanders's trial opened as scheduled on that date, but when the prosecuting and defense attorneys were unable to seat an impartial jury after two days of questioning, Judge John Thurman ruled that the location of the trial would have to be changed. He subsequently decided upon Ocala as the new location and rescheduled the date of the trial for July 22nd.

The delay gave prosecutors the opportunity to work out a plea bargain with John Barrett's common-law wife. If she would testify against Dorsey Sanders III, the four accessory-after-the-fact charges against her would be dropped, and she would be released from jail on five months' probation.

The Ocala trial opened as scheduled, and after four days of listening to testimony, the Marion County jury found Dorsey Sanders III guilty as charged and recommended that he be sentenced to four life terms for the deaths of the four victims in Floral City. Judge Thurman subsequently followed the jurors' sentencing recommendation on August 19, 1991, in Inverness.

In the meantime, the trial of John Barrett, the alleged hit man, began on July 29, 1991, in St. Petersburg, following a change of venue from Tavares. After seven days of testimony from such witnesses as Dorsey Sanders's mother, the medical examiner, the blood-spatter analyst, a lab technician, John Barrett's relatives and friends from Butler County, Ohio, and, finally, John Barrett himself, the jurors began deliberating at three o'clock on the Tuesday afternoon of August 6th.

The six men and six women did not reach a unanimous verdict until the following afternoon. At that time, the jury foreman announced that they had found John Barrett, now 26, guilty of the killing of the four men in Floral City during a botched murder-for-hire scheme. After another 2 hours and 15 minutes of deliberation, the jurors recommended that Barrett be sentenced to life in prison on each of the four killings.

On Tuesday, September 3, 1991, Judge Thurman overrode the jury's recommendation and sentenced John Barrett to die in Florida's electric chair for each one of the four murders. For Thurman, a former public defender, the four death sentences were the first he had imposed since becoming a circuit judge in 1984.

With Sanders sentenced to four life terms and Barrett sentenced four times to death in the electric chair, the focus of the Floral City murder case now shifted to Scott Burnside. Burnside had fled the area after learning that the plot to kill Sanders's mother had gone awry and that four men had been brutally murdered instead. But he had not escaped the watchful eye of Citrus County investigators.

Following the finding of his car in Casselberry some three weeks after the slayings, the detectives turned up an obvious reason why he'd flee to that area: he had relatives living in neighboring Orlando. Shortly thereafter, the investigators received a tip that the fugitive had been sighted in Washington, D.C. The sleuths, believing that his Orlando relatives would eventually lead them to Burnside, kept the relatives under scrutiny.

When the couple's business was closed down in March 1992, detectives tracked them on a trip to a tiny island in the South Pacific. There, they found Burnside living under an assumed name and working in the building trade.

On Friday, April 24, 1992, he was arrested by the fugitive squad of Hawaii's Honolulu Police Department and held for extradition to Florida. Two Citrus County sheriff's officers subsequently traveled to Honolulu to pick Burnside up and return him to Florida to face charges of criminal solicitation to commit murder, conspiracy to commit first-degree murder, four counts of first-degree murder, and being an accessory after the fact.

Scott Burnside was convicted on all charges at the Lake County Courthouse in Tavares on January 9, 1993. On January 25th, he received the same sentence as his co-conspirator, Dorsey Sanders III — four life sentences, to be served consecutively.

EDITOR'S NOTE:
Donald Williams and Patsy are not the real names of the persons so named in the foregoing story. Fictitious names have been used because there is no reason for public interest in the identities of these persons.

"THE HIT MAN STRUCK AT 12 O'CLOCK HIGH"

by Michael Litchfield

Nottingham, Eng.
May 9, 1980

The clairvoyant at the seaside amusement park took one look at John Hansard's hand and turned pale. Fortuneteller Madame Amie Tundrell saw death written all over the middle-aged man's hand.

Should she tell him? Should she keep her deadly secret to herself? This was her dilemma that Saturday afternoon in June as she sat in her little cubicle on the opposite side of a crystal ball.

Madame Tundrell decided that it was her duty to give an honest reading of the client's hand. After all, he had paid $20 for the service, and she felt it was her duty to warn of bad tidings, as well as of good ones.

"This may come as a shock to you," she said tentatively, as she fingered Hansard's hand. "But your lifeline is very short. It ends abruptly. It appears that disaster may be just around the corner. All my training tells me that you don't have much longer to live.

"I'm not trying to frighten you. I hope very much that I'm wrong. I'm not always right, so please take comfort from that."

Hansard, who was something of a hard-headed business tycoon, roared with laughter.

"You're talking nonsense," he said, a hot flush spreading up his neck and face. "I only came in here as a joke, just to amuse my family. I've never been in better health. I've only just had a thorough routine six monthly checkup at the hospital. I've passed A1 — as fit as it's possible to be for my age.

"No blood pressure problems, no dicky heart, perfect vision and sound lungs. And here you are telling me I'm about to snuff it. You should be ashamed of yourself! You could make people ill, you know. There ought to be a law against this kind of thing. It's scandalous!

"It's lucky I'm not a person with a nervous disposition. But I'm angry because it's a waste of money. I can't wait to tell my wife and kids what you said. They'll split their sides with laughter."

Hansard stormed out of the cubicle, without waiting for a reply or explanation. He considered the whole thing a pack of mumbo jumbo; a complete fraud.

His wife, Pauline, and children Francis, aged 11, and David, aged eight, were waiting for him outside.

"What did she say, Daddy?" David asked eagerly. "Did she say you're going to be very, very rich one day?"

Looking at his wife, Hansard answered, "She doesn't think I'm going to live long enough to become a millionaire. The silly old bat said I hadn't much longer to live."

Mrs. Hansard saw the worried look on the faces of her children and quickly put her arms around them, saying: "It's a joke, darlings. Those people can't really tell the future. They make it up. That's all."

"Why would anyone make up such a nasty story about Daddy?" David persevered.

"Because there are a lot of vindictive people about; that's

why," replied his mother.

"What does vindictive mean?"

"Spiteful. Now let's forget all about fortunetellers, shall we, and get back to enjoying ourselves?"

Sideways, Pauline said to her husband, "Fancy saying something like that in front of the children. Can't you see how you've upset them?"

"I thought they would laugh, the same as I did," Hansard answered, with a shrug.

"You have no understanding whatsoever of children, have you?" Pauline wailed.

Minutes later, everything that the fortuneteller had said had been forgotten as the Hansard family enjoyed the experience of a ride on the Big Wheel. They were thriving on all the fun of the fair as the Big Wheel stopped to let people on and off, with the Hansards suspended in their little swaying cage right at the top.

The view out to sea was quite beautiful. The day could not have been more clear. There wasn't a cloud to be seen in the sky, and a brisk east wind blew in from the North Sea. Out at sea, little fishing boats rose and fell with the swell, as if diving and resurfacing like serpents of the deep. In the opposite direction, the streets of Skegness, a holiday resort on the English east coast, were brimful with holidaymakers, just as many on foot as in cars. The date was June 30, 1979.

The Big Wheel started to spin again.

"Thank goodness for that; I thought for a moment it got stuck," said Mrs. Hansard, pinching her husband's arm.

But John didn't answer. Instead, his head rolled to one side onto his wife's shoulder.

Young David was the first to spot the blood on his father's face.

"Daddy's bleeding!" he cried, "Daddy's cut himself. Why isn't Daddy speaking?" the anguished youth cried.

HIT MEN

Pauline Hansard took one look at her husband's face and screamed, bringing the Big Wheel to an instant halt. She was still screaming when the cage was opened by amusement park attendants, who believed there must have been some kind of accident, or that the man had gotten ill.

It was only after John Hansard was carried from the Big Wheel that the bullet hole in the middle of his forehead was spotted.

The fortuneteller's prediction and frightening warning had been sensationally accurate. Madame Tundrell really did seem to have a hot line through to Destiny!

Detective Superintendent Harvey Miller arrived at the crime scene within a few minutes. He was backed up by his regular partner, Detective Sergeant John Parsons, and a team of detective constables. The forensic experts, ballistic specialists and a police doctor were hot on their heels.

The investigation force quickly swung into action, rather like a traveling circus, with each member getting on with his and her allotted task, without fuss or frenzy.

After a superficial examination of the body, Dr. Vernon Voss told Miller: "One shot through the head. That's all it took."

"Kind of weapon?" Miller asked tersely.

"Can't be sure of that until we get out the bullet. Certainly it would have been a high-velocity job. I would have expected the bullet to go straight through his head; in one side and out the other, but it didn't. It must have been blocked by the skull. It must be wedged in the bone."

A reconstruction of the crime revealed that for Hansard to have been shot through the forehead while the Big Wheel was stationary with him at the top, he had to be looking down at the ground at the precise moment that the trigger was squeezed.

From the angle of the bullet entry into the victim's head, Miller was able to pinpoint fairly accurately the spot from which the killer fired—a shooting range among the amusement park's sideshows.

"What an ideal cover," Miller told reporters.

"No one would pay much attention to anyone messing around with a rifle at a shooting range. There must have been 10 or 12 people holding rifles, quite legitimately, at the time of the murder. No one would notice that one rifle was different from all the others.

"The murder weapon would have been fitted with telescopic sights and a silencer. Immediately the trigger was pressed, I've no doubt the assassin disappeared into the crowd," Miller said.

"What kind of rifle was used?" one reporter asked.

"Can't tell you that, yet," replied Miller, honestly. "We'll know the answer to that as soon as the pathologist has dug out the bullet."

Miller then gave permission for the corpse to be taken to the town's morgue, where a pathologist was preparing to perform an autopsy.

The stunned and just-widowed Pauline Hansard told Miller about the uncanny prediction of death made by the clairvoyant just a few minutes before her husband was killed.

"What made your husband have his fortune told?" Miller asked her.

"I don't know," she replied tearfully. "It was just a joke. You know, we were having such a good time, laughing and joking. We don't often get together as a whole family. John is . . ."

Suddenly, she realized that it was no longer appropriate to use the present tense when referring to her husband. The impact of that realization brought a flood of tears cascading down her cheeks.

Miller was patient with her, and allowed her to go along in her own time. They were back at police headquarters by this time, and Mrs. Hansard was given a cup of tea, and a doctor was called to give her a sedative shot.

When Mrs. Hansard was ready to continue, Miller pressed her: "Whose idea was it for your husband to go to a clairvoyant?"

"I don't really know," she said. "I think we all started daring him. I don't think it was any one person's idea. It sort of developed. You know, the way things do in happy families.

"As I was saying earlier, John was totally wrapped up in his business. He would be away from home for days on end. When we did all get away together for a few days, we tried to make the most of it."

At that moment, the memories got the better of her once again, and Pauline broke down in a fit of tears.

Miller decided that further questioning of Pauline Hansard that day would be counterproductive. A policewoman drove her and the children back to their hotel, and stayed with them until Pauline's parents arrived from the East Midlands city of Nottingham—famous for its lace and Robin Hood.

Miller then returned to the amusement park, which had been cordoned off since the moment he and his men had first arrived there. Miller's next line of inquiry was to closely question Madame Tundrell, while Det. Sgt. Parsons concentrated on the shooting range and any possible witnesses to the murder.

Although the amusement park had been cordoned off, Miller did not hold out much hope of catching the killer within the confines of the fairground. He suspected that the killer had made his escape before the police had arrived—unless he worked on the site, of course. Unless she worked there . . .

"I've never seen Mr. Hansard before in my entire life," Madame Tundrell told Miller.

"He came in and paid his $20 just like anyone else," the clairvoyant said. "I had a real shock when I examined the palm of his hand, though. I knew right away that I was looking at a dead man.

"It frightened the life out of me. I didn't know when he'd die — I'm not that clever! But I knew that he didn't have long to live, and I told him so. It took a lot of soul-searching before I decided to tell him the truth, but he'd paid his money for good or for bad. So I gave it to him — the worst news anyone could possibly have to hear. But I was being honest. You can't blame me for being honest, can you?"

Tundrell also told police that Hansard had mocked her when she gave him "his reading."

Although he did not like the woman or her way of earning a living, Miller quickly decided that Madame Tundrell was in no way implicated in the dramatic killing.

"It was pure coincidence, as far as I'm concerned, that she foretold Hansard was going to die," Miller concluded. "We can't take seriously any of that fortunetelling mumbo jumbo."

Establishing a motive for the murder was the biggest problem facing the police. The investigation seemed to show that the dead man had been very happily married. Certainly he had no financial worries. Neither did he appear to be having an affair with another woman.

It was a complete mystery.

True, John Hansard had made numerous business enemies, but no more — and no more serious — than most successful businessmen. Yet his murder bore all the signs of a professional, hit man killing. That meant someone hated him sufficiently to spend a lot of money on his murder.

In business, John Hansard was the chairman and managing director of a textile company. This meant that he was always on the move, always catching planes or making long journeys in the back of his chauffeur-driven car, working as he went along. He was always driving hard bargains. Of course he had a few enemies among his competitors in the trade. Hansard also had a few enemies on his own board of directors. What boss doesn't? But there's a big step between having a row with the boss and hiring a hit man to kill him.

Sergeant Parsons was unable to come up with any witnesses of the shooting. The owner of the shooting range had seen a man hurrying away from in front of his range, but all he'd seen of him was his back.

Miller fully realized that there was no guarantee that the man running from the range was the killer, though the odds were good he was the assassin.

One thing the range owner did remember about the man was that he was wearing a long, dirty raincoat.

"I remember thinking at the time how odd it was he should be wearing a raincoat on such a glorious day," the owner told police. "It was a sunny day, not a cloud in the sky, and was very warm for the time of year. Yet he was all wrapped up in a raincoat that almost reached his shoes."

"Can you recall whether he'd had a go on your range?" Miller asked.

"I wouldn't know. As I said, I didn't see his face. But I don't think he did, though I wouldn't swear to it."

And then he remembered something else.

"As he hurried away, he seemed to be hobbling," the owner recalled. "It was as if he had a slight limp, although he was able to run, but one of his legs appeared to be a bit stiff."

"Could be that he had the rifle stuffed down inside the raincoat," Miller theorized. "That would be a good reason why he'd be wearing the raincoat—so that he could conceal the rifle as he made his getaway. We'll work on it. Thanks."

Every other line of inquiry in the amusement park drew a blank. No one could tell the police a thing. Everyone had been too busy enjoying themselves to take notice of the behavior of other people.

The autopsy revealed that the bullet had come from an army rifle, but police refused to name the exact make or the caliber. It was subsequently determined to be a 6.5-mm Italian carbine.

"We're making certain inquiries and, for reasons I'm not prepared to disclose, we believe it's best to keep secret certain matters regarding the murder weapon, for the time being," noted Miller.

However, at the inquest on July 10, it was stated by the police pathologist that Hansard had died from a single shot from a long range, high-velocity military-style rifle, which had almost certainly been equipped with telescopic sights.

Answering questions from the coroner, the pathologist agreed that the killer had to be a marksman. "He either shoots with a club, or he's an ex-serviceman who reached a very high standard while in the army." As an afterthought, he added, "He could still be in the army, of course."

The only other evidence came from Miller and the widow. The coroner then recorded a verdict that John Hansard had been murdered with one lethal bullet wound to the head by "a killer or killers unknown."

From that point on, the police investigation moved along slowly. As detectives dug deeper into the life and background of Hansard, they found out that he was insured for 500,000 pounds, approximately $1.25 million. His life insurance policy had been increased from 100,000 pounds to 500,000 only three months before his death.

At a top-level police conference some three weeks after the murder, Miller told his men: "The only person who seems to have stood to gain from Hansard's death was his wife, and yet they appear to have been wonderfully happy together.

"With their house, the insurance money and the property

Hansard owned, his wife becomes a millionairess now in her own right.

"She inherits the lot, but she seems genuinely broken-hearted. It just doesn't add up. Why kill her husband for the money when she already has it as his wife? There's a vital missing link somewhere that we have to find before we'll solve this case," Miller noted.

After a thoughtful pause, he told his men to "keep on digging." Miller added: "I'm not sure what we're looking for, but the moment you dig it up, I'll recognize it. Get to it!"

On Wednesday, August 1, Herbert Robinson, a man of modest means, was knocked down and killed by a hit-and-run driver as he stood on the edge of the sidewalk waiting to cross the road.

The incident happened in busy Trafalgar Street, near the downtown area of Nottingham, a few minutes after 5:30 p.m. in broad daylight. It was an unusually cold day for mid-summer, and there were literally scores of eyewitnesses to the blatant crime.

"He was just standing there, looking left and right, like you should, and along comes this car and heads straight for him" said one woman witness.

The witness continued: "Suddenly he saw what was happening and tried to jump clear, but it was too late. He didn't have a chance. He caught the full impact. It threw him into the air, as if he was being tossed by a bull, and he landed in the road.

"Then the car just carried on. It was going really fast. It came fast along the road, and then veered off course just before reaching the man, mounting the pavement (sidewalk), and turned back onto the road immediately after hitting him. It couldn't have been more deliberate. It was murder, I'm telling you! Someone set out to kill that man," the witness told police.

"Did you get a look at the driver?" she was asked.

"Not a good look," she replied. "Not so that I could pick out anyone in a lineup; not that sort of look. But I can tell you this—the driver of that car was a woman! That I can tell you."

The two detectives interviewing her both whistled and gave each other looks that said more than a million words.

"What about the car?" one sleuth asked.

"I think it was dark green. I can tell you the make, for sure. It was a Volvo."

"Registration number?"

"NAR 62, I think, but I didn't get the last number nor the final letter after that number," she answered.

"It doesn't matter," the detective said, his heart racing. "If you're right about the letters and numbers that you've given me, it'll be enough."

Other eyewitnesses told a similar story, though only one other could definitely say that the driver was a woman. No one else had gotten any part of the car's registration number, though there was general agreement that the vehicle was a Volvo, of a dark color, probably green.

The dead man was quickly identified as Herbert Robinson, aged 48, who was the head mechanic of a garage in downtown Nottingham.

His wife, Jane, aged 42, officially identified the body in the city morgue. The mother of two teenage children, she told police that her husband had left for work at 7:30 that morning, and that was the last she'd seen or heard of him.

"I was expecting him home at six o'clock," she said. "He always started work at eight in the morning and he finished at 5:30, when he would always come straight home. He would often go out afterwards—for a drink, and that kind of thing—but he'd always come home first for a meal."

The Robinsons lived in a small semi-detached house at West Bridgeford, a suburb on the city's west side.

HIT MEN

At first, there was absolutely nothing to connect this hit-and-run killing with the Hansard murder. In geographical and MO terms it would be hard to think of two crimes more different.

For a start, the killings had taken place 60 miles apart. Hansard had been shot. Robinson had been knocked down by a hit-and-run driver. Hansard was a tycoon. Robinson was a man of modest means. The only tenuous connection was that they had both lived in Nottingham.

Mrs. Jane Robinson immediately became the prime suspect in the case of her husband's death. She was interrogated for 48 hours, and during that time she protested her innocence.

She did, however, reveal that she suspected her husband of having an affair, which gave her a motive for murdering him — jealousy. She claimed that she didn't know who the other woman was in her husband's life — if, indeed, there really was one — except that she "had plenty of money" and was married.

Chief Det. Insp. Arthur Quigley, of the Nottingham City Police Division, started making inquiries around all the bars, hotels and restaurants. He got lucky about three days later.

The waiter at a fashionable restaurant on the outskirts of Nottingham, the Fir Tree, recognized Robinson's photograph.

"I didn't know his name," the waiter said. "But he would come for dinner here once a week with Mrs. Hansard — you know, the wife of John Hansard, the textile tycoon, who was murdered at Skegness a few weeks ago!"

Suddenly the two cases had come together. That evening, Quigley telephoned Miller at his Skegness headquarters, and they arranged a midnight conference for that same night in Nottingham.

There was now a motive for Mrs. Hansard having her

husband killed. But who had slain Robinson—and why? Was it his wife—or was the case more involved?

Mrs. Robinson, during close interrogation, had been unable to verify her movements during the afternoon of her husband's murder. She said that she was alone in her house, but one neighbor said she thought she saw Mrs. Robinson leave the house in her car at about 4:30, though she could not be absolutely certain. She had not seen Mrs. Robinson return.

The Robinsons' car was a white Ford Cortina. That seemed to let her off the hook, unless . . .

The police car registration computer at Swansea, in South Wales, came up with a Volvo with a registration very similar to the one hurriedly jotted down by one of the witnesses of the hit-and-run killing. The car belonged to a rent-a-car company in downtown Nottingham, called Dexter's Private Car Hire.

Nottingham police searched the garage where Robinson had been employed as a mechanic. In a bolted locker they found a rifle, plus more weapons, all of them the kind that would be used by a hit man.

The rifle was fitted with telescopic sights and a silencer. Ballistics tests proved, beyond all doubt, that this was the rifle that had been used to shoot Hansard. A thorough check into Robinson's background also revealed that he had been a marksman in the army for six years, just after leaving school.

Now the police knew that Robinson had murdered Hansard, only to be killed himself by someone else. Who? And why?

From further intensive inquiries, detectives learned that Herbert Robinson and Pauline Hansard were meeting regularly. Sometimes they would dine together. On other days they would meet for lunch. And one evening a week, Robinson booked a bedroom at a hotel 12 miles outside the city—just for the evening—but Mrs. Hansard always paid the bill!

The next shock came when police probers got Dexter's Private Car Hire Company to look up its records for the week during which Robinson was run down and killed with one of their Volvo cars.

The car may have been driven by a woman when Herbert Robinson was run down, but it had been hired the night before by a man. And that man was Herbert Robinson himself! He had hired out and paid—in cash—for the car that was to knock him over and kill him the following evening!

"This case is getting more and more like a Hollywood whodunit every minute," Miller commented.

Neighbors of the Robinsons recalled seeing Herbert talking with a woman in the Volvo car about 200 yards from his house, at around 11 p.m., the night before his death.

When one neighbor was shown a photograph of Mrs. Hansard, she said, "Yes, I'm sure that was the woman with him."

An official for Dexter's Private Car Hire Company told police that the Volvo had been returned to them "in mysterious circumstances." On the evening of Robinson's death, a woman had telephoned to say that the car had been left in a multistory parking lot just two blocks from their office, with the keys in the ignition.

It was not until a couple of days later that a dent in the front fender was spotted, although the damage was only slight. There had not been any damage to the front wings or the headlights. "We just thought that something had backed into it, while parking, at a very slow speed," said the company official. "We didn't take much notice. We were just glad to have back our car."

The most alarming piece of evidence, however, was a love letter from Mrs. Hansard to Mr. Robinson, her lover, which police discovered among his personal belongings in a deposit box at his bank.

Part of the letter said: "After you get rid of John, I shall inherit his fortune and we can go away together.

"He's well insured, as you know, and he has plenty of cash, plus lots of valuable property. But I'd rather not know how and when you're going to do it."

The letter ended with the reminder: "Make sure you destroy this letter. Remember, if it's found, it incriminates you as well as me."

Pauline Hansard thought he would be too afraid to keep such a self-incriminating document. Unfortunately for her, Herbert Robinson had failed to destroy that letter, thinking, no doubt, that it was his insurance policy should she try to double-cross him.

On August 22, Pauline Hansard was arrested at her home and charged with the murder of Herbert Robinson and of conspiring to kill her husband, John Hansard.

When faced with all the material evidence, Mrs. Hansard made a full and frank statement. "I had no intention of going away with Herbert," she said. "I only used him to kill my husband, whom I hated. I wanted all his money to myself. It was greed, I'm afraid. Sheer greed.

"Then I decided to get rid of Herbert because I knew I would never be fully safe while he was alive. I asked him to hire a car, saying that mine was too well known and that people would suspect us of having killed John if they saw us together. We went out for a drink in the hired Volvo on the night before I killed him.

"We arranged that he would leave the rented car just around the corner from his house that night, so it wouldn't be seen by his wife. Then the following morning he would drive to work in it, leaving it in a multistory car lot, with the keys left in the car in case I wanted to use it that day.

"I called him on the afternoon of August 1 to tell him

that I'd taken the car from the car lot and I'd meet him in Trafalgar Street, near the No. 16 bus stop going south.

"You know the rest. I was waiting on Trafalgar Street for him. When I saw him waiting, I drove straight for him. I dumped the car back in the car lot and later telephoned the hire firm, telling them where they could find their vehicle. I didn't want them reporting it missing to the police."

Sentencing her to life in prison at Nottingham Crown Court on May 9, 1980, the judge commented: "You are the most frightening Lady Macbeth I've ever been unfortunate enough to encounter."

EDITOR'S NOTE:
The name Madame Amie Tundrell is fictitious because there is no public interest in her true identity.

"DIAL-A-DEATH SLAY SCHEMES!"

by Terrell Ecker

Gainesville, Fla.
August 23, 1985

A light, misty rain was falling on north Florida's rural Bradford County when a young woman enroute home from a visit with her parents spotted the car in the ditch with its lights on at 11:30 p.m. Saturday, February 2, 1985. She drove past it, curious but not inclined to stop and get out of her car alone in the middle of the night. But after a quarter mile, the woman yielded to her conscience, turned around and went back. She parked her car on the left shoulder of County Road 18, headed northwest, and approached the blue 1984 Ford Escort on foot. Its engine was running.

She couldn't see anyone in the Escort and couldn't get close enough for a good look inside because its front wheels were on the far side of the water-filled ditch bottom, its midsection and doors straddling the water. She called out but got no response, then followed the little car's tracks southeastward along the ditch and shoulder to the point where it had left the pavement, calling out as she walked. Still no response. She got back into her own car and continued homeward, stopped at the first pay phone she came to and called the sheriff's office.

Deputies David Adderholdt and John Tilley found a

man in the car, apparently dead but warm, with his feet under the steering wheel, his torso across the floor-mounted stick shift and his head on the passenger side floor. They quickly got him out of the car and onto the ground where they tried to revive him with mouth-to-mouth resuscitation, but rescue paramedics arrived within a few minutes and declared the man dead. The victim's identity was easily established through a license tag check and the driver's license and other papers in his wallet. He was a 41-year-old telephone systems installer named John Joseph Banister who lived with his family in a residential area off U.S. 301 just south of Starke, the Bradford County seat.

Florida Highway Patrol (FHP) Trooper J. H. Horler reconstructed the accident but was frankly puzzled about its cause. The Escort had been headed northwest toward U.S. 301 when it ran off the right side of the roadway, traveled 450 feet on the right shoulder, then crossed the road and eded up in the left ditch with its lights on and its engine running. Other than a shattered driver's side-door window, there was little damage, no more than $400 worth, and no apparent reason for Banister's death. Banister's body bore a few minor bruises and two fairly minor-looking cuts on the head. Obviously at least one of them was more serious than it looked or there was a fatal internal injury of some kind. Apparently Banister's head had hit the door window hard enough to shatter it, and there were trails of blood droplets along the roof inside and outside the car. But why? It was a mystery, but apparently a one-car traffic mystery without any indication of foul play. Banister hadn't been robbed, and the only things found in the car, besides the body, were two magazines in the storage area behind the rear seat — one a publication devoted to handguns and the other a copy of the November 1984 issue of *Soldier of Fortune*.

Sheriff's deputies impounded and sealed the Escort, and FHP Lieutenant Winston Barber notified Debra Ann Banister of her husband's death after recruiting a neighboring family to help comfort the 29-year-old widow and her two small children. Banister's body was taken to Gainesville, the seat of adjoining Alachua County, for an autopsy by Dr. William Hamilton, medical examiner for both counties.

Dr. Hamilton's autopsy put a whole new light on the seemingly mysterious "mishap." For one thing, Banister's blood alcohol level had been .14 percent, a fairly ambiguous reading by itself because it could mean anything from reasonably sober to stumbling drunk, depending on the individual's tolerance for alcohol. Far more serious was Hamilton's finding that Banister had suffered from pulmonary congestion and edema and severe coronary arteriosclerosis. His arteries were so plugged up that he could not have lived more than six months to a year longer.

But most serious of all were the bullet wounds in Banister's head. One .22-caliber projectile had passed from left to right through the rear extremity of Banister's head and would not have been fatal, Hamilton said. But a second bullet had struck just above and behind Banister's left ear, passed through the left lobe of the brain and lodged in the right lobe, causing death within minutes. On Monday morning, Dr. Hamilton called the Bradford County Sheriff's Office and told the preacher about it.

At five-feet-eleven and 255 pounds, 44-year-old Don Denton could pass for a stereotypical southern redneck movie cop if he kept his mouth shut. But when he opens it he turns out to be a soft-spoken college graduate and Methodist minister as well as Sheriff Dolph Reddish's very sharp chief investigator. When Saturday night's traffic fatality became Monday morning's murder case, the Reverend Detective Denton took over.

While technicians were processing the victim's Escort and finding the other, nonfatal bullet, Investigator Denton visited the newly widowed Debra Ann Banister at her home in Gainesville. He explained as gently as he could that Joe Banister had been murdered, listened to her protestation that her husband of six years had had no enemies and answered her probing questions about the autopsy. But he evaded her question about the type and caliber of the murder weapon by answering truthfully that he didn't know what type of weapon had been used since ballistics tests had not yet been completed on the bullets. When he asked her to reconstruct Saturday from the time she and her husband got up until she was notified of his death, Debra said, "Let me start with Friday," and talked for an hour and a half, crying softly now and then as she talked.

Debra said that Joe had agreed to spend Saturday helping a friend do some work around his house in Palatka, a town on the St. John River.

On Friday morning, Debra called the friend's wife in Palatka and suggested that the two couples go out for dinner Saturday night. The wife agreed and Debra arranged for her sister Marlene, who lived in a trailer behind their parents' home in Gainesville, to keep the kids Saturday night.

Saturday morning, Joe Banister left home around 9:15. Debra and the children went to Gainesville and did some shopping, had lunch and visited with her parents and sister. Then she drove to Palatka, leaving the kids with Marlene, and arrived at the friends' home around 5:30 p.m. The two couples had dinner in Green Cove Springs and arrived back at the house in Palatka around 10:15. The Banisters only stayed a few minutes. Debra asked Joe to spend the night there because he had been drinking too much to drive, but he refused and they left. Joe headed home on the Starke Highway and Debra said she went to Gainesville, picked up the kids and went home.

Joe should have been there but wasn't. Thinking he may have taken her advice and returned to his friend's house to spend the night, she called, but he wasn't there. Debra explained that she had been frightened enough to call the highway patrol and ask about accidents, but none had been reported. Then, a little later, Lieutenant Horler had showed up with the bad news.

Asked about guns, Debra explained Joe had been a collector and Denton could come to her home and examine the weapons any time he wanted to.

The friends in Palatka and Debra's parents and sister, Marlene Watson, verified her story, and Banister's friends and co-workers echoed Debra's claim that he had had no enemies. As one co-worker said, "He was a real good guy. I've been working with him for seventeen years, and I didn't know of any enemies he had. He got along well with everyone. A person doesn't make enemies installing telephone system equipment."

Investigator Denton had to face the possibility that Joe Banister had been the random victim of a sniper. There had been some recent incidents of cars being hit by sniper bullets in adjoining Alachua County, but, so far, no person had been hit, unless that was what had happened to Banister. Other than that there were no suspects, and the bullets retrieved from Banister's head and car weren't much of a help with a weapon for comparison. It was a .22-caliber weapon, but what kind? It could be a revolver, a semiautomatic pistol or a rifle. As to the killer's identity, there simply weren't any clues.

The night after the funeral, a relative of the victim called Investigator Denton at home and said the family was wondering about something that the detective might want to check out. "It's probably nothing," she said, "but who is John Hearn?"

"I don't know," Denton replied. "I don't think I've ever

heard the name."

"Well," the relative explained, "he accompanied Debra to Joe's funeral. She introduced him as a cousin, but none of us have ever seen or heard of the guy. Somehow it just doesn't — well, we were just wondering, you know?"

In his office the next morning Denton got a call from Alachua County Sheriff's Investigator Charlie Sanders in Gainesville. Sanders was investigating an apparently unrelated murder but said there was one rather nebulous connection. Probably nothing more than coincidence, but Sanders thought there might be some mutual benefit in comparing notes.

Sanders said his victim was a 35-year-old tree surgeon named Cecil Lee Batie. Batie had been asleep on his couch during the early morning hours of Sunday, January 6th, when he was killed by a shotgun blast through a living room window. The puzzling case had been assigned to Sanders and his partner, Farnell Cole.

And the connection? Well, Batie was an ex-husband of Debra Banister's 28-year-old sister, Marlene Watson, and lived across the street from their parents, Franklin and Iris Sims. Batie and Marlene had been divorced in 1975 and had been entangled ever since in a chronic custody squabble over their two children. Anyway, Investigators Sanders and Cole were going to question Marlene's other ex-husband — the middle of her three husbands — and thought the Reverend Detective Denton might like to join them. Denton did, and took State Attorney's Investigator Wiley Clark with him.

Marlene's second ex was, frankly, scared; he said he seemed to be a member of an unlucky group of men. Marlene's current husband was brain-damaged from having been run over by a car recently, and, right after that, her first ex, Batie, had been murdered. No, he didn't know who might have killed Batie or Banister. Yes, he knew

Debra, of course, and knew she had a boyfriend whom he had noticed hanging around the Sims' house now and then. Fellow named Hearn or something like that. Drove a pickup truck with a Georgia license tag.

Then, back in Starke, Investigator Denton got a call from a Georgia official regarding a Florida woman who had called him. The woman had requested information on John Hearn. She gave the Georgia official Hearn's truck's license plate number in hopes that the information would help locate him. Thinking the woman was with a law enforcement agency, he had checked and found that the license tag number was registered to another name and another make of truck. He was calling Denton both to pass along the information and to ask what was going on? Denton explained the situation and accepted the information, which meant nothing at all except that here was a third person bringing up this fellow Hearn. Denton called Debra Banister.

Debra told Denton that John Hearn was an old friend of the family, basically a friend of her father's who traveled between Gainesville and Atlanta. He was a freelance photographer. Hearn had visited with the family in December when her father had a heart attack, and, when he heard that her husband had been killed, he came down to help with the funeral and all. She had introduced him as a cousin simply to spare the feelings of Joe's relatives because they didn't know Hearn and she hadn't felt up to any explanations at the time. If Denton wanted to talk to Hearn, Debra would have him come in. Denton did.

In the meantime, Denton called Florida Department of Law Enforcement (FDLE) Agent Joe Ubehler in Jacksonville and asked him to find out whether his agency's Georgia counterpart, the Georgia Bureau of Investigation (GBI), had any information on a John Hearn. A few minutes later Ubehler called Denton back and said the GBI did, indeed, have some information on Hearn because the FBI had been asking about him. Apparently Hearn had been trying to buy a hundred silencers, which had aroused the federal boys' curiosity.

John Wayne Hearn was a mercenary of some kind who had a "Have gun, will travel" type classified ad in *Soldier of Fortune* magazine. The ad listed an Atlanta telephone number. The telephone was in Hearn's Atlanta apartment and was equipped with an answering machine and a recording device that Hearn could call from anywhere in the country and play back messages.

Soldier of Fortune? That was the name of one of the magazines in the late Joe Banister's Escort, which was still impounded. Denton got the magazine from the car, turned to the classified section in the back and found Hearn's ad:

"EX-MARINE—67-69 Ex-DI, weapons specialist—Jungle warfare, Pilot, M.E., high risk assignments—U.S. or overseas."

That was very interesting, but Denton and Investigator Wiley Clark didn't mention it when John Wayne Hearn came in for lengthy interviews on Wednesday, February 13th, and Thursday, the 14th. They just let him tell what he claimed was his life history and asked a few questions when he came to Debra Banister.

Hearn explained that he earned his living as a truck driver and had met Debra about seven years ago at a Dothan, Alabama, truck stop. Debra was living in Cottondale at the time—that was before she married Joe Banister—and was drilling with the Army Reserve in Dothan. The following year he was in Gainesville and looked up Debra's father, Franklin Sims. They became good friends, but he hadn't seen Debra again until this past December when Sims suffered a heart attack. Debra called, and he came, even rented an apartment in Gainesville so he could be around if the family needed him.

The weekend Joe Banister was killed, Hearn said, he was visiting a relative in his hometown, Columbia, South Carolina.

After concluding their session with Hearn on the 14th, Denton and Clark drove to Columbia and questioned his relative. Irma Benedict verified that Hearn had arrived there around 8:00 p.m. Saturday, February 2nd, and stayed until the following Tuesday. Mrs. Benedict impressed the detectives as very protective toward Hearn.

Back in Florida, the detectives visited Hearn's Gainesville apartment manager and learned that Hearn hadn't rented the apartment himself. It had been rented for him on December 19th by Debra Banister and Marlene Watson. Hospital records confirmed that Debra's and Marlene's father, Franklin Sims, had been admitted with a heart complaint on December 27th. Sims was a retired insurance executive.

The detectives also learned that Debra Banister expected to collect $109,000 for the death of her husband, and Marlene Watson had expected to collect $30,000 for Cecil Batie's death. But in Marlene's case, it turned out that Batie had changed beneficiaries shortly before his death, and in Debra's case the insurance company was balking at the payoff, pending "further developments."

The next immediate development was that Denton and Clark ordered records of all toll calls made during the past few months from or to the telephones in the Banister home, the friends' home in Palatka, the Sims' home, Hearn's apartments in Gainesville and Atlanta and Irma Benedict's home in Columbia, South Carolina. Then, leaving Captain Bubba Roundtree's Alachua County detectives to decipher those records, Denton, Clark, Farnell Cole and Assistant State Attorney Mack Futch headed for Atlanta.

Hearn's Atlanta landlady recognized Debra Banister from a photograph as Hearn's fiancée, a young widow who said she was going to sell the Florida home her late husband had left her so that she and Hearn could build a nice log cabin in the Smoky Mountains. When had she said that? Why, when she spent that weekend with Hearn in Atlanta. Let's see. That was December 15th. The landlady even produced some nice color photographs that Hearn had taken of Debra with the landlady's camera that weekend.

The group's next stop was the Richland County Sheriff's Office in Columbia. Lieutenant Fred Riddle knew Hearn's relative, Irma Benedict, and called her. She came to the sheriff's office and identified Debra Banister from a photograph as Hearn's fiancée, a nice young widow from Florida whom she had met in December when Hearn brought her to Columbia. A very nice young lady.

The next morning the group of lawmen went to Mrs. Benedict's home and struck gold. It seemed that a couple of years back John Wayne Hearn had been having some post-marital difficulties and had attached a tape recorder to Mrs. Benedict's telephones. Mrs. Benedict had developed and still continued the habit of not only recording all telephone calls to and from her home but also dating and photocopying all mail that arrived addressed to Hearn. She gave the Floridian sleuths several tapes and several dated copies of letters. One of the letters, from a man in Bryan, Texas, named Robert Black, was accompanied by a dated photocopy of a $1,000 cashier's check. That was interesting but didn't mean anything at the time.

Back at the sheriff's office, Farnell Cole got a call from his own office in Gainesville. While working his way through the toll calls to and from the various telephones of which the toll records had been subpoenaed, Sergeant Kenny Mack came across a curiosity. He had tried several times to call a number in Bryan, Texas, and never got an answer, so finally he had called the Brazos County Sheriff's

Office and asked whether the sheriff had any information about that number. And Sheriff Ron Miller said he did indeed know something about that particular telephone number. He was in the middle of investigating a very recent murder at that particular number. A 36-year-old housewife, mother and day-care center operator named Sandra Kay Black had been shot twice in the head by an intruder in her home, apparently a burglar. Her jewelry was missing and some of it was pretty expensive stuff, handmade by a relative who was a jeweler. As far as leads were concerned, the case was devoid of those.

Not anymore it wasn't. Back in Starke Friday night, Denton called the Texas sheriff's office and put Mack Futch on the phone with a Texas prosecutor. Futch explained Hearn's apparent involvement in all three murders and said that, at the moment, the Texas case was the strongest of the three. He convinced the Texan that his case was in fact strong enough to justify an arrest and persuaded him to get an arrest warrant for John Wayne Hearn and teletype it to Starke. Then, maybe with a little luck, the solving of all three cases would be a simple matter of picking Hearn up and letting the Reverend Detective Denton preach him a sermon and listen to his confession.

The only problem with that line of thinking was that, with the teletyped warrant in hand, the Florida cops couldn't find Hearn. He didn't seem to be in Starke, Gainesville, Atlanta, Columbia or Bryan. Well, maybe he was off on another "mercenary" mission. On the assumption that the lovesick soldier of fortune wouldn't be able to stay away from Debra Banister for very long, she was put under constant surveillance. An elaborate surveillance network was established, including officers from both sheriff's offices, the state attorney's office and the FDLE. Even an Alachua County sheriff's airplane was used.

The surveillance was called off on Friday, March 15th,

when John Hearn turned himself into the Brazos County Sheriff's Office in Bryan, Texas. He told Sheriff Ron Miller that he was innocent of any wrongdoing but was turning himself in because he was afraid someone was gunning for him. He was so afraid that he had gone all the way back to Texas to surrender.

Pleased with that development, Bradford County Sheriff Dolph Reddish told reporters, "We were out to get him all right. Everywhere he looked for the past three weeks, Don Denton and Wiley Clark had either already been there or were coming up the road. I guess he was afraid some Bradford County rednecks might catch up with him and march him out to the prison and sit him in the electric chair without due process."

Bradford County is the home of Florida State Prison and its least popular chair, Ol' Sparky.

At 7:00 a.m. Saturday, Denton, Clark and Cole departed the Gainesville airport aboard an Eastern flight to Texas. Clark had authority from State Attorney Eugene Whitworth to promise Hearn life sentences in return for confessions, guilty pleas and testimony against Debra, Marlene and their parents. Brazos County Investigators Chris Kirk and Charlie Owen met the Bradford County lawmen at the College Station airport and took them to the sheriff's office in adjoining Bryan.

Hearn didn't accept the deal he was offered, nor was he interested in a similar bargain offered by the Texas officers. (The Texas lawmen had arrested Robert Black, a 38-year-old electrician who had been having so much trouble with his wife Sandra that he had increased her life insurance to $150,000 shortly before she was murdered. Their Florida colleagues had given them a photocopy of the $1,000 cashier's check that they believed was Hearn's down payment for the murder, possibly along with Sandra's missing jewelry.)

In his first interview with the Floridians, Hearn admitted all three killings, but he said they were all accidents and there were no accomplices involved in any of them. He had merely been doing unsolicited favors for old friends and just sort of bungled it. Marlene Watson had been having custody problems with her ex-husband Cecil Batie, and Hearn decided on his own to give Batie a good scare, hoping it would make him back off. He didn't realize he had killed the guy until he read about Batie's death in the newspaper. Debra Banister had been beaten by her husband, and Hearn had decided to give Joe a good scare hoping it would persuade him not to do it again. He didn't realize he had killed the guy until he read about Banister's death in the newspaper. Sandra Black had been blackmailing her husband, and Hearn had decided to give her a good scare hoping it would make her stop. He didn't realize he had killed the woman until he read about her death in the newspaper. Just bungled, unsolicited favors for old friends, was all, Hearn told probers.

Could he back up his story with any physical evidence? Well, yes, Hearn said. There was Joe Banister's gun. Hearn explained he stole Banister's .22-caliber AR-7 semiautomatic rifle and used it to give Banister a good scare. Afterward, he had broken the weapon down into its five component parts and had thrown the parts separately into Payne's Prairie. He described exactly where and how he had thrown them.

Denton decided to go on back to Florida and look for the weapon, leaving Clark and Cole to carry on with Hearn. Payne's Prairie, a state preserve south of Gainesville in Alachua County, is a huge marsh mostly covered with palmettos, saw grass, alligators and rattlesnakes.

Denton and a friend, Sergeant Cromer from Florida State Prison, found the butt, stock and clip from an AR-7, but no barrel. The three parts they found gave some credence to at least part of Hearn's story, but the lack of a barrel precluded a ballistics test. And a records search failed to turn up any record of Banister having bought an AR-7. That eventually led to the revocation of a gun dealer's license and other problems, but in the meantime, Investigator Denton faced the problem of proving that the gun had been Banister's, and that it was the weapon that had killed him.

At Denton's request, Debra brought in "all" of her late husband's guns, but said he'd never owned an AR-7, as far as she knew. She'd never seen nor heard him mention one anyway. And she let the Reverend Detective Denton know that she was plenty mad about being treated like a suspect, too. The insurance company was even holding up the payoff on account of Denton's unwarranted and ungentlemanly suspicions.

Debra was so mad that she insisted on being interviewed by a newspaper reporter. The result was a long and sympathetic article about her plight in which she denied any involvement in her husband's death and any romantic involvement with John Wayne Hearn, and told the world what she thought of Don Denton and his so-called criminal justice system.

Denton had better luck with Banister's friends and relatives. Several told him that Joe had indeed owned an AR-7, and one relative said he had fired the weapon. The best news of all came from a next-door neighbor. The neighbor said that, one day, he had discovered a rattlesnake coiled against his house—right up against it so that he couldn't shoot the snake without damaging his house. So Joe Banister had climbed onto the roof with his AR-7 and, lying on his belly, fired straight down at the rattler. Emptied the weapon without hitting the snake. But, the neighbor said, he had thrown some more ammunition up to Joe, and Joe had reloaded and killed the reptile.

The neighbor showed Denton exactly where the snake had died, and the detective found eight spent .22-caliber cartridge casings, eight spent bullets and one live round. He sent them and the two bullets that had pierced Joe Banister's head to ballistics expert Dave Warniment at the FDLE crime lab in Jacksonville. They matched.

Denton and Clark went back to Texas, and found John Wayne Hearn a changed man. He had read Debra's interview article. Debra didn't love him—told the whole world she didn't love him. No love, no marriage with Debra, no happy ever after, no nothing. Debra had just used him.

Hearn accepted the plea bargains he had been offered by both states and confessed to all three murders. He wasn't a friend of the Sims family at all, he said. He met Debra for the first time in October 1984 when she answered his ad in *Soldier of Fortune* magazine. After he returned her call, they met in a restaurant. She allegedly wanted him to kill her sister's ex-husband, Cecil Batie. He said he would for $10,000. She agreed to the price, and the deal was made. She kissed him on the tip of his nose and walked away with his heart. By the time he got around to killing Batie, they were engaged, and he had agreed to kill Debra's husband. She allegedly paid him the $10,000 for the Batie killing. Apparently the money came from the Simses, who had guaranteed payment, because Marlene didn't get the insurance money she had expected. Then Robert Vannoy Black had answered his ad, and he had gone to Texas and killed Sandra Black after receiving a $1,000 down payment. Sandra's jewelry was part of the payoff. As for Banister's AR-7 survival rifle, Hearn said Debra had brought it to him.

Hearn was indicted along with Robert Black for the murder of Sandra Black, pleaded guilty and agreed to testify against Black.

Hearn then returned voluntarily to Florida with Denton

and Clark and pleaded guilty to the first-degree murder of Joe Banister, the first-degree murder of Cecil Batie and conspiracy to commit first-degree murder, and agreed to testify against Debra Banister, Marlene Watson and Franklin and Iris Sims. All of them were indicted for conspiracy to commit first-degree murder and the first-degree murder of Cecil Lee Batie. Debra was indicted for the first-degree murder of Joe Banister, and their children were placed in the care and custody of Banister relatives.

Hearn's relative from Columbia, Irma Benedict, at whose home Hearn and Debra stayed prior to Joe Banister's murder, called Denton and said there were more telephone tapes. Tapes of conversations between John and Debra. Wiley Clark flew to Columbia and got them.

As it turned out, the taped conversations, which consisted for the most part of Hearn telling Debra he loved her and trying to coax her into saying she loved him, and getting an admission that he was quite a stud, could be interpreted as plotting Joe Banister's murder. But they also could be interpreted otherwise, and so they didn't amount to proof of the plot. The telephone toll record provided better evidence. The records showed that Debra had called her friend in Palatka from Hearn's Gainesville apartment to make the Saturday night dinner date. Banister had been killed at about 11:30 Saturday night. At 12:15 a.m. Sunday there was a call from the Hearn apartment to the Banister home, followed by calls from the Banister home to the Palatka home, from the Banister home to the Florida Highway Patrol and another call from the Hearn apartment to the Banister home. There were calls from the Banister home to the Hearn apartment at 4:30, 7:30 and 9:30 a.m.

Debra was tried first in Starke. On Friday, August 23rd, after a week-long trial in which both Hearn and Debra testified, calling each other liars and both crying on the witness stand, a capital jury of six men and six women retired to the jury room, elected a foreman and took a vote on the first-degree murder charge. Eleven voted for conviction, one for acquittal. After three hours of arguing, they emerged with a verdict of guilty of second-degree murder. Following Florida's controversial sentencing guidelines, Circuit Judge R. A. "Buzzy" Green sentenced Debra Banister to 17 years in the state prison for women at Lowell. He added, "Mrs. Banister, I am sorely tempted to comment on the offense, but I shan't."

If Don Denton or the prosecutor, Assistant State Attorney Tom Elwell, were disappointed in the relatively mild outcome, they didn't let it show. "Obviously it's not the verdict we asked for," Elwell said, but added: "There's never disappointment when a person charged with a crime is convicted."

The Reverend Detective Denton said, "The jury was very merciful and should be commended. I am satisfied with the sentence of the court because justice has been met."

Well, partly anyway. Debra still faces trial in Gainesville, along with her sister and parents, for the first-degree murder of Cecil Batie and conspiracy to commit first-degree murder. Of course, they must be presumed innocent of all charges against them unless proven otherwise in a court of law through due process. Robert Black must also be presumed innocent of his wife's murder unless proven otherwise in a court of law.

EDITOR'S NOTE:
Irma Benedict is not the real name of the person so named in the foregoing story. A fictitious name has been used because there is no reason for public interest in the identity of this person.

"A TANGLED WEB OF CONTRACT MURDER!"

by Olga Kogan

Prospect Heights, Ill.
May 10, 1988

When a police officer is shot in the line of duty, his colleagues on the force spare no effort in launching an all-out investigation. The cop killer naturally knows this better than anyone and he'll use every trick in the underworld book to avoid capture in his desperate flight to stay free. The open-and-shut cop killing is a rarity, so that when officers in Cook County, Illinois, arrested their suspects within hours of the killing, they were naturally pleased with their work. But as they soon discovered, it wasn't just a cop killing case they'd opened, but a case of mystery that just wouldn't stay shut.

The case began on October 17, 1985, not with a homicide, but with a routine response to a complaint from a citizen living in Chicago's northwest suburb of Prospect Heights. It was a sunny fall morning. The complaint had been assigned to Police Officer Michael Ridges of the sheriff's office in Maybrook. Prospect Heights is an unincorporated area of Chicago, and law enforcement there is provided by the Cook County Sheriff's Police Department.

Ridges arrived at an address that already had a history in his department. The previous August, the resident there, Raymond Brown, had called police to report that someone had tossed a brick through one of his windows. The same person had also smashed Brown's car while the vehicle was parked outside.

At the time, 38-year-old Brown claimed he did not know who might be behind the vandalism, but even as he was telling his story to a police detective at his home, a highly suspicious incident occurred.

The telephone rang and as Brown responded, he called the police officer to listen in. The officer did so, and he distinctly heard a man's voice uttering a death threat against Brown. Immediately after, the caller hung up.

As though that wasn't ominous enough, less than two months later, on the evening of October 5th, Brown was driving along West Cornelia Avenue when another car passed him. As the two vehicles drew level to each other, a gunshot rang out. Brown jolted back in his seat, apparently hit by a bullet. The other car accelerated out of sight.

But luck was with Raymond Brown that night. What was certainly intended as a death bullet had come close to fulfilling its purpose and would have if not for a device that's designed to save lives in a somewhat different way— Brown's seat belt harness. The bullet hit the harness, which had acted much like the padding of a bulletproof vest. The intended murder victim got off with nothing more than a minor flesh wound.

Still, Brown was badly shaken by the attack, a normal reaction in anyone who's ever been on the bad end of a firearm. Unfortunately for the police investigation, Brown had been concentrating on watching the road and had not seen what his assassins looked like.

Ten days later, on October 15th, there was another unnerving incident, this time at Brown's home. The house actually belonged to his mother, and it was she who answered the knocking that evening. She opened the door to see a stranger on the doorstep. The man had a surprised look on his face, as though he'd expected to see someone else answering. It might also have had something to do with the big dog that stood growling next to the lady of the house.

The man stammered that he needed some water for his overheated radiator, but the woman smelled something phony and told the stranger to pray for rain.

She later recounted the incident to her son, who again telephoned the police. It was crystal clear by now that whoever was after Raymond Brown wasn't about to give up.

As a consequence of Brown's report, Officer Ridges went out to Brown's house to see if he couldn't get to the bottom of the threats and attacks.

As a veteran lawman who had come from a law enforcement family — his father was a Chicago police captain and his brother was also on the police force — Ridges knew all the investigative ropes. He was also no paperwork lawman, even having taken a slug while breaking up a fight at a local nightclub eight months before.

Brown's interview with Officer Ridges shed a little light on the reasons for the persistent attack, but much remained shrouded in darkness.

His problems began eight months earlier, Brown explained, when he was abruptly fired from his job at the Chicago city clerk's office. The man behind the decision to fire him was a high-ranking official of long-standing in the office. But the reasons for the dismissal, Brown suggested, had nothing to do with his competence as a city worker. Instead, they were of a personal nature bordering on the intimate.

Armed with a potential scandal affecting City Hall itself, Officer Ridges returned to his unmarked car, prepared to file his report. He had just placed his officer's notebook beside him and started the car engine when he spotted an old Cadillac without any license plates sliding down the street.

Dutifully, the officer turned on his dashboard police light and sped off in pursuit of the offender. Following procedure, Ridges called into the dispatcher, describing the car as a 1975 blue Cadillac with three males inside. He also routinely requested some backup assistance.

Whoever was driving the Cadillac was apparently in no mood for an argument. The car pulled over at the first sign of the pursuing officer. The three men inside waited as the lawman stopped, got out of his car and slowly approached their vehicle.

Seconds later, there was a gunshot. Another gunshot quickly followed. Officer Michael Ridges, 29 years old, fell to the pavement.

A woman living in a house nearby peeked out her window at the sound of the gunshots to see a Cadillac moving away from a parked sedan and a man lying on the road. She could make out a red light flashing in the sedan's windshield, and putting two and two together the woman realized that a law officer had been shot, perhaps fatally.

Her telephone call to police came within seconds of the shooting, but in any case, officers were already on the scene in answer to Officer Ridges' earlier request for backup. They were not happy with what they found.

Their colleague lay near his car. Both of the bullets fired at him had found their deadly mark. His own gun was still in his holster. In one hand he still held the driver's license of the driver of the car he had stopped for a tag check. It was obviously a valuable clue, but at that point, the information offered by the local resident had greater urgency. She confirmed that the killers' car was a blue Cadillac, the same car that Ridges had reported a short while earlier to the dispatcher.

Within minutes, every lawman in northwest Chicago was grimly beading an eye for sight of the wanted vehicle. They did not have to search long: the big Caddie stuck out like a sore thumb speeding downtown on the Kennedy Expressway. The spotting patrol car was soon joined by another and then a third. Shortly, the Cadillac was once again pulled over by the side of the road. This time it was approached not by a sole lawman but by a passel of grim-faced officers.

With the officers' drawn guns speaking louder than words, the three men in the car got out and quickly spread arms and legs wide. Eerily, one of them looked almost like a police officer himself: he wore a blue lawman's shirt and even had a patch on one shoulder signifying Chicago police. Another had a flesh wound on his left leg.

The injured suspect was immediately identified from the photo on the driver's license found in the murdered officer's hand. Because of his wound, the man, 22-year-old Allen Falls, was taken under guard to nearby Northwest Hospital. His two companions got a fast trip to Maybrook Sheriff's Office headquarters.

Captain Frank Braun led the team of detectives that interrogated the suspects one by one. Besides Falls, they were identified as Ira Jackson, 23, and Dwayne Coulter, 27, all from Chicago's tough south side. None of them had a job, and in the beginning, they claimed their search for work was the reason they were cruising the north side. What was not explained was why they had been carrying guns and why they found it necessary to shoot a lawman in cold blood. Two firearms were found in their big Caddie: a .38 and a .22.

A check showed the .22 revolver belonged to Allen Falls.

Both Coulter and Jackson had previous police records. Coulter had once been convicted for impersonating an officer, and it was he who was wearing the police shirt at the time of the trio's arrest. He also had a charge for theft outstanding and was only out on bond. Jackson, too, was a burglar out on parole. Although Falls had no criminal record, lawmen held him for interrogation on a charge of unlawfully using a weapon.

What detectives had to deal with was a trio of small-time hoodlums who suddenly took it upon themselves to kill a cop.

Under the suspects' interrogation, however, the killing aspect suddenly got quite a different slant. The trio was looking for a victim, all right, but hardly the one they ultimately found.

The whole shooting incident, in fact, was rather bizarre. After their Cadillac had been stopped, the three men got out following Officer Ridges' order and prepared to be frisked. The driver, Allen Falls, handed over his driver's license.

Taking it, Ridges noted Coulter's officer's garb and asked if he was in law enforcement. Coulter answered that he was a security guard. Ridges saw that Coulter also wore an empty holster from a belt around his waist. When asked if he had a gun, Coulter admitted he did. Coulter began slowly removing the gun from concealment inside his pocket, apparently prepared to give it up peacefully. Then unexpectedly, he pumped the trigger twice in quick succession. After hitting the police officer, one of the bullets ricocheted off the street pavement and struck Allen Falls in the leg.

According to his own account, Coulter suffered immediate remorse for his action, even going so far as apologizing to the slain officer for shooting him. Police officers later recalled that Coulter offered more apologies while being taken into custody. Whether feigned or real, the suspect's remorse might as well have been saved for a sentencing judge, for it cut little ice with interrogating lawmen who knew that only one of their own had died while performing what should have been a routine duty.

Was it then a petty criminal's nervousness that had caused the murder gun to go off or was there another reason? Suspect Ira Jackson began implying the latter, and the more he talked, the more interrogators held their breath. Officer Ridges, he said, had stopped not just three guys cruising in their Caddie, but a trio of hit men out on a job. The intended victim had lived in the Prospect Heights area and it was just bad luck that a law officer had been on patrol there.

Jackson then bowled over the interrogators when he said the hit victim was named Raymond Brown, the same Brown whom Officer Ridges had interviewed just minutes before his death. By a grim stroke of irony, Ridges had stumbled into a murder plot in which he himself had inadvertently become the victim.

Now the big question: Who had hired Jackson, Falls and Coulter to do Brown in and why?

For the second time, Jackson stunned his interrogators. The contract, he explained, had been put out by a high-ranking City Hall employee by the name of John Annerino. Annerino worked in the city clerk's office as the director of its licensing bureau. A murder accusation was a serious indictment against someone who'd worked in government for more than 25 years, but the new piece of information made a lot of sense in the murder puzzle.

Brown had been fired from his post in the city clerk's office after having worked there only a few months. Some checking determined that Brown had been hired by the same man who had so quickly fired him, John Annerino.

Police Captain Braun decided it was time to do some serious talking with Raymond Brown. Brown readily agreed, badly shaken by the thought that his case had somehow become connected with the death of a policeman.

He admitted that he and John Annerino had been more than colleagues at work. They had first met in 1984 when Brown was working as a security guard for bars along Chicago's north side. Annerino had explained his work for the licensing bureau and had lamented over the "restrictions" that his position placed on him. He wanted, for example, to buy a tavern, but could "not put his own name on the license because of his official duties." When Brown swallowed the story, it looked like Annerino had found his patsy.

Annerino continued to play his baloney. He told Brown he was not only in the tavern trade but a "spiritual leader and minister of the church." As impressive as that might have sounded to security guard Brown, the truth was that Annerino was just a dime-store Ayatollah operating out of his south side home. His "church" was in the basement. Half of the basement area was devoted to matters of the spirit while the other half was set up as a weightlifting gym. Annerino liked inviting acquaintances to work out in his mini-gym which had an intimate, club-like atmosphere.

Brown got to know the Annerino home well. Just two months after first meeting Annerino, he was invited to move in. Their cohabitation, however, was short lived. As Brown soon discovered, Annerino had a liking not only for weightlifting, but for weightlifters. Although Brown had been grateful to him for arranging his job at the city clerk's office, he was not grateful enough to have sex with him. Denied what he considered his due, Annerino had quarreled with Brown and their live-in relationship became strained. When Brown made no secret about preferring to date women, Annerino's jealousy exploded. Brown had no choice but to move out and take up residence at his mother's home in Prospect Heights. But if he thought his problems with John Annerino were over, he was seriously mistaken.

HIT MEN

As the man who had smoothly arranged Brown's city office job, Annerino could just as smoothly arrange giving Brown the boot. Within days of leaving Annerino's house, the one-time security guard-turned city worker was out of a job.

But even then Brown was not out of Annerino's vengeful shadow. Annerino filed two lawsuits against Brown, the first alleging that Brown had stolen money from the city clerk's office, the second alleging that Brown had stolen valuable objects from Annerino's home.

Then Brown's house and car windows were smashed, phone calls threatened death, and strangers fired at him from passing cars. It all seemed a bit extreme to be motivated by spurned love alone, and under interrogation, Brown provided a pregnant clue as to the real reason behind all the harassment.

He told interviewing lawmen that at one point while he was living in Annerino's home, Annerino had casually boasted of having a little money tucked away in the bank. The little money totaled a cool half million dollars, and it was clear that even with his solid government paycheck, Annerino could not have amassed such a large sum by legal means alone. The specter of corrupt government loomed its head as lawmen turned their murder probe toward City Hall.

While this was going on, police officers did not forget to pay their respects to their slain comrade, Michael Ridges. More than a thousand uniformed officers mourned as his casket was lowered for burial.

Court orders approving search warrants provided access to the homes of John Annerino and the three men already in custody. At one of the suspects' homes, detectives found Raymond Brown's photograph. Other photos of Brown were found in Annerino's home along with copies of gay men's magazines. But the strongest link in the chain between Annerino and the three suspects was a list containing the suspects' names and phone numbers.

It was getting hot under Annerino's collar and he requested and received a leave of absence from work.

More search warrants now sent detectives poring over the records at the city clerk's office and here they had a field day. They found that not only had Raymond Brown been getting paid for time he did not work, but so were many other employees under John Annerino's supervision. The motive for Annerino's generosity was simple: each worker paid Annerino holy kickbacks with a donation to his basement church. The proceeds all ended up in one of his 12 bank accounts.

The pressure now apparently became too much for Annerino and early in November he took to a hospital bed for some rest. There would be no flowers of sympathy for him, however, just an indictment from a Cook County grand jury charging him with plotting murder. Indictment in hand, Annerino left the hospital on November 7th, a man with a lot on his mind.

His problems came to an end sooner than he expected, though not in quite the way Annerino might have wanted. That same day, November 7th, as he stood on a street on the city's west side, an unknown gunman drilled him through the stomach.

His pooling blood in the dusty street prompted an emergency medical team to hold out little chance for his recovery. Their prediction proved on the money. John Annerino expired on the operating table a couple of hours later. The only suspect in the shooting was a white man seen walking away from the crime scene, apparently a hired assassin.

Detectives were in for a surprise several days later when they discovered who'd done the hiring. Shortly before being shot, Annerino had been visiting with a friend who lived near the murder scene. Police learned that just before leaving, Annerino had made a telephone call to a local number. Phone company records traced the number to a man named William Rubio. Officers knew that Annerino was under a lot of pressure from the court indictment on the day of his death. He had no time to waste on trivialities and if he made a phone call, it was a good bet the call was something important.

Officers drove out to talk with William Rubio. The self-described home handyman got the shock of his life when he saw the badges flashing on his doorstep. Under mild interrogations, he cracked like corn flakes.

Yes, he confessed, he had shot John Annerino. It was a hit job for which he got $600. When Rubio announced the name of the man who hired him, the words struck like lightning. The man who'd wanted John Annerino shot was none other than John Annerino himself!

The shooting, Rubio explained, was all supposed to be a sham. Annerino was not supposed to be killed, only slightly wounded in an arm or a leg. Annerino had figured that by making himself an attack victim, he would divert police suspicion away from him. At the very least, he would get a hospital bed instead of a jail bunk to relax in while waiting the long months until his trial.

Rubio explained that the shooting had been an accident. At the last moment, he claimed, he wanted to pull out of the deal, but Annerino had become violent. They scuffled and the gun went off. Although his story sounded a bit too much like the movies, Rubio showed an admirable willingness to cooperate. He even led lawmen to the place where he had concealed the murder gun, a .38-caliber revolver. Detectives recovered it buried by a rail embankment not far from the murder scene.

On November 12, 1986, Rubio was booked for murder.

Four months later, still another intriguing piece was added to the Annerino puzzle. A boy working in suburban

Palos Park had his youthful curiosity aroused by a lumpy pillowcase lying in a drainage ditch. When he turned the pillowcase upside down, piles of legal papers, bank books and hundreds of Illinois state lottery tickets tumbled onto the ground. The legal documents were insurance policies bearing the name of John Annerino. The bank deposit book added up to 60 grand. How the pillowcase treasure found its way into the park ditch has never been explained.

In September of 1987, the trial of Dwayne Coulter began with Assistant State's Attorney Richard Kaplan prosecuting and Judge James Bailey presiding.

Coulter's defense lawyers did not try to contend their client was innocent of killing Officer Michael Ridges, but they brought evidence to show that Coulter had been abused as a child. Guns and violence, they contended, had been a daily part of his upbringing, so that Coulter used violence as a natural recourse of action.

Prosecutor Kaplan, by contrast, called Coulter a simple, cold-blooded killer, reminding the jury that Coulter and his pals had been out on a hit job when Officer Ridges was killed. Coulter was a gunman looking for a target, Kaplan contended, and it didn't make any difference to him who that target might be.

On September 17th, the jury found Coulter guilty as charged. The following month, Judge Bailey sentenced him to life with no chance of parole.

Coulter's accomplices had to wait a little longer for their day in court, but the verdict was much the same. In May 1988, Allen Falls received a 40-year prison stretch for murder and conspiring to murder. Ira Jackson got a similar sentence.

The same guilty verdict also greeted William Rubio, the bumbling hit man who had "accidentally" killed John Annerino.

Curiously, Annerino was not the first in his family to die

a violent death. His cousin, Sam Annerino, had also been blown away in Chicago by hit men in 1977. That case had been a clear gangland hit connected with Sam's work in the mob. Theories that cousin John was also working for the syndicate were never proven.

EDITOR'S NOTE:
Raymond Brown is not the real name of the person so named in the foregoing story. A fictitious name has been used because there is no reason for public interest in the identity of this person.

"VIXEN'S QUICK-KILL SCHEME"

by Bruce Gibney

Huntington Beach, Ca.
July 31, 1987

It was late Monday evening, September 3, 1984, and a thick fog hung over Huntington Beach, California, clinging to the wet streets and bringing traffic to a crawl.

Barry Ford, 31, had no intention of going out into the night. He was perfectly content to spend the last few hours of this Monday night watching television and snuggling up with his pretty, 27-year-old wife Anita.

Then the phone rang. Barry excused himself and went into the kitchen. Minutes later he slammed down the receiver and stormed back into the living room.

"I'll be back in a few minutes," he fumed.

"Trouble?" Anita asked, curling her legs underneath her.

"Yeah, sort of," Barry replied. He gave Anita a good-bye kiss. "Nothing serious."

"Hurry back," Anita purred.

Barry hurried all right. Roaring his old pickup to life, he sped across the nearly empty streets, watching for stop lights and the occasional car that moved cautiously in the thick fog. It was a lousy night to be outdoors.

Barry consoled himself with the fact that if all went well, he could take care of his errand in a few minutes and be back home within 40 minutes.

But things did not exactly go well.

At 10:40 p.m., a Huntington Beach, California, police officer was patrolling an industrial park in the southeast part of the city when he saw a pickup truck in the middle of the street. The motor was running and the headlights were on.

The patrol officer pulled over parallel to the vehicle and looked inside. The driver was gone. The driver had apparently parked the car in the middle of the road and then for whatever reason, had simply walked away.

What a stupid thing to do, the officer thought, stepping from his patrol car, ticket book in hand. He walked around to the front of the vehicle to get the license plate number — and stopped cold in his tracks.

A man was sprawled on the asphalt face down, one arm flopped out by his side, the back of his head glistening with fresh blood.

Putting away the ticket book, the cop crouched beside the fallen man and pushed two fingers against the bloodied side of the man's neck. He got a pulse — albeit a weak one — but the man was still alive.

Returning to the cruiser, the officer radioed for help.

Several minutes later, a medic van screeched to a halt in front of the car. Attendants in white uniforms spilled from the van and crouched beside the unconscious man laying in the blood pool. One paramedic placed an oxygen mask over the man's mouth while the other inserted an intravenous tube into a fresh vein.

Seconds later, the van with its precious cargo inside, was racing toward the hospital.

In the emergency room, doctors worked feverishly to stabilize the comotose gunshot victim. The wound which was still oozing a small amount of blood, was cleaned and X-rays were taken to determine how severe the man's injuries were.

Plenty severe, as it turned out. The man died later that morning without ever regaining consciousness.

The case was given to Detectives Richard Hooper, Patrick Clemens and Dale Mason of the Huntington Beach Police Crimes Against Persons Unit.

The sleuths were notified at their homes and all met at the shooting scene in the industrial park at 2:30 Tuesday morning. Joining them was a team of technicians from the Orange County Sheriff's Crime Lab.

After questioning the officer who had discovered the corpse and after making a brief examination of the crime scene, the detectives went to the hospital, where they learned the victim had died.

"He was completely unconscious," one of the emergency room doctors informed them. "There was nothing we could do for him. I am surprised he lived as long as he did."

The victim's wallet was empty of money, but a driver's license and credit cards identified him as Barry Ford, 31, of Huntington Beach, California.

The small color picture of the smiling, bespectacled driver matched the lifeless corpse in the emergency room who was now covered with a bloodstained sheet.

Ford lived on a cozy, tree-lined street in an older, affluent section of Huntington Beach. A light was on in a front room of the house when detectives came knocking on the front door.

A pretty woman with long, dark-brown hair, answered. "Yes?" Anita Ford asked. Her large, almond-shaped eyes were puffy; apparently she had been sleeping.

The detectives identified themselves. Puzzled, Anita Ford nodded and asked, "Is something wrong?"

Trying to break the news as gently as possible, Detective

HIT MEN

Mason replied, "I'm sorry to report that your husband is dead. We would like to talk to you for a few minutes."

Anita gasped in disbelief and stumbled backwards into the living room. Her jaw dropped and her eyes suffused with tears. "No," she gasped, then burst into tears.

The detectives comforted her as best they could. After she had calmed down, they asked if she was up to answering a few of their questions.

Anita nodded, then asked, "Can I call my brother, first? He should know."

"Sure, go ahead," Detective Mason responded.

With hands shaking, Anita pressed the receiver to her ear and punched in the telephone number. In a trembling voice, she blurted out the bad news. "Somebody shot Barry," she gasped. "He's dead."

Detective Mason glanced over at Detective Hooper who returned the surprised look.

They waited until Anita Ford had finished her phone call and had calmed down enough to answer their questions.

Anita told them about the strange phone call Barry had received Monday night. She said she didn't know who it was from, but apparently it was important enough to drag Barry out of the house.

"He said he would be back in a couple of minutes," Anita cried.

"You think it was a friend?" she was asked.

"I don't know," she replied. "Maybe. Barry was always doing favors for people."

Maybe this was the one favor he shouldn't have done, the detectives agreed, as they left the house and the sobbing widow.

It was close to daylight when the sleuths returned to the industrial park where Barry Ford had met his unexpected and bloody demise.

The victim's pickup had been searched and towed to the

police station for fingerprinting. Lab technicians were now searching the asphalt for cigarette butts and scuff marks and other physical evidence.

They finished the search as employees began arriving at the industrial park. The technicians headed back to the station.

The autopsy conducted later that day produced a few interesting clues. According to the coroner's report, Barry Ford had been shot twice in the back of the head at almost point-blank range. The fateful slugs had been fired from a small-caliber weapon, such as a .22-caliber pistol.

The path of the bullets and the shape of the entry holes indicated the weapon had been fired from a downward angle and that the 31-year-old businessman had likely been bent over when shot.

An execution slaying pure and simple, detectives agreed. But why?

When the patrol officer stumbled upon the scene just minutes after the shooting, it appeared as if Ford had been forced from his car then shot during a botched robbery. The car door was open, the lights were on, and Ford's wallet was cleaned of cash.

The theory, however, did not bear up to close inspection. If Barry Ford had been the victim of a robbery, why was his wallet returned to his pants pocket? Even the most considerate of robbers would not have bothered with such a nicety after pumping two slugs into the back of Ford's head.

And detectives could not explain what the cheery, 31-year-old Ford was doing late Monday night in the industrial park. Had he gone there to meet someone? If so, who? And why?

Searching for answers, the detectives returned to Barry Ford's neighborhood. Residents received the grim news with shock and disbelief. Barry was one of the more popular persons on the block, they agreed.

No one knew why he had been shot.

No one looked more anguished than John Aldridge, Ford's neighbor and friend for many years. Grief-stricken, he pointed to a picture hanging on the kitchen wall of him and his friend Barry. The photo had been taken at a recent outing.

"We did a lot of things together," Aldridge told sleuths. Crossing his fingers, he gave the detectives a fierce look and said, "Barry and I were like this. We were that close."

Aldridge said Barry ran a tow truck business out of his house, while Anita was self-employed as a trucking broker. He described them as "good people" who would do anything to help a person in need.

"Barry got calls at all hours of the day and night," Aldridge said. "He never turned anyone down."

He said neither Barry nor Anita had told him about receiving crank calls or being in trouble. He said he was unaware of any trouble on the block that might be related to the murder.

"This is a good neighborhood," Aldridge said proudly. "If this could happen here it could happen anywhere."

Probers learned that Barry Ford was well liked on his block. The outpouring of grief for the 31-year-old tow truck operator seemed sincere. Everyone seemed to like him.

Not everyone, however, liked his vixenish wife, Anita. High on the list of her detractors were members of Barry Ford's family. To them, Anita was just too frisky and full of the devil to be a good enough wife for Barry.

"A lot of us just never accepted her," one relative confided to probers. "We tried to make Barry reconsider marrying her, but he wouldn't listen."

Initially, Barry was deaf to all criticism about his young wife. But lately, friends said, he had begun to reconsider.

Witnesses told police that Anita had a fiendish cocaine

and alcohol problem. Her appetite for the drug plus a penchant for hitting the bars and dancing till dawn had put a strain on the couple's marriage.

The two argued often and, police learned, Barry once stormed out of the house yelling he wouldn't be back until Anita straightened herself out. The two reconciled, but Anita was soon back to her old tricks.

A discreet check revealed that Barry had become so concerned about his wife's expensive habits that he had removed her name from their joint bank account and had frozen their credit cards. That hardly made Anita blink because she used income from her job as a self-employed trucking broker to feed her drug habit.

Detectives suspected that Anita knew more about her husband's murder than she was letting on. They had been tipped off when Anita had rushed to the telephone to tell her brother that Barry had been shot to death.

That was true—but how did she know? Detective Mason had only said Barry was dead and had mentioned nothing about a shooting.

From that point on, the investigation quickly focused on the young widow. Some digging revealed that Anita had plenty of motive. Barry had a $140,000 life insurance policy naming Anita as sole beneficiary. And in the event of his death, she also stood to inherit the house, the car and all the family possessions, not to mention her husband's thriving tow truck business. But to get those things, Anita had to act fast.

According to friends, Barry had just about given up on his wife and her wild ways. He was thinking about divorcing her and writing her name out of his insurance policy, friends told sleuths. And that would have left Anita out in the cold.

Anita had every reason in the world to want her husband dead, police agreed. But they doubted she had been the one to pull the trigger.

The Fords didn't have any firearms and as far as anyone could tell, Anita did not know the first thing about shooting.

"She'd probably end up shooting herself before shooting someone else," a friend noted.

Who then had shot Barry?

Police learned that in the weeks before the shooting, Anita had approached several people in the bars she frequented and had asked them if they knew where she could hire a hit man.

No one, however, took her seriously, apparently dismissing her as a pretty but slightly shrill housewife who had apparently had too much to drink.

Obviously, someone had taken her seriously—serious enough to pump two slugs into the back of Barry Ford's head and leave him to die in a pool of his own blood.

But who? Detectives didn't have an answer to the question until they got a tip that a neighbor of the Fords, Brad Chase, had been seen visiting the Ford home almost daily prior to the shooting.

Chase, 24, had already been questioned during the initial neighborhood canvass. A solemn-looking young man with a nervous demeanor, Chase told police he was friends with Barry Ford and had once called him to have his car towed.

Now, according to the new information, Chase had not only been friendly with Barry, but also with Anita, who he would trot over to visit almost daily while Barry was gone.

It didn't seem like much, but investigators gave it a try and brought Brad Chase to the station.

Under the lights, it was obvious why Chase was so nervous and pale. He had a ferocious cocaine habit that had nearly consumed him for years.

With a monkey on his back, Chase was no match for the relentless detectives and their barrage of questions. When asked what he knew about the Barry Ford murder, he replied quite correctly, "Everything!"

Chase wasn't lying. In a detailed statement which he would later repeat in court, Chase said Anita Ford was the mastermind behind the plot to kill her husband and that she had convinced two men to carry out her wishes.

The gunman was her brother, George Wright. His accomplice was the Fords' neighbor, John Aldridge.

Detective Dale Mason nearly leaped off his chair in the interrogation room. "Hey, wait a minute, Aldridge is Ford's best buddy!"

But, as police learned, with friends like John Aldridge, who needed enemies?

Chase related that he had been stopping by the Ford home after Barry was at work to smoke marijuana and snort coke with Anita. He said that while getting high, Anita would chat incessantly about being tired of her husband and wanting to get rid of him. Chase said he thought Barry was an okay guy and that he only listened to the incessant chatter because he wanted some of Anita's potent drugs.

"I didn't take her seriously," he admitted.

Chase said he realized she was serious when Aldridge and Wright entered the picture. Wright was a big guy with a face full of whiskers who bragged about killing more than 200 men while in Vietnam. Aldridge also didn't look like someone to mess with.

Chase said he didn't know how he had gotten mixed up in the plot to kill Barry, a guy he actually liked.

"It was just something that sort of got out of hand," he admitted.

Chase said they were sitting around the Ford home drinking beer and getting high. Naturally, the talk got around to getting rid of Barry. Barry had already talked about getting a divorce and writing his wife out of the

$140,000 insurance policy, so the conspirators agreed that if they were going to do it, it had to be done soon.

"We started talking about ways to get rid of him," Chase said. In one scenario, they decided to shoot Barry then dump his body in the desert. In another scheme, they thought of disposing of Barry's body in Mexico.

Neither idea was greeted with much enthusiasm.

"We also brought up the idea of killing Barry in a car crash, but Anita nixed the idea," Chase said. "She said she wanted the car."

Chase said they finally decided to lure Barry from his house on the pretense that Aldridge's car had broken down. That seemed like a pretty good idea. Aldridge, after all, was an old friend and Barry would do anything for a friend.

They scouted locations and came up with the industrial park in southeast Huntington Beach. It was secluded and lightly patrolled at night.

On September 3, 1984, Aldridge telephoned the couple's home around 10 p.m. and asked Barry to come help him start his car. Barry agreed to help his old buddy. But when Barry got to the industrial park, he wasn't in the best of moods, according to Chase, who had tagged along to get in on the action.

Chase said that, as the two old friends talked, George Wright materialized out of nowhere, stuck a gun to the back of Barry's head and fired two shots.

Barry dropped like a stone; a puzzled look on his face was his last expression.

The men then jumped into Aldridge's car and got out of there in a hurry, leaving Barry on the asphalt, with his car door open and lights still on.

Chase admitted he was worried when police started poking around but cooled off when no arrests were forthcoming. Convinced he was in the clear, Chase started boasting about murdering poor Barry Ford—a big mistake since word about his boasting became a hot gossip item and put Brad Chase in the hot seat.

After his confession, Brad Chase was arrested and booked into the county jail on suspicion of murder. Word got back to little Anita, who could not have been happy about the arrest, but chose to stick around the house rather than run.

That didn't last for long, though.

Anita Ford was arrested on October 24, 1984. No one looked more shocked or upset than the sultry, little housewife who had cried so convincingly when informed of her husband's unfortunate death. Taken away in handcuffs, she insisted, "I didn't do it."

A similar statement peppered with obscenities was given by Anita's brother, George Wright. "I don't know what the hell this is all about, but I am innocent," the fuzzy-faced, Vietnam vet said.

Also claiming innocence was John Aldridge, Barry Ford's former neighbor and best buddy.

With the suspects in jail, detectives continued their investigation. A key piece of evidence was the .22-caliber pistol that was used to shoot Barry. Police found .22-caliber ammunition in George Wright's trash-strewn home, but no weapon. Brad Chase later told detectives the weapon had been tossed into the ocean, where it would never be found.

He was right. Despite several searches by the police department's volunteer search and rescue team, the weapon was never recovered.

The defendants were arraigned on murder charges in Orange County Municipal Court and ordered to stand trial. The charges carried the special penalty provisions of murder in commission of a robbery and lying in wait. This meant the conspirators could receive the death sentence if they were convicted.

Brad Chase had also been charged with murder. He was, however, later allowed to plead guilty to a charge of voluntary manslaughter in return for his testimony against the others for an automatic sentence of only seven years.

Bright-eyed and drug-free, Chase proved to be a credible witness and absolutely devastating to the defense.

In February 1988, John Aldridge pleaded guilty to murder charges and was sentenced to 15 years to life in state prison.

A few months later, triggerman George Wright was found guilty of first-degree murder and conspiracy. He was sentenced to life in prison without parole.

Of the three, only Anita Ford took the witness stand. At her May 1987 trial before Judge John McCartin, the sultry brunette took the witness stand to tell her own story.

Glancing occasionally at the jury, she described life with her ex-husband Barry Ford as anything but a barrel of laughs. According to Anita, Barry verbally abused her, beat her and, in general, made her life sheer hell.

"Did you kill him?" her attorney asked.

"No," the sultry widow replied.

"Did you plot or have anything to do with the murder?"

"No."

Who did then?

Anita had an answer: her brother, George, she maintained. She said George didn't like Barry and when he learned that Barry had beaten her up, he decided to mete out a little justice of his own.

By the time she learned what George was up to, Anita said, it was too late; Barry was already dead.

It was also too late for Anita Ford. On June 3, 1987, an Orange County jury found her guilty of conspiracy and murder for financial gain, which triggered an automatic life sentence without the possibility of parole.

Upset at the verdict, Anita's attorney told reporters, "I

knew we were going to lose on the first-degree murder, but I thought we would win on the special circumstances. If she did participate in her husband's murder, I had hoped we could convince the jury it was just because she hated him."

If that had been the case, Anita would have been eligible for parole.

Anita appeared less disturbed about the verdict than her attorney. She sat emotionless as the verdict was read, then shrugged at a court bailiff with whom she had become friendly.

Before leaving the courtroom, Anita asked her attorney to make sure Judge McCartin did not sentence her on July 30th.

"It's my birthday," she said.

A good sport, the judge went along with the request and sentenced Anita to life in prison on July 31st.

EDITOR'S NOTE:
Brad Chase is not the real name of the person so named in the foregoing story. A fictitious name has been used because there is no reason for public interest in the identity of this person.

"'HIT CONTRACT' CLIMAXED THE FAMILY TRAGEDY!"

by Bud Ampolsk

The setting was all wrong. There was no way this pretty 17-year-old high school cheerleader should be here. Nor did it make any more sense that her clean-cut looking 17-year-old homeroom classmate should be seated on a rear bench, his expression stony and apprehensive.

And yet the lovely brunette, neatly dressed in a white knit sweater and gray wool skirt, her brown hair softly touching her shoulder, was not only here, she was the prime reason for the jam-packed assemblage which strained the stern, forbidding confines of Suffolk County Court in Riverhead, Long Island.

Every eye was trained on Cheryl Pierson as she stood trembling at the rail before Judge Harvey Sherman's bench. Every mind was focused on the particular stress the teenager suffered.

Inexorably, the 20-minute proceeding inched forward. Looking down from his high vantage point, the grandfatherly-appearing jurist showed his own sense of compassion. Frequently he asked whether Cheryl would care for a glass of water or would like to sit down. Each time the question was put to the girl, she would dab at her eyes, wiping away the tears which flowed from them. Then in a nearly inaudible voice she'd whispered, "No."

At last came the question, the answer to which the crush of court officers, attendants, spectators and working press had been awaiting for well over a year.

Judge Sherman leaned forward and asked if Cheryl would like to change her plea from not guilty of murder in the second degree to guilty of first-degree manslaughter. The nearly hysterical girl broke into a new series of wrenching sobs.

For everybody who had had anything to do with the bizarre and tragic case, the moment of ultimate truth was at hand. Cheryl Pierson was about to make her first public statement concerning the slaying of her 42-year-old father, James Pierson.

Now Assistant District Attorney Edward Jablonski, Chief of the Major Offense Unit of the Suffolk County District Attorney's Office, stepped forward.

"Why," he asked, "were you looking for somebody to kill your father?"

Cheryl fought to get the words out. At first no sound would issue from her trembling mouth. She was overcome by still another fit of bitter weeping.

"Because . . ." she managed at last. Spectators leaned forward, trying to catch her words. A deathly pall spread through the courtroom. She went on, "He was sexually abusing me."

Expanding somewhat on the statement, Cheryl told the court that she had offered Sean Pica a $1,000 fee for ambushing and slaying her father because James Pierson had been sexually abusing her since 1979. In the days prior to the shooting of her father, she had become terrified that the elder Pierson was now turning his sexual attentions towards Cheryl's younger sister.

According to Cheryl, the sexual abuse started at a time when the girl's mother, Cathleen, first came down with a kidney disease which was to prove fatal on February 13, 1985.

As had Cheryl, Sean Pica, who had been charged with second-degree murder, told the court session that he was guilty of first-degree manslaughter as the hired hit man who gunned James Pierson down in the Pierson driveway on the morning of Wednesday, February 5, 1986, as he left for work.

As the plea-bargaining session ended in Judge Sherman's chambers on Tuesday, March 24, 1987, the jurist noted that under terms of the worked-out compromise, Cheryl would receive no more than two to six years in prison. Also, it provided that she could be considered for youthful offender status under which she could be freed on probation.

For his part, A.D.A. Jablonski said he would ask that Cheryl be ordered to serve at least a year in prison.

The prosecutor also felt that Pica, as the triggerman, should receive the maximum possible penalty of eight and a half to 25 years for his part in the conspiracy killing.

Dramatic as it was, the court session which featured the two guilty pleas provided a forum for only the sketchiest details of the Long Island tragedy. There was much more to the story than that.

Included in the saga were inspired police work, deep splits among family and friends concerning the motivations behind the slaying, divergence of expert opinion in the reactions of sexually abused children, widely varying evaluations of the personality and traits of the slain man and new thoughts about justifiable homicide.

For Captain Robert Savarese of the Suffolk County

Police Department Homicide Squad, Suffolk Detective Chief John Gallagher, Detective James McCready and other dedicated lawmen, it all started in the bitingly cold early morning hours of February 5, 1986.

It was shortly after 6:00 a.m. when, as was his habit, the muscular James Pierson arose. The union electrician, who also owned a rather lucrative side business installing cable television boxes in private homes, donned a hunting jacket and jeans before leaving for work. On his way out of the wood shingle home he shared with his two daughters on Magnolia Street in Selden, Long Island, he checked on the girls to make sure they were up and about. Satisfied, he opened the kitchen door and departed.

Pierson got no farther than his driveway. Although no neighbors in the modest community heard the five shots ring out, the bullets were none the less lethal.

All that detectives had been able to glean as they rolled up to the Magnolia Street address was that a 911 had been called in by a young girl who told the dispatcher that her father had just been shot. First examination of the dead man showed that five slugs had found their way into his back. The marksmanship involved and the neatness of the execution-style slaying indicated that Pierson could possibly have been the victim of a mob-style professional hit.

Lending support to this line of reasoning was the fact that Pierson had been active in union affairs. With racketeering of certain locals a problem, police began a close check of the dead man and the labor organization to which he had belonged. Both came up squeaky clean.

For his part, Pierson enjoyed a top-flight reputation among his co-workers and those with whom he did business in his own enterprise. Although he had been a union delegate and somewhat active as a unionist, he had not been an official of any labor group.

The union in which the dead man had held membership was highly regarded for its integrity. There was not the slightest hint of racketeering infiltration which might have led to a labor-sponsored contract hit.

Something else was disturbing Detective Chief Gallagher. That was Cheryl Pierson's original reaction when she first met the homicide specialists who came to Magnolia Street in answer to her call.

Said Gallagher, "Here was her father lying maybe fifteen feet away, dead as a mackerel in the driveway and she didn't seem overly upset, even though she had found the body.

"She was very indifferent to detectives, greeted them as they came into the house and even asked them airily, 'Who's wearing that nice after-shave lotion?'"

Although reactions of close relatives are frequently bizarre and unpredictable at the scene of a sudden and violent death, this one got detectives to wondering. It might have been that the girl subconsciously refused to accept the finality of the grisly tableau. By remaining composed and paying attention to seemingly trivial things, she could have been denying to herself that anything dire had occurred.

On the other hand, in the first stages of an investigation no enterprising police officer will take anything for granted. With this in mind, Suffolk County authorities now began checking out Newfield High School where Cheryl was a member of the junior class and also belonged to the cheerleading group.

While this phase of the police probe was going on, members of the Pierson family, relatives and friends prepared to pay their last respects to James Pierson.

The funeral was held on a brutally cold and snowy Saturday, February 8th, with about 150 in attendance. They heard a eulogy read by a priest. It had been written by Cheryl and another close relative.

In part, it said, "Our father was strong-willed, but soft-hearted. He treated some people like a brother or sister and some like a father or a son. He was our best friend."

The mourners were witness to the extent of bereavement shown by Cheryl. She wept uncontrollably throughout the funeral mass and burial services. At the graveside, the teenager kissed the coffin which bore her father's remains.

But the questioning of schoolmates by detectives was beginning to produce another picture of the girl.

Several reported having heard Cheryl complain about how hard it was to find someone who was willing to kill for a price, Detective Chief Gallagher reported.

A few days after James Pierson's funeral, an unidentified student called Suffolk County Police and told them that Cheryl had been looking for a "hit man" to kill her father.

Armed with this knowledge, Detective McCready went to the home in which Cheryl was staying with her grandmother. The teenage girl was asleep at the time. Her grandmother awakened the girl, who came into the living room clad in her pajamas. McCready informed her she was under arrest. She was allowed to change to street clothes, and was then taken to Nassau County Police Headquarters at Yaphank and read her rights.

Instead of choosing to remain silent, the girl confessed and implicated Sean Pica.

On February 13, 1986, a stunned community learned that Cheryl Pierson and Sean Pica were being held on charges of second-degree murder and had allegedly confessed their respective roles in the killing of James Pierson. Also being held on charges of conspiracy was Cheryl's 19-year-old boyfriend, Robert Cuccio of Selden, who allegedly had recruited Pica as the hit man. He too, was reported by police to have confessed.

At this point, Cheryl told detectives that she had been sexually abused by her father over a period of seven years and recently had feared that James Pierson was beginning to make sexual advances to her younger sister.

In presenting the state's case at arraignment proceedings, Assistant District Attorney Stephen Wilutis showed a deal of compassion for Cheryl not usually displayed in a criminal court proceeding.

Said Wilutis, "We are taking into account that she believed that her father was about to abuse her little sister. She had no place to turn, other than to her boyfriend. She may have believed she acted morally correctly, but we think she acted legally wrong."

Hauppauge District Judge Armand Araujoin listened to Wilutis' demand that bail for Cheryl be set at $200,000 and reduced the sum to $50,000. Pica was held on $100,000 bail and Cuccio on $5000.

Expanding on the theme, Captain Robert Savarese of the Suffolk County Homicide Squad quoted Cheryl's confession stating that James Pierson had been sexually abusing her. Cheryl had wanted to break off the incestuous relationship.

She'd gotten the idea of having her father killed from news stories concerning a pending case in Mastic, Long Island. In that situation, a housewife was charged with having hired five other persons to kill her husband, whom she claimed had abused her.

Savarese noted that Cheryl had talked openly about

finding someone who would perform the killing for money. However, none of her schoolmates knew of the illicit relationship between James and Cheryl.

According to the charges against him, Pica agreed to do the job. He used a .22-caliber pump-action rifle for the killing, noted the chief of the homicide squad.

Pica had hidden in the shrubbery outside the Pierson home just after 6:00 a.m. on the day of the killing. Shortly afterward, James Pierson began to leave for his job in Huntington. As Pierson passed the shrubbery, Pica stepped out and fired five shots into the marked man's back and torso.

As cited in the confessions, Pica, after shooting Pierson, fled the scene in his own car. According to the plan, Cheryl waited ten minutes before calling police, thus insuring Pica's getaway.

Immediately after the hit, Cheryl allegedly turned $400 over to Cuccio to be delivered to Pica as partial payment of the $1,000 owed to him, said Police Chief Gallagher. Pica used the money to pay off some debts.

Defense Attorney Paul Gianelli, representing Cheryl, gave a capsule version of what his approach to the case would be when he said that after the death of his wife, James Pierson had become even more violent toward his daughter. At that point, he had begun to have sex with her.

"He subjected her to brutal beatings. Many times she was seen black and blue. She didn't speak to anyone except her boyfriend," said Gianelli.

As more information on the case was developed, it was learned that the February 5th slaying marked the second attempt on Pierson's life.

Just before Christmas of 1985, a plan had been devised whereby Pica would throw a rock through a window of the Pierson home. Cheryl was to awaken her sleeping father to go outside and check for burglars. Pica would be lying in wait. He would fall upon the elder Pierson and stab him to death. The plan allegedly aborted when the father refused to get out of bed to investigate.

On February 19, 1986, Cheryl and Pica were indicted on second-degree murder charges by a Suffolk County grand jury. Assistant D.A. Jablonski said the twin indictments would be handed up to Suffolk County Judge Morris Weissman for further court action. Both Cheryl and Pica were still lodged in the Riverhead Jail while their respective families tried to raise bail.

The following week, having pleaded not guilty to the murder and conspiracy charges, Cheryl was released on $25,000 bail.

On March 20th, there was another startling twist in the tangled case. It was revealed by Suffolk County Medical Examiner Charles Hirsch that Cheryl had suffered a miscarriage of an eight-week pregnancy. Blood samples of the girl and her father were taken in an effort to determine the paternity of the dead embryo. (Later, the authoritative *New York Times* would report, "Laboratory tests proved that James Pierson could not have been the father of the aborted child.")

Now, as new legal developments were awaited, the suburban community of Selden, situated in the middle of Suffolk County some 50 miles east of Manhattan, began to take stock. The shaken townspeople could not find a common meeting ground on the allegations of sexual abuse as the motivating factor in the killing.

Town officials pointed out that Cheryl had never shown any signs of delinquency nor any other psychological problems which would have called attention to her.

Said one assistant principal of Newfield High, "It's all been quite a shock to the staff, to students and to the community."

He noted that there were resources within the school available to troubled young people. One example he gave was "The Time Out Room."

There students could speak in confidence to specially trained teacher volunteers, who in turn could send them to professional counselors.

However, Dr. Urie Bronfenbrenner, a psychologist and professor of human development and family studies at Cornell University, said that sexually abused children are often reluctant to seek help.

"There must be a pre-existing bond with an adult they trust," he said. "Sexual abuse is not something a child is going to want to discuss with a stranger. This entire situation appears to be a symptom of the breakdown between adults and kids, and not just in the one community. It's a generic problem."

Dr. Vincent J. Fontana, chairman of the Suffolk County and New York City commission on child abuse, noted that "there are no simple answers."

"But there is a lot to be learned from a case like this," he continued. "The problem of sexual abuse is far more common than most people might suspect.

"The statistics are just beginning to surface. We estimate that one out of every five girls and one out of every nine boys will have reported being sexually abused at least once by an adult during childhood years."

What was at issue among those who had known the dead Pierson and his accused daughter was whether there were signs of abuse which should have been perceptible to discerning people.

One clergyman, who had known Pierson casually for

about eight years, recalled him as a friendly and well-accepted man. He recalled that while Pierson had not been a regular churchgoer, he had coached the boy's baseball team.

Some of her schoolmates agreed with Defense Attorney Gianelli's contention that there were signs of physical abuse on Cheryl's person. A number of students reported that they had seen Cheryl bearing black-and-blue marks. However, her teachers, including those who had coached her cheerleading activities, had not noticed the contusions.

On this point, the assistant principal stated, "The majority of our teachers are very attuned to the kids and aware of what's going on. And legally, they must report suspected abuses."

He added that no such reports had ever been turned in concerning Cheryl. "There's nothing in her health record to indicate that this was indeed true. I've researched this," he said.

Several classmates said that Cheryl had asked a number of students if they knew anybody who would kill her father. But she had not given any reason for the query.

Like Cheryl Pierson, prior to his involvement in the Pierson homicide, Sean Pica had been thought of at Newfield as "an average kid."

Said a faculty member, "These kids were not identified as troubled kids. Often the kids give off only hidden signals. The symptoms can be very difficult to recognize."

There was growing interest in the background and personality of the slain James Pierson during the trial period.

It was learned that Pierson had lived in Selden since his teen years. He'd graduated from Newfield High School in 1962. Three years after his graduation, he'd married Cathleen. He'd been a good provider and an industrious worker. Bringing a feeling of prosperity to his immediate family seemed to be the center of his life.

The Piersons had had three children. With the kids he'd been a strict disciplinarian. He was of the old school when it came to such admonitions as "silence is golden" and the importance of good manners.

Although he was not known to inflict corporal punishment on the youngsters, he would threaten them with "a smack across the face" if they got the least bit out of line.

Proper behavior brought rewards in the form of gifts.

Some described him as rough and foul-mouthed. But they added that he was also both generous and loyal.

"He was the kind of man whose bark was worse than his bite," said one acquaintance. "He would raise his voice and the next minute he had his arm around you," he went on to say.

The crisis which developed when Cathleen was diagnosed in 1979 as having a fatal kidney disease caused tremendous stress within the Pierson family. There were frequent visits to the hospital for therapy. There was talk of kidney transplants.

More and more Cheryl was forced by her mother's illness to take on the responsibilities of the woman of the house. At about that time James allegedly began paying more physical attention to his older daughter. At first she welcomed this, but later sensed that it was wrong.

After Cathleen died in February of 1985, James Pierson confided in friends that his grief at her loss had been mixed with a sense of anger that she had left him with three children to raise on his own.

Still, on Cheryl's 16th birthday, celebrated some three months after her mother's death, her father threw a lavish Sweet Sixteen party for his daughter. This was in keeping with plans which had been made while Cathleen was still alive. Father and daughter danced alone at the height of the party as guests stood in silence watching them.

More and more, Cheryl looked to Robert Cuccio for her sense of comfort and strength. She confided in him, and nobody else, of her sexual problems with her father.

Yet there were times when the relationship between father and daughter appeared to be typical of what one might expect in a normal and untroubled family.

One of these occurred on the night before James Pierson's death, according to a family member.

Pierson is said to have picked up his daughter at the high school gym after a basketball game and driven her home. There, the woman relative met the pair and delivered two stuffed animals to the elder Pierson. She says he was planning to give the toys to his daughters as a Valentine present.

Following the killing and in the months while court action was grinding slowly forward, family members took differing views of who was to blame for the tragedy which had engulfed the Piersons.

One relative said that he had not known of the alleged sexual abuse Cheryl had suffered until after her father's slaying. He is quoted as saying, "If I'd known, I would have killed him myself."

Another reported having seen Pierson make a sexual advance toward his teenage daughter while they were shopping at a convenience store.

However, several women relatives, as well as a number of James Pierson's friends, contended that Cheryl had fabricated stories of sexual abuse. They held there were other reasons why she might have wanted to see her father dead. One was James Pierson's sense of strict discipline at a time when the attractive teenager was becoming interested in boys of nearly her own age. Another was that by hard work and frugality, James Pierson had amassed a tidy fortune of approximately $500,000 from which she might have benefited in part. The third concerned her pregnancy.

The question of whether Cheryl had reason to believe that the only means she had of protecting her younger sister and herself was to enter into a conspiracy to have her father killed, triggered spirited debates between professional law enforcement authorities and specialists expert in dealing with abused children.

For his part, A.D.A. Jablonski held that there was no direct evidence to support Cheryl's claim of having been sexually abused. He argued that even if such evidence did exist, the real issue was that she should be punished for having taken her father's life.

Whether she was or wasn't abused "has nothing to do with the fact that all she had to do was to go to the police. That's what they're there for," Jablonski commented.

Defense Attorney Gianelli countered by pointing out that the defendant had suffered the same type of emotional trauma from her experiences with her father as do battered wives and victims of chronic violence. He said that because of this "she was in an extreme emotional state."

Support for the defense position came from mental health experts.

Said Dr. Fontana, "The problem is the system is unable to deal with abused adolescents. When we deal with an adolescent who asks for help, we always question whether it is a disciplinary matter or one of legitimate abuse."

Meg O'Regan, executive director of the Center for Women's Rights in Mineola, Long Island, also cited lack of adolescent trust in the system. She stated, "Our history is not believing children. A lot of kids don't think the system will help them, and they're right. Battered children are supposed to call the police, but they know they will either not be believed or their lives will be completely disrupted."

On September 15th, a pretrial hearing was convened in jam-packed Suffolk County New York State Supreme Court to determine the admissibility of Cheryl's and Pica's confessions as evidence at their pending trials.

Cheryl, neatly dressed in a gray flannel skirt and blazer and a ruffled white blouse, sat at the defense table sobbing as Detective McCready described how he placed the girl under arrest at her grandmother's house. A stoic Sean Pica, wearing a tan jacket and striped tie, was seated beside his attorney, Martin Efman, listening to the witness.

Detective McCeady then recalled the conversation he'd had with Cheryl's grandmother—it had been around midnight on February 12th—the night of Cheryl's arrest.

"I know who killed your son and you're not going to like what I have got to tell you," Detective McCready said he told the grandmother.

"James Junior?" the detective recalled the woman as having asked. (She was referring to her 20-year-old grandson who had left home because of frictions between him and James Sr.)

"No," McCready told the court he'd answered. "But it's Cheryl."

The detective said that the woman had wept when she heard the news. He said that he asked to speak to

Cheryl, who was asleep. Her grandmother, he said, then awakened the girl and Cheryl came into the living room clad in pajamas. She was placed under arrest. After changing into street clothes, according to the witness, Cheryl had been taken to police headquarters for questioning and had been informed of her constitutional rights against self-incrimination. She then confessed to the plot with Sean Pica, McCready testified.

Under direct examination by Jablonski, McCready then described how Pica had been taken into custody the next morning at 7:30 a.m.

At first, Pica had denied any involvement in the crime, the law officer reported. But when told that both Cheryl and Robert Cuccio were already in custody, Pica also confessed.

Under cross-examination, McCready steadfastly denied that Pica had been subjected to abuse by police.

He told Efman that Pica had been subjected to a strip search before the questioning. He rejected Efman's charge that the teenager had been handcuffed to a file cabinet or otherwise mistreated.

McCready went on to testify that Pica had told of firing the .22-caliber rifle at James Pierson.

Asked by Efman whether Pica had requested that an attorney be present during his questioning at the police headquarters, McCready said he did not. He also said the youth did not want to call his parents.

On the following day, it was learned that Cuccio had pleaded guilty to criminal solicitation charges and was prepared to appear as a state witness against Cheryl and Pica. The announcement by the prosecution sent a ripple through the courtroom. Cuccio's role in the slaying had been known from the outset, but he had never been formally charged.

According to the authorities, Cheryl had told Cuccio that she wanted somebody to kill her father because he had been sexually abusing her. Cuccio then contacted Pica to carry out the slaying. The Cuccio confession said that Pica had been paid $400 for his services.

With Justice Harvey Sherman presiding over the pretrial proceedings, Defense Attorney Efman voiced strong objections to captions on four pictures introduced in court. The sequential photographs purportedly showed Pica recreating the throwing of the murder weapon into the waters off Cedar Beach in Brookhaven, Long Island.

Efman took issue with captions written by Suffolk County Detective Daniel Quinn categorically stating Pica's part in the disposal of the weapon. He was overruled by Judge Sherman.

The defense attorney also attacked procedures used in the arrest of Pica once again. With Detective Stephen Cleary on the stand, Efman questioned him on why he and the other three arresting officers had not obtained a warrant before taking the teenager into custody. He also wanted to know why Pica had been picked up on the street in front of his house instead of at home in the presence of Pica's family. Cleary said the move was not his decision.

According to Cleary, Pica was grabbed as the youth was on his way to catch a bus at 7:00 a.m. The detective said Pica had been read his rights and asked if he wanted a lawyer.

He quoted Pica as having replied, "No, I don't need a lawyer. I didn't do anything." Cleary also said that Pica did not want his family notified.

Thus was the stage set for the highly charged scene which took place in Judge Sherman's courtroom on March 24, 1987.

Spectators who had come expecting the final showdown in the struggle precipitated by James Pierson's slaying waited expectantly as prosecution and defense lawyers disappeared into Judge Sherman's chambers.

As the behind-the-scenes plea-bargaining dragged on, Cheryl sat disconsolately at the defense table. Her head was down. She spoke to nobody. Pica was seated in the rear row with his parents. He showed no emotion until Efman returned and told him that he would be remanded to jail under terms of the agreement hammered out.

Then Pica placed his head between his knees and began weeping.

Still sobbing, Pica then admitted to the court that he had gotten the rifle from a friend and shot Pierson as the older man walked down the driveway.

Following the guilty plea, Judge Sherman revoked Pica's bail and remanded him.

Of his client, Efman said that Pica did not slay Pierson for the proffered $1,000 fee alone, but out of compassion over the girl's abuse. "He felt like Rambo, saving somebody from their fate," commented the defense attorney.

On October 5, 1987, Cheryl Pierson appeared before Judge Sherman and, under terms of a plea-bargain, was sentenced to a six-month term in jail for manslaughter.

For cooperating in the case, Robert Cuccio was promised and received probation.

After pleading guilty to manslaughter, Sean Pica was sentenced to an 8-to-24-year term in prison, with eligibility for parole in eight years.

Under the terms of her sentence, Cheryl Pierson was to be treated as a youthful offender, with record sealed. She was assigned to Minors North, a section for teen-

HIT MEN

agers in the Suffolk County Correctional Facility in Riverhead, Long Island. Upon being paroled, she was to remain on probation for five years and to continue psychological therapy during that time. After that, her debt to society would be considered paid in full.

"SHE TRIED TO KILL FOR HER KID!"

by Bill G. Cox

To understand the bizarre events that occurred in the small Houston, Texas, suburb, it helps to understand the mystique that surrounds Texas high school football. Elevated to everlasting popularity in Texas small towns back when there wasn't much else to do on Friday nights and Saturday afternoons, the high school sport and all of its attendant traditions, on and off the playing fields, peaked in the dire Depression years of the 1930s. Football wasn't just a game to rural Texans. It was war, and it was enthusiastically backed by all citizens, whether they had kids on the playing field or not.

The soul-deep pride, the bitter rivalries, the tooth-and-nail competition more times than not wound up in fist-swinging free-for-alls for which there were not enough unsportsmanlike-conduct penalties on the whole earth.

A son who made the varsity football squad was a town hero. A daughter who was on the cheerleading squad—or pep squad, as it was called then—was a heroine. As propinquity would have it, football hero often married cheerleader heroine, promulgating the fierce football spirit generation by generation.

That's a simplified explanation of Texas high school

football and the supporters who carried it high on their shoulders for decades and decades. But the unindoctrinated might find it useful to understand what happened in Channelview, Texas, in 1990 and 1991. The series of events claimed the media spotlight from around the world, making headlines and TV patter for months. Some of the more poetic called it the "Case of the Pompom Mom."

Involved were two pretty women and their pretty teenage daughters, two families who lived around the corner from each other in almost identical houses. One of the moms was what the press would later call "the ultimate stage mother," a determined lady who initiated unprecedented action in the Harris County Courthouse.

If looks truly did kill, the case might not have gone as far as it did, at least from the standpoint of the mom who suddenly became the subject of an intense undercover police investigation.

Wanda Holloway, 36, was thought an achiever in the minds of those who watched her grow up in the blue-collar industrial town of Channelview, whose economy depends on the vast petro-chemical complexes in the area. Straddling Interstate 10, the town is just east of Houston. It gets its name presumably from the view residents have of the oil tankers that move along the ship channel.

Wanda grew up in a family that was poor but respected by the locals. As a girl, she had wanted to be a cheerleader, a spot of stardom in her small-town junior and senior high schools. But Wanda's father thought the skimpy costumes worn by the pompom girls were too revealing for God-fearing folk, and he forbade his daughter from joining the squad.

Wanda swallowed the bitter pill of disappointment and, despite it, went on to achieve a degree of social success—at least by the time of her third marriage to an older man with a successful oil field servicing business. By her first husband, Wanda had a daughter and a son, whose custody she had retained.

Besides marrying well, Wanda had been a secretary and was the pianist and organist for her church. She was well spoken, had refined manners, and always dressed exquisitely. She was active in school projects involving her kids, especially where her pretty, 14-year-old daughter Shirley was concerned.

Shirley was the pride of her mother's life. Wanda always wanted the best for her daughter, but most of all, she wanted Shirley to have what she herself had been forbidden to have: a place on the junior high school cheerleading squad.

But Wanda saw a barrier to Shirley's being chosen for this recognition. That barrier was another student at the school, the daughter of Wanda's friend of several years, Evelyn Terrell. Wanda and Evelyn had become friends when their daughters were in elementary school. The Terrells lived just around the corner.

That Vicky Terrell, a member of Shirley's freshman class, was a dark shadow on Shirley's cheerleading prospects was not merely a figment of Wanda's imagination. Wanda saw evidence that Vicky was a formidable rival the year before, when the girls were in the seventh grade.

The girls had always been in friendly competition for school offices, though they usually ran for different offices. But in the seventh grade, Shirley and Vicky found themselves competing for the vacancies on the cheerleading squad.

Both youngsters were popular among their classmates. Vicky was named "friendliest and most spirited" in the yearbook. Shirley, like Vicky, was an honors student with a long list of class accomplishments.

The girls were friends, too. They said that theirs was a

natural enough friendship because they were alike in so many respects. They even attended a fancy cheerleading school together in nearby Pasadena, where they studied the complicated twirling and gymnastic techniques so necessary to the modern-day cheerleader.

The rift between Shirley and Vicky widened in 1989, when both were trying out for the cheerleader spots. According to published reports, Wanda Holloway had taken Shirley out of the private elementary school she attended and enrolled her in the public school so that she would be eligible for the cheerleader tryouts the following year, when she would be in the seventh grade.

Vicky had stayed in the private elementary school, but her mother obtained permission from the public school officials for Vicky to try out for the cheerleader spots, since she would be a student there next fall.

Evelyn Terrell took her daughter to the school to help her campaign during tryouts. Wanda Holloway had complained that this was unfair, since the teenager wasn't even enrolled at the school that year as Shirley had been.

But when it was all over—there were three candidates for two slots—Vicky won and Shirley lost.

That had been in 1989. Now that the girls were in eighth grade, Wanda wondered if history would repeat itself—for, once again, the girls were competing for cheerleader honors. Wanda needed some advice on how to gain a victory for her daughter this time. She consulted a male relative of her first husband. He suggested that Wanda buy some rulers, print a campaign slogan on them, and distribute them around the school.

Wanda thought it was a neat idea, but after she had handed out the rulers, school officials decided that such parental campaigning violated school rules. A parents' meeting was called. Among those attending was Evelyn Terrell, Vicky's mom. When the meeting ended, Wanda was prohibited from circulating any more campaign rulers on behalf of her daughter Shirley.

It was around this time, according to a witness, that Wanda Holloway's obsession with her daughter's cheerleading career took a twisted turn. This time, Wanda sought out her campaign adviser with a cold-blooded request.

It was now January 1990. The cheerleader tryouts were scheduled for March, some three months away. Wanda, according to later courtroom testimony, was frantic to the point of desperation.

Wanda arranged to meet John Wright, the male kin of her ex-spouse, at a convenience store. After an exchange of trivial pleasantries, Wanda told Wright that she wanted two people "taken care of," and she wasn't particular about how it was done. When he learned the identities of the two would-be victims—Vicky Terrell and her mother Evelyn—Wright said he wasn't interested.

But in the days that followed, Wanda persisted in her request.

According to his later statements, Wright tried to talk Wanda out of such a horrible idea. Finally, realizing the woman was serious, Wright decided to go to the authorities.

Wright contacted the Harris County Sheriff's Department in Houston and was referred to veteran investigator George Helton. A member of the department's organized crime and narcotics task force, Helton had also worked successfully as an undercover agent in cases involving people wanting to hire professional killers. Helton had occasionally posed as a hit man, when the situation called for it.

The investigator had seen and heard a lot of strange things in Channelview, but when John Wright told him that he knew someone who wanted to "hit" a cheerleader and her mother, Helton was slightly skeptical at first.

Eventually, however, after several meetings with Wright, Investigator Helton decided there was something to what the man was saying. Calling in another officer, wiring expert Sergeant Flynt Blackwell, the investigator obtained an agreement from John Wright to wear a hidden microphone when he had future conversations with Wanda Holloway.

In all, Wright taped six different meetings with Wanda. The final conversation had the effect of convincing investigators that Wanda Holloway was serious about her deadly mission and was ready to pay a hit man for the job.

There was, however, a disagreement over prices. Wright had relayed the fee purportedly quoted by the hired assassin he had lined up (Helton): the hit man wanted $2,500 to do Evelyn Terrell, Wright told Wanda, but the price for hitting teenage daughter Vicky came much higher—$5,000.

Wanda couldn't see it, according to later police reports and court testimony. She said she would settle with offing the mother. Wanda speculated that Evelyn's death would leave Vicky so emotionally upset that she wouldn't be able to concentrate on winning the school cheerleader competition!

When payment time came along, Wanda handed over two diamond earrings to Wright, which she claimed were worth $2,000.

Armed with the taped conversations between John Wright and the scheming mother, Sergeant Blackwell and Investigator Helton went to the D.A.'s office and obtained a warrant for the arrest of the suspect on a charge of solicitation of capital murder.

Wanda Holloway was dressed to the teeth in stylish perfection when officers took her into custody on January

30, 1991. Strangely enough, officers recalled later, Wanda didn't show much reaction to her situation. That wasn't true with the rest of Channelview's population. The community was rocked with the story when it broke in the papers and on TV.

On February 19, 1991, the suspect was indicted by a Harris County grand jury on the solicitation of capital murder charge. She was released on a bond of $10,000.

Early in March, the same month that the school cheerleader tryouts were to be held, Wanda Holloway entered a plea of not guilty in state district court. Meanwhile, the cheerleader competition was held at the school on March 22nd.

Vicky Terrell once again won a spot on the cheering squad, one of four students chosen that day. Shirley did not participate in the competition. Both girls had stayed out of school for a short while after the arrest of Wanda Holloway. But both had returned and were seemingly going about a fairly normal routine.

That same month, Wanda's first husband, the father of Shirley and her brother, filed in court for joint custody of the children, which was given by the judge.

Wanda's trial was first set for June, but was postponed for various reasons until August. A jury was selected in district court in Houston on August 23rd. Testimony began on August 26, 1991.

When the trial got underway, reporters from the far points of the globe, eager representatives of both the print and electronic media, were present.

In their opening arguments, the prosecutors and defense attorneys outlined what they hoped to prove to the jury. The prosecution said it would show that Wanda Holloway had conspired to kill a rival parent over an eighth-grade cheerleading battle, that she hired a hit man to kill the mother of a 13-year-old girl (Vicky) who at-

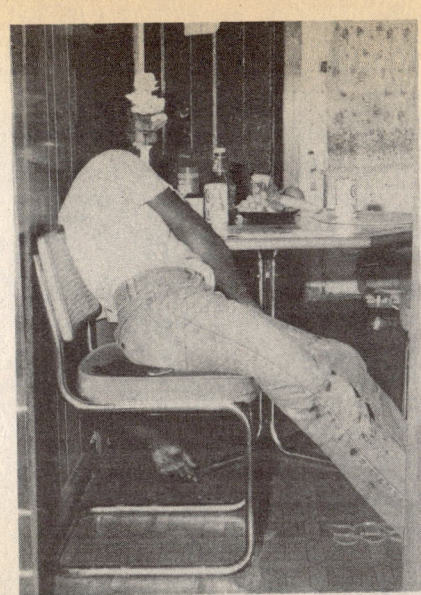

Ronnie Mitchener was drinking a beer when a man entered his house in Baltimore and shot him dead.

Helen Wright of Baltimore, ambushed on her way home with Chinese take-out.

Geraldine Parrish, mastermind behind the Baltimore hits.

Edwin Gordon, 4-time contract killer.

Pamela Mason, 42, was shot four times in her garage.

John Mason ordered the hit on his ex-wife.

Andrew Cantu killed three people for $10,000.

Gregory Summers was convicted of hiring a hit man to kill his parents.

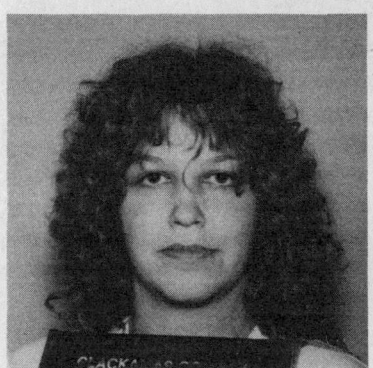

Tamara Maurer hired two men to kill her ex-husband.

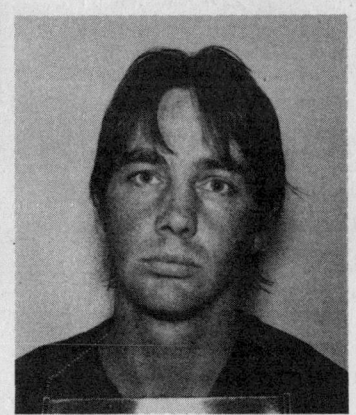 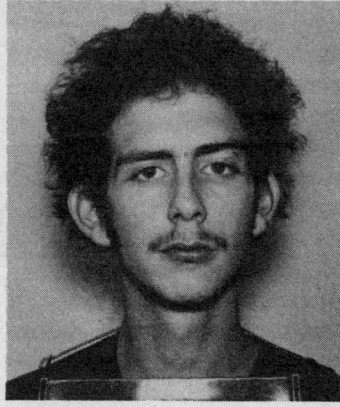

Barry Lynn Larson and Jon Patrick Thompson killed Maurer.

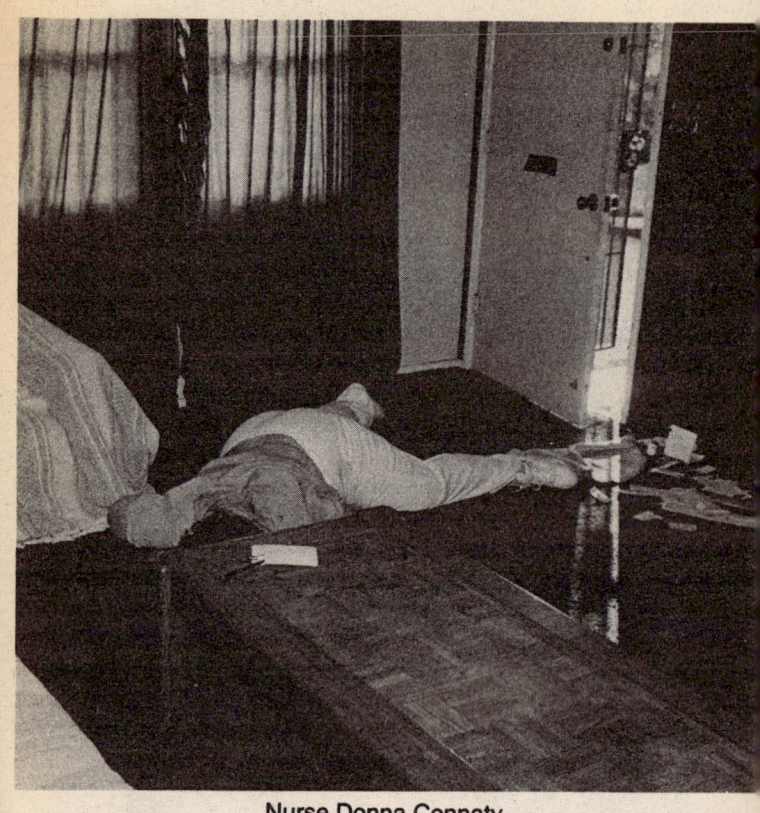

Nurse Donna Connaty.

27-year-old victim Scott Campbell.

Campbell's killers, Donald DiMascio and Larry Cowell.

Robert Levine.

Ronnie Cook broke out of prison—only to end up murdered.

Linda Calvey hired Danny Reece to kill Cook, then finished the job herself when Reece only wounded him.

Bill Curtis hired his young lover, Todd Plamondon, to kill his wife.

Bloody valentine left on hit victim Leonard Fowler's rug.

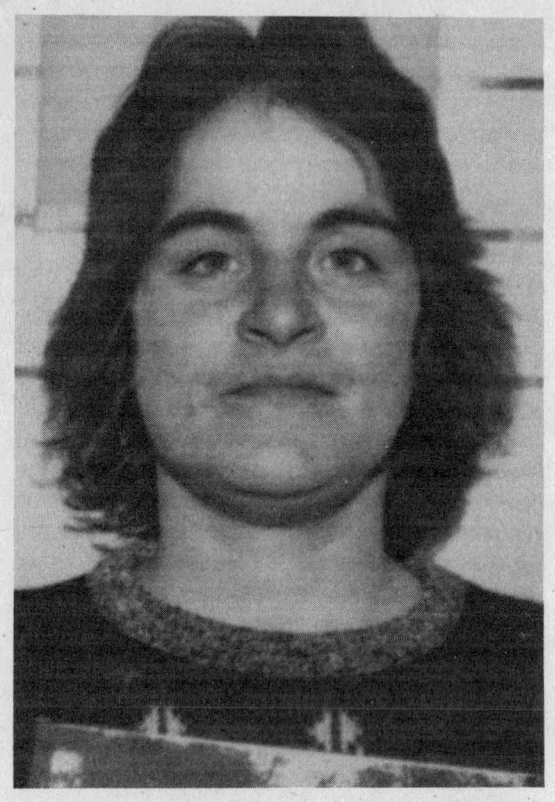

Cindy Landress, who plotted the murder of boyfriend Leonard Fowler.

tended the same school as the defendant's daughter (Shirley).

Prosecutor Mike Anderson said Wanda hoped that Vicky would be so upset about her mother's death that she would drop out of the cheerleader competition, thus improving Shirley's chances of winning the coveted slot.

Speaking of the woman on trial, Prosecutor Anderson said, "Everything bad that happened to her became [Evelyn Terrell's] fault. Wanda began to talk about having her done away with."

The prosecutor said that on a tape that would be played to the jury, Wanda Holloway talked about killing Mrs. Terrell or having her sold into slavery. On the tape, Prosecutor Anderson said, Wanda can be heard saying, "I don't care what you do with her. I just don't want to see her in Channelview again."

As Judge George Godwin looked on from his bench and the jury sat transfixed, Wanda's attorney took a different stance on the events, saying, "There's a whole lot more to this than two mothers who have daughters running for cheerleading."

The defense lawyer claimed that the whole thing had been a scheme devised by John Wright to help his relative, Wanda's first husband, gain custody of their two children. Wright was the "black sheep" of the family and was looking for a way to get back in its good graces, the defense attorney contended.

Wanda was against the plot from the start, claimed the defense. "She was trying to find ways not to do this. You will hear Wanda say [in a taped conversation], 'Blow it off. I don't want to go through with this.' Then Wright says, 'Have I got a deal for you!'"

The attorney told the jury that Wright, having learned of Wanda's disappointment about her daughter's failure to secure a cheerleader spot, said, "I can take care of that for you." And Wanda answered, "That's crazy."

But testifying as the state's key witness, John Wright told a far different story. "She kept saying, 'I hate this girl. I want to get rid of her. I hate her mother. I want to get rid of her, too. I want these people done away with.'

"She asked me what I would do. I said, 'You could get one of these Colombian drug lords and have her taken to Colombia and have her sold into slavery.'"

That testimony brought chuckles from the spectators in the courtroom, for some reason.

When Wanda asked how much this would cost—and Wright estimated up to $20,000—she expressed surprise, the witness testified. To which he had answered, "Look, lady, this ain't no five-and-dime burglary. This is a federal offense."

John Wright explained why he had gone to the police with Wanda's story, saying, "I wanted to cover me. If anything happened to this woman or little girl, I wanted them to have heard it from me first."

Wright said that during one of his conversations with the mother bent on murder, he told her he wasn't sure he could find anyone to kill the girl. He explained, "I said I'd look into it for her, but I don't know anyone who would kill a thirteen-year-old girl. She said, 'There's car wrecks. Houses burn down.' I said, 'Yeah, but not on purpose.' She kept saying, 'I hate this girl. I want to get rid of her. . . . I want these people done away with.'"

When the tapes themselves were played for the jurors, Wanda Holloway was heard saying, "I would like it done. I'm serious about it. I've just got to come up with the money."

In the tape-recorded conversation of their final meeting on January 28, 1991—when Wanda had given Wright a pair of diamond earrings valued at about $2,000 and also promised to pay for the hit within a month—the woman told Wright, "I can't afford to do both. The mother's the one who screwed me around, the mother's done all the damage."

"You want her dead?" Wright asked on the tape.

"I don't care what you do with her," Wanda answered. "You can keep her in Cuba for fifteen years. I want her gone."

Throughout the recorded talks, Wanda Holloway spoke rapidly, and both she and Wright joked and laughed. At one point, the woman expressed concern about getting caught.

"If I ever get tied into this, I know I'd have to move. . . . But I know I want to do it."

The courtroom audience watched with anticipation as Evelyn Terrell, a pretty woman with long hair, took the witness chair. She told the jury, under quizzing by the prosecutor, that she was startled when she learned of the murder-for-hire plot. But she added that Wanda's jealousy did not surprise her.

Her friendship with Wanda had deteriorated after Vicky Terrell won the cheerleading spot in the seventh grade, said the tearful witness.

"I felt tension," she related. "I felt she had trouble with Vicky being able to do something that Shirley could not do. She was very upset because Vicky got cheerleader. . . . We really didn't speak. We didn't communicate. . . . We did not have the same relationship we had before the cheerleading [competition]."

Evelyn Terrell said the idea that Wanda Holloway had tried to arrange for her death made her life miserable.

"I've had nightmares at night, and when I get in my car I'm afraid to start the engine because I've often felt like my car was going to blow up," Evelyn Terrell said with a break in her voice and tears running down her cheeks. "I've not been able to be as good a mother because I've been concerned about his ordeal."

She said her children were also affected. They'd become fearful and less successful in school. She added that she had undergone counseling. Once during the testimony, the woman had to leave the stand briefly to regain her composure.

After the state finished its case, the defense started hammering away at John Wright's version of what happened. Called as a witness was Wright's estranged wife, who testified that Wright and his relative, Wanda's first husband, schemed to set up Wanda Holloway so that Wanda's former spouse could get custody of the children. She said Wright wanted to get back in good standing with his family after being on the outs with his family for a long time.

The witness for the defense told the jury that she once overheard Wright tell Wanda's former husband over the phone that "he had finally gotten her [Wanda] where he wanted her." She said the men began talking about the plan on New Year's Eve.

Wright wanted to get back in the good graces of the family because Wanda's ex-husband was executor of the family will, which Wright had been cut out of, the witness said.

"He [Wright] said [Wanda Holloway] came to him and wanted someone scared," the woman testified. Wright had said on the phone that he suggested to Wanda Holloway that someone "take the mother out. Then you wouldn't have to worry about the daughter."

The witness related that Wright bragged about what he could do to Wanda with the scheme. She quoted Wright as saying to her, "[The ex-husband] is finally going to get his kids." She recalled Wright saying that "they were going to burn Wanda, that he was going to get her to say things with him wired with a recording device."

The witness, quizzed on her marital background, said she and Wright had been married twice in the past two years. She claimed to fear Wright because he abused her mentally and physically. The estranged wife also related that Wright beat her the week before the trial in an attempt to persuade her not to testify in the case.

Recalled for cross-examination by the defense, John Wright admitted discrepancies between his trial testimony and depositions he had given earlier.

"My memory was a whole lot better in February than it is now," he explained. Regarding his estranged wife's testimony, Wright said, "I've never ever got her to change her mind, never ever." He said that her testimony about him beating her up to keep her from testifying was "definitely" a lie.

Wanda's first husband took the stand to say that he and Wright did not talk about the ex-husband gaining custody of the children from Wanda.

He said that when he sought custody of the children two weeks after his former wife was charged, he had done so to "use it as a tool" to take the daughter and son to a counselor, which his ex-wife refused to do. About Wanda's involvement in the murder-for-hire plot, the ex-husband testified, "I was somewhat shocked but not totally surprised. I wouldn't put it past her."

The witness who the courtroom audience and the press had been waiting for took the stand as the defense neared the close of its case. As usual, Wanda Holloway, her hair styled in the latest do and her apparel reflecting current fashion trends, testified quietly and with composure.

She claimed she was dragged into the murder-for-hire plot by John Wright.

But her calmness quickly gave way to tearful testimony. In the beginning, Wanda related, she thought Wright was joking about hiring a hit man. And, after he persisted, she thought he wanted to bilk her for some money.

"I have never wanted Vicky or Evelyn killed," Wanda said.

She testified that she ran into Wright, a man she rarely saw since divorcing her first husband in 1980, at a convenience store in the fall of 1990.

Talking about her children, Wanda mentioned that Shirley had been disqualified from the cheerleading competition, something that she blamed Evelyn Terrell for. She also had been angry with Vicky Terrell for laughing at Shirley, Wanda said.

She recalled that Wright appeared to be sympathetic to Shirley's troubles.

She said that he acted angry and mentioned knowing people who "could take care of those problems." Recalling that she had laughed at such an idea, she added, "I didn't want her killed or kidnapped. But I was still mad about all the cheerleading stuff."

When Wright later called to say he had contacted a hit man for her, she didn't think he was serious.

"But I was a little curious about what he had to say," the witness admitted. Wanda said that when she realized Wright was serious, she phoned him to call it off.

"I had no intentions of having anybody killed."

Wright responded with a threat, saying it was too late now because he had already contacted the hit man. Wanda quoted Wright as telling her at that time, "When he [the hit man] gets mad at me, I'm going to turn him onto you, tell him where you live."

"I was afraid. . . . I didn't know what he was going to do," she said.

Wanda testified that she and her current husband were worth about $2 million and regularly kept $5,000 to $7,000 cash in their house. She said she became suspicious when Wright suggested the hit man be paid with the diamond earrings instead of cash.

"I thought then that [John] was just trying to rip me off for some money." Wanda said she gave him the earrings to get rid of him.

With Wanda's testimony closing out the defense presentation, courtroom observers and the news media speculated about the outcome. One reporter from the *Houston Chronicle* observed that when the jurors started their deliberations after closing arguments, "they'll be in a who-do-you-believe situation."

On Tuesday, September 3, 1991, Prosecutor Casey O'Brien stepped before the jury in the small, third-floor courtroom to tell them why the state believed Wanda Holloway was guilty as charged. The theme of his forceful argument: A woman plotted for months to have her former friend killed just so her own daughter could be a cheerleader. It was a potentially lethal obsession, as outlined by O'Brien.

The state attorney replayed several parts of the damning tapes for the jury, saying, "You listen to the tape. You don't hear fear in her voice. You hear hate. She's consumed with hate."

An excerpt from the tape was highlighted:

Wright: If you don't want to do it, I'll understand.

Wanda: It's not that I don't want to do it. I just have to get the money.

The attorney referred to Wanda's testimony that she was afraid of Wright and the hit man as ludicrous. He said that Wanda was so intent on the hit that she obtained the make of Evelyn Terrell's car and the license number.

But the defense attorneys claimed that the state had not proven its case. They described John Wright as "unbelievable, a liar."

"Without his testimony, Wanda Holloway is innocent,"

said one attorney, adding that no other witnesses had substantiated his story. The defense harped on the theory that Wanda was framed by Wright and the woman's ex-husband, a move by Wright to restore his relationship with the executor of the family will.

The state always has the final word before the jury. And Prosecutor Mike Anderson heaped on the coals, labeling Wanda Holloway "a vicious, vengeful" woman. Said Anderson as he summed up for the jury of eight men and four women:

"You might think this is such a weird reason to kill somebody . . . so bizarre. . . . But can you give me a good reason for having anybody killed? This is not about cheerleading, folks. This is about someone who hated two other people so much that it gnawed at her day and night to the point of obsession. It's about not getting what you want . . . and then deciding, I'm going to get it above everything else, no matter what I have to go through. . . . It's putting a price tag on lives."

Anderson said the motive involved jealousy, greed, ambition, and hatred. Listen to the tapes, he urged the jury. "You can hear her voice. You can hear her emotions. You can hear the words she chose."

The jury did listen to the tapes, avidly, as jury members would later tell the press.

The jury deliberated six hours. When they returned their verdict, it was one finding Wanda Holloway guilty as charged. The defendant showed little emotion as she stood, looking grim, while the verdict was read. She hugged her daughter for a long time before being led from the courtroom by a deputy.

The same jury would return the sentence after hearing testimony from witnesses. The convicted woman could be given up to a life term in prison.

The jury heard Evelyn Terrell tell how the plot had affected her family's life, leaving them under a mantle of fear and mental distress.

The defense called to the stand the convicted homemaker to issue a plea for probation to the jury. Wanda said she had been punished enough by the trial and the events that caused it.

Breaking into sobs, Wanda cried, "I never meant for anything to happen to her or her daughter, and if I could do anything to take it back, I would."

Wanda acknowledged the terrible effect on the Terrell family. "It's totally destroyed her life and her family. I lost sight of a right from a wrong."

Maybe the emotional outburst had some bearing on the jury's final actions, maybe not. No one will really ever know for sure. But after deliberating for three hours on the punishment, the jury returned a verdict giving Wanda Holloway 15 years behind prison walls plus a fine of $10,000.

Perhaps the man who did the undercover work that brought the strange case to trial summed up best the actions of the convicted mother.

Investigator George Helton said, "I think it was probably a case of a mother trying to live her life through her daughter. Reasonable people like you and me can't understand how in the world cheerleading can be so important, but I think these people are just a bubble off."

Helton's excellent investigative work certainly had burst Wanda Holloway's bubble. Helton said that in his 17 years as an undercover officer working would-be hit cases, he had never seen a murder-for-hire plot with such a frivolous motive.

"The thing that amazes me," he said, "is that ten years from now, what difference would it make if she was cheerleader?"

In the long run, maybe it all goes back to the high

school football frenzy that roared into being in Texas in the Dust Bowl years of the 1930s. When it's the only game in town, some players will try anything to win.

EDITOR'S NOTE:
Shirley Holloway, Evelyn Terrell, Vicky Terrell, and John Wright are not the real names of the persons so named in the foregoing story. Fictitious names have been used because there is no reason for public interest in the identities of these persons.

"EVIL 'PUPPET MASTER' MADE THE GARDENER DO HIS KILLING!"

by John Railey

Deputies from the Columbus County Sheriff's Department in Whiteville, North Carolina, roared down N.C. Highway 410 past rolling farmland in the late afernoon sun. It was August 18, 1991, an otherwise quiet Sunday. As they neared a community called Pine Level just after Rural Paved Road 1004, the lawmen found the murder scene they'd been dispatched to: a one-story, red-brick ranch with a carport on one side that was set far back from the road in a stand of tall pine trees.

Emergency workers pronounced the victim, 53-year-old Cecil Floyd Edwards, dead at the scene. A relative, who had found the lifeless body minutes earlier, identified the victim for the deputies.

The body, lying on its back in the dining room, bore several apparent gunshot wounds. Realizing they were dealing with a homicide, the patrol deputies notified their supervisors, who called in detectives Greg Cole and Alexander Singletary.

The case would soon shock residents of Columbus County, a rural county in eastern North Carolina with a population of about 50,000. About 50 deputies, under Sheriff Harold Rains, patrol within its borders.

By the time the veteran sleuths arrived, deputies had cordoned off the crime scene. The investigators went to work with their fellow officers, shooting photos and studying the body and crime scene.

On a stand near the body, detectives noted, was a blue telephone that was missing its receiver. Had the killer—or killers—grabbed it?

The victim was partially clothed; his blue jeans and shoes were in a heap near the body. The officers finished taking photos and carefully turned the body over. When they did so, they found a large-caliber bullet protruding from Cecil Edwards' back.

The investigators carefully pried the slug out, then bagged and tagged it. Later they would ship it to the State Bureau of Investigation (SBI) laboratory in the state capital of Raleigh for analysis.

Pathologists conducting the autopsy would surely produce more slugs for analysis, the sleuths agreed. The body bore several bullet wounds to the head and chest. The autopsy would show that Edwards had in fact died of the bullet wounds—six in all. Apparently, the killer had made certain that he got the job done.

There was no evidence that anything had been taken: the house was stocked with several relatively expensive items. If it wasn't a robbery, was this a "hit" of some sort? sleuths pondered.

Aside from the slugs, deputies scouring the house found very little physical evidence to work with—and no shell casings. Sleuths speculated that the killer might have used a weapon that doesn't eject its casings. Or worse, they were dealing with a killer sharp enough to have picked up the spent casings.

As the sun went down on Sunday, Detectives Cole and Singletary, realizing this would be a tough case, called in

HIT MEN

SBI agents to help them. Agents arrived on the scene later that night with a mobile crime lab.

As Sunday night surrendered to Monday morning, the deputies and SBI agents combed the house, looking for any evidence. They canvassed the neighborhood, looking in vain for elusive pieces of the puzzle. No one had seen or heard a thing.

The officers interviewed Edwards' relatives. They soon learned that Edwards, a septic tank installer, was separated from his wife and lived alone. The last time anyone had talked to him was about 10:30 Saturday night, when a relative had chatted with him on the phone. Edwards had seemed fine then, the relative said.

But Edwards may have been killed soon after that. County Coroner Linwood Cartrette said after exmaining the body that Edwards was probably slain late Saturday night.

As to why Edwards' blue jeans and shoes were found lying on the kitchen floor, detectives learned he sometimes undressed there.

From family members, detectives learned that Cecil Edwards was a good father, a salt-of-the-earth country man who worked hard all his life but never got rich. He was the kind of guy who had few enemies. But as the sleuths dug deeper, they learned there was one man whom Edwards had had some trouble with.

Relatives told the sleuths a story that was later confirmed by other officers and court records.

Edwards and the man, a heating and air-conditioning installer, had done business together in the past. But the previous month, they had allegedly argued about a woman. Edwards and the man got into a fistfight in Whiteville, and each one pressed assault charges against the other in connection with the incident.

Two days after he was killed, Edwards had been set to appear in court on the case.

On Monday afternoon, the sleuths checked on the heating and air-conditioning installer at his Chadbourn house. He'd heard that Edwards had been killed from news reports, he said, but he told lawmen he hadn't had anything to do with it.

Would he mind if they searched his house? the sleuths asked.

The man agreed.

In the house, the investigators found a box of .45-caliber bullets, which they confiscated. They would send those bullets off to the SBI lab for comparison with those recovered from Edwards.

But for now, Detectives Cole and Singletary had nothing on the man. They left his house to continue working on other leads in the case.

In the days ahead, the frustrated sleuths slaved away to little avail. SBI Agents K.T. Moser and Matt White joined them on the case. But the four probers couldn't get anything on the man, and he sure wasn't talking.

A records check showed the man was clean, save for the pending assault charge. And prosecutors would have to dismiss that misdemeanor charge since the alleged victim was dead.

The bullet tests would take several weeks, but even in the best of all possible worlds, if the bullets taken from the man's house were a conclusive match with the slugs found in Edwards' body, that still wouldn't be enough to hang a murder charge on, even with the story about the assaults.

Then, about two weeks after Cecil Edwards' death, luck surfaced in the form of a talkative Whiteville man. Witnesses called the investigators, giving the name of a man who was running his mouth about a slaying he said he'd been involved in.

The sleuths were familiar with the name the tipsters gave. Daniel Ray McMillian, 31, of Whiteville was a petty thief who'd been in and out of trouble for some time. But did he have it in him to be involved in murder? He didn't seem the type, but he bore checking out. The detectives looked him up on Tuesday, September 9th.

It wasn't long into an interview at the sheriff's department headquarters before McMillian was spinning a bone-chilling tale for Detectives Singletary and Cole and Agents White and Moser.

On the day of the killing, McMillian did yardwork for a local man. He drank beer all day. That afternoon, the man he was working for asked him to kill Edwards for him. McMillian made no commitment. The man drove McMillian by Edwards' home.

"This is where the man lives [who] I want dead. I want him dead tonight," the man told McMillian.

The man gave McMillian five $100 bills and said there'd be $400 more when he finished the job. McMillian took the money, but he still didn't agree to go through with it.

The man gave McMillian a loaded World War I vintage .45-caliber revolver and showed him how to use it. The man also loaned McMillian a dump truck to drive to Edwards' house.

About this time, a friend of the man ordering the hit, Vernon Wayne "Babe" Godwin, threatened to kill McMillian if he didn't do the job.

After smoking pot and drinking liquor, McMillian decided to go ahead with it late Saturday night. McMillian took a friend from Chadbourn with him, 26-year-old Mills Evans. Just after midnight, McMillian parked the heavy truck on the road by Edwards' house. Leaving Evans in the vehicle, McMillian walked up to Edwards' house and knocked on the side door under the carport.

When Edwards came to the door, McMillian shot him at least twice. After Edwards fell, McMillian stood over him and shot him at least four more times. McMillian pulled the phone receiver off and threw it away outside. He then ran back to the truck, and he and Evans roared off.

The next day, McMillian returned the dump truck to the man who hired him. And the day after that, the man paid McMillian the rest of the money, $400.

McMillian had chucked the old revolver. Sleuths later tracked down the frame to it, but they never found the cylinder. It would have been invaluable as forensic evidence.

The man who McMillian said hired him was none other than the heating and air-conditioning installer, 52-year-old George Douglas Larrimore. A law enforcement official would later describe Larrimore as a "puppet master" who pulled McMillian's strings.

Outside the interview room, the investigators conferred. McMillian's tale of how the actual shooting went down jibed with the physical evidence at the scene. The petty thief had apparently become a hit man, albeit a bizarre one. So much for the image of a shadowy hit man in a sleek sports car with state-of-the-art weaponry. This one showed up for his lethal assignment in a dump truck and armed with a World War I sidearm.

The sleuths charged Daniel McMillian with first-degree murder and conspiracy to commit murder and placed him in the Whiteville Jail. Now it was time to round up George Larrimore, Vernon Godwin, and Mills Evans.

The cocky Larrimore, arrested at his home that afternoon on first-degree murder and conspiracy counts, went peacefully. He refused to make a statement and was placed in the local jail without privilege of bond.

Officers arrested Evans a while later as he walked along a local road. Talking to him, the sleuths quickly realized that he knew nothing about the plans for the slaying: he'd just happened to be in the wrong place at the wrong time. Since he knew about the murder and didn't report it, however, the sleuths charged Evans with being an accessory after the fact and jailed him, as well.

Detectives Cole and Singletary, and Agents Moser and White got an unwelcome surprise when they tried to arrest Godwin. They got to his house about 5:00 p.m. that Tuesday. Nobody answered their knocks on the door, so the lawmen couldn't be sure whether Godwin was inside or not. They wondered: Had Godwin gotten word that his friends were arrested earlier that day?

The detectives chose to wait their man out—provided he was inside the house where he lived alone. They decided they wouldn't storm the house and risk hurting a suspect who might provide much needed evidence.

The sleuths called in an SBI SWAT team for help. Outside the house, team members set up an electronic listening device to track noises inside the structure. Soon, they heard noises indicating that someone—most likely Godwin—was inside.

The officers settled down for the long haul, blocking off roads leading to the house. Curious residents gathered through the night and early morning as the deputies and SBI agents conferred in a nearby church parking lot.

Finally, at 6:50 a.m. Wednesday—after a tedious, 14-hour vigil—Godwin opened his front door and surrendered peacefully. He was unarmed.

Godwin, who refused to make a statement, was placed

in the Whiteville Jail without bond.

Detectives Cole and Singletary and the SBI agents didn't stop working after the arrests. McMillian had indicated he would testify against his co-defendants, but the sleuths knew defense attorneys would likely attack McMillian's character in an attempt to discredit that testimony.

The test results on the .45-caliber bullets found in Larrimore's house came back. Forensic scientists had found that the slugs pathologists had recovered from Edwards' body were .45 caliber, and that the lead composition in those slugs was very similar to the lead composition of the bullets from Larrimore's house. It was good evidence, but they needed something stronger.

So the investigators reinterviewed witnesses and hunted for more evidence. The stakes were high. District Attorney Rex Gore would be seeking the death penalty against Larrimore.

Days after Larrimore's arrest, a magistrate set his bond at $500,000. Larrimore made the bond and walked out of jail, but he remained in the county under the watchful eyes of Detectives Cole and Singletary.

In January 1992, Daniel McMillian pleaded guilty in Columbus County Superior Court in Whiteville. In exchange for his guilty plea and his agreement to testify against his co-defendants, the state reduced the count against McMillian to second-degree murder and dropped the conspiracy count altogether. McMillian got a life sentence, but he might otherwise have gotten the death penalty.

The next month, Mills Evans pleaded guilty as charged: to accessory after the fact of murder. His sentencing was delayed until after Larrimore's trial, as prosecutors planned to use him as a witness against Larrimore.

In July 1992, a month before Larrimore's trial was to begin, Vernon Godwin was found hanged in the backyard of his Chadbourn home. Officials ruled that he took his own life.

As George Larrimore's trial began in Columbus Superior Court on Monday, August 10, 1992, McMillian, testifying for the state, told the jury the story he'd previously told detectives, about how Larrimore had paid him $900 in two installments to gun down Cecil Edwards.

The next day during cross-examination, Defense Attorney J. B. Lee III questioned McMillian about his motivation for testifying.

"The whole point of this entire exercise is to save you from the gas chamber," Lee told the witness.

He also questioned McMillian about the amount of pot he smoked and booze he drank on the day of the killing.

The witness said, "I was drunk, but that ain't going to change the fact that [that] man gave me the gun and the money," McMillian said, looking at Larrimore and pointing at him.

As the defense began their case on Friday, August 14th, Larrimore took the witness stand on his own behalf. The defendant contradicted McMillian's testimony that Larrimore had paid McMillian to kill Edwards.

"I don't know nothing about it," Larrimore maintained. "I had nothing to do with it." He said he didn't know why McMillian had testified against him. He claimed that the first time he ever met McMillian was when they were in the Whiteville Jail together after their arrests.

The defendant said McMillian had never done yardwork for him, as McMillian had testified. Another man had done that yardwork, Larrimore said. A relative of

Larrimore's later took the stand and backed him on that contention.

Larrimore denied ever owning a .45-caliber pistol. He did acknowledge that he and Edward had "exchanged licks" the month before Edwards' death.

As lawyers prepared their closing arguments, it was down to a question of whom the jury would believe: Larrimore, who said he had nothing to do with the murder, or McMillian and the other state witnesses.

In his closing statement on Monday, August 17th, Defense Attorney Lee banged away at McMillian's testimony. He contended that McMillian had cut a deal with prosecutors to avoid the death penalty. Co-defense counsel Marvin Tedder agreed, arguing in his closing statement that the case came down to a "swearing contest" between his client and McMillian.

"McMillian is a thief, a robber, a murderer, and a liar," Tedder told the jury. "And the state says, 'Don't believe George Larrimore,' who has a perfectly clean record."

In his closing, Assistant District Attorney Don Kelly told the jurors they should believe McMillian, despite his record.

"You don't get witnesses from Sunday School in a conspiracy of murder," Kelly said.

"There sits one of the most dangerous people in this state," the prosecutor continued, pointing to the defendant. "He's the puppet master, hiding behind the screen, manipulating people. Without the George Larrimores in the world, there wouldn't be the Ray McMillians to carry out their deeds."

Summing up his case, D.A. Gore said that, while McMillian admitted to pulling the trigger, Larrimore was just as guilty in Edwards' death. The head D.A. described Larrimore as the "mastermind and paymaster" in the murder.

The jury got the case the next day, Tuesday. After deliberating for six hours, at 8:20 p.m., they sent a note to Judge William Gore (a distant relative of the prosecutor). The note said, "We cannot come to a unanimous verdict. We have people on both sides."

When the judge read the note aloud in the courtroom, Defense Attorney Lee moved for a mistrial.

D.A. Gore objected, saying the state had spent a lot of time on the case and the jury should be given every chance to reach a verdict.

The judge denied the motion for a mistrial, and ordered the jurors to be sequestered at a local motel that night and continue deliberations the next morning, Wednesday. But by noon Wednesday, after about nine and a half hours of deliberation, jurors were hopelessly deadlocked at 8 to 4, the jury foreman said. He did not say which way the jury was leaning. Judge Gore declared a mistrial a few minutes later.

The state maintained that Larrimore had intimidated its witnesses and the judge granted a defense request that Larrimore's bond request be revoked. Larrimore returned to jail to await a new trial.

By North Carolina law, when a judge declares a mistrial, the defendant still faces the original counts and double jeopardy does not apply since the jury did not reach a verdict. For all involved, a mistrial is one big headache and it's back to square one.

The judge granted a defense motion that the new trial take place in adjacent Brunswick County. The defense attorneys had argued that the trial publicity would make it tough to pick a second impartial jury in Columbus County.

D.A. Gore told reporters that the mistrial was disappointing, but, "These jurors had reasonable differences between them and acted accordingly. That's the way the system works." He said he didn't plan to change his evidence at the next trial, although he might change the way he presented it.

As detectives and prosecutors prepared for the new trial, new witnesses came forward with information that bolstered the state's case. Those witnesses included a neighbor of Larrimore's who said that McMillian had in fact been working in Larrimore's yard on the day of the killing, contradicting Larrimore's denial of that fact.

The new trial took place the following November in Brunswick County Superior Court in Bolivia, North Carolina. McMillian repeated his incriminating testimony against himself and Larrimore, and Larrimore once again took the stand and denied that testimony. After five days of testimony, the case went to the jury on Monday, November 16, 1992.

After about 55 minutes of deliberation, the jury came back with their verdict: Larrimore was guilty of first-degree murder and conspiracy.

After a court clerk read the verdict, Judge Donald Stephens ruled there were no aggravating factors in the case warranting a possible death penalty. The next day, the judge sentenced Larrimore to life in prison.

D.A. Gore didn't get his chance to pursue the ultimate punishment against Larrimore, but the first-degree murder conviction was sweet enough after the agonizing mistrial the previous summer.

After bailiffs led Larrimore away and Judge Stephens recessed court, Gore told reporters that he felt he'd presented a more precise, compact case this time. He said he "was relieved that justice was done."

In return for cooperating with the state's case, Mills

Evans was released from jail after the trial. A judge gave him credit for time served on his accessory conviction.

EDITOR'S NOTE:
Mills Evans is not the real name of the person so named in the foregoing story. A fictitious name has been used because there is no reason for public interest in the identity of this person.

"A LOVE TRIANGLE TRIGGERED THE FREELOADER'S LETHAL SCHEME!"

by Gary C. King

**Spokane, Washington
February 15, 1983**

At approximately 6:15 p.m. on Thursday, January 8, 1981, the telephones at the Whitman County Sheriff's Department in Colfax, Washington, began to ring. A part-time radio operator answered the phone on this otherwise quiet winter evening, only to be told by a near-frantic woman that her husband had been shot.

"My husband's been shot by a burglar," cried the caller, who identified herself as 48-year-old Neva Henning of nearby Rosalia. The radio operator, rather than take down the information and have to repeat it for the dispatcher, told Mrs. Henning she was handing the phone to the dispatcher. However, when the conversation resumed it was between Duane Henning, also 48, Mrs. Henning's husband, and the dispatcher. Mr. Henning told the dispatcher that he'd gone out to his shop, which was basically an outbuilding on his 40-acre farm where he kept the family camper pickup housed, where he'd been met by a man and was subsequently shot in the back when he turned to run back to the house.

As a result of the call, a sheriff's patrol unit was dispatched to the Henning farm to investigate the burglary-shooting. Deputy Sheriff Rich Gay, the first officer to arrive, was urged to exercise extreme caution because it was believed the perpetrator was still on the Henning property. In addition to Gay, the Whitman County Sheriff's Department "rolled" backup units of its own, as well as SWAT team and units from the Washington State Patrol, according to Whitman County Undersheriff Dalton E. Lewey.

At approximately the same time the first officer dispatched to the scene arrived, Duane Henning was being loaded into a waiting ambulance that had been called in from nearby Rosalia, a farming and agricultural community of about 600 located just two-tenths of a mile south of the Henning farm. As Deputy Rich Gay got out of his patrol car, the ambulance left the area, its siren wailing and its lights flashing, hastily enroute to a Spokane hospital some 35 miles to the north.

Deputy Gay surveyed the Henning farm after briefly talking with his dispatcher by radio and noted there were several buildings on approximately five acres of the 40-acre farm. There was the main house where Mr. and Mrs. Henning lived with their teenage daughter and a permanent boarder, a rental house next door, a large barn, a tool shed, a couple of smaller buildings and the workshop where Duane Henning said he'd been shot after encountering a burglar. The dimensions of the crime scene covered a large area, around which Deputy Gay put up an outer perimeter and secured the area until the SWAT team arrived.

A short time later the SWAT team arrived and, under

the direction of Undersheriff Dalton Lewey and Investigator Bill Rodgers, its members were strategically positioned, their weapons accurately trained on each of the farm's buildings. However, a security sweep of all the buildings failed to yield a suspect originally believed to have been hiding in one of them.

Knowing the importance of talking with the victim, an officer from the sheriff's office was dispatched to the Spokane hospital where Mr. Henning was taken with the hopes of interviewing the shooting victim, if at all possible, as well as other family members who'd been present at the Henning residence at the time of the shooting. A female communications officer was sent along to assist in accomplishing the critical task.

According to the reports filed by the officers dispatched to Spokane to interview the victim, Duane Henning had already been taken into surgery by the time they arrived. However, according to the reports, Henning had been talking to his wife and the ambulance attendants on his way to the hospital and, judging from his statements, he had not been too worried about surviving the gunshot wounds he'd sustained.

"Call the office and tell them I won't be in until Monday morning," Henning reportedly said to his wife enroute to the hospital. "And don't forget to take the church deposit to the bank (he was treasurer of his church)."

Upon arrival at the hospital, according to the reports, Henning was immediately taken to X-ray where it was determined that the bullet had lodged itself in the inferior vena cava, one of the large veins in humans by which blood is returned to the right atrium of the heart. At this point his situation was listed as serious, but not critical.

However, when Henning was opened up in the operating room the surgeons discovered, much to their dismay, that the bullet was no longer there. As a result, he was taken back to the X-ray department, where additional X-rays revealed that the bullet had traveled into the heart. Henning was taken back into surgery and the bullet was removed from his heart and was subsequently given to authorities as evidence.

Meanwhile, the crime scene investigation continued at Henning's Rosalia farm until approximately 3:00 a.m. Although the investigators had worked throughout the evening and into the early morning hours, they conceded that little could be accomplished until daybreak, at which time a thorough grid search of the grounds could begin. However, from the evidence they did have, the investigators felt that by the time they were ready to leave that morning they either had a burglary-shooting or a domestic dispute with an assault, but, of course, it would be premature to arrive at a conclusion based on the sketchy details and scant evidence they had so far obtained.

The case suddenly took a different turn about an hour after the investigators left the Henning farm. In spite of valiant efforts to save his life, Duane Henning died in a Spokane hospital at approximately 4:00 a.m. The Whitman County investigators now had a homicide on their hands, and they returned to the Henning farm in large numbers a few hours later, just after daybreak.

Once organized, the investigators and their deputies performed a thorough grid search of the Henning property, as well as a search of the house and the several outbuildings. During the course of the search the cops turned up a clock radio outside lying next to a fence post near the shed or shop where Henning had been shot. The significance of the radio was not immediately known, and detectives did not immediately develop any theories regarding it. A flashlight was also found, at an undisclosed location.

The investigators noted that the temperature outside was cold but not freezing and, naturally, they reasoned that since the ground was soft enough to leave footprints or shoe impressions there should have been some, either near the entrance to the shed where Henning was shot or near the fence post where the radio was found. But there were none to be found.

In the shed where Henning was shot, the sleuths noted that there were a few hand tools lying about, an old car battery, cans of paint, tires, and an old wrecked pickup truck. The search of the shed revealed to the probers that there was nothing of particular value inside, certainly nothing a burglar would normally go after. Additionally, lawmen were told that a rifle, a .22-caliber Ruger carbine that Henning normally kept stored in the garage, was missing.

The detectives were troubled by the entire affair. Originally focusing on a burglary-homicide attempt, the sleuths had been unable to come up with any evidence of a burglary with the exception of the clock radio. Giving a benefit of the doubt on that point, the investigators reasoned that the suspect may have dropped part of his loot while attempting to cross the fence where the radio was found. And the ground was sufficiently soft, so there should have been footprints made by the fleeing burglar. But there weren't any, and things just weren't adding up.

According to Undersheriff Dalton Lewey the only people present at the time of the shooting, aside from the victim and the suspected burglar, were Neva Henning, the victim's wife, and Richard Miller, their 20-year-old permanent boarder. Lewey said that Mrs. Henning told him during initial interviews that at approximately 6:00 p.m.

on January 8th she was busy in the kitchen preparing foods for a surprise birthday party for one of her daughters who was still living at home. Although the birthday party was not to be held until the following evening, Mrs. Henning told Lewey that she was taking advantage of the fact that her daughter was taking part in an extracurricular school sports activity that evening and was not expected home until after 7:00 p.m. because practice was being held later than usual.

Mrs. Henning told Undersheriff Lewey that she asked Duane, her husband, to go outside to the shed and get an old cookie sheet from inside the camper they kept stored there, that she wanted to use it for cookies at her daughter's birthday party the following evening. According to Mrs. Henning's statement, her husband went out to the shed at a few minutes past six, surprised a burglar and was shot. He was able to run back into the house, she told Lewey, where he called the sheriff's office and an ambulance.

Right from the very beginning, the investigators felt there was something wrong with the story they were being told, but they were unable to immediately pin it down. "It just isn't a normal thing for burglars to shoot people, at least not around here," said Lewey. "I don't think we've ever had one (burglary-homicide) around here, to my knowledge. So we were suspicious that there was something more going on here than met the eye."

Meanwhile, a background check was done on the victim, which ultimately failed to turn up anything significant. The investigators learned that Duane Henning was raised in the community, was involved in church work and was employed in nearby Colfax at the grain inspection station. Henning was characterized by the people of this farming and agricultural community as a quiet person, a calm and collected type of guy who never seemed to get upset or angry about anything. He was well thought of by all who knew him, and was generally regarded as a very "gentlemanly" person. So why was he killed? And why would someone shoot such a man in the back? The detectives wanted to know, before the killer's trail had a chance to get too cold.

Analysis of the bullet recovered from Duane Henning's heart revealed that he had been wounded, and eventually died, as a result of being shot with a .22-caliber long-rifle projectile. A ballistics expert from the FBI crime lab in Washington, D.C., flew out to Whitman County and demonstrated that the projectile or bullet that killed Duane Henning was similar in its characteristics (lands and grooves) to those fired from a Ruger carbine, the same type of rifle missing from Henning's garage.

Another FBI crime lab expert told the Whitman County investigators that several items of evidence, such as the clock radio, the flashlight and items inside the shed, had been wiped clean of fingerprints. "That fact alone was significant in and of itself," said Lewey. "You just don't handle several objects without leaving *some* ridge impressions."

Results of the autopsy on Henning's body showed that the .22-caliber bullet struck the eleventh rib from behind on the right side. The bullet entered Henning's body about half the distance between his shoulders and his hips, deflected at a slightly downward angle and struck the rib, deflected even further downward, rupturing the spleen and nicking the liver, and lodged itself in the inferior vena cava, one of the large veins by which blood is returned to the right atrium of the heart. The bullet at some point began to traverse, or move, through the inferior vena cava and travel into the heart.

While still at the preliminary stage of the investigation, a close female relative of the victim told the detectives that Richard Miller, the Hennings' permanent boarder, shot Duane Henning. However, the sleuths were unable to pin down the accusation, and the relative later denied that she even made the statement. Just the same, the homicide investigators began to focus on Miller as a suspect, and further investigative inquiries turned up inconsistencies in Neva Henning's initial statements to police.

Originally Mrs. Henning told the investigators that she sent her husband out to the shed to get a cookie sheet, but when questioned again later she told the detectives that she had sent her husband to the shed for a carrot peeler instead of a cookie sheet. Why the two different statements? probers wondered. Was she involved with Miller in a murder plot? Or was she just trying to cover up for Miller by attempting to confuse the police? If so, why? What was her relationship with Miller? Was it sexual?

Things just were not adding up, and investigators felt they were not being told the truth. As a result, Miller was taken in for a polygraph examination as an attempt to determine whether or not he was telling the truth. Although he did not admit during the examination that he shot Duane Henning, investigators said, he did make statements that were not in his best interests. However, his statements were not enough for investigators to make an arrest, but they were sufficiently incriminating for the sleuths to continue focusing on him as their prime suspect.

Further interviews with family members and friends of Duane Henning revealed that Henning was not at all pleased at having Richard Miller living at his home. Although Henning was easygoing, perhaps even stoic or impassive most of the time, close relatives told sleuths he was nonetheless displeased about Miller's presence in his home. So why did Henning accept Miller? The probers wanted to know.

Miller, originally from Lewiston, Idaho, came to Rosalia, Washington when he was a high school senior, police learned. At the time he befriended the Hennings, he was basically flunking out in school, having never been a good student. Apparently the Hennings, especially Neva, felt sorry for the young man and decided to take him in. In exchange for room and board, he was supposed to do chores and generally help out around the farm. But according to witnesses, Undersheriff Lewey said, Miller did very little to help out around the place, a fact which upset Henning and prompted him to characterize Miller as lazy. In spite of Miller's laziness, though, Henning put up with him in order to please his wife.

In a contrasting point of view, according to Lewey, Neva Henning considered Miller their "foster son," and said that Duane really enjoyed having Miller living with them because Miller's presence relieved Duane's "female-dominated world" (Henning and his wife raised their three daughters, but no sons). According to what Neva told Undersheriff Lewey, Duane was happy to have a male around the house to talk to, help him do chores, and so forth.

"However, that appears not to be totally accurate," said Lewey. "From what we understood, from (information obtained from) other family members, Duane was really not pleased with having Miller around because his wife would show all of her attentions to Miller."

According to Lewey, though, Henning put up with Miller because of his wife's wishes. Lewey characterized Neva Henning as the head of the house, the controlling force and the decision maker. As a result of his wife's forceful personality, Henning apparently felt that the situation would be easier to deal with if he let Neva have her way. Little did he know that his passivism would ultimately cost him his life!

After graduation from high school, detectives learned, Miller joined the Marine Corps but was discharged about six weeks later. He got out of the military through the help of Neva Henning, who hired an attorney for him. Apparently he was discharged because of "fraudulent enlistment" on the part of his recruiter, who had promised him a job in the field of scuba diving; but evidently the Marine Corps didn't have a job classification for scuba divers and, as a result, Miller was able to obtain a discharge.

At that point Miller returned to Lewiston, Idaho, to attempt to find work. After several weeks and unable to land a job, he got in touch with the Hennings and again asked them for help. Neva talked to her husband and persuaded him to help Richard get a job with a local grain storage company. He was hired as a warehouseman, and his duties included loading grain into storage elevators, loading out trucks for grain shipments, general cleanup, and occasional driving to pick up equipment. It was an easy job, one that didn't require much mental or physical ability. But in spite of that fact, Miller was lazy, would hide from supervisors to avoid work and would go off and find a place to sleep when he was supposed to be working. He laid off work frequently, and Neva Henning would call his supervisors and report that he was sick when he wasn't; after nearly one year of this type of behavior, Miller was caught sleeping on the job and was fired.

A background check on Miller revealed that he had no

major criminal history. All that turned up was the usual teenage traffic tickets, and one incident of malicious mischief involving him and a couple of other young men who connected a heavy chain to a woman's porch and dragged it away with their car. Other than that, his record was clean.

At one point in the investigation, the detectives learned that Miller's school grades substantially improved when he moved in with the Hennings. Interestingly, Miller went from failing grades in Lewiston to Bs in Rosalia. However, this was explained through further interviews with Neva Henning, who at that time was a library instructor at a Rosalia school. According to Mrs. Henning, she was responsible for Richard Miller's scholastic improvements; in actuality she was doing his work for him by taking exams on correspondence courses and exams at Rosalia School. Miller confirmed these facts later.

As the investigation continued detectives learned that, prior to Miller taking up residence at the Henning home, when Duane and Neva Henning's daughters brought their boyfriends home with them Neva would take them off into the kitchen and, before they knew it, the girls were being excluded. "The girls felt Neva was their rival for their boyfriends," said Undersheriff Dalton Lewey. According to Lewey, these young men, aged 16 and up, would either end up staying at the Henning home for some time or they would actually move in for several months, like Miller did. Miller lived there the longest period of time, it was discovered—approximately 18 months. It was never revealed whether or not any sexual encounters occurred between Neva and the young men prior to Miller.

After a lengthy investigation spanning several months, Whitman County authorities finally had sufficient information to bring charges of first-degree murder to Rich Miller, and Whitman County Prosecutor Ron Carpenter felt that Duane Henning's death and Miller's alleged involvement had become a jury question. As a result, in November 1981, Richard Miller was tried and convicted on charges of murdering Duane Henning. Miller was sentenced to life at the Washington State Corrections Center in Shelton, Washington. But the story was far from over...

Following Miller's conviction, Neva Henning continued to visit him at the Whitman County Jail. During those visits Miller expressed his concerns to Neva about having been convicted and having to go to prison for seventeen and a half years before becoming eligible for parole. Neva told him to be calm, according to Dalton Lewey, that they would appeal his conviction and would beat the rap on appeal. When he protested about being in prison while awaiting appeal, Neva purportedly told him to be calm and go along with her, and as a reward for being good, she would give him $10,000. She told him she would set the money aside for him, which he could have when he was released upon winning the appeal—if such a time came.

Miller later told Dalton Lewey that he wasn't worried, that he thought Neva could get him off. Instead, Miller went to prison, and Neva would write to him from time to time. At one point Miller and Neva Henning became embroiled in a dispute involving Miller's stereo and cassette tapes, which Miller believed Neva had given or thrown away. In response to Miller's accusations regarding the stereo and tapes, according to Lewey, Neva wrote to Miller and said, "I thought you were my friend. People are accusing me of things, and here I thought you were my best friend and now you're doing this to me. I guess I'll have to take you off my friends list," Lewey said Neva had written to Miller.

As a result, according to Lewey, Miller began thinking and saying, "Here I am down here (in prison), there she is out there, and now I'm off her list." After talking the situation over with relatives, saying that he wanted to tell the truth about Henning's death, he was urged to come forward.

Miller, of his own volition, began to contact the prosecuting attorney's office, as well as his own attorney, saying that he wanted to talk, to tell just what had happened regarding Henning's death. Whitman County Undersheriff Dalton Lewey, Prosecutor Ron Carpenter and deputy prosecuting attorney Jim Hickman traveled to Shelton to see Miller. Miller wanted to make a deal, but before they would commit themselves, the Whitman County officials wanted to hear what he had to say. His story would implicate Neva.

According to the original plan or scenario laid out by Neva Henning, Duane Henning was supposed to die at the time he was shot in the shed. Miller was to do the shooting, after which he was supposed to leave the shed, climb over a fence where he had planted a clock radio at approximately 3:00 p.m. the afternoon preceding the shooting, run through soft mud, climb over another fence, run a short distance along some railroad tracks, and climb up an embankment near a Catholic church in Rosalia (it is important to remember that Henning's farm is situated on the outskirts of Rosalia city limits, making Miller's journey a short one) where he would wait for Mrs. Henning to pick him up. While Miller was making tracks, Neva was to have left the family house in her own car, pick up Miller along the road where he was waiting, go on into town and buy something in a store and be seen by someone, so they could fabricate an alibi. Afterwards they were to have returned home, where Miller was to have packed his things for a trip he would make to Lewiston. When Henning's daughter came home and asked, "Where's dad?" the plan called for Miller and Neva to act innocent and say they didn't know where he was, at which point they would look around for him and discover his body in the shed. But when Henning lived, said Miller, it screwed up the original plans.

According to Lewey, Miller said Neva had promised to pay him $3,000 and provide him with a place to live for the rest of his life in return for killing her husband. Miller told the investigators that he became acquainted with the Henning family through dating one of their daughters, and shortly thereafter was invited by Neva to move in.

Miller told the investigators that he and Neva *did* have sexual relations, on more than one occasion. He said the sexual encounters ceased however, prior to any involvement where Neva discussed killing her husband. According to Miller, Neva told him that her husband had been abusing her, hitting her, that life was miserable with him but that she couldn't divorce him because of their daughters. During these times she would show him bruises on her legs and arms, and would say, "He did that to me."

The day before Duane Henning was shot, according to Dalton Lewey, Miller and Neva drove to Spokane where Neva shoplifted a ski mask for Miller, after which they set the scenario and put the plan into motion.

The next evening, the night of the murder, Miller told Lewey that Henning came home early from work, about 5:00 p.m. instead of the usual time of about 5:30 p.m. The three of them had dinner together; afterwards, Neva sent Duane out to the shed for a carrot peeler that was in a cupboard in the camper. Miller was waiting in the shed, and watching Henning get the carrot peeler out of the camper. But he couldn't bring himself to pull the trigger, so Henning returned to the house unharmed. Miller put the gun away, came back into the house and told Neva, "I just can't do it. I can't shoot somebody like that."

However, Neva convinced Miller that they had to do it on that particular night (January 8th) because they knew where everybody was. The daughter was gone and wouldn't return until after 7:00 p.m., so it had to be that night, according to Miller. Convinced, Miller went back out to the shed, got the rifle and positioned himself in a corner by the camper and laid in wait.

The second time, Neva sent her husband out to get a cookie sheet from the camper. When Henning came out of the camper holding the cookie sheet he apparently heard something and turned around with his flashlight, shining it into Rich Miller's eyes. (Miller was wearing a ski mask at this time.) Miller said that he had originally been squatting down, but when he realized that Henning had spotted him he stood up and pulled the trigger. The bullet struck Henning in the back as he was running away from the shed, but he made it to the house.

At this point Miller took the rifle, placed it in the trunk of his car parked in the driveway, and was preparing to leave. But Neva came out of the house and approached Miller, telling him to come back inside because Henning didn't know it was Miller who shot him.

"I thought he knew who I was, that it was me who shot him," Lewey said Miller told him. "I thought it was all over, and I was gonna run." But Neva convinced Miller that Henning didn't know, coaxed him to come back into the house and "play it cool," which he did.

"If Mr. Henning did know (who shot him)," said Lewey, "he didn't say anything, at least (not) to the people present." Lewey said that Miller told him he took off after facing Henning, saying he was going to get help. In reality, though, Miller drove to a location about one mile south of Rosalia where he tossed the rifle, ammunition, ski mask and flashlight into a ditch. When he returned Henning had already been loaded into an ambulance and was enroute to the Spokane hospital. Miller then took Neva's car and drove to the hospital.

When Miller returned from Spokane, which was after Henning had died, he got inside his own car which was parked in the driveway near the house and drove to the area south of Rosalia where he ditched the evidence a few hours before. After loading the rifle, ammunition, ski mask and flashlight back into his car, he drove to Lewiston, Idaho, where he tossed the incriminating evidence into a river. The evidence was never recovered.

As a result of Miller blowing the whistle on Neva Henning, Whitman County Prosecutor Ron Carpenter agreed to work out a deal with Miller in return for his testimony against Neva. Mrs. Henning was charged as an accomplice to first-degree murder, to which she pleaded innocent, and her trial was set for December 1982, after nearly two years of lengthy and exhaustive inquiries into the death of her husband.

The much-publicized trial opened to a standing-room-only crowd in Spokane County Superior Court, heard before Judge Michael Donohue. Prosecutor Ron Carpenter went through his case against Mrs. Henning step by step for the seven-woman, five-man jury, calling Richard Miller as the main prosecution witness. Miller outlined the circumstances surrounding his relationship with Mrs. Henning, saying that at first the defendant had taken care of him in a motherly fashion. But after awhile the relationship changed, and he became emotionally and sexually involved with Mrs. Henning, ultimately agreeing to kill her husband at her request.

"She used to visit my room late at night and rub my back and neck," Miller told the jury. "Something happens to a man when a woman does that. One night we had sexual intercourse. I don't know how many times in all, but it was always in my room late at night. It was a short-lived love affair.

"During these late night visits," he continued, "she used to tell me how miserable she was, saying that Duane had beaten her and that she couldn't tolerate it anymore. I asked her why she didn't get a divorce but she said she didn't want the children to be hurt.

"One night I jokingly said, 'Why not hire a third man to do away with your husband?' She said she feared blackmail from such a person, and besides, she didn't know how to go about hiring an assassin." Miller told the jury that a short time later he broke his shoulder and was required to go to Spokane for treatments, and during these trips to the doctor, as well as their nighttime encounters, Neva discussed the murder plans. "Finally, she somehow asked me if I'd do the job," he said, saying that Neva promised him $3,000 from one of four life insurance policies on her husband's life. He added that she also promised him that he could live on her farm for the rest of his life.

"It (the murder) was set up to appear as though her husband had been shot during the course of a burglary," said Miller as he explained the setup for the jury. Miller said that the first time Neva sent her husband to the shed to get carrot or potato peeler, he "froze and couldn't shoot." But Neva convinced him to go back into the shed a second time and wait. Miller said that "she influenced me to go back, like it was a debt I owed her.

"I heard him cursing when he entered the shop," Miller continued, describing the second time Neva had sent her husband out to the shed to get the cookie sheet. "He went into the camper to get the pan. As he got out he must have heard me rustling in the corner. He shined his flashlight in my eyes, saw me, and turned to run. I had the gun and I . . . just fired . . . I was in an upward position and he fell immediately. I think he tripped over something. He got back up and ran out of the building and towards the house. I just sat there, frozen. I couldn't believe I'd shot the gun."

"Mr. Miller, when you've told so many different stories, it's hard to recall, isn't it?" asked Jeff Morris, Mrs. Henning's attorney, in an attempt to discredit Miller's testimony. Morris contended that the case boiled down to a matter of credibility, Mrs. Henning's against Richard Miller's. However, Miller maintained that he and Neva Henning were lovers, and that she convinced him "to do the dirty work" for "$3,000 and a place to live on the farm."

Following nearly 20 hours of deliberations, the jury found Neva Henning guilty of first-degree murder in connection with the death of her husband. On Tuesday, February 15, 1983, in spite of a plea from the pastor of Mrs. Henning's church to release her on probation in his custody, Spokane Superior Court Judge Michael Donohue sentenced Neva Henning to life in prison.

"I feel under a monumental pressure that I've never felt since I've taken on this office," Donohue said at Neva Henning's sentencing. "The penalty has to fit the crime and that's the position I'm left in." However, Judge Donohue has allowed Mrs. Henning to remain free on a $50,000 property bond pending an appeal, soon to be heard in the Appellate Court.

"She was the most controlled person I have ever been associated with," said Dalton Lewey regarding Mrs. Henning. "She showed zero outward emotion . . . is a very calculating person . . . the way she had (laid out) the scenario, Miller took all the chances."

In return for his testimony against Mrs. Henning, Prosecutor Carpenter asked that Miller's appeal be returned to Superior Court where, in essence, he let his appeal go and was allowed to plead guilty to the lesser charge of second-degree murder, for which his sentence would be reduced to 20 years. However, he could be released on parole after serving six and a half years.

"THE VICTIM REFUSED TO DIE!"

by Tom Basinski

The two young boys backed the small pickup truck into an empty space on the large apartment complex parking lot. They parked next to another truck bearing a construction company's name and logo on the driver's door.

The two boys had arrived about 5:00 a.m. They sat there, the driver staring straight ahead, his collar pulled up for warmth. He shivered from time to time. He may have been cold, or he may have been nervous.

It was the morning of January 31, 1989, and the boys were in a small community called Cardiff-by-the-Sea, an affluent section of northern San Diego County. Januarys are cold in San Diego, especially in those areas on the Pacific Coast.

The boys had stolen the pickup they were in just a few hours before.

The passenger dozed off and on. Finally dawn started to break and the area began to lighten up. The driver whispered, "That's him!" The passenger strained to look.

"Are you sure? Wait and see where he goes. He'll come to his truck."

The person they were watching climbed into a tan Buick and drove away from the lot. The driver said, "That wasn't him. Take it easy. When he leaves, he'll have to come right here."

At about 5:55 a.m., a stocky man emerged from the apartment building. He walked across the lot with a strong, purposeful stride. "Oh Jesus, it's him," said the driver.

As the man approached the construction company truck, the passenger silently slid from the cab of the stolen truck where he was sitting. With catlike quiet, he walked around the truck and was behind the man.

The driver stepped from the truck. When he first started to speak, nothing came out. The man eyed him as he took his keys out of his jacket pocket.

Finally the driver could speak. " 'Scuse me. Can you tell me what time it is?" The man paused near his door, held up his left wrist, and said, "Yeah, it's. . ."

Before he could get the hour out of his mouth, the passenger, who had circled around the man, plunged a knife into the man's back.

The man looked at the boy who had asked him the time. The man's eyes were wide open and his mouth was poised as if to ask for help. The driver reached inside his jacket and brought out a small construction hatchet. The driver raised the hatchet and smashed it into the man's face.

And the melee was far from over. The prey was 40-year-old Robert "Wayne" Pearce. He was a strapping six-footer who weighed 198 pounds. He'd worked hard all his life. He was tough. He was strong and he was not about to lie down and die—not without a

HIT MEN

fight, that is.

While this brief eye contact was going on between Wayne Pearce and the driver, the passenger from behind had managed to stab Pearce four more times in the upper back, thinking all the while, "Damn, they don't die like this on TV."

Wayne Pearce raised his arm, hoping to deflect the hatchet blows. The arm received the full force of the strike and was split.

Pearce moved in and grabbed the hatchet man. He got him in a headlock and started to punch. By now the stab wounds in Pearce's back were up to over 15 and Pearce became aware of his assault from the rear. Some muscles had been severed and he could not hold onto his attacker.

The onslaught was taking its toll. Pearce went down to his knees, letting go of the hatchet man and turning to the knife wielder. The hatchet man put a hard right to Pearce's nose and knocked him down. It was finally over.

The fight had carried out into the middle of the parking lot. The hatchet man said, "Let's get out of here."

The duo ran to their pickup truck and got in. To their horror, they saw Wayne Pearce back on his feet stumbling for the apartment. "Damn, he's alive. Come on." The two ran for Pearce and got to him when he reached the lawn.

The attack started anew. The hatchet man raised the weapon and brought it down hard on Pearce's collarbone, then the top of his head, then one more blow to the forearm that was raised in self-defense.

The knife continued to find its mark, hitting Pearce in the neck. Pearce turned to fend off a knife thrust, and the blade split his hand between the middle and ring fingers. Pearce punched the knife wielder in the face.

Finally Wayne Pearce went down again. There had been yelling and sounds of a struggle, and the attackers were fearful of witnesses.

"Come on. He's dead. Let's go," one of the attackers said. They ran to the truck again. As they were driving off, they looked back and saw Wayne Pearce on his feet once more, stumbling up to the door of the apartment with the knife sticking out of his back.

The attackers were breathless and panting hard. "He wouldn't die. He just kept fighting. I don't believe it." Both attackers were bloody. The driver said, "Son of a bitch. I left that hatchet there." The passenger said, "Screw it. Just drive."

Meanwhile, Wayne Pearce had stumbled to the double glass doors. His left eye had a piece of forehead skin hanging down, obstructing his vision. Blood was flowing from his head into his right eye. Pearce felt his way along the hallway to the elevator where he pushed the "up" button.

Pearce fell to his knees. When the doors opened he rolled in. He reached up and felt the buttons, pushing "3."

When the door opened, he crawled out on all fours and pulled himself to his feet. He stumbled along the hallway leaving smears of blood along the walls.

Pearce pounded on his own door and slumped to his knees. His roommate, Amy Wren, answered the door. It was a nightmare out of the horror-movie tradition. A blood-covered man with a knife sticking out of his back fell facedown in the doorway.

Amy screamed. The man was wearing Wayne's

clothes. She looked at the face, or what was left of it, but could not be sure. Amy ran to the phone and dialed 911. The emergency medical equipment and sheriff's department logged the call at 6:02 a.m.

Pearce had crawled across the living room floor. He rolled over, moaning. The knife dislodged. By now Amy knew it was Wayne. He had on Wayne's watch. What hair that was not covered with blood was Wayne's color.

Amy was too terrified to cry. She looked at this apparition on the floor. Then she ran to lock the front door in case the attackers came back to finish the job.

Within minutes, paramedics and sheriff's deputies were banging on the door. Amy peered through the peephole, then let them in. They examined Pearce and hooked up IVs immediately. Pearce's blood loss was substantial. He had gaping wounds in his neck, back, face and head.

They called for Life Flight, the county helicopter equipped with a full medical staff. Within 25 minutes, Wayne Pearce was being airlifted to Palomar Medical Center in nearby Escondido.

Patrol Sergeant Ken Takeshta had responded to the call with the medics. When Takeshta saw the blood on the walls and saw the IVs from Pearce, he called for homicide. Why not? He knew it was going to end up being one.

Homicide Detectives Robert Fulmer and Russ Oliver were nearly ready to leave their respective homes when their phones rang. The two were told to go to the 2200 block of Carol View in Cardiff on a case that was not yet a homicide but probably would be by the time they arrived.

As Russ Oliver was driving to the scene, the sun was

up. There were no clouds and it was going to be a bright, warm day. Oliver was grateful he had had a full night's sleep.

Many was the time he had sat on the couch reading, his head drooping to his chest. Oliver would have changed to his sleeping clothes and been ready to crawl into bed, only to have the phone ring informing him of a call-out. In spite of his fatigue, it would be at least 24 hours before he would be in bed again.

Today, on the other hand, was great. Russ Oliver had shaven, eaten breakfast and had a full night's sleep. He was ready for anything.

When he pulled into the parking lot, he could see patrol cars and the yellow plastic crime scene tape. There were deputies near a pickup truck.

Oliver knew his colleague Fulmer would take a little longer to arrive so Oliver began to get an idea of what the team had to do. The first thing was to establish what the crime scene was and decide whether or not he needed a search warrant.

The patrol deputies introduced him to Amy Wren. She explained that, that morning, Wayne Pearce had done the same thing he did every weekday morning of the one month they had lived together.

Wayne was a foreman for a construction company. He got up, ate breakfast and went to work. The only thing different was that this time he'd come back covered with blood. His only words to Amy were, "Two guys . . ."

Detective Oliver noted that Pearce was 40 years old and Wren was 24. They had been living together with another female roommate for about one month.

Pearce did not gamble or use or sell drugs. Amy Wren consented to a search of their apartment. Oliver was especially interested in any address books they might find. Strangers do not come up and do what they did to Wayne Pearce for no reason. The patrol deputies said Pearce still had his wallet in his trousers pocket.

By now Robert Fulmer had arrived. He was a five-year veteran of homicide investigation and had worked numerous cases. Even he was amazed at the amount of blood he had seen outside and in the hallway and apartment.

The patrol deputies relayed to Fulmer and Oliver that Pearce had died at 7:08 a.m. Neither detective had seen Pearce, but Sergeant Takeshta told them it was hard to believe he had survived as long as he did.

Amy Wren did not have any old boyfriends who would have done this, she told probers. In fact, her last boyfriend had broken up with her, and their parting was cordial. Oliver knew he would have to verify that version with the boyfriend.

The other roommate had no boyfriends, having just moved to California from the Midwest. She was a friend of Amy's and rented one room of the two-bedroom apartment until she could save enough money for a place of her own.

After taking some preliminary notes on things to do and people to interview later, the two homicide detectives left to concentrate on the crime scene.

Next to Pearce's truck in the parking lot the detectives found the construction hatchet. It was covered with smeared blood. The detectives were not strangers to blood, gore, and violence. But when they saw the hatchet they winced as they visualized the damage it could do. The hatchet was preserved for possible fingerprint lifts.

On the ground the detectives also found a hat, a ballpoint pen, and keys (all later found to belong to Pearce).

On the grassy area where the second part of the attack began, probers found some chunks of flesh.

The knife that had been in Pearce's back was collected from the living room floor. It, too, was smeared with blood.

As far as the crime scene went, that was about it. The evidence technicians shot a few hundred pictures of the area. But there were no tire tracks, footprints or fingerprints.

Pearce's truck was dusted for prints from headlights to rear bumper. There were a few lifts. The truck was a typical construction foreman's truck. It was dirty on the outside. It was dirty on the inside with a few gasoline receipts, empty paper coffee cups, and aluminum soft drink cans.

Sometimes a crime scene is extremely important in a homicide investigation. This crime scene was important too, but not as important as what the detectives would find when they began interviewing people.

The apartment complex was canvassed for witnesses. Most of the occupants were working people, however, and they had left by the time the deputies knocked on their doors.

The crime scene work took most of the day. Detectives Fulmer and Oliver began the task of learning all they could about Wayne Pearce, Amy Wren, and the roommate.

Wayne Pearce was separated from Roberta, his wife of 14 years. Roberta was a teacher's aide at a local high school. Oliver made a note to talk to her soon and to find out about Pearce's life insurance. In Oliver's experience he learned that love and money account for a lot of the evil men do. He had seen men killed for a nickel and seen men killed for giving a wrong look to some guy's girlfriend.

The detectives learned that Wayne Pearce was a stay-at-home guy. He worked from 6:30 a.m. to 4:00 p.m. every day. He liked movies and liked to cook. He was a college graduate.

Pearce's bosses were contacted. There was no union trouble within the company, they told sleuths. Pearce was a good foreman who was well liked by his crew. There were no recent firings or disciplinary actions against any of the men who worked for Pearce.

Sometimes after work Pearce would stand around with his crew and pop the top on a couple of cold ones while the crew sat in the backs of their pickup trucks, as was the construction workers' custom.

Wayne never stayed too long, though. He socialized with the guys a little, but would leave so they could be among themselves. It was good therapy for the workers. They respected Wayne and liked him.

By the end of the day, the detectives had nothing. The veteran sleuths did not panic. This brutal murder had an explanation and they would find it.

The next day Dr. John Eisele performed the autopsy on Pearce. It was a case of overkill. Pearce had been stabbed 27 times. He had two gaping wounds in his left abdomen. He had been whacked numerous times in the face, head and arms with the hatchet.

He had died of massive head injuries and loss of blood. The pathologist found clumps of hair in each hand, indicating Pearce's desperate fight with his attackers. The hair was preserved for possible comparison later.

Meanwhile, a check of the computer showed that the pending divorce between Roberta and Wayne Pearce was stormy.

Patrol deputies had been called to the Pearce household in the 29000 block of Yellow Brick Road in Valley Center on three occasions. On one of the calls, Mrs. Pearce placed Wayne under arrest for domestic violence. Mrs. Pearce never bore any signs of physical violence, yet she claimed that Wayne had beaten her.

The patrol deputies knew someone of Wayne's size would leave marks on anyone he decided to hit. The responding deputies told Detective Russ Oliver they believed Roberta was making up the physical violence part in order to get Wayne arrested.

The homicide detectives had worked plenty of cases where the going was difficult. For example, a convenience store robbery in which a clerk was murdered simply to eliminate a witness was a tough one to solve.

The Wayne Pearce case was not like that. Somebody wanted Pearce dead, and it should have been a relatively easy task to find out why. But it wasn't.

The crime occurred on Monday, January 31st. By Wednesday, February 2nd, information was trickling in, none of it usable—yet. The deputies first started receiving anonymous phone calls telling them Mrs. Pearce had been trying to find someone to kill her husband.

This bit of information made sense. A normal check of records revealed Wayne Pearce had $200,000 worth of life insurance, with Roberta as the beneficiary. Detective Robert Fulmer would say, "I've seen 'em killed for a lot less."

The Pearce vs. Pearce divorce was due to have become final on March 1st.

More anonymous phone calls told the deputies, "Mrs. Pearce and Hector killed that man in Cardiff." When the deputies asked who "Hector" was, they were told to check at the school.

Rather than immediately interview Mrs. Pearce, Detectives Fulmer and Oliver decided to let her stew for awhile. If she had killed her husband, she was expecting the cops and would be mentally prepared for them. To wear her out by ignoring her for awhile was a good strategy.

The detectives went to the high school in Escondido where Roberta Pearce worked. After a few formalities of protocol with the principal, the deputies interviewed Roberta Pearce's immediate supervisor.

The supervisor appeared to want to protect Mrs. Pearce and not make any rash accusations. But she did say she had had to "counsel" (a new buzzword in employee supervision: it means "chew out") Mrs. Pearce for becoming too familiar with the students.

While teachers are encouraged to be friendly and accessible to students, there should be definite boundaries to the relationships.

Mrs. Pearce had been wearing one of the student's jackets. Detective Oliver was interested. "Who is this student?" he asked.

The teacher said his name was Hector Ruiz. The teacher also said that word had floated around the school that Mrs. Pearce had held parties for some of the kids. The teacher was now starting to get uncomfortable, fidgeting and looking away. "Oh yes," she said. "There was also some talk about Mrs. Pearce having a, uh, sexual relationship with Hector."

As the detectives were walking to their car, Russ Oliver said, "This is a damn sight different than when I went to high school."

The detectives also learned that a young high school girl named Freda Sipe was actually living with Mrs. Pearce. They contacted Freda at school and learned she came from a broken home. She had moved in with Roberta about one month earlier.

Freda was evasive and hesitant. The detectives did not think she was an actual participant in the killing, but they were confident Freda knew everything about it.

After about one hour of listening to Freda answer, "I don't know," "I can't remember," and "Mrs. Pearce would never do anything like that," the detectives became very direct with Freda.

They told her they were going to solve the case and arrest the killers. They did not know exactly when—in a day possibly, or a week for sure. Nonetheless, it was going to be done. There was going to be a trial, and the killers were going to jail.

They told Freda to decide what side of the field she was going to line up on. Was it going to be with the killers, or was it going to be with them? Then they gave her a brief explanation of the legal terms "accessory" and "accomplice."

They told her the word was out everywhere that Mrs. Pearce had hired some students to kill Mr. Pearce. They told Freda they knew about the parties and knew she was there when the killing was planned. Finally, they asked Freda if she wanted to be a witness or a suspect.

The 16-year-old girl looked as though someone had asked her if she would rather die by poison or by hanging. Neither choice was very pleasant.

Freda decided to tell the truth—sort of. She stumbled over her sentences, saying she did not know who committed the killing, just some guys who showed up at the house. She did say that Mrs. Pearce was going to pay the boys $50,000 each and give them each a car. Mrs. Pearce had a nice blue late-model Lincoln and a red Corvette.

Finally, Detective Robert Fulmer closed his book and shook his head wearily. He told Freda that, the way all the kids at school were talking, it would only be a short time before they knew the names of the killers. It would look a lot better if Freda was the one who supplied those names since she already knew them.

Freda slumped in her chair. "All right," she sighed. "The boys are Anthony and Isaac. That's all I know. Anthony was a friend of Hector's and he brought Isaac into it.

"They talked about it a lot," said Freda. "Once, Mrs. Pearce drove them to where Mr. Pearce lived. She showed them a picture of Mr. Pearce so they'd know him. At first they was going to shoot him. Then they took the ax and some knives.

"After they killed him, they came back to Mrs. Pearce's house. They was all bloody. They cleaned up. I had to wash their clothes twice in the washing machine. Then they left. I think they went to Mexico."

The detectives knew they were on a roll. Freda had overheard enough of the plan to tell them that Hector, the 16-year-old student who was sleeping with Mrs. Pearce, invited Anthony to do the killing. In turn, Anthony invited his friend Isaac.

At first, none of the youths thought Mrs. Pearce was serious. She initially offered them $3,000 each. Then the price went to $6,000, $10,000, and finally $50,000 and a car.

The boys bit at that last offer. Mrs. Pearce's reason was that her divorce would be final March 1st, and according to community property laws, the house would be sold and the proceeds split. Mrs. Pearce could not afford to buy another house, even if she received a hefty cash settlement for her half.

Her teacher's aide salary was meager. Wayne Pearce did not care about the house. He had an apartment and a young girlfriend to go with it. His cash settlement would go for glitter and pleasure while Mrs. Pearce would be out on the street.

With Mr. Pearce dead, Mrs. Pearce would get $200,000 life insurance, the house, and the cars. She would pay $100,000 to the boys and give them the cars. With the remaining $100,000, she would be in good shape.

The detectives knew that finding out who Isaac and Anthony were and locating them would not be a problem. They both knew what the problem would be: they needed to get enough evidence on Mrs. Pearce that could withstand an attack by her defense counsel, since she was not present when the murder was committed.

The detectives contacted Deputy District Attorney Mike Carleton. He drew up an affidavit for a search warrant for Robert Pearce's house. The affidavit summarized all they knew about the case so far.

On February 3rd, shortly before midnight, the detectives knocked on the door of Judge Zalman J. Sherer, now deceased. He authorized the search of Mrs. Pearce's house on Yellow Brick Road.

When the detectives went to Mrs. Pearce's house an hour later, on February 4th, they found her to be up and awake. She was nervous but in control. She told the detectives she was packing to go to Illinois for Wayne's funeral.

The detectives interviewed her about their suspicions. They confronted her about arranging Wayne's murder. She denied it, but admitted knowing Anthony, Isaac and Hector. Haughtily she said, "Of course I know them. They're students where I work." She denied the sexual relationship with Hector.

The detectives laid out the entire case as they knew it. Roberta Pearce denied everything. They offered her a polygraph. She said she would have to talk to an attorney before doing that.

They asked Roberta why she had never called the sheriff to check on the progress of the case. In their vast experience, surviving family members, even estranged ones, call to see how things are going.

Roberta said, "I didn't call the sheriff because I had too many other things to deal with."

Detective Oliver said, "Like cleaning the house? Like getting rid of Anthony's and Isaac's fingerprints? Cleaning the car? Cleaning their bloody clothes? Taking care of a couple of people in Mexico?"

Roberta did not acknowledge that Oliver was speaking with her.

After awhile the detectives knew they were getting nowhere. Roberta was strong. She was a good liar, too. She could keep straight what she had previously told them.

Roberta finally said, "Are you going to keep me from going to Illinois?"

"Yes."

"You are?"

"Yes."

"How can you do that?"

"How? It's real easy. We put you in jail." And they did just that.

The veteran detectives knew the case was in pretty good shape. They found a knife set that matched the one in Wayne's back. However, the detectives needed the boys who had actually committed the murder.

The case would actually be two-pronged. First, sleuths would have to prove the solicitation on Roberta's part and then prove the murder on Anthony and Isaac's part.

A check at the school revealed the boys were a couple of 16-year-olds, Anthony Pilato and Isaac Hill. The detectives remembered the violence and the hacking done to the body of Wayne Pearce. How could a pair of 16-year-olds have done such damage as to render the poor man unrecognizable?

The detectives learned the word on the street was that the boys were in Mexico, as Freda Sipe had said. The boys were going to wait there until things cooled off.

Robert Fulmer said, "Mexico? Who do they think they are, Butch Cassidy and the Sundance Kid?"

The detectives heard that Mrs. Pearce had given the boys some money and had taken more money to them while they were in hiding in Mexico. With Roberta in jail, their money source would be gone. The officers believed Anthony and Isaac would be back soon. Tijuana is no place for two young Caucasian boys.

In the meantime, the detectives located Hector Ruiz, the 16-year-old purported lover of 42-year-old Roberta Pearce. When one of the detectives not assigned to the case heard about the Ruiz-Pearce relationship, he asked, "What does that woman teach out there, sex education?"

Ruiz was a large, Baby Huey-type boy. The detectives could not see what Roberta saw in him. For that matter, they could not see what Hector saw in her, either.

Hector's interview was a series of lies heaped one

upon another, liberally sprinkled with "I don't knows." Hector thought he was being cagy and streetwise with the veteran cops.

In truth, Hector was a horrible liar. When he thought he was being cool and in control, he was actually looking quite stupid. Hector did admit to the detectives that he regularly bedded the older lady. There were always a lot of kids at the Pearce house, he said. There was some marijuana, alcohol, and even crystal methamphetamine.

Hector said that, when the murder was being planned, it was always done away from the rest of the youths, with only Isaac, Anthony, Hector and Freda present to discuss it.

After the interview with Hector, Detectives Oliver and Fulmer went to the Juvenile Department of the district attorney. They spoke with bureau chief Carlos Armour. After hearing the facts, Armour, an 11-year veteran, drew up arrest warrants for Isaac Hill and Anthony Pilato. Cops put deputy district attorneys in different categories. Armour was considered to be "cop-friendly."

Some D.A.'s delight in finding minuscule things wrong with an investigation so they can ask the officer, "Why did you guys do *this?*" Carlos Armour worked with what he had and always tried to cooperate.

After the juvenile court petitions had been filed, Detective Fulmer and Oliver headed up to the North County Courthouse in Vista. The case against Roberta Pearce was assigned to Deputy District Attorney Tim Casserly.

Casserly is a young, articulate, athletic deputy who worked in Sacramento County for five years. He has been with the San Diego District Attorney's Office for four years and done five murder trials.

Casserly looked at the growing file and whistled softly. His main concerns were: Would the jury believe those dope-smoking, school-ditching, wild kids? And how could he get Isaac and Anthony on the witness stand?

The two killers were not required to testify and Casserly was not inclined to give them a "deal." Casserly also had seen the autopsy photos and the savagery of their attack on Pearce. Casserly decided not to worry about the things he could not control.

Finally, on February 8, 1989, a full week after the murder, Isaac Hill and Anthony Pilato gave themselves up. They had obviously tired of the life in a strange land. Their dreams of money and a car had turned into a droning, fearful existence of rice, beans, tortillas, and noisy diesel buses outside their hotel.

No cars materialized. The only money that came their way was $300 split between them—not the $50,000 each had expected.

Both boys agreed to be interviewed by police without an attorney. They admitted to the killing to Detectives Oliver and Fulmer, but insisted they had forgotten key details, such as how many times they had stabbed Pearce and what they did when they returned to Mrs. Pearce's house.

Their story was right on line with the available evidence regarding the murder solicitation, however. When Roberta first asked, they said they refused. They thought she was kidding. When she continued to raise the price, they believed she was telling the truth and eventually agreed to do it.

Meanwhile, the detectives learned that Roberta Pearce had cashed a $300 personal check on the day the boys said she drove to Mexico and gave them that amount. It was not a lot of overwhelming evidence, but a jury would find it interesting.

Also, Roberta's phone records showed she had received collect calls from Tijuana at the time the boys said they called her.

In a case this brutal, the detectives normally would try to get the juveniles certified as adults to increase the sentence. That option is available only if the defendant is 17 years old. Since both boys were only 16, they had to be tried as juveniles.

Carlos Armour was ready to put the case on. Before he could, both Isaac Hill and Anthony Pilato pleaded guilty to first-degree murder and were sentenced to the California Youth Authority until they turned 25, the maximum term.

Both boys were remorseful and wanted to undergo counseling to deal with what they had done.

With the juvenile aspect of the case over, that left only Roberta to deal with. Carlos Armour and Tim Casserly talked at length about the case. Neither Anthony Pilato nor Isaac Hill had received a special deal. Armour had not made them promise to testify against Roberta Pearce in exchange for their plea.

D.A. Casserly was understandably concerned. Without the boys he had a largely circumstantial case. The knife on the floor matched her kitchen set. The personal check for $300 and collect phone calls from Tijuana corroborated what Anthony and Isaac had said. But would the killers testify?

Both agreed. The trial of Roberta Pearce began in mid-February 1990 in the Vista courtroom of Judge Franklin J. Mitchell Jr.

Since she had planned the murder by laying in wait and for financial gain, the district attorney said he would attempt to prove "special circumstances" which made Roberta eligible for the death penalty if convicted.

The trial began with arguments from the media on whether the two boys could be photographed. They could. Public interest was considerable.

The trial was predictable. Both Anthony Pilato and Isaac Hill testified. They were not Rhodes scholars, to be sure. But in spite of their imperfect memories, they gave the appearance of honesty. Their saving grace was that they had already pleaded guilty to their crime and received the maximum sentence. So they were not testifying to save their own skins, but because they wanted to put their lives back together.

Roberta Pearce took the stand in her own defense. She was hardly a sympathetic figure. Short and buxom, she told how the teenagers had taken over her house against her wishes. They told her, on their own, that they would kill Mr. Pearce so she could keep her house.

Roberta did admit to having sex with Hector Ruiz, and on one occasion with one of the killers. She could not explain the cashed $300 check, nor the collect calls from Tijuana.

The jury deliberated for 15 hours and came back with a first-degree guilty verdict on March 13, 1990.

During the penalty phase, Casserly urged the gas chamber for Mrs. Pearce. Her attorney begged for the mercy that Wayne never enjoyed.

The jury elected to sentence Roberta to life in prison without possibility of parole. On May 11, 1990, Judge Franklin Mitchell Jr. meted out that sentence.

Hector Ruiz, the teenage boy who recruited Isaac Hill and Anthony Pilato to do the killing, was sentenced to the California Youth Authority until he turned 25. Ruiz blew any chance for a lighter sentence when he was arrested for car theft shortly before his conspiracy sentence. He had been out of custody on "house arrest" status.

EDITOR'S NOTE:
Freda Sipe, Amy Wren, and Hector Ruiz are not the real names of the persons so named in the foregoing story. Fictitious names have been used because there is no reason for public interest in the identities of these persons.

"GRISLY CASE OF THE 'GORILLA' HIT MAN"

by Walt Hecox

When Detective Sergeants Mike Destro and Dalton Rolen of the San Jose, California Police Department examined the body and then looked over the murder scene in the Round Table Apartments, they could be sure of only one thing. Twenty-three-year-old Jerome Nance had been executed. Why or by whom was a mystery which would remain unsolved for a long time. The killers were careful. They did not leave clues. It was 9:30 a.m., May 29, 1980.

Nance had been found by a relative at about 8:55 that morning. He was slumped over a couch with his upper body lying across it and dressed only in his bathrobe and undershorts. An expert opinion was hardly needed to determine he was dead. He had been shot twice in the head.

Both Sergeants Destro and Rolen could tell immediately that Nance had been shot at close range. Neither was there any question about the intent of the person who shot him. The killer of Jerome Nance wanted him dead. He took no chances.

Later the detectives would be told by Dr. Richard Mason, Santa Clara County pathologist, that the first bullet to strike the recently deceased Mr. Nance pierced his left cheek, fractured his left jawbone and, traveling at a downward angle, lodged in the fatty tissue on the right side of his neck. From powder stippling on the dead man's face the detectives could tell the barrel of the weapon used to shoot Nance had been very close to his face. Dr. Mason informed them the distance was 10 to 12 inches.

One shot was not enough for the killer. When Nance crumpled over the couch, he had fired a second shot. It was an obvious coup de grace. The bullet entered Nance's skull behind the upper portion of his left ear, bounced off the right side of the dead man's skull and then came to a stop in his brain. Dr. Mason labeled it a contact wound. Powder burns indicated the gun was held from two to four inches from Nance's head.

As they examined the apartment, Detectives Destro and Rolen found no obvious motive for the killing, such as a fight or a robbery. The apartment, aside from the body and the blood-soaked couch beneath his head, was undisturbed. There were no clues. Hit men stay in business because they are adept at not getting caught. The man, or men, who had killed Nance were obviously professionals. They had left the police nothing with which to work.

Leaving the apartment for criminalists and technicians to process, the detectives began searching for the lucky break which might make the case solvable. That lucky break would consist of someone in the apartment complex who had seen something, or someone who might have seen the killer and be able to identify him, or at least provide a clue to his identity.

From a young man who lived in the apartment directly below Nance, the investigators learned that two people, a man and a woman, had left the murdered man's apartment at about 11:30 p.m. on the 28th. Shortly after midnight, the witness said, he had seen a shadowy figure climb the stairs to Nance's apartment and the door close directly above him. Because the lights in the complex yards had been, to a large degree, extinguished at that time, the young man had not been able to see the person climbing the stairs clearly.

Once he had heard the door close, the young man told the investigators, he heard the sounds of an argument during which he heard one man say clearly, "Why did you hit me?" The argument continued in muffled tones, he said, which were indistinguishable. It ended suddenly with two sharp reports which the witness believed to be either gunfire or firecrackers. They were followed by a dull, thudding sound, then silence.

Immediately after hearing the shots, the witness said, he pulled the curtain over the front window through which he had seen the people enter and leave Nance's apartment, turned off the television set which he had been watching, went to the bedroom and told his mother what he had heard and instructed her to stay in bed, then returned to the living room and peered out into the open area between buildings.

Shortly thereafter, the witness said, he saw the same dark figure descend the stairs. Once again he could not make out the figure clearly. He added, however, he had heard a clicking noise as the figure moved down from Nance's apartment that sounded to him like a woman's high heels moving over a hard surface. For that reason he suspected the person was a woman. Later, he told Jim Morris, an investigator for the Santa Clara County District Attorney's Office, that he did see a person silhouetted by lights from the rear standing in a doorway leading to the complex parking area. Because all he could see was the outline of the person, he was unable to describe him or her. He did say that he saw what looked like heavy, braided, frizzy hair which made him believe the visitor was a woman.

The apartment complex in that area included four buildings arranged in a square. Each building contained four units, two on each floor. The witness lived in apartment six, directly below the one occupied by the murder victim. The tenant in apartment 13 had moved in with his live-in girlfriend and her two-year-old son about two weeks before the shooting. Joined by Detective Sergeant Richard Arca, the investigators continued to canvass the area. They discovered that few people had heard gunshots and almost no one had seen anything.

The detectives did discover that Nance, until early on the evening of the 28th and shortly before the murder, had shared his apartment with another man. His roommate had moved out and into an apartment a few hours before Nance was killed. Sergeants Destro, Rolen and Arca decided they should pay a little extra attention to Nance's former roommate.

Later, as they continued canvassing the complex, the detectives discovered the woman who lived directly under apartment 13, which adjoined Nance's living quarters, had been visiting the tenant in apartment eight in the building across the interior yard of the complex.

The two women reported they had been visiting in the kitchen of apartment eight when they heard what sounded like gunshots originating in the general direction of Nance's rooms. The tenant in number eight had left the kitchen and looked across the court but told the detectives she saw nothing. Her visitor confirmed her story. She said the woman had returned to the kitchen and told her she hadn't seen anything.

From the criminalists, the investigators learned that one slim clue had been found in the apartment. A complete set of fingerprints, which did not match those of any of Nance's friends or associates, had been found on the hinge plate of the murdered man's front door.

The prints, the criminalist explained, had to be made when the door was open. Any fingers in contact with that plate at the time the door was closed would have been crushed. The detectives knew a long, slow process would follow before the prints could be compared with those of known criminals on file in hopes of locating the murderer.

Aside from the fingerprints, the investigators came up with almost nothing after 15 days of investigation. The killer, or killers, of Jerome Nance had worked with professional precision. There appeared to be no one who could positively identify them and they had left no clues in their wake.

The only possible suspect, Nance's former roommate, who had moved out a few hours prior to the murder, had a foolproof alibi. He had attended a party across town after moving from apartment 14 the night Nance was killed and stayed on until the small hours. A wide variety of people, some of whom did not even know each other, had seen him there at midnight. It would have been impossible for him to have returned to the Round Table Apartments and shoot Nance. The detectives did not believe everyone they questioned on the matter could be lying.

On June 13th, hoping they might uncover fresh information which had been overlooked in the original canvass, Sergeants Destro, Rolen and Arca returned to the apartment complex and began requestioning everyone who had heard shots at the time Nance was murdered. This time they learned the woman who had been visiting apartment eight had a different story to tell.

She said that when the shots were fired her hostess in apartment eight had gone to the front window and looked out, as reported earlier. But she had seen two men leave Nance's apartment and enter apartment 13. She had not described either man in any detail other than to say one of them was wearing a watch cap.

One small flaw marred the woman's story. The woman who had lived in apartment eight was gone. She had returned to Philadelphia, Pennsylvania, her home city, shortly after the murder and her friend did not know her new address. Through the Philadelphia Police Department, the San Jose investigators were able to locate the woman. She was interviewed by the eastern detectives and confirmed her friend's story. She had seen two men leave Nance's apartment immediately after she heard the shots and seen them enter apartment 13. The woman explained she had been raised in a ghetto and learned early in life that people who saw a crime committed and told the police what they saw often paid a high price for talking. She said she believed most people who talked after witnessing a crime had their homes dynamited or worse.

Immediately after the murder, Sergeants Destro and Rolen had spoken with the man who lived in apartment 13. He told them he had visited his mother, who was scheduled for surgery, in the hospital early in the evening and returned home at about ten o'clock. At that time, he said, he had seen Nance standing on the balcony shared by both tenants, had spoken and shared a marijuana cigarette with him, then returned to his apartment. At that time, he said, he and his girlfriend had eaten dinner and retired. They had not heard any disturbance or gunfire that night.

In view of what they had learned from the former tenant in apartment eight, the detectives wondered if the man in apartment 13 was telling the truth. The testimony, however, was not enough to pin the murder on Nance's neighbor.

Through the months that followed the detectives tracked down lead after lead, all of which led them down blind alleys. Ten months passed and the murder was still not solved.

On March 10, 1981, a badly mutilated body was found at the corner of Las Plumas Avenue and North Marburg Way in San Jose by a man who worked in the area. Patrol officers, responding to his call, saw signs the body had been struck by a car and dragged from one side of the road to the other toward the north for about 300 feet.

The badly battered body was lying at the side of the road with blood flowing from the head. The man had taken a terrible beating. In addition to the scraping and bruising over his entire body which had occurred when he was dragged, he had been stabbed repeatedly. His skull also appeared to have been punctured several times by pellets from a shotgun. There were several obvious depressive skull fractures. Three items regarded as possible evidence were collected at the murder scene. They included a maroon coat with three keys in one pocket, a hat and a brown, fishhead cane.

One strange thing happened while the San Jose police were securing the scene. Officer Mike Schembri, who was directing traffic around the area, was approached by two men, riding in a tan automobile, who asked him for directions. Told how to get to the location they inquired about, they immediately drove off in the opposite direction to the one the patrolman had indicated.

Once again, the police, including Detective Sergeant Arca, who was assigned as one of the lead investigators on the case, discovered they had a corpse and no leads. The sergeant probed through San Jose's underworld and came up with a couple of offbeat names. Sergeant Arca soon discovered the names were Swahili in origin. Swahili names, he knew, were often taken by members of the Black Gorilla Family, a notorious, prison-oriented gang, after a new member had taken the oath and sworn lifelong loyalty to the organization. Among themselves, at least, they used the names in place of what they referred to as their "slave names"—those given them at birth.

A wallet tentatively identified the dead man as William Fisher, a rotund black man whose killers had been excessively vicious. As was the case with Nance, there could be no question that whoever had ended his life wanted to be doubly sure he was dead. An autopsy performed that morning by Dr. John Hauser, another San Jose pathologist, revealed exactly how vicious and cruel the killers had been.

Dr. Hauser found that the 5-foot-11-inch, 230-pound, 32-year-old Fisher could have been killed by any one of several traumatic wounds or fractures. His body was a mass of internal injuries. Alcohol and drug tests showed he was neither drunk nor was under the influence of drugs.

There were three puncture wounds in his head, his skull was fractured and his brain had been lacerated. There were four stab wounds in his chest. His left lung had been perforated three times and there was extensive blood trauma within the pleural cavity. Fisher's right lung was virtually collapsed. Even his right knee was fractured and the leg reduced to literal pulp.

The pathologist listed the causes of death as puncture wounds to the lungs, puncture wounds to the head, laceration of the brain and extensive blood trauma. Any of these could have killed the victim. The dead man's skin on both the front and rear had been peeled off as though he had been flayed. His sex organs were torn and hanging loosely held by flaps of skin to his body. His head was mutilated. There were areas where great flaps of skin and hair was torn loose or split through. In places, his brain showed through the mutilated flesh.

Members of the dead man's families, along with friends, were contacted by Sergeant Arca and others

HIT MEN

of the investigating staff, but they had little or nothing to offer. No one came up with a logical motive for the cruel murder of William Fisher.

On March 24th, 14 days after the body was found, the apparently unrelated arrest of a suspected parole violater opened the first crack in the case which would eventually grow to a king-sized fissure. One Harvey Joe Hensen was arrested at about 12:15 a.m. and scheduled to be turned over to his parole officer. Hensen was carrying several credit cards the arresting officers believed to be stolen. Chance and Lady Luck moved in on the police department's side. Officer Mike Schembri, the same policeman who had been directing traffic around the investigation when Fisher's body was found, was directed to interrogate Hensen. Something in the officer's mind clicked when he saw Hensen. After brief probing, he contacted the San Jose Police Department Intelligence Division.

"This guy is apparently a member of the Black Gorilla Family and he seems to have some information to give," he reported.

Officer Dave Byers of the Intelligence Division arrived to question Hensen. The parolee promptly mentioned several details concerning the Fisher murder which had never been published in the San Jose newspapers.

Hensen told Officer Byers he had been in a San Jose bar on March 9th and had seen William Fisher in the bar with one Harold Bernard Shamburger and another man. That, he said, was the last time he had seen Fisher alive. Hensen added that he had heard that Shamburger had killed Fisher during a dispute over a drug deal.

The parolee told Officer Byers he had heard that Fisher had been beaten in the head with a shotgun after the weapon had failed to fire and had also been stabbed three times in the chest. To this, he added, that he heard the shotgun and knife had been put in a plastic bag and buried in a field on the southwestern drive of a home on Scotsdale Drive in San Jose. He said that he, a woman, and a man named Lloyd Henry Brice lived there.

Brice, he said, was aware of the homicide and could have ordered it. He was, Hensen indicated, a general in the Black Gorilla Family. Shamburger, he said, was a hit man for the organization. Hensen explained he was afraid he would lose his job if his employers discovered he had been arrested, and that he was already worried about the stolen credit card charge. In return for his freedom, he said, he would return to the house, get what added information he could, and pass it along to the San Jose police.

Officer Byers considered the alternatives. On one hand, he had at best a weak charge that could be levied against Hensen. On the other, Hensen might help solve a particularly cruel and inhuman murder. He elected to free Hensen in return for information.

Hensen did not keep his promise, but on April 21st, almost a month later, he was arrested in Stockton, California for failing to report to his parole officer. At that time, Hensen was questioned by Officer Byers and Sergeant Arca. Hensen expanded on his version of the Fisher murder at that time.

The parolee said there was a contract out on Fisher

and he believed the portly black man knew it. He added that Brice, whose Swahili name was Heshamu, had told him about the contract. Hensen said Shamburger and a certain Black Gorilla member were supposed to make the hit.

On the night of March 10th, Hensen said, Shamburger had gone to Brice's house covered with blood and carrying a sawed-off shotgun and a knife. Hensen added that he was told by Brice to put the weapons in a plastic bag and bury them across the street in an open field. The parolee said he followed orders.

Hensen said he was also told to follow Shamburger and get rid of Fisher's car which the hit man had driven back to the house on Scotsdale Drive. Hensen said while he followed in a beige Dodge Duster belonging to Brice, Shamburger left, drove to a market where he bought some Thunderbird wine and charcoal lighter fluid, then to a location which he had second thoughts about. Shamburger continued then, Hensen said, to Hellyer Park off Coyote Drive where the hit man stopped, wiped Fisher's car down carefully, sprinkled charcoal lighter fluid in it and pushed the aging automobile down an embankment.

The car, Hensen said, rolled down into a small field where it struck a tree and failed to ignite. Shamburger moved down into the field, sprinkled more lighter fluid in it and used a match to start the fire. After the old car was burning, Hensen said, Shamburger had told him what had happened to Fisher. He said he had met the doomed man in a bar. Fisher, Hensen explained, was under the influence of a drug of some kind and ready to pass out. Shamburger had offered him a ride and taken him to Las Plumas Drive and

North Marburg Way. At that time, according to Hensen, Fisher was asleep in the back seat of the car. Hensen said Shamburger told him he had put a sawed-off shotgun against his head and pulled the trigger but the gun misfired. Next, Hensen said, Shamburger had taken a knife and stabbed Fisher in the chest. That awakened the doomed man, but did not kill him. Instead, he jumped out of the parked car and started to run.

Shamburger, Hensen said, followed but could not catch him. Hensen said the hit man then jumped into Fisher's car and caught the fleeing man in it, jumped out and began stabbing him, shouting, "The Dragon is here!" The Dragon is, according to Hensen, a Black Gorilla symbol.

The parolee told the officers that Shamburger said he had stabbed Fisher five or six times in the chest, hit him over the head with the stock of the shotgun and then run over him. The hit man, according to Hensen, said he had a hard time getting Fisher out from under the car and that he had to back into a ditch before he finally succeeded.

At that point, Hensen said, Shamburger said he had left his leather jacket at the scene and he was worried because it had some keys in it. Returning to the crime scene to pick up the jacket, Hensen said, Shamburger drank some Thunderbird and, as the wine took a trip on him, announced that he felt good, that he had another notch in his belt, and talked about how great it was to be a hit man.

Then, Hensen said, Shamburger added that the last time he had pulled a job he had to rent an apartment next to the mark. Sergeant Arca, who had worked on the Jerome Nance case, listened with interest. Sergeants Destro and Rolen had spoken to Nance's next-door neighbor. The detective wondered if Shamburger was that man. Later that day, he learned that the hit man had been the occupant of apartment 13, at the Round Table Apartments.

Sergeant Arca and Detective Sergeant Larry Demkowski, also assigned to investigate the Fisher killing, discussed the case with Officer Byers and Sergeants Destro and Rolen and the five investigators decided that, since Hensen indicated Brice and Shamburger frequently worked together, they would compare both men's prints with those found on the hinge plate of the door in Nance's apartment. Brice's prints matched perfectly.

Certain that they were finally close to solving a crime which appeared to be getting closer and closer to the inactive list, the authorities filed murder charges against both Shamburger and Brice for both the Jerome Nance and William Fisher killings.

Hensen, meanwhile, was taken from Stockton to San Jose, where he assisted the detectives in locating a sawed-off shotgun and folding knife buried in the field across from house on Scotsdale. At that point, Sergeant Demkowski, a veteran investigator who had not yet talked with Hensen, asked for an interview. The homicide specialist could not believe that a man could have such detailed knowledge of how the crime was committed unless he was present when Fisher was killed.

Under careful questioning by both Sergeants Arca

and Demkowski, Hensen finally admitted he had followed Shamburger to the murder scene from the bar where Fisher was first picked up. Earlier, Hensen said, he and Shamburger had been in Brice's home and the shotgun had been given to the hit man by their host. At that time Shamburger was ordered to go to the bar and pick up Fisher. Brice, Hensen said, knew that Fisher had fought with his girlfriend the preceding night and would be alone.

With the exception of the fact that Hensen admitted getting out of his car after the shotgun had misfired, he told almost exactly the same story he had previously. Shamburger, he said, had descended from Fisher's car when the shotgun misfired and handed Hensen the weapon. He then handed Hensen his coat. Holding the shotgun, Hensen had put the coat on top of Fisher's car. Shamburger returned to the car and attempted to stab Fisher. The doomed man ran. Shamburger got out, grabbed the shotgun, tried to follow, then hopped back into the car and caught his mark and killed him the way Hensen had described earlier.

Hensen had followed in the Duster and arrived at the murder scene in time to see Shamburger sitting atop Fisher and stabbing him while shouting, "The Dragon is on you!" Later, Hensen said, Shamburger had used the shotgun stock to beat Fisher over the head. Next, Shamburger had run over his victim and the body was dragged under the car until the hit man drove into a ditch to free it.

Hensen was given two polygraph examinations and passed them both. His attorney allowed him to plead guilty to accessory after the fact to the Fisher murder in return for a statement declaring his description of the killing was true and correct.

On May 22, 1981, armed with search warrants, the investigators went through the home of a relative of Shamburger's, his girlfriend's house and Brice's home. Sergeants Rolen and Destro and Officer Byers allegedly found complicated bomb timers in Brice's home. They also said they discovered a barrel to a sawed-off shotgun.

Criminalist Wilken Fong, meanwhile, had matched the shotgun cocking mechanism to the marks in William Fisher's skull and discovered they matched perfectly. He also determined that the barrel end, found in Brice's home, was consistent with the barrel of the shotgun which had been used to club Fisher to death.

The keys found in the pocket of the maroon coat at the Fisher murder scene were tried in the door of Jerome Nance's apartment and opened it easily, thus establishing Shamburger's presence there. The coat had already been identified as Shamburger's.

Lloyd Brice was arrested for both murders on May 22, 1981. Harold Shamburger was not apprehended until October. A patrol officer, seeing him walking down the street, addressed him by his Swahili name and, when the hit man responded, promptly arrested him.

The Shamburger and Brice trials were separated in the case of Nance, and eventually the Nance murder charge against Brice was dismissed by a superior court judge for insufficient evidence. Shamburger was found guilty of the murder June 4, 1984, after extensive legal bickering. He was sentenced to serve from 25 years to life in the California prison system.

Both Shamburger and Brice were to go on trial for

the murder of William Fisher at a later date.

Joe Hensen, in return for his evidence, was allowed to plead guilty to being an accessory to Fisher's murder and has already served his sentence.

It must be assumed that Brice and Shamburger are innocent of the charge in the Fisher murder unless and until they have been found guilty by due process.

EDITOR'S NOTE:
Harvey Joe Hensen is not the real name of the person so named in the foregoing story. A fictitious name has been used because there is no reason for public interest in the identity of this person.

"CALIFORNIA'S BIZARRE WEB OF 4-WAY LETHAL SEXCAPADE"

by Don Lasseter

Even though she had just made his heart sink, the two lovers held hands as they strolled through Reid Park, in Anaheim, California, in the early evening of November 23, 1990. It was the day after Thanksgiving, and Donna Connaty and Vince Peterson were discussing their plans for the weekend. Vince had been assuming they would spend the evening together until Donna started her night shift at the hospital as a registered nurse. But Donna told Vince that she was going to take the night off and go out with some friends.

They weren't teenagers anymore. Donna was 34 and Vince two years older. But for Vince, the announcement struck a sensitive nerve. It was hard enough to swallow Donna's occasional visits with her husband, Richard "Rick" Connaty, even though they were divorcing. But Vince certainly didn't want Donna to date anyone else.

Vince was, for the most part, happy with their year-old relationship. When Rick moved out from the home on Jackson Circle in Buena Park, Donna and her three children stayed on, and Vince was an occasional overnight guest. Then, Vince and Donna decided to live together, so she relinquished custody of the house and children to her estranged husband.

After five months, Vince and Donna realized that cohabitation put a strain on their finances, so in August 1990, they agreed to live separately again, with their respective families, while Donna struggled through the turbulent divorce proceedings with Rick.

Now Vince was concerned that Donna had a date with someone else. But, she explained, she was just going to be with some friends, both male and female, and she would be happy to see Vince on Sunday afternoon, after she had finished her Saturday night shift and had a few hours of sleep. Partially placated, but still uneasy, Vince accompanied Donna back to the nearby shopping mall where they had spent the afternoon.

Donna Connaty, despite what she had told Vince about spending the evening with friends, reported to her job at 7:00 p.m. that Friday.

Two days later, Donna's relatives were panic stricken. They had received a call on Saturday at 7:30 p.m. from Donna's supervisor at St. Joseph's Hospital, inquiring about her failure to show up at work. A flurry of telephone inquiries failed to provide any hint of where Donna might be. No one had seen her since she left work Saturday morning, after the Friday night shift. The family tried to call the Jackson Circle house that Rick Connaty now occupied to see if Donna was there, but no one answered. Finally, in desperation, they telephoned Rick's family, who lived in the Jackson Circle neighborhood, with a request to check the Connaty house to see if anything was wrong.

At 2:00 p.m. on Sunday, a member of the Connaty family walked the short distance and pulled open the unlocked metal security door. No one answered the bell, so the man unlocked the front door and opened it. A rectangular shaft of light illuminated the threshold, revealing a grisly scene that froze the relative in stunned silence.

Just inside the door, on the bright red carpet, Donna Connaty lay face down, her left cheek submerged in a pool of blood that formed a dark halo around her matted blonde hair. Her right arm was awkwardly twisted underneath her chest, while her left arm, the elbow slightly bent, was extended outward. The blue short-sleeved blouse she wore as part of her medical uniform was wrinkled and pulled up slightly, baring her midriff. Her legs, clad in white pants, were spread so that her white tennis shoes were nearly 30 inches apart. A stethoscope protruded from under her neck.

It was obvious to the relative that Donna was dead. Trying to overcome his shock, he trotted as quickly as he could to a neighbor and asked them to call 911. He then walked home to tell his family the bad news, then returned to wait for the police.

Officer Alex Holguin of the Buena Park Police Department arrived at 2:09. He met the relative at the door and stepped into the house to examine the prostrate victim. Her flesh was cold to the touch. Three minutes later, paramedics from the Buena Park Fire Department joined Officer Holguin. They guessed that Donna Connaty had died the previous day.

After securing the crime scene and while waiting for homicide investigators and coroner's personnel, Officer Holguin glanced around the room. A brown leather purse, its contents scattered around on the red carpet, lay open near the victim's left foot. If there had been any money in the purse, it was now missing. Close to the victim's left hand, Holguin spotted a white wristwatch with a broken white plastic band. Without moving it, the officer took a closer look. The crystal was shattered, and the hands were stopped at one o'clock. In old murder-mystery movies, Holguin knew, that was a sure sign of the time of death. He wondered if it would prove to be true in this case.

A few spatters of blood on the interior side of the door suggested to Holguin that the victim had been attacked with the door closed. More blood spots were on a coffee table, close to her head. A wall unit had apparently been ransacked.

Outside, the officer noted that a brown station wagon sat in the driveway. He examined the windows and back door of the house. There were no signs of forced entry, such as splintered frames, or pry marks in the wood. His inspection was interrupted by the arrival of a relative of the victim's, who had been notified by the neighbor who called 911. Holguin informed the man, as gently as possible, that Donna was deceased. The shocked relative told Holguin that Donna was going through a messy divorce.

Sergeant Harry Dock and Officer Bill Mentzer had just arrived on the scene when a female relative of the victim's walked into the yard. When she was told of what had happened, the woman screamed and collapsed in hysterics. After she calmed down, Officer Holguin learned from her that Donna sometimes slept at the Jackson Circle house when Richard Connaty wasn't there.

Meanwhile, Detective Gaylen "Buck" Buchanan was relaxing at home on Sunday afternoon, enjoying leftover turkey and watching a football game in his cozy den. Ordinarily, the 42-year-old investigator would be using leisure time to coach his church softball team, play golf (handicap of 13), or bowl (average 189), but on this Thanksgiving weekend, he was taking it easy. A 19-year veteran of the Buena Park Police Department (BPPD),

Buchanan had served stints with traffic, vice, and narcotics before landing in the homicide unit. He liked police work, having known members of the BPPD as a teenager when the officers patronized his parents' restaurant. Near the end of his tour in the Air Force, Buchanan had applied to join the department. He was hired three weeks after leaving the service.

At 2:30 p.m., Buchanan's leisurely holiday ended with a phone call from the watch commander. Buchanan quickly combed back his thick brush of short, sandy-colored hair, put on some work clothes, crammed his solid 6-foot frame into the car, and headed west for the 45-minute commute from Riverside to Buena Park.

Buchanan would have the support of a team of officers and specialists, but he would miss his partner, Detective Dan Flanagan, who was on leave until the end of the year.

Upon his arrival at the crime scene at 3:30, officers filled Buchanan in on the facts. It didn't seem a very likely place for murder, Buchanan thought. He could see, just two blocks away, the shimmering tower of a full-scale replica of Independence Hall. It was part of Knott's Berry Farm, the popular Southern California theme park that competes with Disneyland.

After the briefing, Buchanan decided to delay any additional searching for evidence until a warrant could be obtained. But the victim's husband, Rick Connaty, showed up at 4:30 and signed a consent-to-search form. Detective Buchanan asked Connaty to remain close so that he could be interviewed a little later. Buchanan wanted to have a look at the interior of the house first.

Officer Holguin showed Buchanan into the master bedroom. Signs of burglary were readily apparent. Drawers in a chest and a desk had been pulled out and the contents scattered. Clothing was strewn on the top of the chest. Both men noticed, however, that two walkie-talkies, a telephone, and a digital clock—all loot a burglar would be expected to take—were still sitting on the desk. When the detectives shifted the items, a fine layer of dust left outlines that proved nothing had recently been moved. Two other bedrooms were completely undisturbed. If there had been a burglary, it had been extraordinarily ineffective.

To verify the exact hours Donna had last been seen at the hospital, Detective Buchanan called her supervisor who told him that Donna had worked from 7:00 p.m. Friday, until 9:00 a.m. Saturday.

Crime Scene Investigator (CSI) Kenneth E. Patrick, an expert photographer, shot pictures of the victim and as much area inside and outside the house as possible before he began dusting for fingerprints. Clear latent prints showed up on the knob of the rear door. The same print was found on the telephone. Another latent was on the master bedroom doorknob. Patrick would laugh later when the third print turned out to be his own. The other two belonged to Rick Connaty, who lived in the house.

Patrick then set up the Omnichrome Argon Ion Laser to make a visual examination of the victim. This state-of-the-art process is used to detect trace evidence on the body. Patrick was disappointed when it produced nothing of importance.

It was obvious to the investigators, even before Deputy Coroner Richard McAnnally confirmed it, that Donna Connaty had been repeatedly bludgeoned to the head with a blunt instrument. The medic noted a number of wounds, plus a probable defensive injury to the left forearm. The victim's thick hair, matted with blood, prevented an exact count of injuries until the autopsy could be performed.

The investigators launched an intensive search of the house and yard for a hammer, length of pipe, ax, or any other heavy object that might have been used as the murder weapon. Eventually, a rusting clawhammer was retrieved from the backyard, but there were no bloodstains on it.

In the midst of the busy crime scene work, Donna's boyfriend, Vince Peterson made an appearance in the late afternoon. Officer Bill Mentzer took him aside for a preliminary interview. Peterson said that he was in the neighborhood looking for Donna when he saw the police activity and felt compelled to stop at the house. Recovering quickly from apparent shock, Peterson told the detectives about the last time he had seen Donna and their conversation at Reid Park. On Saturday afternoon, Peterson said, he decided to drive over to Donna's family's residence where she lived, but he swung by the Jackson Circle house first. He was surprised to see Donna's station wagon sitting in the driveway. He went to the door, Peterson said, and knocked, but no one answered. He had seen a note attached to the security gate.

There had been no note when the police arrived. "What was on the note?" Office Mentzer asked.

"Something like, 'Rick, we missed you.' There wasn't any signature."

Peterson said that he drove away, puzzled, and then stopped to visit Donna's relatives. They were all worried, wondering where she could be. Mentzer asked Peterson to wait around so that Detective Buchanan could talk to him.

Buchanan was, indeed, anxious to talk to Rick Connaty, Vince Peterson, and the Connaty relative who had discovered the body. At 6:00 p.m., he left the crime scene investigation in the hands of the expert technicians and asked Peterson and Connaty to drive their cars to headquarters while he transported the relative.

Buchanan interviewed the Connaty relative first. The man nervously related his shocking discovery of the victim. He told Buchanan that Rick and Donna had fought viciously and were going through a bitter divorce, but he thought that in recent weeks, they were putting the relationship back together. He also described an incident on a local freeway in June 1989, in which Rick and Donna argued on the way home from a marriage counseling session. Rick had struck Donna in the head with a tire jack. The injury had required 11 stitches, and Rick had been arrested for it. Buchanan made some notes, then released the weary witness to be transported home by another officer.

Vince Peterson was interviewed next. He portrayed his loving relationship with Donna and told how he used to stay overnight with her when she had custody of the Jackson Circle house.

"Were you ever worried that Rick would catch you there with her?" Buchanan asked.

"No," Vince confidently replied. "There was a restraining order to keep him away from the house."

Peterson said he had received three telephone calls from Donna's family over the weekend, wondering where she was. He thought she had gone out with friends and was surprised to learn that she worked that night. When he dropped by the Jackson Circle house on Saturday, he saw the note on the security door and left. When he returned on Sunday, he was shocked to see all of the police activity.

Yes, Peterson said, he did know about the freeway incident. He also knew that Rick Connaty was a violent man.

After Detective Buchanan concluded his interview with Peterson, he recorded some observations in his spiral notebook. "It should be noted that Peterson provided exact dates, which I thought was unusual, and also displayed a great deal of nervousness. At times, he would shiver and shake. He also attempted to cry at times, but was unable to complete the act."

The third interview on that Sunday night was with Rick Connaty. In a somber voice, the victim's estranged husband disclosed that he and Donna were married in 1976 and bought the Jackson Circle house in 1978.

"When did you start having problems with your marriage?"

"In April of '89," Connaty replied, with unusually specific recall. "Donna went back to school to become a nurse, and she was never home." They had three children, he said, and he always had to care for them. Donna had kept them while she stayed in the house, but when she moved in with her boyfriend, Connaty took custody of the house and the kids. He recently worked at a supermarket as a mechanic, but he hurt his knee and was on disability leave.

Regarding the freeway incident, Connaty said he could not remember striking Donna. But he had been receiving counseling and had learned to accept the divorce, he said. While Donna occupied the house, Connaty had lived with a buddy in Santa Ana in a mobile home park. Yes, he had met Vince Peterson a few times.

"Was there an insurance policy on your wife?"

"I think it lapsed in 1978."

"When did you last see Donna?"

"On Friday, after Thanksgiving, about six-thirty that evening," Connaty recalled. He and his children were leaving to spend the weekend camping in the desert, and they met Donna at the hospital just prior to her work shift. She had commented that she would like to go to the desert with them, but had to work.

"So just you and the kids went to the desert?" Buchanan asked.

"Well, a couple I know in Santa Ana, in a mobile home, were supposed to go with us to ride dirt bikes. I met them when I lived over there. We planned to leave Saturday morning, but I decided to go Friday night. So I called them, but Neill had to work Saturday morning."

Connaty said he picked up his friend's child on Friday night to accompany his own kids on the ride to the desert. He told Buchanan that the couple, Neill Matzen and Gloria Lynn, arrived at the desert campsite, near Victorville, on Saturday afternoon.

"What time did you arrive out there?"

"About eleven o'clock, Friday night. The kids went to sleep in the back of my truck, and I slept in the cab."

"Did you talk to anyone there?"

"Yeah, I met a guy who was interested in dune buggies. We talked and even exchanged phone numbers." Connaty fished a business card from his wallet and read Buchanan the man's number.

The group left for home after lunch on Sunday, Connaty said. Whimpering, he told of arriving at his family's home, learning about the tragic circumstances, and driving immediately to the Jackson Circle house.

If Connaty was telling the truth, he had been over 100 miles away when Donna was killed, sometime after her shift ended on Saturday morning. Buchanan made a mental note to verify his story by interviewing Rick's camping companions. In his report, Buchanan wrote that Connaty had tears welling in his eyes during the interview. "Either his acting ability is good, or he was sincerely bothered by the loss of his wife."

Detective Buchanan let the victim's boyfriend and husband go home. It was past 10:00 at night, but the detective couldn't quit yet. There were too many unanswered questions. He telephoned Connaty's friend in the Santa Ana mobile home park, the pal with whom Rick had lived. The man told the sleuth that he had seen Connaty on Friday evening in the mobile home park.

"Does someone named Neill Matzen live there?"

"Yes, right next door," he told Buchanan, "but they don't have a phone." He volunteered to go to Matzen's residence and invite him over to speak to Buchanan. Within a couple of minutes, Matzen was on the phone.

Neill Matzen verified Connaty's story about picking up the child on Friday evening. But Matzen said he didn't realize that Connaty was leaving for the desert that same night, so he and Gloria went to Connaty's house on Jackson Circle on Saturday morning at 9:00 and found that Rick had already departed. At Matzen's request, Gloria left an unsigned note on the screen of the security door, saying, "Rick, Where were you? We were here at 9:00! Catch you later."

"Did you notice anything unusual around the house?"

"No. We saw a brown station wagon in the driveway." They returned to Santa Ana, Matzen said, then left for the desert, where they arrived about noon on Saturday, November 24th.

Detective Buchanan thanked Matzen and said that he would probably be contacting him soon for more details.

It had been a hectic day. As Buchanan made the long drive home to Riverside, he mulled over what he had learned. Donna's boyfriend might have been jealous enough to kill her when he saw that her station wagon was at Rick's house. Rick Connaty seemed to have a convenient alibi, but could he have left the desert, killed Donna, and returned? And now, there was Neill Matzen. How did he fit into the picture? Buchanan had a lot of investigative work yet to do, starting the next morning.

The first order of business on Monday was a task Buchanan dreaded—the autopsy. Joined by Crime Scene Investigator Ken Patrick, Buchanan observed the final indignity for the pitiful murder victim. Dr. Ronald Katsuyama, whose 25 years of experience included more than 15,000 autopsies, identified 14 multiple laceration wounds in the blood-encrusted scalp. When he refracted the scalp, he revealed three fractures. The cause of death, the pathologist said, was massive head trauma caused by a blunt object, perhaps a wrecking bar or crowbar. Donna Connaty had probably died on Saturday morning.

Glad to be out of the coroner's lab, Detective Buchanan contacted St. Joseph's Hospital where Donna had worked. A security employee had seen Donna leave on Saturday morning around nine o'clock. He also had some other interesting information. About a year before, a suspicious person had been seen loitering around the hospital parking lot. When confronted, the man said he was waiting to give Donna Connaty a ride home and wanted to talk to her about an argument she'd had with her husband. Ordered to leave the premises, the man jumped into Donna's red Honda and drove away. The car was seen back in its normal parking place an hour later. The man was identified as Neill Frank Matzen.

Odd, Buchanan thought. He thanked the security person, and called Rick Connaty to ask about the incident. Yes, Connaty said, Donna had been driving his red Honda at that time; it was before he had given her the brown station wagon. But Connaty denied knowing any-

HIT MEN

thing about Matzen's mysterious appearance at the hospital.

"Did Matzen have any reason to dislike Donna?"

Connaty said that Donna had once given Matzen a dog that later bit Matzen's child. Matzen had sued Donna over the incident, and after that, Donna and Matzen didn't get along.

Wanting to know more about Neill Matzen, Detective Buchanan called Connaty's buddy in the mobile home park. The man said that Matzen worked as a tow truck driver, but was having financial trouble. He and Gloria Lynn were always behind on the mobile home payments and rental for the space. They recently had a car repossessed and their utilities had been discontinued for payment failure. The informant added that he thought Gloria was sexually attracted to Rick Connaty, and might be having an affair with him.

Detective Buchanan's interest in Neill Matzen was growing by leaps and bounds, but he wanted to talk to Vince Peterson and Rick Connaty again. Peterson complied with Buchanan's telephone request to come to the police station, arriving just before 3:00 p.m.

Asked to describe again the events of Friday and the last time he saw Donna, Peterson told the sleuth that he and Donna had gone to her family's house that afternoon in separate cars. He had followed her and was surprised when she detoured and went to Jackson Circle. He saw Rick Connaty's truck and trailer, loaded with dirt bikes, parked in front of the house, so he waited in his car while Donna talked to Rick. A little later, at the mall, Donna told Peterson that Rick was taking their children to the desert. Then he and Donna went to Reid Park, where she mentioned that she was going out that night with friends. He had been bothered by the idea of it and he still didn't understand why she said it but worked that night anyway.

"Why did you go to the Jackson Circle residence on Saturday at two o'clock?" Buchanan asked, his voice firm and all but accusatory.

"Well," Peterson stammered, "I—I was on my way over to her family's place and I decided to go by the house. I saw her car, and thought she would be there."

"Why did you select that particular time?"

Peterson mumbled something, and Buchanan entered in his notebook, "He could not give me a satisfactory answer."

To see how Peterson would react, Buchanan growled, "I'm beginning to think that *you're* responsible for her death."

Instead of showing anger or denial, the detective noted, Peterson turned his hands upwards, sighed, and said, "I couldn't do something like that. I loved her."

In his coldest manner, Detective Buchanan asked very simply, *"Did* you kill Donna?"

His voice low, Peterson replied, "No, I did not, Mr. Buchanan."

Before releasing Peterson, Buchanan took photos of him and his car.

It was already dark when Rick Connaty arrived at the police station with his three children. Buchanan talked to them separately. The 10-year-old verified that they had left for the desert Friday night after picking up the Matzen child, that Neill and Gloria arrived at the campsite on Saturday afternoon, and that they didn't leave the desert until late Sunday. His father had been with him the whole time, the youngster insisted.

The second child, age eight, told the same story. The third one was too young to question.

Rick Connaty told the detective that he knew Matzen and his wife were having marital and financial problems. Gloria had been to his house because he was helping her with her math. No, Connaty said, he wasn't having an affair with her. Gloria had made sexual advances to him, but he had turned her down. The couple had wanted to move in with him, but he refused.

When Connaty and his children left the police station, Detective Buchanan was convinced that the man had not killed his wife, but he wasn't sure that Connaty was totally innocent of complicity in her death.

Detective Buchanan spent much of Tuesday on the telephone. He heard from a divorce attorney that Donna "was the typical battered woman" but for some reason, kept delaying the divorce. The dune buggy enthusiast who had met Connaty in the desert confirmed that Rick was there the whole time until Sunday afternoon.

Trying to learn more about Vince Peterson, Buchanan talked to an elderly member of his family. She stated that Peterson had told her on Sunday morning, before Donna's body was discovered, "You know, Donna is dead, and her sister will probably want to come and get her things." But Buchanan didn't put much weight on the statement, since the elderly relative seemed to confuse several dates and events. She had added that if Peterson was in trouble, ". . . he would have to deal with it."

A neighbor had seen Peterson on Sunday evening, rearranging furniture in his garage. He informed Buchanan that he had commented to Peterson about cleaning up the garage, and Peterson had just looked at him, "seeming edgy and nervous."

During the next few days, Buchanan made inquires at eight of the homes on Jackson Circle. Using his photograph of Vince Peterson's car, he asked if any of the residents had seen it in the neighborhood on Saturday morning. None of them recalled seeing Peterson or his car that day.

A relative of Donna's told the detective that Rick Connaty had threatened Donna a number of times, and speculated that "Rick would hire a hit man and make it look like Donna's boyfriend did it."

In between interviews, Buchanan pulled the police report regarding Neill Matzen taking Donna's red Honda from the hospital. The officer who handled the case had interviewed Donna Connaty at the time. She had told him that she had not given Matzen a key to her car or permission to use it, and she did not consider him a friend. The officer wrote, "Mrs. Connaty said she was in fear of her personal safety and considered Matzen to be a threat."

Buchanan knew it was time to confront Neill Matzen. On Friday, Buchanan called Matzen to request that he come to the police station for an interview and to be fingerprinted "for elimination purposes." Matzen agreed, but he quickly volunteered, "Well, my prints will be all over the house. I helped Rick move back in."

On Saturday morning, December 1st, Matzen sat face to face with Detective Buchanan. He told the detective again how he had planned to go to the desert with Rick, but that Rick had picked up Matzen's child on Friday night and gone directly to the desert. The next morning, Matzen said, he and Gloria went to Rick's house where they left the note on the security door. The investigators had been wondering what happened to the note until another of Donna's relatives explained that he had dropped by very late Saturday night, seen the note, and removed it. He later handed it to the police.

Asked if he had any ill feelings for Donna, Matzen

HIT MEN

candidly told of the dog-biting incident and the subsequent small claims suit, which had been dismissed in court. "After that, we didn't get along."

"Did Richard Connaty ever talk about killing Donna, or wanting her killed?"

"No, man," Matzen replied. "I've never thought of Rick as a violent person."

Explaining the circumstances of the day he drove Donna's red Honda away, Matzen said that he went to the hospital, at Rick's request, to talk to Donna about the divorce and to take the Honda. Rick had given him the keys, telling Matzen that if Donna had no transportation, he hoped she would call him and ask for a ride. That would give him an opportunity to talk to her and smooth things over, Rick had told him. Matzen acknowledged taking the car but said he returned it within a few minutes because he didn't want Donna to have to walk and perhaps be accosted.

At the end of the interview, Matzen told Buchanan that he thought his wife Gloria was having an affair with Rick, but he could never confirm it.

Detective Buchanan finally had a day off. Sunday, one week after the discovery of Donna Connaty's body, the detective tried to relax, but he couldn't get the case off his mind. He was now convinced that Neill Matzen had killed Donna at Rick Connaty's request.

After attending a parole hearing on Monday morning, Buchanan walked into his office at 9:30 a.m. and was hit with news that nearly knocked him off his feet.

Apparently, Neill Matzen and Rick Connaty had been in a gunfight earlier that morning at the mobile home park. Both men were hospitalized, Connaty in critical condition. Buchanan learned that Connaty had walked into Matzen's mobile home, stood over his bed, shouted,

"You killed my wife!" and shot Matzen in the left arm with a .380 automatic. Matzen had grabbed a .357 Magnum, leaped to his feet, chased Connaty outside, and shot him in the chest.

Absolutely amazed at the incident, Buchanan hurried to the hospital. He found out that Connaty was near death and unable to speak. Matzen was not seriously injured and was able to talk, but he told Buchanan that he had nothing new to tell him.

Then Matzen asked an odd question about the date of Donna Connaty's murder. "Are you concerned with the specific time period of one o'clock on November twenty-fourth?" he asked. Without waiting for an answer, Matzen continued, saying that he had receipts at home to prove he was not at the Connaty house at that time.

Buchanan was quite sure he knew why Matzen had asked such a specific question about the time. Donna's watch had been found on her wrist, stopped at one o'clock, even though she had probably been killed several hours earlier. Buchanan theorized that Matzen had set the watch, then crushed it, with plans to make an alibi for that specific time.

It was a day for surprising events, and at noon, Detective Buchanan was stunned again. Responding to a radio message to telephone headquarters, Buchanan was told that Gloria Lynn was spilling her guts in the Santa Ana P.D., giving Detective Irma Vasquez information that linked Neill Matzen with the murder of Donna Connaty.

Buchanan raced to the Santa Ana station, where Detective Vasquez gave him a tape of Gloria's statements. In it, Gloria said that the murder weapon, a steel pipe, was hidden by Matzen under a closet trapdoor in the house on Jackson Circle. Immediately contacting his own office, Buchanan asked CSI Patrick to go to the Connaty

HIT MEN

house and see if the weapon was in the alleged hiding place. Patrick found the bloodstained 30-inch steel rod, almost an inch thick, just where Gloria said it was. There were no prints on it.

Meanwhile, Buchanan faced Gloria Lynn. She said she had papers belonging to Donna that Neill had taken when he killed her. Detective Buchanan drove Gloria to the mobile home she shared with Matzen, where she turned over three bank savings books in Donna Connaty's name.

Back at headquarters, Gloria Lynn, with a videocamera running, told Buchanan that she had taken Matzen to the Connaty residence at 6:00 a.m. on Saturday, November 24th, "when the sunlight started to appear on the eastern horizon." On the way, they stopped at a convenience store and noted the number on a nearby pay phone. Gloria then dropped Matzen off near the house, she said, then, after filling the tank at a gas station, she drove to Boisseranc Park, about a mile away. There she parked the car and dozed off.

When she woke up, Gloria rushed back to the convenience store pay phone, arriving at 10:00 a.m., just in time to receive Matzen's call to come pick him up. When she arrived at the Connaty house, Matzen stepped out, locking the front door behind him. He instructed Gloria to write the bogus note, putting down the time as nine o'clock.

As they drove away, Gloria said, Matzen told her that he had killed Donna. Gloria claimed she didn't believe it because she had heard Matzen and Rick Connaty talk about doing it many times, but it never happened. Later, en route to the desert, Matzen showed her the bank books he had taken to prove that Donna had money Rick could get.

"Did Richard Connaty know about the murder before he came home from the desert?" Buchanan asked. Gloria was positive that Matzen had told him while they were out there.

She continued her account, saying that Matzen had entered the house through a rear door that Rick had deliberately left unlocked. Her own prints were probably in the residence, Gloria said, and on the murder weapon. She had seen the pipe in the bedroom a month earlier, had tripped on it, and picked it up to place it under the desk.

Buchanan's face didn't register the skepticism he was feeling.

At 1:30, Buchanan made another quick trip to the hospital to talk to Neill Matzen. When he arrived, he learned that Richard Connaty had died one-half hour earlier. There went any chance of corroboration by a third party.

Buchanan confronted Matzen with Gloria's statement and asked, "Why don't you tell me all about it?"

"What difference does it make?" Matzen croaked. He reiterated that he had nothing new to tell and suggested that Buchanan was lying and trying to trick him. He wanted a lawyer.

Detective Buchanan advised Matzen that he was under arrest in connection with the murder of Donna Connaty. The suspect was transported in an ambulance to a medical facility behind bars.

The case was far from over, though. The Orange County District Attorney's Office was forced to announce, the next day, that Neill Matzen was released and would not be charged with the murder. California Penal Code 1111 states that testimonial evidence from a possible co-perpetrator must be corroborated. There was no evidence to fulfill that requirement. Furthermore, the killing of Richard Connaty was apparently self-defense, and Matzen could not be held for that. The D.A. was frustrated, and Detective Buchanan was beside himself.

On Tuesday morning, Buchanan interviewed Gloria Lynn once more, hoping to find something that would help land Matzen back in jail. She repeated her previous story and added a few specific details. Matzen had said, on the way to Jackson Circle, that "he had a job to do for Rick, and he wanted to wait for Donna." Lying in wait, Buchanan knew, was a special circumstance of murder that could get Matzen the maximum penalty, if they could nail him with some more evidence.

Matzen had attacked Donna as soon as she entered the house, Gloria said, striking her with the bar and yelling, "This one's for Rick!" As he struck, again and again, he kept saying, "The rest are for me and for her [Gloria]." Matzen disclosed to Gloria that he had hit Donna 25 to 30 times. Donna had started pleading with him and whimpering. Matzen checked for a pulse, and figuring that Donna was dead, he ransacked the master bedroom before he left to make it look like a burglary. Gloria described how Matzen had adjusted the white watch "which had a bold face" to 1:00, then stepped on it, breaking the crystal, to "throw the police off."

As Gloria Lynn spoke, Buchanan formed an opinion that grew stronger by the minute. Gloria knew too many details. The detective was convinced that she had been in the house during the murder, and maybe even struck some of the blows herself.

"Why did Rick Connaty want Donna dead?" Buchanan asked.

"He wanted her out of the way so he could keep the house and the kids."

"Why would Neill do it?"

"To help Rick," Gloria shrugged. Then she added that Matzen may also have been planning to blackmail Rick Connaty. If so, Buchanan realized, that might explain Connaty's attempt to kill Matzen in the fatal gunfight.

"What was Neill wearing when he did the murder?" Buchanan asked, thinking that if he could recover clothing with the victim's bloodstains on it, he would have the needed evidence.

"He was wearing blue work pants and a flannel shirt," Gloria said. The clothes had probably been buried somewhere in the desert, but his shoes were thrown out on the way down there. She described the area to the detective.

Following Gloria's directions, Buchanan and a team of volunteers drove nearly 100 miles into the Mojave Desert. Miraculously, after hours of searching in the December chill, they found the beat-up sports shoes, which Gloria verified were Matzen's. Unfortunately, there were no usable bloodstains on them that could place Matzen at the murder scene.

While Buchanan kept searching for the evidence he needed, Neill Matzen disappeared. No one had any idea where he was, until he finally made a fatal move.

Sixteen days before Christmas, Detective Buchanan received an unexpected present. It was a letter dated December 7, 1990, at 11:00 p.m. from Neill Matzen:

"I sent a full confession to the newspaper and told them to print it compleaty [sic]. It is the truth and fact. Information only known to myself and Rick Connaty as God is my witness and on my death bed. See because by the time you get this note I will also be dead and you and [Gloria] and the newspaper will all find out together what the real truth is and also that I am dead."

A quick check with the *Orange County Register* revealed that Matzen had, indeed, sent them a letter of confession, four pages long, containing many more details than the one Buchanan received. In it, Matzen wrote, "These are the facts known only to me and a dead man, and by the time you get this letter, I will also be dead, out in Chiriaco Summit, 30 miles east of Indio."

The remote site, east of Palm Springs, was in the barren Orocopia Mountains, where General George S. Patton trained his army for desert warfare.

Matzen, describing in the letter how he had met Rick Connaty, wrote, ". . . then one day he and [Gloria] decided to have an affair together. It lasted 14 months." Connaty wanted to do away with Donna, Matzen noted, and would pay $15,000 for the job. He had caught Connaty and his wife making love in Rick's truck, but he sneaked away before they knew it. Matzen thought that Donna and Rick were going to be reconciled, and wrote, "He was getting her back and at the same time rolling around with [Gloria]. When I thought of this, I got madder and madder."

The amazing document continued, describing the circumstances leading up to the murder. "He [Connaty] also told me where the pipe was gonna be and then told me to open the hall closet. The floor has a trapdoor. Throw the pipe down there. The cops won't think of looking there. Besides, you won't get out of the house with it. And then make the place a little messy to look like a burglary."

Several passages in the letter were clearly designed to exonerate Gloria. Matzen ended by writing, "This letter contains only the truth and facts and open for full print, so that the truth will finally be known."

Gloria Lynn also received a letter from Matzen, addressed to "My Dearest . . ." and containing the words, "Yes, I killed Donna." Matzen included a will and an apology to his child, along with a comment that his body could be found in a canyon hut they had visited the previous New Year's Eve. Gloria turned the letter over to Detective Buchanan.

Now the sleuth and the D.A. had the corroborating evidence they needed, but the suspect was missing, perhaps lying dead in the dusty hills around Chiriaco Summit. Gloria Lynn gave them directions to the remote canyon where she and Matzen had sometimes camped. Buchanan led a team of searchers to the makeshift, rocky lean-to. There, they found notes that the couple had left a long time ago, but Neill Matzen was nowhere to be found. If he had committed suicide, his body was somewhere else.

But Matzen had not committed suicide, and if he had not made one more major error, he might have successfully vanished "into thin air." In Fontana, near San Bernardino, he lived for a week in a storm drain, then in a decrepit shack, filthy, hungry, and desperate. Finding some discarded copper, he tried to sell it in a scrap metal shop. The proprietor recognized him from newspaper photos, and called the police. Matzen was arrested and returned to Buena Park on December 14th, almost three weeks after Donna Connaty's murder.

Deputy D.A. Pat Donahue, an ex-marine, military history buff, and one of the top prosecutors in Orange County, had faced public misunderstanding 10 days earlier when he announced to the press that the suspect in the killing of Donna Connaty had been released. In February 1992, Donahue, who had prosecuted 22 murder trials, was happy to present the state's charges against Neill Matzen. He had the confession letters as the backbone of his case. Gloria Lynn asked for immunity in exchange for her testimony against Matzen, but Donahue suspected, as Detective Buchanan had, that she was more involved in the crime than she admitted. He refused to offer a deal of immunity. But he managed to let the jury hear her words anyway. Buchanan's interviews with the woman had been taped, and they were played in court.

The defense, as presented by Deputy Public Defender David Biggs, made even more explicit accusations against Gloria Lynn. Biggs focused his case on the proposition that Gloria had actually perpetrated the murder. "She had the best motive for killing Donna," Biggs argued, "because she was having an affair with Richard Connaty and was furious when she thought that Rick and Donna might reconcile their marriage." Matzen had written the confession letters, Biggs said, just to protect Gloria.

Prosecutor Donahue agreed that Gloria was a participant, but pointed to Matzen as the person who mercilessly battered the life out of Donna with a steel rod.

Gloria Lynn took the stand, but with the aid of her lawyer, she refused to answer any questions. Matzen did not testify.

After three weeks of evidence and testimony, the jury came back on February 24, 1992, finding Matzen guilty of first-degree murder. They also agreed with Donahue that the special circumstances of lying in wait and murder for financial gain applied to Matzen's crime. That made him eligible for a sentence of life in prison without the possibility of parole.

On April Fool's Day 1992, Superior Court Judge David O. Carter called the case a "bizarre and twisted tale" as he pronounced the sentence of life in prison with no parole. Carter looked sternly at Matzen and said, "With all likelihood, sir, you will die in state prison."

Officially, the case against Gloria Lynn is still under

investigation.

EDITOR'S NOTE:
Vince Peterson and Gloria Lynn are not the real names of the persons so named in the foregoing story. Fictitious names have been used because there is no reason for public interest in the identities of these persons.

"A LAWSUIT GOT HIM SHOT IN THE FACE!"

by Bruce Gibney

The black sedan with no license plates crept along Gascony Road, a tree-lined street in the beach town of Encinitas, California. It was 8:00 p.m. on September 17, 1988.

"Is that it?" the driver asked, pointing to a house nestled behind two palm trees.

"I can't see the number," said the man in the passenger seat.

They pulled to the curb and killed the lights.

Both men looked at the pretty, beach-style home set back from the street.

"No that isn't it," the driver said.

He pulled away from the curb. As they continued south, the driver said, "I'll be glad when this is over."

The passenger watched the scenery go by. "Before it's over, we first have to find the house," he said.

On the next block, the driver pulled in front of another beach-style home. The passenger looked at the address painted on the curb and checked it against the one he carried in a spiral notebook. It was the right house.

The two men parked and got out. Looking both ways, they crossed the street and went up the front walk. The driver tried the screen door. It was locked. He knocked loudly. A pretty, middle-aged woman came to the door.

"Is Sal here?" the driver asked.

The woman disappeared into the house, leaving the late-night visitors on the front steps. They heard talk inside and a heavyset man with gray hair came to the door.

"Sal?"

"Yes," the man said.

The man who carried the notebook stepped forward. With no expression, he whipped out a pistol from inside his jacket and fired four times.

Sal screamed once and fell backwards into the hallway.

The two men hurried back to their car. They retraced their route along Gascony Road back to the freeway. Maintaining the speed limit, the driver weaved into the center lane, careful to avoid any quick turns that might arouse the attention or suspicion of others.

"Jesus! That was loud," the driver said. "My ears are still ringing."

The gunman looked out the window. Dusk had turned to darkness. They had two more stops to make before returning to Los Angeles, and he was starting to get hungry.

San Diego's sheriff's deputies, led by Lieutenant John Tenwold, began arriving at the home on Gascony Road. In the doorway, they found "Sal" Ruscitti, 58, sprawled on his back. He was dead, shot once in the face and twice in the chest. More deputies arrived, followed by Detectives Terry Wisniewski and Mark Parmely.

The victim's wife was stunned and shocked. She told detectives about the two men who had come to the front door and gave their descriptions. The one who asked for her husband by name was Latino, about 30 years old, 5 feet, 5 inches tall, 170 pounds, with collar-length dark hair and a dark bushy mustache. He wore a large belt buckle with a blue stone. The second man, also about 30 years old, was 5-foot-8, of medium build, and with long curly hair tucked under a beige baseball cap.

"I never saw them before," the woman said. "They asked for Sal by name so I thought they knew my husband." She said she called her husband to the door and returned to the family room. She heard gunshots and rushed back to the front door. Her husband was in the doorway, his face half-blown away, and the two men were gone.

It was that fast and that violent. And apparently, that pointless.

Sal Ruscitti was a bighearted guy, lawmen learned, a man's man who was liked by just about everyone. As a kid growing up in West Allis, Wisconsin, he played minor league baseball and hoped one day to follow his hero, Joe DiMaggio, into the big leagues. But at age 17, he joined the Army and trained for the military police. Stationed in Panama after World War II, he learned Spanish and took up boxing, fighting 60 amateur bouts and winning all of them. Sal now had two heroes, Joe DiMaggio and Rocky Marciano.

After being discharged, Sal returned home, only to learn that the Korean War had broken out. He joined the Air Force and was stationed in northern California. Returning to Wisconsin after the war, Sal put a sports career on hold and became a Milwaukee cop.

It was tough duty. On patrol alone, Sal enforced the law unaided except by quick fists and a hard nightstick. He often came home bloody. After a year of walking the beat, he quit for a quieter job. He had taken marketing courses in college, but his first foray into the business disagreed with him.

One night, he told his wife that he wanted to quit marketing and try something different—selling cars. "That sounds crazy, but that is really what I want to do," Sal told her.

His wife said three words: "Go for it."

Sal did go for it—and he never looked back. "It was the best decision I ever made," he declared later.

Over the years, Sal worked for several Milwaukee car agencies and became the top salesman at each. Twice he was promoted to manager's position, but he always went back to sales.

In 1981, tired of Milwaukee and the cold winters, he moved to San Diego County. He went to work for two Ford dealerships in San Diego, moved to a dealership in Pomona, near Los Angeles, then returned to San Diego.

Sal Ruscitti earned a very good living. He owned a house in Encinitas, the beach town north of San Diego. He drove expensive cars and took good care of his family.

Now he was dead—gunned down by two gunmen who had sought him out by name. But why?

Investigators quickly came up with a reason.

In the previous two years, Sal had filed a legal complaint about the amount of commissions he was making at Center City Ford. A company employee later tipped off Sal that that company and another one in Pomona were adding on false charges and that Sal was "getting screwed."

Sal did a little investigating of his own and later went to an attorney. He filed a lawsuit with 300 current and former co-workers alleging that the two dealerships had swindled them out of the full sales commissions they were entitled to. The lawsuit alleged that both dealerships had fraudulently and systematically inflated the dealer invoices on new automobiles, thereby diluting the profit margin.

The lawsuit stunned the elderly couple who owned the San Diego dealership, but outraged their 37-year-old son, Will Nix.

"What the hell is wrong with you, Sal?" Nix had asked Ruscitti after he filed the suit. "If that goddamn thing gets off the ground, you will ruin us."

"You shouldn't have cheated us," Sal had replied.

Nix was part owner with his parents of the dealership in San Diego, and he owned his own agency, Will Nix Ford, in Pomona, 90 miles to the north. Nix had recruited Sal to work for him.

True to form, Sal Ruscitti, police learned, became the top salesman. But the relationship between Nix and Ruscitti soured.

For one thing, Ruscitti didn't much care for Nix, a loud, flashy character who lived in an $850,000 home in the foothills of the nearby San Bernardino mountains and drove a $150,000 red Lamborghini Countach, a car so fast and low that you could drag your knuckles on the pavement at 150 miles per hour.

Nix was also a womanizer, cocaine addict, alcoholic, and high-roller gambler with a $25,000 marker at a Las Vegas casino.

If Sal Ruscitti and the other plaintiffs won the lawsuit, lawmen agreed, that might seriously cut into Nix's high-profile lifestyle.

So Nix had motive—plenty of it—to want Sal Ruscitti dead. Hostilities reached a head when Ruscitti and a friend, who was part of the lawsuit, confronted Nix at one of his dealerships. Nix ordered them off the lot and called Ruscitti a grease ball.

"Will," Ruscitti responded, "you better keep your mouth shut—or I will own this store."

Brimming with anger, Nix yelled, "You are dead meat!"

In February 1988, Sal received the first of several death threats warning him to lay off the case. The last threat came in August. Sal ignored them all, saying, "I'm not letting those bastards scare me."

A month later, Sal Ruscitti was shot to death.

Detectives Wisniewski and Parmely went to Will Nix's dealership and later his home. Nix, however, shrugged and told detectives it was too bad about his former salesman. He referred all other questions to his attorney.

Nix's employees didn't have much to tell sleuths, either. After several months, the case languished.

On December 16, 1989, Dennis Ames called the Milwaukee Police Department and was put through to the detective detail. When a detective came on the line, Ames asked to speak to Sal Ruscitti's relative, a Milwaukee detective.

"You're too late," the detective said. "He's retired. What is this about?"

"It's about his brother, Sal," Ames answered. "I know who killed him."

For almost a year, Ames said, he had carried the awful secret. It had twisted his guts. Now, he had a chance to unload it.

A lieutenant came on the line. "I knew Sal," the lieutenant said. "He was a friend of mine. What do you have?"

After the conversation, the lieutenant called the San Diego Sheriff's Office. They put a tail on Dennis Ames, then later questioned him.

Ames didn't want to talk. It meant giving up his friends. On the other hand, he didn't want to live with his secret any longer.

"It was Nix," Ames told detectives. "He was behind it. It was no secret. He bragged about it."

Dennis Ames had known Nix and his family for almost 30 years. He had watched Nix grow up, and later he worked at Nix's Pomona dealership.

"Will has got troubles," Ames admitted. "Heck, we all do. But you got to draw the line."

Nix had been dating Ames' daughter. Ames thought they were going to get married. So did his daughter. But at the last second, Nix dumped her — and married another girl he had been secretly dating.

Ames didn't like that, but Ames hadn't turned his old pal in because he had dumped his daughter. He had called Milwaukee police because he couldn't live with the horrible realization that a family friend for 30 years was a cold-blooded killer.

"He is reckless," Ames told police of William Nix. "He talked about killing Ruscitti all the time. It was his favorite topic of conversation."

Nix was obsessed with getting rid of Ruscitti. Ames said that Nix had called a meeting at his dealership to plan the whole thing out with the help of other employees. Everyone knew about it but they were afraid to talk. Just like Ames had been, except, perhaps, they did not feel the pain that Ames did.

Ames' statement was hard, solid evidence connecting the lawsuit to Sal Ruscitti's murder. According to Ames, Nix had planned the whole thing in front of witnesses. The trick was getting them to talk.

With the case already a year old and leads getting colder by the minute, investigators went to the U.S. Attorney's Office.

FBI Agents Ed Gaffrey, Russell Baker, and Jake Gregory took over the case. They ran crime checks, traced checks that Will Nix wrote on several accounts, tapped phones, and questioned over 100 witnesses. The story that emerged was shocking.

Whether he was motorcycle riding with his buddies, snorting coke at one of his all-night parties, or off on a Las Vegas gambling junket, Nix couldn't get Sal Ruscitti out of his mind.

Nix, according to FBI information, never had any intentions of killing his former top car salesman himself. The impending lawsuit made him a natural suspect, and he didn't want to get his hands dirty.

But he did want Ruscitti dead. The question was how. In the summer of 1988, Nix put the question to a group of employees he assembled at the Will Nix Ford dealership. The after-hours meeting included a body shop foreman, his girlfriend, and two other employees.

"Sal Ruscitti is suing Will Nix Ford," he told the employees. "If he wins that suit, you could all lose your jobs."

Nix said he didn't want to lay off anyone; in fact, he wanted everyone to be employed and happy. "I have given this some thought," Nix said, according to the one employee. "I see the only way to resolve this problem is to get rid of Sal."

The late-night meeting then took a bizarre turn, as the employees discussed different ways of getting rid of their much-liked former salesman.

One plan was to run him down with an automobile and make it look like an accident. Another was to hire a Las Vegas hit man to do the job. Nix said he knew where to get such a hit man. Unfortunately the hit man was out of action; he had been arrested and was not available.

There were other ideas. None seemed quite right.

Finally, a woman raised her hand. "My boyfriend might help," she offered. "He told me that he has connections with the Mexican Mafia and knows a lot of guys who would kill for money."

The Mexican Mafia was a tough organization—as brutal and nasty as anything dreamed up in Sicily. And according to the girlfriend, the hit men were hired from Mexico, so they would be doubly hard to trace.

"Will was very excited," she told detectives. "He told me to contact my boyfriend at home and instruct him to come to the dealership. I did."

The woman's boyfriend was Paul Gonzalez, 42, a heroin addict and convicted criminal. According to the girlfriend, Gonzalez met with Nix, then later told her, "It looks like I have to take care of a personal matter for Mr. Nix."

On May 10, 1991, FBI agents armed with warrants arrested Will Nix at his hillside home near Pomona. In the bedroom they discovered an Uzi machine gun, equipped with a laser-sighting mechanism that made it an excellent weapon for shooting at night.

In a simultaneous raid, Paul Gonzalez was arrested at his home in the nearby suburb of Rowland Heights. "What the hell is this about?" Gonzalez snapped, as he was put into the back seat of a sheriff's car. He soon found out.

The sheriff's detectives drove to the Nix estate and parked beside a sedan with Nix in the back. The car dealer and would-be hit man saw each other but could not speak as detectives searched the house.

On the trip back to San Diego, the federal officers used the ruse of car trouble to pull into a rest stop. The sheriff's car pulled in behind.

While investigators looked under the hood, Nix was put in the caged sheriff's car with Gonzalez.

"What do they know?" Gonzalez asked nervously.

"Nothing," Nix replied. "Just don't tell them a word."

Unbeknownst to the men, the conversation was secretly being monitored and recorded on tape.

"I don't think I have ever had a case with so many underhanded, sneaky tricks in it," FBI Gaffrey would later tell Prosecutor Larry Burns.

Nix and Gonzalez were booked into the Metropolitan

Correctional Center in San Diego, charged in connection with Sal Ruscitti's murder. Others were also arrested.

The search for a third suspect, 27-year-old Albert Vargas of Los Angeles, continued. He was not at his home when Nix and Gonzalez were arrested, and no one had seen him.

Then, in September 1991, a Los Angeles man named Bill Jones, was arrested for drunk driving and he put police back on the chase.

Bill Jones and Albert Vargas had been high school buddies. Jones hadn't seen Vargas in three years when, on August 24th, he bumped into him by accident. After exchanging handshakes and bearhugs, Jones asked Vargas how he was doing.

"Not so hot," Vargas told him, "The cops are after me. It's a murder thing."

Vargas explained to Jones that in 1988, he went to San Diego with his father-in-law Paul Gonzalez to kill a man. He said his father-in-law was being paid by his boss, a guy named Will Nix, to do the killing.

"I went down there with this wetback," Vargas said, according to Jones. "The wetback did the killing."

Since then, Vargas had been hanging low. "I haven't seen my father-in-law since May," Vargas told his buddy Jones. "He's in county. So is his boss. They're down in San Diego."

Vargas gave his old buddy his new address. He said they should get together, share a few beers, and talk about old times.

That seemed like a good idea. But Jones was now in jail. And it was every man for himself.

Albert Vargas was arrested on September 11, 1991. He gave up peacefully. He was charged in connection with the Ruscitti murder. Like Paul Gonzalez, he was a key player in the execution-style slaying and faced a possible

HIT MEN

life sentence behind bars. In federal prison, there's no such thing as parole; "life" means life.

However, that didn't appeal to Vargas, who figured he had a lot to live for. And Gonzalez wasn't too happy at the bleak prospect either.

In a plea-bargain deal, both men agreed to plead guilty to participating in the Ruscitti murder. In return, the judge could offer leniency—perhaps a sentence of less than 20 years.

It was a stiff jolt. But better than a life term.

Vargas and Gonzalez made detailed confessions and later testified before a federal grand jury. They told a harrowing, frightening story.

Gonzalez was a drug addict. His boss, Will Nix, was also a drug addict—a cocaine abuser. They got along just fine. In the summer of 1988, Gonzalez said Nix called him to the office to say that he had a job for him. "I asked him what the job was," Gonzalez said. "He said a guy was blackmailing him for one hundred thousand dollars, and he wanted to get rid of him."

Gonzalez said he suggested that Nix pay him off, but Nix didn't go for it. "The only way to get rid of the snake is to cut off its head," Nix told him.

That, then was the job—to cut off the snake's head.

But Gonzalez was a shooter of heroin, not people. He didn't want to kill anyone. Still, he knew someone who would.

"There was this guy," Gonzalez told authorities. "He claimed to be a hit man. I went to him and said, 'Here is the deal.' He said, 'Great. I will do it for ten grand.'"

Gonzalez took the offer back to Nix. "Will didn't even blink," Gonzalez said. "He reached into the safe and pulled out ten thousand dollars cash."

Nix said the blackmailer was a guy named Sal and explained that he had to be hit at the Ford dealership where he worked. "Will said it had to be done while he was on vacation," Gonzalez explained. "He said he'd provide a car."

Gonzalez said he put the money in the safe and tried to reach his hit man buddy. "I finally said to hell with it and decided to return the money," Gonzalez said. "I decided I wanted nothing to do with it. I told Vargas what I was planning to do, and he said no way."

Vargas agreed to be the middleman. "He said he would set the whole thing up in return for two thousand dollars. I said all right."

On September 17th, Gonzalez drove to the Los Angeles suburb of Maywood to pick up the hit man and drive him to San Diego. But when Gonzalez arrived, the hit man said he wasn't going to do it. "I was pissed," Gonzalez said. "We had gone through a lot of trouble and now this guy had bugged out."

But it was not a complete loss. The hit man didn't want to do the hit. But he had located a friend nicknamed Tonto, who was interested in the job.

Gonzalez about flipped. Tonto was not like the Lone Ranger's faithful Indian companion. This Tonto was from Mexico, he was a member of the Mexican Mafia, and he was one tough dude.

"We went to Tonto's place," Gonzalez told detectives. "I offered eight thousand dollars for the hit. He said no way, he wanted fifteen thousand dollars. We settled on twelve thousand dollars."

Gonzalez said he called Nix and told him that the hit was on for that evening but would cost an extra $4,000. "Will said no problem. He would have the money ready."

At 4:00 p.m. Saturday, September 17th, Gonzalez, his son-in-law Vargas, and Tonto left Gonzalez's Rowland Heights home, looking for Sal Ruscitti. They went to the car dealership but Sal wasn't there.

Gonzalez called Nix and told him the bad news. "I figured that would be it for today," Gonzalez said. "But Willy Boy was real excited. He said he had just learned Sal was home in Encinitas and said we should do the hit there."

Gonzalez was semi-illiterate and handed the phone to Vargas to write down the directions. That done, they were all set for murder—except Gonzalez, who still had misgivings about it.

"It didn't seem right," he told detectives. "I don't know. Maybe I got cold feet. But Vargas and Tonto were very hot. Vargas said go for it."

Vargas *was* hot for it. As he later explained. "I had a one hundred-dollar-a-day habit. And when you got that big a monkey on your back, you will do a lot of crazy things."

Tonto apparently felt the same way. It was easy money. So after further discussion, Vargas and Tonto agreed to go to the Ruscitti home, with Gonzalez and his son-in-law waiting for them at a rest stop at Aliso Creek.

With Vargas behind the wheel, the hit men continued to Sal Ruscitti's home. They had little trouble finding it. "It was really a very nice place," Vargas recalled.

Going to the front door, Vargas said he rang the doorbell, then asked for Sal by name. When Ruscitti came to the door, Tonto pulled out a 9-mm pistol from his jacket and shot Ruscitti four times.

Gonzalez and Tonto later went to the Will Nix Ford dealership to pick up the rest of the money. Nix was showing off his motorcycle to a circle of friends. When they told him the job was done, they went to the office and Nix pulled out $4,000 in cash from the safe.

"He was real happy," Gonzalez recalled. "We all shook hands and he wished us the best."

Gonzalez drove Tonto to a nearby restaurant. They

shook hands and Tonto walked away from the car toward the restaurant. "That is the last I saw of him," Gonzalez said.

In 1992, Will Nix went on trial before Judge J. Morgan Lester with Larry Burns as prosecutor. Nix adamantly insisted that he was not guilty. Jurors had no difficulty finding him guilty of murder. On August 22, 1992, he was sentenced to life in prison without the possibility of parole. In pronouncing sentence, Judge Lester said, "You will have your last Christmas in prison, your last meal will be there. The last time you ever go to sleep at night will be in prison. You will spend the rest of your natural life in a prison in the state of California."

Nix stared back blankly as if the judge was speaking to somebody else.

Before sentencing, the victim's widow told the defendant, "When you took my husband's life, you took everything from me, including the future. My wish for you is that you feel the same isolation and loneliness that starts and ends all my days and nights."

The one-time high-flying playboy will serve his sentence at Pelican Bay Prison, described as a dismal high-security facility near the Oregon state line, where cells are made of steel instead of concrete and inmates spend 23 hours a day in lockup.

Nix insisted he was innocent, but Judge Lester told him to give it up. "It is unfair for your relatives to believe the fairy tale you have woven," he said. "You know you did it, I know you did it, and the jurors know you did it. Your relatives should be given the truth. That would give you some dignity and honor."

The search continues, meanwhile, for Jose "Tonto" Miranda, who is reportedly hiding in Mexico. A warrant is out for his arrest and a reward has been offered for his return. He must be considered innocent of all crimes until proven guilty in a court of law.

Will Nix once had his philosophy stamped on his license plate, which said, "I want it all." Nix gave away motorcycles and gold jewelry, dressed in $1,000 suits, drove $200,000 cars, snorted a king's ransom worth of cocaine, and gambled with the high rollers at Las Vegas.

"The funny thing is," observed Prosecutor Larry Burns, "he had it all and then he threw it away."

EDITOR'S NOTE:
Dennis Ames and Bill Jones are not the real names of the persons so named in the foregoing story. Fictitious names have been used because there is no reason for public interest in the identities of these persons.

"THE COKE DEALER'S BRUTAL HIT MEN"

by Bill Kelly

Anaheim, CA
January 26, 1990

It certainly was weird the way fate dealt the cards to the Campbell family. One family member, a racing entrepreneur named Mickey Thompson, was shot to death along with his wife, Trudi, in front of their home in Bradbury, California, March 16, 1988. The killer was never caught.

And now, it had been two weeks since Scott Campbell's family had heard from him. Scott had called to say he was taking a business trip to Fargo, North Dakota. The last words he spoke to his family were "call you tomorrow."

But tomorrow never came.

The 27-year-old Scott was busy with his computer business in Anaheim, but, as Scott jokingly told his buddies, "I always call whenever I go out of town because mom is a worrywart."

Enormously concerned when Scott failed to return

their calls, family members called every airline at the Los Angeles Municipal Airport, as well as Long Beach Airport and the John Wayne Airport. In each case, they were told that no one had purchased a ticket under the name of Scott Campbell, heading for North Dakota—or anywhere else for that matter.

Scott's family repeatedly went to his house, peered through the curtained windows, frantically banged on the door and rang the bell. A prophetic silence was their only reply. When their disquietude developed into genuine concern, the police were notified.

A police spokesman said: "We don't have indications that there has been a crime, but due to the circumstances we feel that Scott Campbell could be a victim."

When the police failed to turn up a lead, his family decided to tackle the dilemma themselves. They piled into their car and roamed Orange County, searching for Scott's car.

Their concentrated search of the area took in the parking lot of the John Wayne Airport in Costa Mesa, the parking lots of the L.A. Municipal Airport and adjacent Long Beach Airport. They painstakingly scanned every bus terminal in the vicinity of Orange County and neighboring Los Angeles. They searched under the cape of darkness clear into the glittering neon of the rising sun. There was still no sign of Scott's car.

The sun was high and hot, and a warm wind hooted across Orange County on the third day of their search. Campbell's relatives were cruising Commonwealth Boulevard past the Fullerton Municipal Airport which accommodates only small aircraft. "There!" his mother, Mrs. Campbell screamed. She was pointing to a car angled by the barbed-wire fence surrounding the airport. "There! It's Scott's car!"

She was right. The parking stub wedged beneath the right windshield wiper was dated the day of Scott's disappearance. Additional probing by the family uncovered another bit of startling information—Larry Cowell, whose family were longtime acquaintances of the Campbell's family, had leased a private plane at the airfield the same day of Scott's departure.

It was obvious to Anaheim Police Detective Larry Flynn that the family had every right to be concerned about Scott's mysterious disappearance. He set out to find out what had happened. Flynn took a lengthy statement from Larry Cowell at the Anaheim Police Station. But Cowell steadfastly denied having seen his old school pal on the morning of April 17, 1982. He said it was strictly coincidental that he had leased a plane for a joy ride in the sky, on the very day that Scott's car was ticketed.

Larry Cowell said he often rented planes. He got great pleasure in hovering over Palm Springs, peering down into hotel pools and backyards where sexy, well-shaped females lay sprawled in skimpy bathing suits. If he was lucky enough, he would catch an unsuspecting woman wearing even less. Sprawled out on a towel soaking up the sun, he said.

Flynn checked out his story and discovered that Cowell hadn't gone anywhere near Palm Springs on April 17th.

By this time, the media had been alerted and Scott Campbell's picture graced the front pages of newspapers throughout southern California with the caption: "Have You Seen This Man?" Television stations gave the Campbells ample time to make pleas. Teary-eyed, Mrs. Campbell offered a $5,000 reward for information leading to her son's whereabouts.

It was never collected.

The police were equally concerned. They maintained a 24-hour surveillance on Larry Cowell's movements.

Investigators extended their interviews to anyone who had either professional or casual relations with Scott Campbell. They discovered that he was a citizen of good repute, well liked and so conscientious that he owned his own computer business before his 26th birthday. He was also a fast-talking string-puller who always carried around a wad of money.

This could have provided the perfect motive. Perhaps someone knew that the computer wizard with the pleasing personality carried a sizeable wad and lured him to the airport, snuffed him, then disposed of his body. The evidence against Larry Cowell was weak, but he nevertheless remained a prime suspect.

During the following year, Scott Campbell's name was almost never mentioned in print. To everyone but the Campbells and Detective Flynn, he was a forgotten man. Then some interesting information turned up during the course of an intensified series of interviews involving everyone remotely connected to the alleged victim.

Apparently, Scott Campbell had lied to his parents. He had not flown to North Dakota on computer business. Curiously, he had made arrangements to sell a pound of cocaine to someone.

That someone turned out to be Gregory Fox. Unknown to young Scott Campbell, Fox was an informant for the Federal Drug Enforcement Administration (DEA).

Detective Flynn learned that on the morning of

April 17th, Scott Campbell was carrying about $1,000 in cash on his person, plus a pound of cocaine valued at $34,000. He was a walking setup for trouble.

This information hit Detective Flynn like a fly ball in center field. He quickly called Gregory Fox and asked him to come to California for a powwow with Larry Cowell. Fox would be wearing a hidden microphone and the conversation would be taped. Fox was to say that he was an organized crime member and that he wanted to know where Campbell was because he (Campbell) was carrying around a little black book that contained some pretty big names of corrupt politicians, and the boys on the East Coast were uneasy.

Lawrence Cowell was a hell-raiser and big. He was 36 years old, of medium height, had light hair that knotted down his back and a thick-cropped mustache that curled nearly to his ears. He had come from Parker, Arizona to open up an automobile shop in Anaheim that specialized in expensive sports cars. He monopolized the local industry.

Cowell kept his appointment with Gregory Fox, the undercover agent, who set up a parley in an Anaheim motel, not far from Disneyland. Fox spoke so glibly that Cowell believed him when he said he represented the underworld, and that he was unconcerned with morals or the code of conduct. His soft, cottony voice seemed to lend authority and significance to whatever he had to say. Cowell went for it like a marlin goes for a mullet.

They met. Cowell's story was even too malodorous for a veteran like Fox to swallow. He claimed his pal Donald DiMascio had murdered Scott Campbell over a drug dispute. DiMascio killed Scott, Cowell said, while he piloted the plane.

Fox went on to explain that his underworld cronies were suspicious of outsiders and they were certain that Scott Campbell was dead. He explained to Cowell that if he was lying, gang members would leave him looking like Swiss cheese. Cowell understood. He said he would arrange for Fox to meet with Donald DiMascio. DiMascio would tell him how he had killed Scott Campbell.

A confrontation was arranged. They would meet at a motel off Harbor and Katella, adjacent to Disneyland, the next afternoon.

"You'll like him," Cowell told Fox. "He believes in the maximum use of force and violence to gain his ends."

Gregory Fox was a congenial host to his friends on that windblown afternoon in March. Mike Patterson, an Anaheim detective, accompanied Fox. Patterson posed as a rub-out expert for the mob. Unaware that he was being taped by a hidden microphone, Donald DiMascio yammered on until Fox pinned him down.

"My bosses are anxious," he told the man with the mustache, who calmly lit up a huge stogie and leaned back in his chair.

The following deposition was taken from the court records of the Orange County Courthouse:

First off, Fox and Patterson asked Donald DiMascio (DM) if he had come alone and whether he was armed.

DM: "No everything's cool here."

Fox: "So talk to me. What I got to know is . . ."

DM: "The dude burned me, OK? The dude burned me."

Fox: "Dope Deal?"

DM: "Yeah."

Blowing huge puffs of smoke that looked as though they were snorted by a dragon, DiMascio crossed his chubby legs and looking relaxed, continued to talk calmly.

DM: "The dude burned me twice."

Fox: "On what?"

DM: "Coke. He burned me, so I broke his neck. About two miles past Catalina. I broke his nose . . . and threw him out."

Fox: "Look, we want to make sure this guy is gone."

DM: "Oh, he's gone."

Patterson: "And he won't be washed up anywhere?"

DM: "No. It's been, what? Almost a year now."

DiMascio was trying to impress his underworld hosts with chitchat about how he had handled the murder with the professionalism of a hit man. When they asked him specific details about the death plane, the fat man mistakenly identified it as a two-prop plane.

Patterson interrupted: "We heard one."

DM: "OK, one prop. I'm sorry. Hey, it's been a year, man."

Donald DiMascio continued to explain how Scott Campbell had asked his school chum, Larry Cowell, to fly him to North Dakota. DiMascio decided to go along for the ride. When the single-engine plane took off from the Fullerton Airport, Cowell aimed toward the puffy white clouds 2,000 feet up and out over the Pacific Ocean. It certainly wasn't North Dakota.

Somewhere between the coast and Santa Catalina Island, DiMascio reached over the passenger seat and snapped Campbell's neck.

"It sounded like a twig," he bragged, giving a wringing sign with his hamlike hands.

Before throwing the body out of the plane, DiMascio said he stripped Campbell naked, then punched his nose into a pulpy mess. He did this, he said laughingly, so the body would be ravaged by fish.

"The fishies took care of him," DiMascio assured them.

Screwing his confession deeper into the socket, Donald DiMascio said he got $700 of the $1,700 Campbell had on him, and that Larry Cowell got the rest. Later, he said, he burned Campbell's clothing in his backyard.

Fox: "All right. What did you take off him? I want the truth."

DM: "Just cocaine."

Fox: "Was it good toot?"

DM: "I sold it."

Patterson: "Where did you burn this stuff at? I want to make sure it's rid of."

DM: "Oh, it's been burned a year. Everything was burned ... I don't get nothing. I was paid to do something and I did it."

Fox: "What kind of money did you make?"

DM: "I only got enough to fix my Cadillac, really."

Fox: "Well, who took the coke?"

DM: "... a pound. Larry took half."

Fox: "You thought there was a quarter-million bucks, didn't you? You thought there was some money in that suitcase?"

DM: "I didn't really know. Larry said there might be some cocaine."

Fox: "Or there might be money?"

DM: "There might be money. There was no money. On his personal body, there was seventeen hundred dollars."

Fox: "Did you kill this guy?"

DM: "Yeah." DiMascio went on to explain that he had hit on hard times and he saw the chance to clean the heap up with one grunt.

DM: "I needed the money because I was out of my pad . . . I was living in my car."

Fox: "Did you do pretty good off the cocaine bag?"

DM: "I put four thousand dollars into my Cadillac."

Fox: "You got four thousand dollars for half a pound?"

DM: "No. I tooted a lot of it and partied."

In tones that occasionally betrayed pique and bitterness, DiMascio laid out for his listeners the ruthless and cold-blooded murder of Scott Campbell, stopping here and there to chew on the stub of his cigar, and to spit tobacco juice on the motel carpet.

DM: "Larry told me it might be coke. He wasn't sure. He said he was going to give me five thousand dollars for offing the dude. I come out with maybe eight grand. Four of it went into my Cadillac. I had my Cadillac completely recherried. The car was a gift from my father for staying out of trouble for four years."

Fox: "You been locked up?"

DM: "Yeah, I got a murder beef in the pen . . ."

Patterson: "Do you want some more killings?"

DM: "If the price is right."

Fox: "You did it for five grand, right? We pay our people better than that. And it seems to me like you did a pretty good job."

DM: "I don't mess around . . . I was trained."

Patterson: "You don't mind, ah, killing somebody then?"

HIT MEN

DM: "If it's worth my while. Yeah, I'll go shoot the mother. It don't bother me a bit."

Fox: "You care who it is?"

DM: "Why, you want me to kill Larry?"

Fox: "If you had a debt to settle with Campbell, why did you insist on money from Cowell to kill him?"

DM: "Cause I told him, 'Hey, I'm not gonna kill the dude for free and take a chance that he don't have nothing on him. So I told him to give me five grand."

That struck the chord that signaled the end. Patterson looked across at Fox. "That about wraps it up, wouldn't you say?" he asked the informant. These words were the given signal for the officers listening in the next room to come storming in. Two detectives entered the room, each waving .38-caliber Smith & Wesson revolvers—pistols generally favored by Anaheim cops.

The intrusion stopped Donald DiMascio in midsentence. He jumped up. "Hey, you guys are cops!" he thundered.

"Put your hands on the table," ordered one of the officers. This statement sent DiMascio into paroxysms of bitter mirth. "What the hell is this? Are you guys serious?"

The officer pounced on that. "Right now! Put your hands on the table!" he repeated, while pointing his weapon at DiMascio's head.

"You move and you're history," the second detective blurted.

Essentially, this new information beamed new light on Larry Cowell's part in the murder of his friend, Scott Campbell. The district attorney's office obtained a warrant for his arrest and he cooled his heels for nine months in the Orange County Jail while legal dickering filtered through the system. Finally, Judge James Perez freed him in December of 1983 in lieu of $250,000 bond.

Contending that Cowell did not qualify for bail because he faced charges that could result in a death penalty, District Attorney Thomas Avdeef strongly objected on four separate occasions. In each case, the judge denied D.A. Avdeef's requests that Cowell's bail be revoked, mainly because Cowell's family went to the trouble to scrape up $25,000 non-refundable fee for the bond. So Cowell was set free.

His freedom was short lived. Campbell's family embarked on a hard-driving campaign, collecting almost 8,000 signatures to have Cowell's bail revoked. Under the gun, Judge Perez was forced to reverse his decision. There was pandemonium in the courtroom as 50 Campbell supporters cheered. But the longtime friendship of the Campbells and the Cowells was over.

Housed at the Orange County lockup in Santa Ana, 36-year-old Donald DiMascio was having his own troubles. His family had been unsuccessful in their attempt to raise his $250,000 security bond. The press didn't help either. Angry newspaper columns condemned DiMascio for perpetrating "the most heinous and revolting crime that has ever been committed in the annals of the state."

The trial began in Santa Ana on November 20, 1985, slightly more than three years after Scott Campbell became a victim somewhere near the choppy waters of Santa Catalina Island. The jury selection had taken nearly a month. The jam-packed audience drew a deep breath.

Meanwhile, after a seventh bail hearing, Judge Perez

reversed his reversal. A local scribe said that the judge ". . . changed sides more often than a windshield wiper." Cowell was again freed on $250,000 bail, and was living with his parents in Parker, Arizona.

Cowell's first trial was conducted before Judge Donald A. McCartin without a jury. Defense Attorney Gerald Reopelle maintained that a jury trial would result in a life without-the-possibility-of-parole sentence. They had learned from a pretrial hearing that Judge McCartin didn't think Cowell deserved anything more than the 25-year-to-life sentence, with a possibility of time off for good behavior.

McCartin sentenced Cowell to 25 years to life on January 6, 1986, for first-degree murder, conspiracy and robbery.

Even though Donald DiMascio was billed second in credits, he was much more interesting than Larry Cowell. He was a rough-skinned killer and a throwback to the climate of the depression.

On Wednesday, July 15, 1987, a jury convicted him of murder for financial gain and he was sentenced to life without parole. That sentence was upheld by the Appellate Court. The 4th District Court of Appeals' Santa Ana division reversed Cowell's conviction. The justices maintained that Cowell's confession had been coerced and should not have been used as evidence against him.

At Cowell's second trial, which took place in December 1989, Deputy District Attorney Thomas M. Goethals relied solely on evidence received from the Campbell family's own private investigation into their son's dilemma, Cowell's confession having been ruled inadmissable.

Goethals told the court that it was the Campbells

who had actually discovered that Cowell had rented the plane from the Fullerton Municipal Airport that carried their son to his death over the rushing waters off Santa Catalina Island. And it was the Campbells who had discovered that Cowell got two friends to lie for him about his whereabouts on the day of Scott Campbell's murder. And it was the Campbells who found their son's car at the Fullerton Airport when all other searches had failed.

It took jurors less than seven hours to find Larry Cowell guilty of first-degree murder for the second time. In murder cases, typically five to seven days of deliberations is normal.

On Friday, January 26, 1990, a judge sentenced Lawrence Cowell to 25 years to life for the murder of Scott Campbell, whose body has never been found. Thus ended eight years of trials and court proceedings, which prompted one Campbell family member to say, "That's a long time to go through a funeral every day."

The Campbells remembered that they had appeared before more than a baker's dozen judges in the two killers' pretrial hearings over the years.

The Campbells the led an initiative—which was on the state ballot in 1990—to make California courts operate more like the federal system. The time between arrest and trial is much shorter in Federal Court and defendants are granted fewer pretrial hearings.

"HAVE GUN, WILL MURDER!"

by Howard & Mary Stevens

Munster is a quiet, affluent community in the extreme northwestern part of Indiana, near Lake Michigan. It hadn't had a single homicide in the last decade, but during the first week of November 1989, it had two. The double murder sent shivers and shock waves throughout the usually tranquil town, which is located south of Chicago.

The bloody fingerprints on a chalk-white schoolroom wall and a bloodstained suit coat on the floor of the principal's office at Munster's Elliott Elementary School were the gruesome reminders of the unexpected carnage that had visited the town, claiming the lives of 53-year-old Marsha Levine and her husband, 55-year-old Donald, and of the near-fatal assault on their son.

The Levines were each shot twice, and both died hours later in Community Hospital. The slain couple's son was bludgeoned about the head with a handgun. He survived the vicious attack by running across the street to the school, where he summoned police. A housekeeper, who was in the basement of the sprawling

Levine residence at the time of the slayings, escaped injury but had to be treated for shock at the hospital.

Munster Police Chief William Sudbury figured that Marsha Levine was the first one shot by a bearded gunman who had gained entry into the home by posing as a deliveryman with a package. After shooting Mrs. Levine and pistol-whipping her son, the neatly dressed assailant came upon Donald Levine in a rear bathroom and shot him in the chest. Both victims were shot first in the chest in order to knock them down, and then in the face and head to finish them off, Chief Sudbury surmised.

The terrible violence broke out as Donald and Marsha Levine were getting ready to attend a ceremony in which their son was to be sworn in as an Illinois lawyer. The day began with a mood of anticipation and happiness, observed investigators, but it ended with death and despair. It was a day, friends of the Levines lamented, that would long be remembered in sorrow.

An all-points bulletin described the gunman as a dark-haired, tall white male weighing about 200 pounds and wearing a tan trench coat over a dark suit and white shirt. Police said that a young woman had briefly followed the suspect, who managed to speed away in a late-model vehicle bearing Indiana license plates. The suspect lost his pursuer in the rush-hour traffic, so she was unable to get an accurate license number. Thus, the killer got away.

Detectives said that nothing appeared to have been taken from the Levine home. They acknowledged that they were interested in determining the exact intent of the home invasion. Particularly alarmed by the violent incursion into the Levine residence were the parents of schoolchildren attending the elementary school located directly across the street from the slaying scene.

Chief Sudbury identified Donald Levine as a Chicago mall developer and a recent gold mining speculator. The veteran lawman said that the victim's business interests and commercial activities throughout the area would be looked into as part of the investigation.

In the community of tree-lined streets and large, luxurious lots, Munster's residents did not take very kindly to the brutal, senseless slayings. One influential citizen offered $50,000 for information leading to the arrest and conviction of the couple's killer. The reward was tendered to police on the express condition that its donor remain anonymous.

Investigators reported that the reward offer produced nearly 100 telephone calls and some interesting leads. None of the leads proved fruitful, however.

Three days after the attack, the victims' son was released from the hospital. He had been treated for a painful skull fracture which produced wrenching headaches. He immediately went into seclusion. During his hospital stay, sleuths questioned him for any useful information he might have had.

For the first time, probers disclosed that the killer may have been after Marsha Levine because she was quite active in the business affairs of her husband's companies. "We haven't ruled out the possibility that the wife may have been the original target of the assassin," Chief Sudbury told the press.

Detectives learned that the Levine interest had spread to Arizona and to a gold-mine speculation in Montana. Over the years, the Levines had amassed a considerable personal fortune and it was speculated that Donald

Levine's aggressive business practices may have made him some enemies. The sleuths were convinced that they had not yet uncovered the motive that would solve the homicide puzzle.

Chief Sudbury learned that in 1990, the slain couple had planned to move to Phoenix, where their relatives had operated Levine business interests. The chief acknowledged that detectives were looking closely at all Levine business holdings in Illinois, Arizona, and Montana. Sudbury added that the Levine mining activities in Montana had come under considerable fire from environmentalists, creating some tensions.

Crime lab technicians reported that the package the killer left behind at the crime scene contained several maps and written directions depicting various routes to the Levine home. Officials at the express delivery firm were cooperative in the attempts to trace the origin of the package. A composite drawing of the killer based on the description given by the victims' son was circulated among the news media in hopes that someone had seen the man in the area.

Illinois firearms experts told Munster authorities that they were unable to determine what specific weapon was used in the slayings. They said that the type of ammunition he'd used indicated that the gunman was a professional.

With few clues to pursue, probers appealed to anyone who might have relevant information to come forward. "The slightest clue might provide just the break we need," said one sleuth.

Cooperating in the probe were members of the Lake County Sheriff's Department and special units assigned to the Hammond Police Department. Also assisting were crime lab technicians from the Illinois State Police and investigators attached to the office of Daniel Thomas, the Lake County Coroner.

Detectives were relieved upon determining that there was no connection between the Levine slayings and an earlier burglary reported in the immediate area. They assured residents that the community was quite safe and secure and that they should not be unduly concerned about their personal safety.

Investigators from the coroner's office took additional blood samples from the murder scene and from one of the victim's shoes. They also removed a household iron and ironing pad from the basement for lab analysis.

Friends and neighbors of the slain couple were reinterviewed and a room-by-room search of the ranch-style residence resumed under the personal direction of Coroner Thomas. The coroner reported that he was certain the assailant had used a handgun equipped with shotgun pellets to avoid leaving behind incriminating shell casings.

Teachers at the elementary school across the street from the Levine home said the bloody appearance of the victims' son sent fear and panic throughout the school. The frantic young man, bleeding heavily from the wounds to his head, used a pay telephone at the school to summon help. The interior of the phone booth and the wall near it were spattered with his blood.

One instructor told detectives that the students were extremely upset and agitated when they heard the young man screaming into the telephone. Some emergency equipment was misdirected to the school grounds when it was first thought that the shootings had occurred there. A number of volunteers responding to the emergency call were directly involved since they had children of their own attending that school.

In an attempt to be tidy, one teacher's assistant cleaned up a bloody spot on the classroom floor, thereby destroying blood samples the crime lab technicians might have identified. The principal sought to calm down some excited students by talking to them over the school's public address system, assuring them that they were in no danger.

The mystery package left behind by the killer did not contain a bomb but it did provide valuable leads. A close examination of the package by the county bomb squad revealed two maps and a hair dryer inside. The hair dryer had been used to provide bulk to the package, and on the maps were marked the location of the Levine residence and the various routes to get there.

One map detailed the Chicago metropolitan area; the other pinpointed the Munster region just across the Illinois state line. Officers studied the maps and some hand-drawn markings in hopes that these might lead them to the rental car agency used by the killer.

In the first week of December 1989, Chief Sudbury made an unexpected announcement. He asked the FBI to enter the probe of what he said appeared to be much like a gangland murder. He labeled the slayings "the work of a professional killer, a hired gun on a hit mission." Sudbury added that the November murders had all the earmarks of a business deal gone sour.

Munster's top lawman ruled out narcotics, saying that Donald Levine had no criminal record or any problem with authorities. "He was an upstanding member of the community," Sudbury declared to members of the press.

Business associates of the slain couple told lawmen that the deaths were hard to comprehend. Chicago coworkers at the Loop-located firm, Commercial Retail Specialists, said that Levine founded the firm in 1983. The company was involved in buying land, developing it, and leasing it to retailers. Donald Levine was the company president; his wife helped him operate the business from offices in downtown Chicago.

Chief Sudbury was pleased that the killer made at least one mistake—leaving the package behind. "I hope he makes others," the chief said.

Coroner Thomas agreed with Sudbury's judgment that the murders had been committed by a professional hit man. "The use of special ammunition and the dispatch the killer made of his victims" reinforced the theory.

Investigators believed that Marsha Levine was dressed to go to the office when she was gunned down. Her husband still wore his dressing robe.

In an unusual development, FBI agents declined to comment on a report that hypnosis was used on the woman who had followed the killer's car for several blocks before losing it in heavy traffic. She had identified the license plate as one issued in Indiana.

Early speculation that the hit man may have worn a fake beard was discounted by investigators following extensive interviews with the victims' son and other witnesses who had observed the killer getting into his car and driving away. All agreed the beard was genuine.

An FBI spokesman admitted that the main focus of the probe had shifted to Arizona, where Donald

Levine's relatives operated the western branch of the firm. Agents were looking into the Levine real estate holdings near Pony, Montana, a site of a gold mine owned by the Levine family.

The feds said they were looking closely at reports that hard feelings surfaced when avid environmentalists had been unable to halt the issuance of county permits for the firm to conduct strip mining on the property.

On the day before Christmas 1989, murder charges were filed against an Arizona man suspected to be the hit man who had murdered the Levines. The dramatic announcement was made by Lake County Prosecutor Jon DeGuilio. Named in two murder complaints as the defendant was 46-year-old Bruce McKinney, of Phoenix. Extradition proceedings were begun immediately to return McKinney to Munster, Indiana.

Prosecutor DeGuilio informed the media that McKinney was arrested outside a restaurant a few blocks from his house in northern Phoenix. The subject had lived in Phoenix for several years and worked as a real estate salesman. McKinney was held without bond in the Maricopa County Jail and additional charges of felony murder were filed. The prosecutor said the charges would allow the state to seek the death penalty if McKinney was convicted.

Cooperating in the investigation and arrest of Bruce McKinney were Munster lawmen and Phoenix homicide detectives who, along with undercover officers, had tracked McKinney to Arizona. McKinney had once worked for the Levine real estate firm in Phoenix, Prosecutor DeGuilio added.

Five weeks after McKinney was seized near his Arizona home, he was returned to Lake County to face trial. DeGuilio reported that McKinney had waived his right to a hearing after the Arizona governor signed extradition papers clearing the way for McKinney's return to Indiana.

DeGuilio indicated that his deputies had a lot of questions for the suspect. Among them, why had McKinney used the driver's license of Robert Levine, Donald's brother, to rent a car that neighbors observed outside the Levine residence on the day of the slayings? Neighbors who were shown photographs of the defendant identified him as the man whom they had seen driving away from the murder scene.

Shortly after New Year's 1991, a federal grand jury in Hammond indicted 46-year-old Robert Levine in the murder-for-hire scheme involving his brother and sister-in-law. If convicted, Levine faced life in prison and a $1 million fine for using interstate commerce in connection with the Levines' deaths.

During the second week of March, McKinney pleaded guilty to having murdered Donald Levine, but he insisted that he had broken the law at the "request, urging and direction of the slain man's brother." McKinney had agreed to plead guilty in exchange for having earlier charges dropped, promises of escaping the death penalty, and testifying against the man charged with hiring him to commit the murders.

The prosecutor said McKinney had been charged only with the slaying of Donald Levine. Charges dealing with the murder of Levine's wife and the pistol-whipping of the couple's son would be dismissed, DeGuilio said. He made it clear that his office had discussed the proposed plea-bargain agreement with the victims' son, who had not raised any objections to the terms.

Although the agreement did not mention any specific prison terms, it was assumed that McKinney would be sentenced to at least 30 years and not more than 60 years. Meanwhile, a two-month manhunt to locate Robert Levine ended when Robert Levine surrendered to federal agents in Los Angeles.

Preliminary hearings for the fugitive conducted by U.S. magistrates in California had concluded that Levine might flee if released on bond. No bail was allowed and U.S. marshals transported the defendant to Hammond to stand trial. It was also ruled that Levine was to remain in custody until his trial.

Prosecutor DeGuilio made it clear that it had been necessary to reach an agreement with McKinney in order to secure the successful prosecution of whoever else was involved in the murders. He also indicated that, under the state law, those who initiate, plan and facilitate murder are as culpable as those who have carried out the crime.

In a sworn statement made public as part of the plea agreement, McKinney outlined his part in the slaying of Donald Levine by describing how he had encountered Levine in a hallway after gaining entrance by posing as a delivery man. No mention of the slaying of Marsha Levine was made in the defendant's statement. The assault on the victims' son was not mentioned, either.

The January indictment of Robert Levine for conspiracy alleged that McKinney had flown to Chicago the day before he killed the Munster couple. He admitted that he had used an alias and had managed to slip the murder weapon past all airport security precautions.

Fearing retaliation because of his plea bargain with prosecutors, McKinney asked to be placed in the federal witness protection program. Under certain provisions of the program, he would be allowed to serve his sentence in a federal prison under a different identity.

In June 1991, Robert Levine heard the first testimony from the government's key witness in his conspiracy trial in the U.S. District Court in Hammond. Testifying was Bruce McKinney, who spent most of the first day telling the jury about how he and Levine had planned and carried out the murders of Donald and Marsha Levine in the couple's Munster residence.

Courtroom seats at the sensational trial were regarded as prize possessions and entry to the first row situated near the witness stand was doled out on a first-come, first-served basis. "This is better than TV," one trial veteran commented as she made her way to her coveted seat in the front row.

Some spectators had already made up their minds about the innocence or guilt of the principals. Others looked on as if they were watching a staged drama or a soap opera. Many viewed the proceedings quietly; others had difficulty restraining their impulses to laugh or cry.

A few onlookers had packed lunches in order not to lose the spots they had staked out in the crowded courtroom. Others brought snacks that could be unwrapped quietly and consumed without violating courtroom decorum. Those persons who couldn't squeeze into the courtroom patiently waited outside until a seat became available. Bailiffs regulated traffic in and out of the courtroom in an effort to maintain the dignity of the proceedings.

Federal and state prosecutors charged that Robert Levine had changed his mind several times about how his brother Donald was to be killed.

During opening arguments, Assistant U.S. Attorney Ronald Kurpiers described the defendant as an "asset-rich but cash-poor" millionaire. Kurpiers labeled Robert Levine as a thief and accused him of stealing from the real estate management firm that was owned jointly by members of the family.

McKinney told the court that Donald Levine was killed because he was going to put Robert out of business, particularly in the Arizona operation.

McKinney testified that Robert had talked at some length about his mounting problems with his brother. McKinney told the court that he had heard Robert Levine angrily lash out at his brother on more than one occasion and that Robert had plotted to push Donald out of the business entirely.

McKinney's testimony portrayed Robert Levine as a man who changed his mind at the slightest whim. At one "planning conference" for the crime, McKinney recalled that the defendant told him that he had permission for this act and "you are going to do it."

The confessed hit man told the court that he couldn't believe anyone would have given permission for Donald Levine to be killed and he presumed that the actual decision to do it had come from the mob. "I was frankly taken aback by the information the defendant had given me," he testified.

McKinney said he used Levine's office as a base while he sought work in the Arizona real estate business. At a series of meetings after the subject of murder had been broached, McKinney reported he was told that killing Donald Levine would not be enough because everything would go into a trust for Marsha and that she and her son would control the assets thereafter.

Robert Levine's timetable for murder had slated Donald's son as the first target. McKinney said he went to Ohio to kill him but then backed out of it because he didn't want to do it. He said he had gotten close enough to do it but balked at the last minute. The money for the murder of Donald's son had come from Robert Levine's daughter's college fund, which amounted to a little over $2,000, McKinney recalled.

Calmly describing how he had pistol-whipped the son before entering the Levine home, McKinney said he shot Marsha in the chest. As Donald bolted out of the bathroom, McKinney shot him once in the chest and another time in the head. Asked why he had not shot Donald's son as he ran out of the house, McKinney responded, "I don't know. I really didn't want shoot anybody."

During cross-examination, the defense counsel jumped on McKinney's statement that he had allowed the couple's son to escape the slaying scene.

Rising to the challenge posed by the defense, the federal prosecutor recalled McKinney to the stand and asked him, point-blank, why he hadn't shot the Levines' son as he ran from the house. "I was afraid of hitting schoolchildren playing nearby," McKinney replied.

In an important decision favoring the state and federal prosecutors, U.S. District Judge Rudy Lozano ruled that a former cellmate of Robert Levine's could testify about the 20 or more conversations he had with

Levine while the pair were jailed in the Metropolitan Correctional Center in Los Angeles. Under the magistrate's ruling, the inmate would be able to testify about the frequent chats he had with Robert Levine.

But the ruling was somewhat tempered when the judge recessed the trial, allowing defense counselors time to prepare a strategy against the unexpected witness from the past. Prosecutors maintained that the inmate was privy to many details of the double homicide told to him by the man who had planned the sordid slayings.

The inmate, prosecutors conceded, had his own problems to contend with. He was awaiting trial on charges of bank fraud. The defense also complained that the inmate was not only a snitch but might very well have taken money from other prisoners in exchange for jailhouse legal advice and opinions.

The defense argued that if the inmate acted as a lawyer during his conversation with Levine, information exchanged between them was confidential because of the client-attorney relationship. The magistrate overruled that argument and permitted the inmate to continue his testimony.

Back on the stand, the inmate resumed his account of talks with Robert Levine and how the latter had planned the murders of the Levines. The witness testified that the murder plot had been planned in minute detail.

Before the prosecution closed their case against Robert Levine, a business associate of Donald Levine's testified before the jury that he had heard violent arguments between the brothers on a number of occasions. He also testified that Donald told him that he was convinced his brother was cheating him in many of their business dealings.

One of the most telling bits of testimony introduced was evidence that the murdered couple had planned to send an auditor to Phoenix to review the firm's books on the same day they were slain. Donald's business associate testified it was common knowledge that Robert Levine was fearful that time was running out for him to play a vital role in the Levine business interests.

The prosecution's last witness was the Levines' son, who related details of the murders and told how he had whispered into his mortally wounded father's ear that he loved him.

During cross-examination, the defense asked the son why he had run from the house and had not gone to the aid of his parents. The witness responded that he had not thought clearly at the time of the ordeal. He said he only wanted to get out of the house.

The day after the July 4th holiday, a federal court jury, after deliberating 12 hours, convicted Robert Levine of hiring a man to murder his brother and sister-in-law. The panel returned guilty verdicts on all five counts of using interstate commerce to effect murder-for-hire in connection with the deaths of Donald and Marsha Levine.

U.S. District Judge Lozano ordered the defendant held in jail until he was to be sentenced in the fall. Levine, now 50, faced life in prison without parole.

On October 18, 1991, Robert Levine, onetime partner of his brother, Donald Levine, was sentenced to life in prison for masterminding the slayings of his brother and sister-in-law. Two months later, Bruce McKinney was sentenced to 55 years in prison for the killings. McKinney was spared the death sentence because he had cooperated with the federal government in their prosecution of Robert Levine. He could have received a prison sentence of up to 65 years.

An impassioned plea by Bruce McKinney before Lake County Superior Court Judge James Letsinger fell on deaf ears. McKinney pleaded that a long prison term would be equivalent to a death sentence, because he suffered from a continuing heart complication.

During his court appearance, McKinney read from a prepared statement. He stood at a lectern placed at one end of the courtroom and, at times, his voice could hardly be heard. Dressed in a baggy, dark-blue prison uniform, McKinney suggested that he'd had no choice but to commit the murders because Robert Levine had threatened to kill McKinney's wife and two children if he didn't carry out his role as hit man.

"I regret what I did. I have committed a mortal sin and violated the laws of the state. I apologize," McKinney said.

In a startling admission, McKinney explained that he would have killed the Levines' son if he had attempted to interfere with the slayings. Speaking directly to the slain couple's son, who was seated in the spectator's gallery, the defendant complimented him on his intelligence. "If you had jumped me, you would have been dead," McKinney said.

Earlier, the son had asked the magistrate to mete out a stiff sentence, reminding the court that the impact of the crime had changed his life dramatically. "I know you can't bring back my parents, but you do have the power to give him as much time as possible. I ask that you do that," he pleaded.

Deputy Lake County Prosecutor James Olszewski also sought an extended term for McKinney. He charged that the defendant represented a risk to society because of his "premeditated, calculated and well-thought-out act.

"In his veins runs ice blood," Olszewski declared.

"GANGSTER'S MOLL URGED HIT MAN TO KILL"

by Philip Westwood

Promptly at 9:10 on the morning of Tuesday, November 20, 1990, the guard knocked on the door of the warden's office at Maidstone Jail in the southeastern English county of Kent. That the guard did not wait for the customary invitation to enter told the warden that something was wrong.

"What is it?" the warden asked, looking up from the batch of papers that, up to that moment, had been receiving his complete attention.

"The bus is back," replied the guard. "And Cook's not on it. Nobody's seen him."

The warden shuffled the papers into a neat bundle, opened one of the drawers of his large, leather-topped desk, placed them inside, and closed the drawer. Slowly, he pushed back his chair, stood up, and took a bunch of keys from one of his pockets. An expression of mingled surprise and puzzlement settled onto his face as he selected one of the keys and inserted it into the lock of the drawer he had just closed.

"That's very strange," said the warden, replacing the jangling keys to his pocket. "I never figured on Cook to do a runner. He's due for release soon. You're absolutely sure?"

"Absolutely sure," the guard responded. "We've made a thorough check. There's no sign of him."

"Very well," said the warden. "Alert the police and get me Cook's file." He thought for a moment. "Call in all of the off-duty officers. I think we're going to be in for quite a day."

Inside a half-hour, two detectives had arrived at the jail. They were shown the warden's office and were soon busy taking notes.

"What can you tell us about the missing man?" the detectives asked.

The warden detailed everything contained in Cook's file and a few things that weren't.

The prisoner absent from roll call that morning was 55-year-old Ronald Cook. Cook was a true professional in crime. The opportunistic stickup at a small bank was not for him. Neither was pointing a shotgun at some terrified cashier and handing her scribbled instructions to "fill the bag with money and don't try to press the alarm." That was strictly small time. And whatever else he was, Ronnie Cook was not small time.

Cook had been born and raised in London's East End. As a child, his playground had been the back streets where the only law was that of the local gang boss. Every Friday, the owners of the tiny shops on almost every street corner turned over a part of their week's earnings to the gang's collector. In return, they were allowed to continue in business, free both from the attentions of any neighboring gang planning to extend its sphere of activity and from the attentions of the local gang, who would have destroyed the shop had the payments not been made.

Cook was a tough kid and was soon recruited into the operation of the protection racket. He showed himself to be pretty adept at inflicting violence on anyone who fell foul of his bosses. By the time he had reached his late teens, he was a full-fledged gangster. He began to be noticed by those who ran the criminal underworld.

But Cook had more than mere muscles. He also had brains, a fact that he demonstrated by organizing several sizable heists. Before long, he had branched out on his own, forming his own gang and carrying out a number of well-planned raids. He became one of East London's most notorious gangsters, a position that he maintained throughout his long career.

But as he got older, Cook became careless. The flair to organize and carry out a job was still there, but his ability to cover his tracks after a raid and remain one step ahead of the law began to diminish.

Ten years earlier, Cook planned an armed raid on a security truck. It went well and Cook himself got away with £800,000, or around $1.25 million. But his luck had run out. The police were soon on his trail and he was arrested. In Britain, justice tends to look unkindly on gangsters who use guns. In 1981, Ronnie Cook was sentenced to 16 years in jail. But at least he could console himself knowing that the proceeds of the robbery had not been recovered. All he had to do was behave himself, do his time, and when he got out, he would be on easy street for the rest of his life.

If there was something Ronnie Cook had learned during his long career on the wrong side of the law, it was how to behave himself in jail. He had no intention of doing his full term. Cook had been a model prisoner in every way and had entitled himself to a full remission on his sentence.

"That's why I can't understand why he should choose to disappear," the warden told the detectives. "He was due to be released in a month's time. And he knew that. It's impossible that he would jeopardize everything now."

When asked how it was that Cook came to be out of jail, the warden explained that it was policy to allow prisoners nearing the end of a lengthy sentence to spend short periods of time away from the institution in order to ease them back into society. Of course, they weren't allowed to simply wander the streets. Their periods of freedom had to be spent in the company of people known to the prisoner. In most cases, this meant that the prisoner went home to his family.

"They're allowed out for one day in a week," the warden explained. "Sometimes they're allowed to be away over a weekend. Of course, it is a privilege that is only granted to men who, it is felt, can be trusted."

"And it was felt that Ronnie Cook could be trusted?" a detective asked, with more than a hint of incredulity.

"Yes," the warden replied. "After all, he was being freed after only nine years. He knew that if he failed to return and was caught, he would have to serve out the remainder of his sentence. That's another seven years. And there would probably be additional time that he would have to serve for trying to escape."

The warden went on to explain that Cook had been due to spend his day of freedom with his girlfriend at her apartment in the Plaistow district of East London. Cook's girlfriend had collected him from prison at the appointed time and they had gone off together, arm in arm. Everything had seemed to be perfectly all right.

"Her name's Linda Calvey," the warden responded in answer to the detectives' next question. "I've tried telephoning her apartment, but there's no reply."

The detectives reported their findings to their colleagues of the London Metropolitan force whose area took in the Plaistow district. To them, the name of Linda Calvey was not unknown. In fact, it was known only too well.

Linda Calvey was 43 years old. She came from a good family, but in her teens, she had been lured by the bright lights of the big city. A taste for the good things of life, combined with a natural disinclination toward the dull routine of a "normal" working life, had quickly led her to the seamier side of London and to the shady characters who lived there.

Linda became fascinated by gangsters and their way of life. She became involved with a particularly vicious hoodlum by the name of Michael Calvey. In 1970, when she was 22, Linda and Calvey got married. Theirs was a marriage of big houses, fancy cars, and exotic foreign vacations, all financed by the proceeds of Michael Calvey's criminal career. But all good things come to an end. And, for Linda, the high life with Michael Calvey came to an abrupt halt in 1978 when he was shot dead by armed police during a bank raid that went wrong. It was an event that earned for Linda Calvey the epithet of "Black Widow."

Friends rallied around to comfort Linda in her tragic loss. And one of those friends was Ronnie Cook. Linda was still dressed in black when Cook called on her at home with a couple of bottles of booze and $1,000 in cash. Linda poured out her tears of grief on his shoulder as they stood in the hallway. Linda was still dampening the lapels of Cook's expensively tailored suit as they sat on the sofa and reminisced about the good old days. But Linda had stopped crying by the time they were puffing on a couple of post-coital cigarettes in the bed that, such a short time previously, she had shared with her late—and increasingly unlamented—husband.

Michael Calvey might have hoped, as he gazed down from the great hideout in the sky, that his memory would have lived on in his beloved wife's mind for a little longer than three weeks. But if he did have such a hope, he was in for a bitter disappointment. For in those few short days, his memory was, to Linda, as dead and buried as the rest of him. Three weeks after losing Michael Calvey, Linda moved in with Ronnie Cook.

For the avaricious Linda, life with Cook was infinitely better than it had been with Michael Calvey. Cook was a much bigger gangster than her late husband, and the money that he acquired through his underworld activities enabled them to live like millionaires. But, again, Linda's grasp on rich living was prematurely broken. This time, it lasted only three years, ending with Cook's capture and subsequent 16-year sentence.

Ronnie Cook was, however, a powerful figure in the criminal underworld. Even from his jail cell, he was able to issue orders to his subordinates and to see that those orders were carried out. One of his commands was that his recently acquired lover should be cared for during his enforced absence. He was concerned for Linda's welfare. He was also concerned for the welfare of the £800,000 haul that he had managed to stash away before the police got to him. There was no doubt that, in his own way, Cook loved Linda. But he was not so naive as to think that she would pass the long years sitting quietly by the fireside, dreaming of the day when they could be together again. It was not in her nature. But what worried Cook even more was that Linda knew where the loot was hidden. And money, for Linda, had roughly the same level of attraction as honey for a bee.

Cook assigned Alfie Robertson the task of looking after Linda. Cook had known Robertson for several years and although he couldn't exactly trust him—Ronnie Cook didn't exactly trust anyone—he had always thought of Robertson as being pretty straight, for a crook. Anyhow, Robertson had been in the game long enough to know that if he crossed Cook, he stood a better than even chance of ending up as an integral part of one of the many bridges that span the nation's freeways.

So Linda and Robertson moved in together. It was supposed to be a platonic relationship, and maybe it was. Nobody can say for sure. But what can be said for sure is that Linda took a much closer interest in Robertson's "business" affairs than she had in those of either Calvey or Cook.

Robertson specialized in robbing post offices. His methods were pretty basic—masks, guns, and a lot of shooting and shouting. It was quite old fashioned in its way, but as Robertson modeled himself on men such as John Dillinger and Machine Gun Kelly, this was not really surprising.

Linda insisted on playing an important part in Robertson's operations. Maybe she was tired of just sitting back and enjoying the proceeds of a robbery without having tasted the excitement of the job itself. Perhaps, with her husband and her lover locked away in jail for 16 years, Linda had seen enough of the mess that her partners eventually got themselves into when left to their own devices. But, whatever the reason, Linda decided to get involved herself in the robberies that Robertson undertook. She became his planner, selecting likely targets and plotting each and every move necessary in order to make their unauthorized withdrawals.

But Linda soon discovered that she was no better at the work than Calvey or Cook had been. Robertson got caught after pulling off a job that Linda had played a large part in setting up, and an unsympathetic judge gave him 18 years in jail for armed robbery. That same judge gave Linda five years' jail time for conspiracy to rob.

Linda did her time, and with the remission she earned, she was out in a little under three years. She took the apartment in Plaistow and had lived there ever since. Local police kept a discreet eye on her, if for no other reason than that Linda was, as they described her, a "gangster's moll." There was also the question of the missing money from Cook's last robbery. Police hoped that Linda might, in a careless moment, lead them to it. But Linda was not the careless type, and she never did.

The police, however, couldn't help noticing that Linda seemed to be living well. She was always well dressed; not simply smart, but expensively smart. Occasionally, she was away from the apartment for two, sometimes three weeks at a time. Routine checking uncovered that these absences were because she was on vacation. And she always went abroad to some exotic location. Police found it strange that a woman fresh out of jail and whose only visible means of income was her social security check could live as well as Linda.

So it was against this background that Plaistow detectives called round at Linda Calvey's apartment on the afternoon of November 20th in search of Ronnie Cook. For a long time, they had been looking for a legitimate reason to get inside Linda's apartment, and now they had it.

No one came to the door in response to the officers' constant pressure on the doorbell. But they had foreseen that the place would be empty. That was why, along with a search warrant, they had acquired a set of keys to the apartment.

The detectives were extremely cautious about entering the apartment after they had opened the door with their passkey. They couldn't be too sure of what might be waiting for them inside. Although they were armed—for both Cook and Linda were considered sufficiently dangerous to warrant firearms being issued to the ordinarily unarmed British police officers on the investigation—the detectives had no wish to turn the place into a shooting gallery.

But they needn't have worried. Linda was not at home.

And although Ronnie Cook was in the kitchen, he was in no position to offer any kind of resistance. The top of his head was missing, and most of his brains had been spread across the tiled floor.

Throughout the remainder of that afternoon, the array of experts who made up the crime scene team busied themselves in their various tasks around the apartment. Nobody said very much. They were simply anxious to get on with it, and get out of there. So it wasn't too long before their work was completed. By early evening, several items found in the apartment were bagged and tagged and taken away for forensic examination. What was left of Ronnie Cook was scooped up off the kitchen floor and taken to the morgue.

The pathologist's report was simple and straightforward. Ronnie Cook had received two gunshot wounds. One had smashed into his right elbow, and the other had blown away the top of his head. Both shots had been fired at very close range from a sawed-off shotgun.

Probing an underworld killing is never easy. Innocent witnesses don't want to talk for fear of the consequences, and those directly involved rarely feel intimidated by the atmosphere of a police interrogation room. They know exactly what to say and what not to say. They know exactly how far police officers are allowed to go. When it comes to the law, few people know it better than a professional criminal.

Tracking down Linda Calvey was no problem. Getting her to talk was. She was as tough as old nails, and she knew her rights. "I don't know anything about it," was all that she would tell detectives. "I don't know who did it or why it was done. I wasn't there."

Detectives had their own theories about the killing. They felt that Linda was responsible, though they could only guess at the reason why she wanted Cook out of the way. But, at least, it was an educated guess.

While her lover had been languishing in his prison cell, Linda, the detectives felt, had been playing around. Not only had she been seeing other men—an offense that, in Cook's eyes, would probably have merited him doling out to her a punishment whose effects would be permanent—but she had also been using Cook's stashed haul in order to finance her high living. And that was something that was certain to ensure that she'd be wearing a pair of concrete boots.

The detectives' feelings were reinforced by something that they learned at Maidstone Jail. During a visit by Linda to see Cook some two weeks before his death, the conversation between them took on a rather sinister aspect. A prison officer, noticing that Cook suddenly started to look serious and threatening while Linda, just as suddenly, became quiet and thoughtful, moved forward to try and hear what Cook was saying. He missed most of it, but he did manage to catch Cook saying to Linda, "I'll either be dead by Christmas, or I'll be back in prison serving life for murder."

The remainder of that visit had been passed in virtual silence. Cook stared at Linda, looking as if he were trying to suppress a burning rage within him. Linda looked at the floor, at the walls, at the ceiling—anywhere but the eyes of Ronnie Cook.

The strange behavior between the couple was never repeated. On subsequent visits, Linda appeared bright and carefree and Cook seemed genuinely pleased to see her. They talked, quite openly and audibly, about his impending release and how they would spend their time together when he had gained his freedom.

They had still seemed happy together on the morning that Linda collected Cook from the prison. But detectives were sure that this was all a show to make sure that

Cook's short spell of freedom was not blocked. Each wanted Cook free; Cook himself so that he could get a few things sorted out, and Linda so that she could get Cook sorted out.

Though the officers were long on theories about how Ronnie Cook had met his death, they were short on hard evidence. They needed something they could take before a court, and they weren't going to get it by sitting around and waiting for it to come to them. They had to go out and find it, and there was only one way to do that.

Detectives started visiting the backstreet pubs and bars that were the known haunts of small-time criminals. Such villains were not in the same league as their big-time counterparts, but they studied their activities and followed their fortunes in the hope that they might learn something that would show them the way to the top. It was a forlorn hope, but everyone has dreams.

These men were useful to the detectives who could manipulate them, work them like puppets on a string. Some were informants, selling information on other criminals, sometimes for cash but more usually for favors. Now was the time for those favors to be called in.

The visits to the sleazy bars proved productive. Detectives learned that the word on the street was that Linda had arranged for Cook to be bumped off. She was terrified of him coming out of jail and discovering what she had been doing with his loot, most of which, the word was, had been frittered away by Linda in an orgy of riotous living.

"And that after the way he had looked after her," one informant told detectives, with more than a hint of bitterness.

Pressed further, the informant told detectives that Cook had lavished money and gifts on Linda. He had taken her on vacation to Las Vegas, where they blew $50,000 in just eight days. He had bought her a car, and had insisted that she buy all of her clothes from the most expensive range at a top London department store. "And his real wife couldn't even afford a winter coat," the informant added.

Cook had also taken Linda on vacation to Spain and Greece. It was first class all the way. Whatever Linda wanted, Cook gave her. Money, jewelry—anything she wanted, she could have. Ronnie Cook would provide. When Linda decided to have her breasts enlarged, Cook was there with the $6,000 necessary to cover the cost of the operation. "He gave her everything she wanted and still it wasn't enough," said the informant. "She got greedy and Ronnie wouldn't like that. He wouldn't like it at all. So she had to get him, before he got her."

But Linda was not going to kill Cook herself. For that little task, she had hired the services of a professional hit man.

"And who was this highly skilled assassin who was prepared to rub out one of the top gangsters in London?" detectives wanted to know.

"Danny Reece," they were told. It was a name that several informants subsequently gave the investigating officers.

"Danny Reece?" detectives asked incredulously. If Linda had hired Danny Reece as a contract killer, then she had made one really big mistake.

The name of Danny Reece was well known to London's detectives. But they did not know him as a professional killer. They knew him as a criminal of a very different kind.

The 35-year-old Reece had a string of convictions, mostly for offenses described as of a "minor sexual nature." He fancied himself as something of a ladies' man. Unfortunately, for Reece, the ladies who he fancied didn't fancy him. Reece, however, was slow to get the message, and, some time previously, his illicit groping of unwilling females had gone much too far. One thing led to another, and Danny Reece finished up with a conviction for rape and a few years in prison in which to reconsider the extent of what he saw as his sexual magnetism.

But as well as being a sex offender, Reece was also a great talker. Whenever he was pulled in on suspicion by police officers, they had no trouble closing the case. Reece seemed to have an aversion to the atmosphere of a police station. He became nervous and needed very little persuasion to tell investigators everything they wanted to know. He was rather like one of those crying dolls that little girls have as toys. When he was squeezed, he squealed.

So detectives on the Ronnie Cook case pulled in Danny Reece and subjected him to a little metaphorical squeezing. And, sure enough, he squealed.

"I didn't do it!" Reece screamed, after detectives had pointed out that his chances of survival were so remote as to be almost nonexistent once Cook's former friends and associates got to hear who had carried out the killing. "It was her! Linda! She did it!" Reece continued. He shuddered visibly, before adding, "That woman is evil! And I mean really evil!"

Reece told detectives that Linda had approached him with the offer of a job. She was willing to pay well and he needed the money. Reece was not long out of jail and he had a cash flow problem: No cash was flowing his way. And with no sign of a road out of his financial desert, he was ready to consider anything—even bumping off the powerful and much-feared Ronnie Cook.

Linda set up everything. She even provided the shotgun that Reece was to use. He thought it would be easy. Cook would walk into the apartment and Reece would blow him away. No warning, no long, drawn-out confrontation. Just "bang! bang!" and Reece would be on easy street.

But when Cook entered the apartment Reece lost his nerve. He just stood there, looking at Cook. Cook stared into Reece's eyes. Not once did he look at the shotgun that Reece held in his shaking hands and pointed, more or less, at Cook's chest. Reece wanted to fire, but he couldn't. All the time, Linda was shouting, "Do it! Do it! What are you waiting for? Kill him!"

Eventually, Cook turned away and started to walk toward Linda. At that moment, Reece pressed one of the shotgun's twin triggers. He didn't know why he fired. It was just an instinctive reflex, he said. He was not aiming at Cook. He was not aiming at anything. But the sawed-down barrels of the gun meant that the lead pellets from the cartridge sprayed out over a wide area. Most of them caught Ronnie Cook in the arm.

Cook shouted out in pain as his elbow was smashed by the shot. Reece stood rooted to the spot, terrified by the spectacle in front of him. Linda was still shouting, "Kill him! Go on, finish it! Kill him!"

But Reece couldn't finish it. He couldn't kill Cook. So Linda, realizing that Reece was going to be of no further use, grabbed the shotgun from his trembling hands. "Give it to me," she snapped. "I'll do the job myself."

And she did. "Kneel!" Linda ordered Cook. He didn't have much choice. The agony of his shotgunned elbow had forced him to sink to the floor. When Cook was in a kneeling position, Linda walked around behind him, put the gun close to his head, and fired off the remaining barrel. There was a dull thud when the shotgun discharged. Cook slumped forward as blood and brains spurted across the kitchen.

Linda Calvey still had little to say when police officers brought her in for further questioning. All she would say was "I didn't do it!"

Linda Calvey and Danny Reece were charged with the

murder of Ronnie Cook and faced trial at the Old Bailey in the latter part of 1991. Both pleaded not guilty and neither gave evidence. On Tuesday, November 12, 1991, both were convicted.

"This crime was carried out in the most cold-blooded and ruthless circumstances," the judge, Mr. Justice Hidden, told Calvey and Reece before he sentenced them both to life imprisonment.

So Linda Calvey has swapped the expensive designer clothes of the top London fashion houses for the more down-to-earth blue denim of the British prison system. It may take her a little while to get used to the change. But that should be no problem. She has all the time in the world.

EDITOR'S NOTE:
Alfie Robertson is not the real name of the person so named in the foregoing story. A fictitious name has been used because there is no reason for public interest in the identity of this person.

"GAY LOVERS' LETHAL PLOT AGAINST SUE ELLEN!"

by David Benson

When Bill Curtis arrived at his home on Cottonwood Lane the evening of April 1, 1991, he hung up his coat, set his real estate books down, and mixed himself a drink. It was a little after 7:30, the end of a long day. Curtis' home in remote Dexter Township was far from the rat race of the larger cities, like Ann Arbor and Ypsilanti, in Washtenaw County, Michigan. The pressures of being a real estate agent would melt in Curtis' martini.

Curtis' wife, Sue Ellen, was cooking dinner for him and their guest, Florence Chartreuse, an old family friend whose busy life in another state was making her visits to Michigan less and less frequent.

It was to be an evening of old friends and old times. The three sat in the living room, their drinks on a marble cocktail table. Sue Ellen briefly checked the progress of dinner and rejoined the pair.

Suddenly, a noise came from the kitchen. Florence heard it first.

"Probably just the cat," Sue Ellen said. The Curtis cats did like to knock their ceramic dish against the hard kitchen floor, making a sound much like the thump they'd just heard.

Florence then caught a glimpse of the stranger barreling his way out of the family room down the hall. The intruder was too big to have been a cat.

"Oh, my God! There's someone in your house!" Florence shouted. She started to get up, but the tall intruder's gun made Florence change her mind.

"Give me your cash and jewelry and drop to the floor," the intruder ordered. He wore a stocking mask over his face. Electrical cords dangled from his jacket pockets.

At first no one moved. Cottonwood Lane is where people move to get away from the crime of the cities. Burglars aren't supposed to barge in and demand money from innocent people.

The intruder repeated his command. "Give me your cash and jewelry and drop to the floor!"

With that, Bill, Sue Ellen, and Florence hit the ground. Florence threw her watch onto the carpet. Sue Ellen contributed a diamond ring and Bill tossed a money clip with $50 into the pile.

"That's not enough," the intruder demanded. Florence removed her earrings and necklace and threw them into the pile.

Sue Ellen began to cry. Bill seemed to be regaining his courage. Raising his 53-year-old body off the floor, Bill shouted, "Take what you want and leave!"

The intruder swung his fist and struck Bill Curtis on the jaw. Curtis went down, striking his head on the marble cocktail table and apparently getting knocked unconscious.

"Come with me," the intruder said, motioning to Florence. Florence got up, stepped over Bill and Sue Ellen, but then she paused.

"I'm not going with you," Florence said. "Just get out of this house, right now! Go!"

As she neared the intruder, Florence grabbed hold of one of the electrical cords that had fallen from his jacket and started whipping him with it. Sue Ellen got up, grabbed another cord, and the gunman now found himself outnumbered two to one. He kicked at Sue Ellen and ripped out chunks of Florence's hair.

Florence looked around and saw the exit. Freeing herself from the struggle, she made it down the hallway and through the front door. Florence didn't turn to look, but she thought Sue Ellen was right behind her. Once out the front door, Florence ran across the lawn, over the berm across the street, and toward two houses in the distance. She was greeted by a neighbor on the other side of the street.

"Help! There's a man in the house!" Florence shouted. The neighbor returned to his house, raced to the telephone, and summoned police.

Florence turned around. Sue Ellen wasn't behind her anymore.

When the authorities arrived, Bill Curtis was on the phone with the police. Sue Ellen Curtis lay on the dining room floor. She had been stabbed at least twice. Her throat had been cut. Her face was badly bruised. A neighbor was trying to stop the bleeding.

Medics realized that an ambulance wasn't going to be fast enough. A helicopter was summoned, and Sue Ellen Curtis was airlifted to an Ann Arbor hospital.

Dinner was still cooking in the kitchen.

"Where's the burglar now?" deputies asked.

The neighbor and Florence Chartreuse had both seen someone get into Bill Curtis' burgundy Cadillac and speed off.

With that information, the detectives put out an all-points bulletin for the vehicle. Law enforcement agencies in surrounding counties posted police cars to watch routes leaving the county.

The burglar's escape in the Curtis Cadillac raised a question in investigators' minds. How did the suspect arrive on the scene? Located in a remote rural area, Cottonwood

Lane is a suburb without a city. It's a dead-end street, and the only road it attaches to is a country road that isn't even paved in the area of Cottonwood Lane. It wasn't like a suspect could take the bus. Or a taxi. Or even walk.

One possibility was that the suspect had driven out to the scene in another vehicle. The suspect might have ditched the vehicle some distance from the crime scene and then walked the rest of the way. The suspect might have driven the Curtis' car back to where his own car was, and then switched cars to make his getaway.

Somewhere out in the countryside, police expected to find the Curtis' car or even the suspect's own getaway car. Deputies began running license plates of cars parked on Cottonwood Lane and the surrounding area to check for suspicious vehicles.

The crime scene yielded a few clues. On the kitchen floor lay what would turn out to be the murder weapon: a simple paring knife. It was bloody and broken in two. The tip of its blade had been broken off.

On the porch were Sue Ellen Curtis' glasses and one of the electrical cords. Apparently, Sue Ellen had made it to the porch only to be dragged back inside to be slain. She had missed her freedom by only inches.

While law enforcement agents continued to look for clues, Bill Curtis went to Ann Arbor to be with his wife.

In the meantime, the burglar was about to run out of luck. One deputy, who positioned himself on Interstate 94 near the Wayne County line, noticed Bill Curtis' Cadillac heading east toward Detroit. The burgundy Cadillac took the Rawsonville exit and headed back toward Ypsilanti on Grove Road. The deputy followed and radioed dispatch for backup. The deputy could see that the stolen car was driven by a lone occupant, apparently a white male with long, blond hair. The deputy could not see anyone else in the suspect vehicle.

Whoever the driver was, he seemed to ignore the deputy's

car and piloted the Cadillac as if it were all just a Sunday drive through the country. A backup unit pulled in behind the deputy's car. Now with a reinforcement, the deputy attempted to make the stop. The Cadillac driver sped off. Twisting and turning through the suburban streets, the chase finally ended when the deputy rammed the burgundy car on a street in Ypsilanti.

The blond man bolted out the driver's side door, with the two officers in hot pursuit. Two and a half blocks later, the officers caught up with their quarry.

The young man, now wearing handcuffs, had blood smears on his hands and sweater. Inside his pocket was a ring that belonged to Sue Ellen Curtis. A search of the car yielded a Smith & Wesson .38-caliber revolver and more jewelry that belonged to Sue Ellen and Florence Chartreuse.

Inside the suspect's trousers pocket was a temporary driver's license that identified the owner as Todd William Plamondon, 24, who lived at an address on Bell Street in Ypsilanti.

After being photographed, Plamondon was placed in a squad car and carted off to the Washtenaw County Jail. The next morning, he would be brought before a district judge and charged with a multitude of crimes, including armed robbery, auto theft, breaking into an occupied dwelling and using a firearm in the commission of a felony. And one more charge would be added: first-degree murder. Sue Ellen Curtis was pronounced dead at 9:24 p.m.

Lawmen stayed at the crime scene until late that night. The more they learned about the case, the less they liked it.

One investigator noted that the burglar had struck at 8:00 p.m. "That's not prime time for burglaries," the investigator said. "The house was well lighted so it was obvious that the building was occupied. Generally, burglars like to avoid occupied dwellings."

But a bigger question remained: How had the suspect arrived on the scene? He obviously couldn't have *walked* the 20 miles from his home in Ypsilanti.

Since Todd Plamondon had been captured behind the wheel of the Curtis Cadillac, the question of how he got to their rural home became even more prominent in the detectives' minds. Deputies finished their search for suspicious vehicles without finding even a bicycle out of place. To investigators, the absence of a suspicious vehicle meant only one thing—Plamondon had an accomplice. Somebody had to get him there. Somebody else was involved in this crime.

When Bill Curtis returned home from the hospital, lawmen asked him a few questions. There wasn't much the grieving man could tell them. All he could say was that someone had broken into his house and stabbed his wife. When he had resisted, the intruder had slugged him. On his way down, he had struck his head against the marble table and was knocked out. When he came to, he found his wife in the dining room with her throat cut. She was making gurgling noises. The suspect demanded the keys to his Cadillac. He had never seen the intruder before in his life.

Police decided to focus their investigation on the man sitting in the Washtenaw County Jail. Todd William Plamondon was hardly a stranger to law enforcement agencies. Although he was only 24, he had been compiling a growing list of petty crimes and had a curious way of making the charges against him much worse.

In 1987, for example, he pleaded guilty to assaulting a police officer. He was fined $300 and sentenced to 20 days on a work program. That might have been the end of it, except that he failed to pay his fine and was caught with marijuana during the work program. He was then sentenced to 40 days in jail.

During 1986, Plamondon received two speeding tickets in the city of Ann Arbor. He didn't pay the tickets and the state suspended his driver's license. He didn't get his license restored until March 20, 1991, two weeks before the Curtis murder.

At his arraignment, however, Plamondon faced his most serious charges yet: five felonies, including one first-degree murder charge. Given the severity of the charges, the judge refused to set bond. Although media organizations were pursuing this story, Plamondon's arraignment was soon overshadowed by another story.

The day after Plamondon faced the judge, the home he rented on Bell Street was gutted by fire. Firefighters were calling the blaze suspicious in origin. Within a day, the real cause was released: arson. Law enforcement officials weren't sure what this meant. Since Plamondon had been safely ensconced in jail at the time of the blaze, some wondered if the fire wasn't part of a conspiracy to destroy evidence.

That same day, investigators executed a search warrant on the Curtis Cadillac. There was plenty of paperwork in the backseat, but one form turned out to be of special interest to the officers. The piece of paper asked the postal service for the current address of one Todd Plamondon. Since Plamondon was the man in custody, investigators studied the piece of paper carefully. In nice, neat handwriting, the form listed Plamondon's full name and previous address. It was dated January 1991. Even more intriguing was the name of the person who had filed for the address — William Curtis.

Detectives found it strange that Curtis had denied ever laying eyes on the intruder when the post office had supplied him with the complete address of his wife's murderer only three months earlier.

Police officers also checked the handgun they had found in Plamondon's possession. It was registered to Bill Curtis.

Investigators began to look into Sue Ellen Curtis' background. There was nothing surprising to learn. The 54-year-old woman had worked as a credit supervisor for an Ann Arbor firm. She had been married to Bill Curtis for almost 30 years. No one detectives spoke with ever suggested the couple had any marital problems. But in interviewing Sue Ellen's co-workers, detectives learned another odd aspect about the case. At quitting time on Thursday, a mere four days before her murder, Sue Ellen and some friends had left work only to discover a man in the backseat of her car.

When confronted, the young man had said he'd taken refuge in her car because some people were chasing him. He then fled the area. After driving home, Sue Ellen thought maybe the young man had been involved in a robbery. She decided to check under the backseat. There, she found a butcher knife, eight inches long.

From photographs, the co-workers were able to identify the young man in the backseat of the victim's car as Todd Plamondon. In the meantime, other detectives were questioning Plamondon's friends to learn more about the young suspect.

"I don't understand why the police say he broke into the house, because they were friends," one Plamondon acquaintance said.

Friends? What would Bill Curtis, a 53-year-old successful real-estate agent with a nice home in the country, want with a 24-year-old punk who lived in a slum?

As police interviewed more of Plamondon's friends, the answer quickly came out. Bill Curtis was paying Todd Plamondon for sex.

It wasn't that the younger man was a homosexual. Plamondon had a girlfriend and had fathered children. But he had a taste for several illicit drugs, and selling his body to Bill Curtis was the only way he could feed his crack habit.

Police also discovered a bar in Ypsilanti where Plamondon and a mysterious older man were regularly seen together. Barkeepers told sleuths that the pair would arrive separately, within five minutes of each other. They would have a few beers together and maybe a meal. The older man always paid. The two men first appeared in the bar in early January. They met on five or six Friday afternoons until at least late February. When the bartenders were shown photographs of Bill Curtis, they instantly recognized him as Plamondon's meal ticket.

Not far from the bar was an adult book store with X-rated movie booths. Bill Curtis was a familiar sight there, the manager remembered. Curtis would show up two or three times a week, collect his quarters, and watch his movies.

Policemen remembered that on the night of Sue Ellen's murder, Curtis had played the role of the grieving husband. When medics arrived, he was still on the telephone, pleading for help for his stricken wife. As medics worked on her, witnesses had seen Curtis go to the living room, drop to his knees, and recite the Lord's Prayer.

But two days following the murder, it was clear that Bill Curtis wasn't all that he appeared to be. Curtis was invited to come into the police station for an interview. Investigators had hoped to put their knowledge of Bill Curtis' relationship with Todd Plamondon to good use. With any luck, their tidbits of information could be used to knock Curtis off guard, perhaps even to make him confess.

Although Curtis agreed to be interviewed, investigators never got to use their strategy to its full effect. The story had attracted the interest of several media outlets in Ann Arbor, Ypsilanti, and Detroit, and at least two media organizations had discovered the Curtis-Plamondon connection on their own. One of them even approached Curtis for a comment. "That's none of your business," was his response.

But when he arrived at the police station, Curtis had had time to amend his story.

Still, early in the interview, Curtis denied he knew or recognized the armed intruder. "Do you know why he used our house?" he asked in a quiet voice. "We moved to the country because we thought we could be safe."

During the same interview, Curtis admitted that the intruder's voice was familiar but, he said, not immediately recognizable. After investigators asked about Todd Plamondon by name, Curtis once said he had hired him to paint his master bedroom. His last contact with Plamondon was December 1990.

"I tried to be kind to him," Curtis told the officers. "I don't know why he would do that to us."

In later interviews, Curtis denied, then admitted, that he had a homosexual relationship with Plamondon. He also eventually admitted that he had given Plamondon money to buy crack cocaine.

In May, police investigating the arson fire that had consumed Plamondon's house developed a suspect. The story surfaced that some of Plamondon's acquaintances had decided to take advantage of his absence. At least three cohorts had arrived at the house with three 40-ounce cases of beer. They cooked some chicken that they found in Plamondon's refrigerator and watched television until the early-morning hours.

One of those present that evening told police that another cohort, a male, walked a woman home and returned to the house very angry. Apparently, he had been in a fight with another male. Angry, he started vandalizing Plamondon's apartment and set it ablaze. The individual was charged with arson and later sentenced to a prison term. The fire, apparently, had nothing to do with the Curtis murder.

After several delays, the wheels of justice began to turn on Todd Plamondon. On June 5th, a preliminary examination was held to determine whether enough evidence existed to require Plamondon to stand trial for the murder of Sue Ellen Curtis.

The pathologist who performed the autopsy on the victim testified. He said that the fatal stab wound had first penetrated the center of Sue Ellen's chest, then cut into some of the right lung and the right side of the heart. Another wound lay between two ribs by the heart and the left lung. The second wound had caused substantial bleeding and might have been a threat to life, although that wound had not caused the victim's death. Another stab wound had gone through the trachea. In addition, there were numerous bruises on the victim's hands, upper face, and head.

Florence Chartreuse told her story of the night of the murder. Then it was Bill Curtis' turn.

Testifying for the prosecution, Curtis said he had known Plamondon for eight months, and that the younger man had even been to the Curtis household twice. Once was in December to paint the master bedroom. Curtis didn't remember the second time. On the stand, Curtis admitted that he had paid Plamondon for sex and that Plamondon had used the proceeds to buy drugs.

Bill Curtis said under oath that he saw Plamondon as late as 5:00 on the evening of the murder. Curtis said he took the young man to buy drugs but then dropped him off in Ypsilanti. When Plamondon broke into the house three hours later, Curtis instantly recognized him by his voice and stature.

Curtis testified that he had been knocked out when he struck his head against the marble cocktail table, but under cross-examination he later admitted that he had been faking. He dared not move, he said, because he was afraid for his life.

Plamondon's attorney attempted to argue that it was just as likely that Bill Curtis had slain his wife as had the intruder. The attorney pointed out that there were no eyewitnesses to the stabbing. He claimed that had Plamondon truly cut Sue Ellen's throat, there would have been more blood on his clothing than what the authorities found.

The judge swept aside the defense attorney's arguments and ordered the defendant to stand trial on charges of felony murder, using a firearm in the commission of a felony, breaking and entering, armed robbery and auto theft. Todd Plamondon was one step closer to spending the rest of his life in prison.

The next day, Bill Curtis showed up at an RV dealership north of Ann Arbor, bought himself a 1973 Winnebago motor home, and drove away. He told everyone that he was going on vacation out of state to get away from his troubles. He took with him a young male traveling companion. There was nothing to stop him. Since Bill Curtis had not been formally charged with anything, he was under no legal obligation to stay. Curtis' attorney said that his client was suffering from depression.

Investigators, however, had been working to prove a case against the real estate salesman. And they knew that the easiest way to do that would be to offer Plamondon a plea bargain. Investigators and prosecutors hoped to be able to incriminate Bill Curtis without the help of the young street hustler, but after a couple of months, the prosecution abandoned that goal.

Plamondon's defense attorneys and the prosecution came up with a deal. In exchange for truthful testimony against Bill Curtis and for a plea of guilty to second-degree murder, the other charges against Plamondon would be dropped.

On August 30th, William Curtis was accused in a nine-count warrant of hiring his homosexual lover to murder his wife. The other counts alleged that he had planned the fatal robbery. A federal fugitive warrant was sought for his arrest.

The real estate agent's life on the run came to an end in early September after a disagreement with his traveling companion. Curtis abandoned his companion in a rest room at a campground 40 miles north of Roanoke, Virginia. The companion notified police.

Police discovered Curtis' motor home at a Roanoke motel at about 4:00 a.m. on September 3rd. A check of the register showed that Curtis had checked in under an alias. Curtis, however, wasn't in his room. Police knocked on his motor home and received no answer, but they heard movement inside. Afraid that Curtis might take his own life, police lobbed tear gas into the mobile home and captured Curtis as he tried to escape the vehicle.

Curtis was eventually on his way back to Michigan. On October 7th, Plamondon entered his guilty plea before a circuit judge.

Curtis' return posed a problem for law enforcement agents who did not want the real estate agent to have any contact with his former associate. Plamondon was moved from the Washtenaw County Jail to the Livingston County Jail in Howell, 25 miles north of Ann Arbor.

Plamondon apparently didn't like his new surroundings. Three days after he pleaded guilty to murder, Plamondon and another inmate escaped. The two men were part of a group being returned to their cells from a religious service at about 8:00 p.m. Guards suspected that the pair separated from the group and ran up a catwalk used only by guards. From there, they broke out a window eight feet off the floor, climbed out onto the roof, and left. The jail is not surrounded by a fence.

Troopers and deputies from two counties fanned out over the countryside in search of the two escapees. They questioned their friends to find out where the two might have headed.

Police soon learned that the other inmate had an accomplice on the outside. By tailing the accomplice, police discovered a wooded area 10 miles west of Howell where the two escapees were hiding out. They waited until the accomplice attempted to drive away with the escapees. Once the pickup left the wooded area, police quickly surrounded it and arrested all three individuals.

Todd Plamondon's freedom had lasted less than 11

hours. One officer speculated that had Plamondon made good his escape or had he been killed in a shootout, the case against Bill Curtis would have been significantly hampered.

Plamondon's version of the truth would come out at a hearing on December 11th.

Plamondon related that he had met Bill Curtis two or three years earlier through a jogging buddy. For awhile, Curtis, Plamondon, and the jogging buddy were a trio, but eventually the jogging buddy faded away.

The young man said that he had been to the Curtis home several times. On a couple of occasions he had sex with the older man for varying amounts of money. At Plamondon's invitation, Curtis and Plamondon met at a bar in Ypsilanti one afternoon in February 1991. During the get-together, the two men went to the restroom. Curtis started pumping Plamondon about his criminal history. Plamondon told him about his troubles with the law and asked Curtis why he was so interested. Curtis replied that he wanted his wife dead. With Sue Ellen out of the way, Curtis could inherit stocks, bonds, and insurance money. He and Plamondon could go travel the country. Eventually Curtis offered Plamondon $5,000 to kill Sue Ellen. Between February and April, Curtis and Plamondon had 10 conversations discussing how and when to kill Sue Ellen.

During the last week of March, Curtis drove Plamondon to Sue Ellen's place of work. Curtis had already supplied Plamondon with a straight razor and keys to Sue Ellen's automobile. Plamondon said he was surprised to see that the keys to Sue Ellen's car actually worked. He briefly considered simply stealing the car and driving away. Once inside, however, he hid in the backseat. When Sue Ellen found him and asked what he was doing, he made up a story about people chasing him. He then fled, leaving the knife behind, and hitchhiked his way home. He later gave the razor to a friend.

When Curtis found out that his wife was still among the living, he became very angry and told Plamondon that he had failed to do what he was supposed to do.

On April 1st, Plamondon met with Bill Curtis again. Curtis said that he and his wife were going to have a house guest, Florence Chartreuse. She would provide excellent cover for the murder plot, Curtis said, because her presence would prove that Curtis had nothing to do with the murder.

To stage the armed robbery, Curtis gave Plamondon his fully loaded gun and a knife, which was to be used to cut the phone lines. Curtis also supplied Plamondon with electrical wire for tying up the three "victims," and a stocking mask to wear over his face.

Two and a half hours before the murder, Bill Curtis and Plamondon met at a bar in Chelsea and drank five or six beers each. Very little discussion was given to the upcoming project. At 6:45 p.m., the two men drove to the Curtis home.

Once they arrived, Curtis got out of the car and told Plamondon to wait 15 or 20 minutes before staging the armed robbery. Plamondon smoked crack cocaine to pass the time away. When the waiting time expired, he donned the stocking mask, put the electrical cord in his jacket, went through the garage door, and entered the house through the back. The door was unlocked, as Curtis had prearranged. Curtis had also arranged for Plamondon to strike at him, so he could pretend he was knocked out. Plamondon's fist never struck Curtis; the older man simply pretended to fall.

Plamondon denied that his goal was to kill Sue Ellen Curtis. He claimed all he wanted was the loot to buy drugs.

The first hitch was the scuffle with Florence Chartreuse. The plan had called for Plamondon to take the women to different bedrooms and tie them up, but Chartreuse had found a cord on the floor and started beating him with it. Sue Ellen joined in the fight. Bill Curtis, in the meantime, lay on the floor, pretending to be unconscious.

After Chartreuse broke away, Plamondon and Sue Ellen continued to struggle. Plamondon portrayed it almost as an accident, but Sue Ellen was stabbed once and fell to the floor. He swore the knife was intact when he left and that he had no idea how it ended up broken.

Plamondon then collected the loot. Curtis sat up. Plamondon said he wanted to leave. Curtis gave him the keys to the burgundy Cadillac, and Plamondon fled the scene.

On January 10, 1992, Todd Plamondon appeared in court for his sentencing hearing. When the judge asked if he had anything to say, he replied, "I'd just like to say I'm sorry for any part that I had in my wrongdoings and any part that drugs played in my life."

The judge scanned the defendant's pre-sentencing report. "The report described you as predatory, meaning that it appears that much of your adult life has been preying upon—or as you put, 'scamming'—other people to facilitate your way of life," the judge said. "That you would be willing to do that to the level of this crime is scary, terrifying to people who are sitting in their homes like Mrs. Curtis, who was minding her own business."

Todd Plamondon was sentenced to life in prison. There was the possibility for parole, but Plamondon's troubles with the law weren't over yet. In July, a Livingston County judge added two to four years to Plamondon's sentence on a felony escape charge for his role in the jailbreak. The sentence was to be consecutive to the life sentence in Washtenaw County. Once again, however, the young street hustler had demonstrated his talent for compounding his legal woes.

Bill Curtis' trial began on May 19, 1992. The prosecution put Florence Chartreuse on the stand once again to tell the horrifying story of the events of the murder night. Plamondon took the witness stand to recite his tale of murder-for-hire.

On the second day, the prosecution played tape-recorded interviews between Curtis and the police. The jury heard Curtis change his story to police officers several times.

The defense countered by portraying Todd Plamondon as an experienced criminal who was peddling a tale to get a lighter sentence.

On the third day of the trial, Bill Curtis took the stand in his own defense. Curtis said that he had been molested at age 11. Although he repeatedly tried to live a heterosexual life, he turned to homosexuality at age 34 and began meeting street hustlers in Ypsilanti. Sue Ellen never knew about his secret life, Curtis said.

He admitted to having sex with Plamondon once or twice a week for seven or eight weeks. Curtis often did the younger man's laundry, fed him, and lent him small sums of money: $20, $40, or $50, sometimes several times a week. Curtis even drove Plamondon to places where the younger man could buy drugs. The loans were never repaid, and Plamondon's demands for money kept increasing.

Three weeks before the murder, Curtis testified, Plamondon suggested that Curtis get a divorce so the two of them could travel together. The real estate agent rejected that idea in no uncertain terms, and a week or so later, the young street hustler began making threats.

According to the defendant, Plamondon demanded that Curtis pay him $5,000, or he would reveal Curtis' sexual inclinations to his wife and his employer. Curtis suggested that Plamondon stage a robbery to collect the money. Afraid, Curtis began storing his handgun in his glove compartment. Ironically, he said, he purchased the gun to protect Sue Ellen.

On the day of the slaying, Curtis said, he went to Plamondon's house to break off their relationship. Instead, he gave the younger man $40 to buy drugs and then drove him to the bar in Chelsea. There, he gave Plamondon another

$20 to buy food, then he went to an appointment.

When Curtis returned, Plamondon was so high on drugs that he made a scene at the bar. When the two men left, Plamondon pulled the gun from the glove compartment and ordered Curtis to drive to the home where Sue Ellen and their guest were waiting, unsuspecting.

Once there, Plamondon commanded Curtis to go inside, leaving the door unlocked, and not tell anyone what was about to happen. Curtis said he didn't immediately call the police because Plamondon had threatened to kill him if he did. Curtis said he hoped Plamondon would stage his robbery, take the money he demanded, and then go away. The death of Sue Ellen, Curtis said, wasn't in the bargain.

On the witness stand, Curtis admitted that he had lied to police officers while under oath. He said he'd lied to hide his sexual orientation and because he was afraid his family would abandon him.

The prosecutor compared Bill Curtis to a "master actor." He pointed out that Curtis had changed his story nine times. The prosecutor put people who worked at the Chelsea bar on the stand. They claimed that Plamondon had acted normally on the day of the murder and did not make a scene the way Curtis insisted.

The jury took some pity on Curtis and acquitted him of the first-degree murder charge. One jury member said the prosecution had not met its burden of proof. But their mercy stopped there. They convicted him on all remaining counts, including felony murder, and two counts each of armed robbery, conspiracy to commit armed robbery, and the use of a firearm in the commission of a felony.

In accordance with state sentencing guidelines, Curtis was ordered to spend the rest of his life in prison without the possibility of parole.

Both William Curtis and Todd Plamondon have appealed their convictions. The State Court of Appeals has yet to make its ruling on their appeals.

EDITOR'S NOTE:
Florence Chartreuse is not the real name of the person so named in the foregoing story. A fictitious name has been used because there is no reason for public interest in the identity of this person.

"LETHAL COUPLE ... 3 KNIVES ... 1 COLD CORPSE!"

by Olga Kogan

Most people in big cities don't realize that they might come into contact with a murderer in the course of their daily lives. Killers, after all, don't wear signs advertising their crimes. Maybe the stubble-faced panhandler on the street corner is actually one of the FBI's most wanted fugitives, or maybe the oddly dressed man muttering obscenities to himself on the commuter platform is really a psychotic obsessed with death.

The chilling fact remains, however, that most killers don't look much different from anyone else—and that works to their advantage, as lawmen have found out time and time again.

The fact hit home for one Indiana state trooper on the evening of April 23, 1988, while he was patrolling Interstate 65, south of Hammond, Indiana. It was a Saturday night, a shift when all officers are just a bit more wary of the people they meet.

It was getting dark when the trooper spotted a pickup truck with Indiana plates parked by the roadside. The truck lights were flashing, so the trooper thought someone might be in need of help. He decided to stop.

There didn't seem to be anyone in the truck as he drew

near it in his cruiser. Even when he got out of his own car, it seemed no one was around to acknowledge his arrival.

It was only when he approached the vehicle that he heard someone coming from the adjacent woods. As the person drew up, the trooper could see that it was a woman in her 30s, with dark hair cut fairly short, and with hard, rather masculine features.

She moved without acknowledging the lawman's presence and swung open the truck cab door as unconcernedly as if she was completely alone. Although irked by the apparent slight to him, the trooper nevertheless asked the woman in a civil tone whether anything was the matter.

The woman turned toward him and shook her head. She just had to stop for a minute to relieve herself, she explained.

The heavy smell of alcohol on the woman's breath told the trooper why she'd needed to stop.

As he stepped closer to her, he could also see that her head was bobbing and her eyes were having trouble focussing. This was a probable DWI if ever he saw one.

At his request, the woman got out of the truck again. Behind her on the cab seat, the trooper suddenly made out another person, a man lying on his side, his head rocking slowly from right to left. Apparently, the woman was one of those who didn't drink alone.

Both the man and the woman admitted they'd been knocking back a few — a few too many, from the trooper's point of view. How they had gotten this far on the highway without any incident was beyond the lawman's comprehension, but in good conscience he could not permit them to take to the road again.

When told that she and her friend could not immediately continue on their trip, the woman's expression suddenly became alert. When the officer asked the couple to get into his cruiser while he routinely filed a report and checked out their vehicle's license number, the woman turned frantic.

The officer tried to calm the woman down, saying it was all routine procedure and there would be no criminal record against them. But nothing he said could stop the torrent of excuses flowing from the woman's mouth. She acted almost as though he was booking her for murder.

Since the pair did not seem to be hardened felons, the officer had the option to be indulgent. It was, after all, Saturday night.

The officer took out the portable breathalyzer kit from his cruiser. If the couple cooperated, he would see what he could do for them.

The man and woman both agreed to take the test. But it was no contest. Both failed miserably. The woman's alcohol level was three times the state legal limit — and she was the one who had wanted to drive!

The look on the trooper's face told the woman everything she feared, and she broke into another series of sob stories: She'd lose her job if she was arrested, her family would abandon her, her friends would shun her.

In the end, the trooper decided that he could fulfill both his duty and indulge the citizen's feelings by driving the couple to the nearest roadside cafe where they could get some black coffee into their systems and sober up in safety. He waved the two into his cruiser.

A short time later, the man and woman muttered their thanks to the lawman and waved goodbye as they staggered into the truck-stop restaurant. Both of them had solemnly promised not to try driving again until their heads had cleared.

The trooper went back to patrolling the Interstate and put the incident with the two drunks behind him. Had he known the dark secret of the couple who'd sat so demurely in his cruiser, he would not have been so complacent.

The nickel dropped about two hours later, around midnight. That's when the Lowell State Police relayed an all-points bulletin for a black pickup truck whose occupants were wanted in connection with a murder that had occurred in Hammond early that same morning.

The state trooper lost no time transmitting back to headquarters a report about his encounter earlier that evening. At the same time, he backtracked to the truck stop in the faint hope that the drunken man and woman would still be there. Of course they were not. Restaurant employees couldn't recall exactly when they had left, but it had been some time ago, they said.

It was a different story, however, with the couple's truck. Another state trooper—acting on the APB—had found it where it had been left by the roadside. Nothing had been touched. Even the emergency lights were still blinking. The trooper ordered a tow truck to bring the pickup in as possible evidence.

The truck's license and registration identified it as belonging to a Leonard Fowler, a 46-year-old auto worker who lived in Hammond. A relative of his had last seen the vehicle parked by his house on Golf Way Avenue when she left for work that morning.

The pickup was gone when she returned in the afternoon. This in itself was not disturbing. However, the tiny blood-like spatters on the driveway were something else. There were about 20 of them grouped in a cluster at one edge of the concrete near the spot where the relative had last seen the pickup parked.

More sun-dried blood spots dotted the walk up to the back door. They acted like tentacles, drawing the relative past the screen door, into the hallway, and through each room in turn.

The bedroom was where the trail ended. The relative let out a scream at the sight there, then somehow found her legs and stumbled outside and into her car. She needed to get to a phone fast. The house phone was out of the question: there was no way on earth that she could have remained in that house a moment longer.

Her call from a nearby restaurant phone brought immediate police action. Both uniformed and plainclothes officers arrived at the ordinary, one-story Fowler residence before the relative made it back there. Two Hammond detectives, Richard Grant and Hershal Byrd, entered the home to investigate the incident.

Prepared for the worst, it was hard for even the lawmen to keep their composure when they got to the bedroom. A man was lying on the floor near the bed. There was so much blood encircling him that at first it looked like some huge blade had been drawn the length of his body. Ruddy streaks and blotches crisscrossed the furniture, walls, and ceiling in a gruesome, bloody pattern.

One lawman pointed to the bindings around the victim's legs. An electrical cord was enmeshed with what looked like a pair of suspenders. The victim's pants had been pulled down as well, perhaps as another means to prevent him from running. Through the blood encrusted on the trouser's seat, the detectives noticed that one of the back pockets had been crudely cut away.

On the floor lay a butcher knife with a strangely irregular edge. Looking more closely, the sleuths saw that the large blade had been snapped off. They could only imagine the savagery with which the knife had been wielded. The killer had used such force that the knife's steel blade had broken against the victim's flesh.

The two detectives touched nothing but awaited the arrival of three crime lab technicians who would process the crime scene according to procedure. While waiting, the two sleuths came across another chilling piece of evidence in the living room—a hunting knife with its blade curled back on itself. Blood covered it from tip to handle.

It wasn't until evening when the crime technicians finally put away their cameras and evidence kits and permitted the victim's body to be removed to the Lake County Coroner's Office for an autopsy. No one who observed the crime scene could ever recall seeing such nightmarish gore.

As distraught as she was, the relative who had reported the crime was able to compose herself enough to answer detectives' questions. Lawmen could only admire her strength of will under such duress. Her story was telling.

It began in the early hours of that morning, she explained. She had been awakened by sounds coming from the kitchen—as a relative, she had her own room in the Fowler house—and she decided to see what the matter was. Perhaps a mouse was loose.

When she entered the kitchen, she saw a figure standing with its back turned in the half-opened door leading outside. She recognized the figure as Leonard Fowler's lady friend. The woman was peering into the night darkness as though expecting extraterrestrials to appear. She gave a little jump as the relative's voice broke the eerie quiet. Was anything wrong?

The woman in the doorway shook her head and told the relative to go back to bed. The relative did so, her worry calmed by the presence of someone from the household in the kitchen.

Now, as she recounted the incident to detectives, the relative had a disquieting feeling that the nighttime encounter in the kitchen might have had some connection with Leonard Fowler's gruesome death—especially since his lady friend was nowhere around.

Detectives agreed. During their search of the house, they had discovered that the woman's clothes were missing from drawers and closets. It didn't look good. Just who was this lady friend of the victim's? they wanted to know.

The relative said the lady friend's name was Cindy Lou Landress. She didn't know all that much about her other than that she was originally a hometown girl who'd left for California several years earlier and returned to Indiana just a few months back. With no job and no place to live, she had it tough; but then Cindy met Leonard Fowler. He took her into his home and eventually into his bed, not a surprising move given that he was unattached. In fact, the last time Fowler's relative saw him alive, he was still in bed with Cindy Landress.

Landress immediately took on prime-suspect status, but what, detectives wondered, could have been her motive in the crime? And could a woman commit such savagery against a man who'd taken her into his home and offered her his tender loving kindness?

Savagery was no exaggeration. The autopsy on the victim's body showed he'd been cut in more than 20 places from his head on down to his chest, groin, and limbs. Three separate blades had left their marks—the butcher knife, the buck knife, and another knife that was not found.

As for motive, lawmen learned that Friday was payday for the workers at the auto plant in Chicago where Fowler was employed. His two-week wages amounted to more than $1,000, and he liked to take the whole bunch home in cold, hard cash—no banks for Leonard Fowler.

Assuming it was a murder-robbery, had Cindy Landress acted alone? That question arose when the victim's relative mentioned to lawmen that Landress had been making time not only with Fowler, but with another man in town as well. But it was no easy task for sleuths this time—the witness knew neither the man's name nor his address.

That was the story up until the moment late that Saturday evening when police issued their APB for a black Ford pickup driven by a 30-year-old brunette woman who was most likely in the company of an unknown male. As lawmen learned too late, the couple had already had one brush with a state trooper and had managed to slither away again into the night. Wherever they were, they apparently were without their vehicle.

One indication of where the pair might be heading came from an indirect source in an unexpected place—the kitchen of Leonard Fowler's house. Sleuths found some old telephone bills tacked to the wall with charges for some long-distance calls to California. Since Cindy Landress was known to have resided there until fairly recently, it was a good bet that the calls were made to people she'd met and was still in contact with.

Further checks on Cindy Landress' background revealed she was no Pollyanna. Besides a federal court conviction for mail theft 10 years earlier, sleuths found out Landress was in the habit of changing her name as often as the weather—a common ploy used by snakes in the grass.

Meanwhile, news of the Fowler murder hit local news desks in time to make the Sunday papers. One of those whose eye fell on the murder's headline was a former lawman. It was more than just professional habit that led him to read the report again and then call the homicide office. He had a story to tell.

The story began early Saturday morning, he related—several hours before Leonard Fowler's murder. An acquaintance had stopped by asking whether he could spend the night. It looked like the man had been on a heavy binge, so the ex-lawman waved him inside and offered him the couch.

Later that morning, around breakfast time, the acquaintance asked another favor—a lift to a place nearby where he was supposed to meet his girl. The former officer said sure, and he drove the man to a corner on Golf Way Avenue. What struck the ex-lawman later was the fact that he left the man just one block from the murder house and within one hour of the time of the Fowler murder.

He gave the man's name as Bill Lewellen.

Detectives quickly punched up an address for William Lewellen—as well as a conviction for drug possession 12 years earlier—and then took a drive over to his residence. There they were directed to another address where a relative of Lewellen's lived.

Puzzled by the lawmen's visit but cooperative, the relative said she'd last seen Lewellen the previous Friday night when he'd come over with his girlfriend. Asked the lady's name, the witness replied, "Cindy."

With the investigative pot cooking, the relative now added more fuel to the fire. Lewellen and Cindy had asked her to give them a lift to Golf Way Avenue at around midnight. Flippant and cocky, the pair had joked during the entire trip, at one point pulling out knives and boasting about the things they planned to do with the blades that night.

Leonard Fowler's date with death had to be postponed for several hours, however, when the murderous couple discovered a second party present in his house. Tired and drunk, Lewellen apparently decided to crash at his friend's place for the night to await a better opportunity to strike in the morning. Landress, meanwhile, nonchalantly crawled into Leonard Fowler's bed as though all was right in the world. Conceivably, she might have even taken her buck knife with her under the covers.

Detectives put calls through to the California phone numbers listed on Fowler's telephone bill. As they suspected, the numbers belonged to friends of Cindy Landress'. In recent conversations, Landress had talked about growing homesick for California and mentioned the possibility of moving back to San Diego soon.

In short order, photos and descriptions of both Cindy Landress and William Lewellen were in the hands of San Diego detectives. The couple was described as armed and dangerous and wanted in connection with murder, vehicle theft, and interstate flight.

Meanwhile, no trace of the fugitives turned up in Indiana or any other midwestern state. To anyone looking at them, the wanted pair might be just any other couple in a coffee shop.

To Officer Tom Wagner of the San Diego Police Department, however, the Indiana couple was like a bull's-eye to a marksman. With their descriptions entrenched in his memory, he stalked the streets where friends of Cindy Landress' said she liked to hang out. There were no guarantees of a payoff for this kind of work, just an outside chance that one or both of them might show up.

Two weeks after the Fowler murder, the suspects surfaced in San Diego. They were ambling like tourists among the pedestrians on University Avenue when they decided to go into a bar where Officer Wagner spotted them. A smart plainclothes lawman, Wagner called for backup before approaching the fugitives.

The uniformed officer who soon arrived was backup and a half. Brandishing the king of shotguns in both hands, he marched into the bar with Wagner and pointed 12 gauges at the head of Bill Lewellen, who was nonchalantly sipping a rum and coke. The suspect put his glass down slow and easy when he found himself staring down the barrels of the shotgun.

News of the arrest brought Indiana detectives to San Diego. Their California colleagues said the fugitives had been just about broke when they were taken into custody. Their combined assets hadn't totaled more than 60 bucks. That was a far cry from the $1,000 in cash they allegedly took from Leonard Fowler just two weeks before.

According to Bill Lewellen, they dropped the first 50 dollars on a ride with a trucker out of the roadside cafe where the Indiana trooper had brought them to sober up. That was the first of many trucker payoffs they made on a trip through three states. It turned out to be a trip that brought them two days later right back to Indiana.

Desperate to get out of the state, they upped the ante to the truckers and finally made it to some Rocky Mountain states, then further west to California. Food and booze cut deeply into their loot along the way.

By the time Lewellen got through telling about their truck run to California, he was ready to sing the whole tragic opera. He gave the starring role to Cindy Landress, a vixen who put fear into his own heart.

Murdering Leonard Fowler for his wad of cash was her idea, Lewellen warbled. At first, all Cindy suggested was rolling the man a little, something Lewellen was prepared to do. On the Friday night before the murder, the two of them knocked off a case of beer as they got psychologically ready for the evening's work ahead.

When they discovered Fowler was not alone in his house, they agreed to postpone their caper for a few hours until the coast was clear. Later, on Saturday morning, Lewellen returned to the house, getting a lift from the ex-lawman who'd kindly allowed him to crash at his place for the night.

Lewellen brazenly knocked on Fowler's door. Fowler himself let him inside — he had no suspicion that he was bidding good morning to his own murderer.

While Fowler busied himself with his domestic chores, Lewellen and Landress plotted their moves. Landress was the brains and the pusher, Lewellen said. At one point he started getting cold feet about the whole thing, but Landress would hear nothing of the kind. When she taunted him about his lack of courage, Lewellen flared. A few beers bolstered his fortitude.

Leonard Fowler was seated at his kitchen table, drinking a second cup of morning coffee, when Lewellen pressed his knife into the victim's back. Together they marched into the bedroom, where Cindy brought cords to tie the victim up.

It was at that instant that Cindy Landress lost control. She was holding a butcher knife in her hand, and all of a sudden she plunged it into the defenseless man's flesh. One thrust followed another. Even when the blade snapped, she hadn't had enough. Cindy took a second knife and went at the man some more. The blood was everywhere. Lewellen considered telling Cindy to stop, but "I was afraid for myself."

Cindy's last act was to cut the back pocket from the victim's trousers in order to free the wallet inserted there.

Then they fled. Fowler's van was in the driveway. They threw Cindy's clothes into the back and sped off. Some blood from a cut on Cindy's hand left the trail along the driveway that was spotted later by the victim's relative as she returned home.

It took them two weeks and just about every cent they'd stolen from the Indiana auto worker to get to the Pacific Coast.

In May 1989, Cindy Landress entered the courtroom of Judge Richard Conroy in Lake County Superior Court, Crown Point, Indiana. Over the four days of the trial, she denied all of the accusations leveled against her by William Lewellen. Lewellen had been the instigator,

Cindy testified, and Lewellen had finally wielded the knife.

But it was a hard sell, and the jury didn't buy it. Jury members pronounced Cindy Landress guilty as charged. On May 19th, she was made a candidate for the electric chair.

One month later, on June 26th, William Lewellen was sentenced to 60 years in prison after pleading guilty as an accessory to murder.

The question remains: How many more Cindy Landresses and William Lewellens are out there sipping drinks in coffee shops among an unsuspecting public?

"WHERE THERE'S A WILL, THERE'S A MURDER!"

by Jayne Schorn

**Port Washington, N.Y.
March 29, 1983**

Forty-seven-year-old Mary Bowen was a woman with strong, sharp, angular facial features. She was slim and carried her body in a stiff, erect manner. Some might say that she had a severe look. Her hair was short and fluffed in a beauty parlor-type setting. She had worked in four states—New York, California, Florida and Nevada—as a waitress/barmaid for a total of 20 some odd years when she decided to come back home to Long Island, New York. It was in 1979 that she began working at a yacht club in Port Washington as a cocktail waitress.

Port Washington, Long Island, is a quiet suburban town, located some 30 miles east of New York City. Tree-lined streets, residential areas with large homes, rambling lawns and gardens that are neat and well kept, characterize this community as the upper-middle-class area that it is. Residents of Port Washington are generally hardworking people who have gotten where they are by the sweat of their own brow. Crime is something they won't tolerate. That's why these residents are willing to pay the extra tax dollars to have their own private police force patrolling the area. The crime rate in this area is quite low, since at any one time as many as three police forces—The Port Washington Police, The Nassau County Police and The New York State Police—are cruising the town.

The yacht club that Mary Bowen began working for is one of the most exclusive clubs on all of Long Island. It is a sprawling brick mansion of the Victorian era, set well back from the road, with numerous tennis and squash courts at its front and Manhasset Bay's breathtaking view from the back. Many yachts moor in Manhasset Bay and the sound of the multitude of ropes on the masts make a pleasing cacophony of noise for the yacht owners as they, drink in hand, watch their boats and those of others coming in and going out.

Everything was going well for Mary Bowen, until she began to burden the yacht club members with her numerous personal problems. The club members did not like it and became even more incensed when Mary pushed them into purchasing various glass figurines while they were in the club's lounge area. The members came to the club to relax and socialize a bit, to escape from the demands of life; they did not come to be solicited and pressured into buying items they did not want. As a result, after repeated warnings, Mary Bowen was fired from the club's employ in 1981.

Soon after Miss Bowen was dismissed, a friend she met at the club, Sylvia Gerard, asked her if she would be interested in a home-health care position. The friend remembered Miss Bowen mentioning that she had once worked with elderly people at a state hospital and thought the position ideal for Mary. Ms. Gerard knew of someone who was in need of such home-health care, a semi-invalid and recluse who was convalescing from a hip operation and used both an aluminum walker and a wheelchair to get around.

Sometime in April, Mary Bowen took this position after insisting that her $325 weekly wage be paid to her off the books. The invalid employer, Mildred Cotter, an extremely law abiding citizen, did not like this idea and refused at first, but she finally relented after learning that professional nurses received between $500 and $600 for their weekly duties. Mildred Cotter figured she was getting a bargain.

Eighty-two-year-old Mildred Cotter was a childless widow. She had been alone since the death of her husband, a New York City homicide lieutenant, in 1960. Her only child had died, many years earlier, not long after birth. Mildred's gray hair was clipped short about her small head, her frame slight, her demeanor mild. She maintained a solitary existence in her later years, rarely leaving her garden apartment, where she had lived since 1963, and ordering food delivered from local groceries.

Soundview Gardens, where Mildred lived, is a garden apartment complex with a multitude of unattached two-story squat brick buildings that are occupied by mostly small familes and older people. Cement paths interconnect one building with the next. It is a neat, quiet complex, situated in downtown Port Washington, away from the town's major thoroughfares.

The only time neighbors ever saw Mildred Cotter was on her infrequent and difficult trips to her mailbox. The widow had no living family, save a distant cousin with whom she was not close. She had few friends and the only person to visit her was her paid health care aides. Indeed, it had become a practice of Mrs. Cotter in her later years to hire these aides. She was one of our "luckier" senior citizens, being able to afford the luxury of personalized care and daily companionship.

The duties of Mildred's aide were basically to be her

friend, to care for her as friends do, talk with her, lightly clean, cook and do laundry, as well as, of course, take care of finances, as Mary Bowen inevitably did.

To repay these kindnesses, Mildred Cotter not only paid Bowen a handsome wage, but after two weeks, put Mary in her will as sole heir to an estate estimated at around $38,000. Possibly, this was an inducement on Mildred Cotter's part to instill loyalty in her employee, to ensure that her helper stayed, or simply to secure quality care.

Months passed and the two women seemed to have worked out an amicable situation. Quiet days were passed in the garden apartment. Mildred Cotter had someone to look after her and care for her. Likewise, Mary Bowen had a job—and a good one at that—one that didn't demand much but rewarded her in an emotional sense in that she was making someone feel a little happier.

On Saturday, October 18, 1981, at 4:30 p.m., Mary Bowen stepped out of Mildred Cotter's apartment 10D, closed the door behind her and locked it with her duplicate key. She had just finished another day of work.

As is the practice of most older people, Mildred retired early that evening. She took off her vividly flowered housecoat and draped it over the aluminum walker beside her bed, before laying her head down upon her green and white striped pillow. Mildred slept until approximately 12:30 when she was violently awakened by two black men who burst into her bedroom and pounced upon her 85-pound frame. She was punched with dark fists repeatedly in the chest until every rib in her body was broken, torn and fragmented, but she did not die. Frustrated, the 185-pound man on top of her wrapped his meaty hands around her frail neck and began to strangle her. Mildred Cotter still hung on until, in desperation, the man picked up a white sports sock that was knotted at the center and wrapped it tightly about her neck. He twisted it viciously and held it firm until Mildred finally stopped breathing.

Reporting for work, on Sunday, October 19, 1981, at 9:30 a.m., Mary Bowen slid her key into the lock of apartment 10D and shortly thereafter discovered the dead body of her employer. At 9:36 a.m. the phone rang at the Port Washington Police Department. It was Mary Bowen calling to report a murder . . .

The Port Washington, Nassau County Police and a representative from the D.A.'s office speedily arrived. The crime scene unit was the first to enter the apartment to photograph the scene. These first pictures taken before the arrival of additional personnel usually prove to be quite valuable. Crime scene photos are a representation and preservation of the scene at the time the incident is reported, prior to a more detailed examination undertaken and before any items are moved or touched the photographer, using a Polaroid, moved around the apartment taking several general view shots at eye level in a clockwise direction. He began at the perimeter and worked towards the victim's body. The photos of the body included a general and a close-up view with at least two full body shots from either side. They were taken before the body was moved. As the photographer went outside to shoot various angles of the apartment house and its surroundings, the crime squad moved in.

The job of the crime squad was to dust for fingerprints. Det. Robert Dempsey of the Nassau County Police Homicide Squad coordinated the efforts of the investigators. He suggested a search method that is the most practical in these cases—one in which you begin at the point where the body is first discovered and work in an outward direction, until the entire room has been covered. The search began with an examination for latent fingerprints. Points of entry and exit, door handles, telephones, windows, glasses, light switches and many more items were dusted.

Detective Dempsey began to examine the body, first noting a complete description of the clothing's position, condition, damage and stains. He then began to examine the body itself, starting with the head and carefully working down to the legs.

Outside of the bustling crime scene apartment, other detectives were busy questioning neighbors of the widow. Every door was knocked on and neighbors downstairs and across the hall said the same things: They hadn't seen or heard anything and Mrs. Cotter was a recluse whom they rarely saw. "She was very frail," said one neighbor. "We seldom ever saw her." Most residents seemed shocked that a murder had occurred in what was a very safe place to live. Another neighbor summed it up saying, "We haven't had any robberies—not even any stolen cars. Nothing."

At 12:00, Detective Robert Dempsey and Assistant District Attorney Edward McCarty questioned Mary Bowen who was the last person to see Mrs. Cotter alive at 4:30 the previous afternoon. She had an airtight alibi for her whereabouts the night before. She was visibly distressed, after all, it was she who had discovered the corpse of her employer and friend, lying on the floor next to the bed, naked from the waist down, blood on the striped pillow. She had seen the deep vertical gouges around the neck, the tongue protruding swollen and thick from the mouth, the face riddled with patches of purple and red. Who wouldn't be upset at such a ghastly sight?

There was no sign of forced entry to the second-story garden apartment, which had a steel front door and strong locks. A bedroom window, however, was open with the screen bent and jutting outwards. Was this the point of entry that the murderers had taken?

The apartment had been ransacked and an unknown quantity of money and valuable property had been taken, officials reported after interviewing Mary Bowen.

The experts on the scene worked diligently amid the mess and it was soon after their arrival that Dempsey and McCarty turned to one another. Seasoned investigators, they simultaneously spoke each other's thoughts: "This doesn't smell like a burglary," they commented. To a layman, it would appear to be so—tables turned over, drawers pulled out and the contents scattered about, clothing and articles haphazardly strewn on the floor of the small apartment. But these investigators *sensed* something awry. Their instincts told them that what appeared to be a burglary was not. On close examination they saw that a table in the dining room was turned on its side, but a vase sitting previously atop the table had been placed neatly on the carpeted floor. This vase should have realistically been broken with the overturned table, but it wasn't . . . it was upright, unmarred on the floor. Why? In the bedroom, clothing was put on the floor in tidy bunches, as it had come from the drawer, folded and in order. In the living room an ashtray and various artifacts were put on the floor prior to the table's upheaval. A fragile tea tray was on its side unbroken. Why? Why would a burglar take so much care and time?

While detectives searched for clues in the apartment's interior, other investigators moved from the actual crime scene building and the questioning of the widow's neighbors to a canvass of the area in a wide search for anyone who might have seen anything. All persons encountered by detectives were questioned extensively and asked if they had seen anything unusual at all the night before. This canvass did not yield much and Detective Sgt. Thomas Mangan explained why. "She was an elderly woman and she didn't have many friends. She stayed inside of her apartment most of the time, and that is making the investigation difficult."

One investigator did record a tidbit of information which at the time seemed insignificant. A man who had been out walking his dog in the complex the night before told the investigator that he saw a yellow sports car in the area. He further revealed that he saw two black males park the car and walk from it at approximately 9:30 p.m. This could mean nothing, but to the detective who realized any seemingly insignificant observation might contribute to the solution of a case, the comment was recorded with the man's name and address.

The medical examiner arrived on the scene at 11:30 and Mildred Cotter was officially pronounced dead. The widow's corpse was removed in a black body bag, after a preliminary examination, to be taken to the medical examiner's office for a post-mortem. Hopefully, the coroner would be able to ascertain incriminating and revealing facts from the body itself. Actually, the coroner had already made certain observations at the scene which enabled him to determine the manner of death as strangulation. There were abrasions, bruises and fingernail marks on the throat of the victim. He also noted petechial hemorrhages or tiny blood clots in the mucous membrane lining the inner surface of the eyelids. There was also evidence of trauma to the tongue. Victims of asphyxiation will often bite their tongue. All of these observations are presumptive evidence of strangulation and while only the autopsy can finalize these assumptions, these findings do give investigators a head start in their murder investigation.

It was later established that besides having every rib in her body broken, Mrs. Cotter suffered severe facial contusions. It also appeared that she had been manually strangled, since half-crescent moons from her killers' nails had left embedded marks in her skin. Obvious finger ligature marks around the victim's neck convinced the coroner that she had been strangled by hand, but that was not the cause of death. A deep indentation at the back of the widow's neck did not come from any pair of hands. It remained to be seen what this object was. The coroner was certain that this latter object had been the cause of death. Mildred Cotter had been fatally garroted with no sexual abuse indicated, even though she was found naked from the waist down.

Investigators intensified their energies in the interrogation of all persons in any way connected with either Mildred Cotter or Mary Bowen in an attempt to uncover a lead. Many fruitless hours were spent involved at the grueling and oftentime dead-end task. Often in the questioning procedure, the person being interrogated will mention the name of a second party, who when duly questioned will mention the name of a third party. All these names, these interconnections, these possible leads must be checked out. Such was the case here.

Probers spoke to friends of Mary Bowen and ultimately hit upon her friend from the yacht club, Sylvia Gerard, who hesitatingly revealed that Mary Bowen had a "nurse friend" by the name of Veronica Pittman. Miss Pittman was similarly questioned and two bits of information were elicited: Ms. Pittman drove a yellow Horizon and Ms. Pittman had a boyfriend — a black, unemployed mechanic by the name of Andre Cartier. Twenty-five-year-old Cartier was likewise brought in for questioning, but no arrests were yet to be made.

Mary Bowen had spoken freely to all investigators involved in the case. She was most helpful to them. She patiently sat with probers and answered questions again and again, explained, reexplained, retold . . . that is until one investigator began to go through Mildred Cotter's papers. He found first, and most importantly, that Mary Bowen was the sole executor to Mildred Cotter's estate. Miss Bowen had been so thorough, so precise, how had she missed telling the investigators so vital a piece of information? Mary Bowen's comments to police cooled off after the discovery of the will and then abruptly ceased when detectives found that large amounts of money, between five and six thousand dollars, had been withdrawn from Mrs. Cotter's account within a short period of time. It was then that Mary Bowen refused any further contact with the police and enlisted an attorney. Found among these various papers were cancelled checks. On close examination it was discerned that checks made out to Mary Bowen for $325, her weekly wage, and signed by Mildred Cotter, had mysteriously become $1,325. The bodies of the checks, it was later found, were made out by Bowen while signed by Cotter.

The crime lab people were busy, in the meantime, checking and analyzing all prints found at the widow's apartment. The most common and practical method of developing prints is through dusting. Most prints at the crime scene in Port Washington were matched to being either those of Mildred Cotter or Mary Bowen. One print, though, a latent thumbprint, was found on a bank withdrawal slip among a mess of overturned papers from the bedside table. This thumbprint did not match those of Cotter or Bowen. These latent prints occur from natural skin secretions such as perspiration. When grease or dirt is mixed with the natural skin secretions, a stable print may be deposited on the surface. Such was the case here; this print was not visible, but dusting brought it out. Now the problem was to match the print with the person it belonged to.

It was soon realized by detectives that this thumbprint belonged to Andre Cartier, who had been brought in ear-

HIT MEN

lier for questioning. Cartier was promptly located and brought in. His Miranda rights were read to him. Confronted with the found print, Andre Cartier did what most frightened murderers do—he waived his rights and spilled the beans, all of them—and implicated his buddy, Roger Powell, as a partner in the murder.

Sometime in September of 1981, Mildred Cotter caught onto the kited checks that had come from the bank, Cartier explained. Detectives theorized that Mary Bowen, in writing out the body of her own paycheck, had left spaces in between the written numbers. This is how she made "three-hundred-twenty-five" into "thirteen-hundred-twenty-five:" a space was left between the 'h' and the 'r' of the three hundred, an 'i' was inserted in this space, then a space was left between the second 'r' and the 'ee,' a 't' was inserted in this space with an 'n' following the double 'e,' making the word "thirteen" instead of three. Eighty-two-year-old Mildred Cotter's eyes were not what they once were and she probably thought these spaces an idiosyncrasy in her employee's writing. Since Mildred did not expect any wrongdoing, she signed the checks, spaces and all, in good faith. Little did the widow know that immediately after her signature was affixed to these checks her employee was busy at work stealing and becoming a thousand dollars richer by the week.

When Cotter realized what was actually happening with her rapidly depleting bank account, she must have threatened Bowen with her expulsion from the will. One detective sergeant of the Nassau County Police said that Mrs. Cotter had been "in the process of getting ready to fire" Ms. Bowen at the time of the killing. Police said they believed Cotter confronted Bowen about thefts from her savings accounts. "Mrs. Cotter was suspicious of the maid's activity," the sergeant went onto say. He explained that an unknown amount of money was missing from the accounts and the balances in the various account passbooks totaled more than $5,000.

The confrontation between the widow and Ms. Bowen, he explained, prompted the health-care aide to seek the employ of two hired killers, whom she met through a relative. A murder contract was arranged after many clandestine meetings between Mary Bowen, Andre Cartier and 28-year-old Roger Powell. Only now Miss Bowen was the employer and her two employees would earn $1,000 each for their night's work, which entailed the murder of the invalid widow. The killers achieved entry through the front door of the apartment with aid of Bowen's key. A 9:30 p.m. reconnaissance mission explained the eyewitness statement of seeing two black men in a yellow car in the garden apartment complex at around this time. Cartier's girlfriend, Veronica Pittman, later admitted to lending her boyfriend her yellow car that night. Cartier and Powell themselves admitted to police that they went to the Soundview Gardens apartments at 9:30 that night to "check out the situation" before returning at 12:30 to commit the dastardly deed.

It also was disclosed during one of these interrogations that the reason every rib bone was broken in Cotter's body was because Andre Cartier, after taking some karate courses, was convinced that he could produce an irregular heartbeat—which would result in death—if the victim was punched in the chest in the correct manner. Cartier had even gone so far as to boast to his friends that he could do this. It was likewise discovered that the actual murder weapon was the white sports sock.

But Cartier and Powell were only on a mission of murder. It was the job of Mary Bowen on October 19, 1981, to ransack the apartment prior to her phoning the police at 9:30 a.m. Investigators' "senses" were right—what seemed to be a burglary was in fact only a poor facade, staged by an inexperienced and greedy inheritor-to-be, who didn't want to break or destroy her possessions of bequest. Hence, the unmarred vase and tea tray and the neatness of her attempt. In Mary Bowen's feeble endeavor to make murder seem motivated by burglary, she had, in fact, alerted the very instincts of the investigators. It was also Mary Bowen who had removed the clothing, from the waist down from her employer's corpse, in another attempt to sidetrack the detectives. It was she, again, who had bent the bedroom window outwards, providing a false motive of entry. And it is she, Mary Bowen, who may still inherit the money bequeathed to her . . .

On February 23, 1983, at the Nassau County Courthouse, the sobs of Mary Bowen rose to wails and drowned out the voice of the jury foreman as he began to read the list of guilty findings. The jury had deliberated ten hours and found Mary Bowen guilty of two counts of second-degree murder and three other felony charges. On March 29, 1983, the weeping nurses aide was sentenced to 25 years to life for setting up the murder of her elderly patient in what the presiding judge called "a cruel and sadistic act." The judge gave her the maximum sentence on each of her charges: 25 years to life for the murder charge, two point three to seven years for grand larceny, eight point three to 25 years for conspiracy and five to 15 for burglary. The sentences, to be served concurrently, mean Mary Bowen must serve at least 25 years before being eligible for parole, authorities said. The judge told her that hers was a "heartless scheme" against someone who had trusted her. Andre Cartier and Roger Powell received sentences similar to Miss Bowen.

Ironically, Mary Bowen may still get the money, which totals some $38,000. Prosecutor Ed McCarty told the judge and jury, "This callous woman who opened the door for her hired killers had the nerve to tell a social worker this week she intends to get the money."

Bowen claims she is entitled to the money because it was in a "Totem Trust"—a form of joint bank account and takes the form of a bequest, said A.D.A. McCarty.

Miss Bowen said the widow told her she'd get the entire estate "if anything happens to me."

The law prohibits profitting from a murder but McCarty admitted that Bowen could get the money if the Nassau Surrogate Court rules the "bequest" was in effect before the murder.

The money is now in the hands of the Surrogate Court where there is a claim on it from a cousin of Mildred Cotter, but Bowen's lawyer will fight in her name for this money in the same forum.

EDITOR'S NOTE:
Sylvia Gerard and Veronica Pittman are not the real names of the persons so named in the foregoing story. Fictitious names have been used because there is no reason for public interest in the identities of these persons.

APPENDIX

"Dial 'H' for Hit Man!" *Master Detective*. June, 1991.

"Femme Fatale and Her Band of Killers" *Front Page Detective*. January, 1990.

"10-G Hit on Pam!" *Front Page Detective*. April, 1993.

"Kill All Three and Torch the House!" *Official Detective*. October, 1992.

"Baby-Faced Angel Was a Cold-Blooded Killer!" *Official Detective*. January, 1994.

"Sent her Stud to Snuff her Ex!" *Master Detective*. February, 1993.

"Murder-for-Hire Goes Haywire: 4 Die in Vain!" *Front Page Detective*. April, 1994.

"The Hit Man Struck at 12 O'clock High" *Front Page Detective*. March, 1981.

"Dial-A-Death Slay Schemes!" *Front Page Detective*. February, 1986.

"A Tangled Web of Contract Murder!" *Front Page Detective*. September, 1989.

"Vixen's Quick-Kill Scheme" *Front Page Detective*. March, 1989.

" 'Hit Contract' Climaxed the Family Tragedy!" *Master Detective*. January, 1990.

"She Tried to Kill for Her Kid!" *True Detective*. March, 1992.

"Evil 'Puppet Master' Made the Gardener Do His Killing!" *True Detective*. August, 1993.

"A Love Triangle Triggered the Freeloader's Lethal Scheme!" *Inside Detective*. October, 1984.

"The Victim Refused to Die!" *True Detective*. January, 1991.

"Grisly Case of the 'Gorilla' Hit Man" *Master Detective*. March, 1985.

"California's Bizarre Web of 4-Way Lethal Sexcapade" *True Detective*. April, 1994.

"A Lawsuit Got Him Shot in the Face!" *Official Detective*. April, 1993.

"The Coke Dealer's Brutal Hit Men" *Front Page Detective*. August, 1990.

"Have Gun, Will Murder!" *Inside Detective*. July, 1992.

"Gangster's Moll Urged Hit Man to Kill" *Official Detective*. December, 1992.

"Gay Lovers' Lethal Plot Against Sue Ellen!" *Official Detective*. June, 1993.

"Lethal Couple . . . 3 Knives . . . 1 Cold Corpse!" *Official Detective*. June, 1991.

"Where There's a Will, There's a Murder!" *Front Page Detective*. December, 1983.

**GOOD VERSUS EVIL. HEROES TRAPPING MONSTERS.
THIS ISN'T FANTASY. IT'S LIFE.
CAPTURE A PINNACLE TRUE CRIME TODAY.**

JEFFREY DAHMER (661, $4.99)
By Dr. Joel Norris
Everyone knows Dahmer's name, but how many of us know the man behind the headlines? Renowned psychologist Dr. Joel Norris sheds light on the dark forces that compelled Dahmer to butcher and consume the men he loved. Based on unpublished facts about the killer's lifestyle and background, it features extensive interviews with his friends and ex-lovers. Readers may never fully understand Dahmer's behavior or find him sympathetic, but Norris's book outlines how a seemingly normal man can degenerate and lash out while silently passing among us.

ARTHUR SHAWCROSS: THE GENESEE RIVER KILLER (578, $4.99)
By Dr. Joel Norris
Despite his parole officer's warnings, child killer Arthur Shawcross was released from prison early. He headed to Rochester, New York, to begin his next chapter. Shawcross's second chance at life spelled death for eleven women. He conducted a horrible slaying spree, reminiscent of Jack The Ripper, that targeted prostitutes and denizens of Rochester's red light district. Strangling them in remote wooded areas, his insane bloodlust drove him to butcher their naked bodies and to devour parts of their flesh before disposing of them. Ironically, police arrested him by luck when he was observed casually eating his lunch while the nude corpse of his latest victim floated past him in the Genesee River.

CHOP SHOP (693, $4.99)
By Kathy Braidhill
Generations of mourners brought their "loved ones" to Lamb Funeral Home. They trusted the sincere staff, appreciated the sympathetic directors, and knew without question that their relations were in capable hands. They were wrong. Grotesque mutilations and sadistic practices flourished at Lamb's. Like a ghoulish twist on a vampire novel, here the living merrily preyed upon the dead. Fingers were severed to claim expensive rings; teeth were forcefully pulled out for the ounces of gold filling; and organs were fiercely removed to be sold to research labs. The crematorium fires blazed fiendishly around the clock as multiple bodies were stuffed into the chambers for mass burnings. It was a scenario worthy of the Holocaust. *Chop Shop* recounts how unspeakable acts of horror were perpetrated against the ultimate victims: dead men who can tell no tales. Thankfully, Kathy Braidhill broke this case and gave a voice to these victims.

SEX, MONEY AND MURDER IN DAYTONA BEACH (555, $4.99)
By Lee Butcher
Florida's society set always makes a splash in the papers: debutante balls, charity auctions, MURDER. Beautiful heiress Lisa Paspalakis surprised her wealthy family by marrying for love. She wed Kosta Fotopoulos, a waiter, after a whirlwind courtship. This fairytale union was ripe with villains and greed. Fotopoulos and his mistress had already laid plans for Lisa's cold-blooded demise. This is an explosive indictment of greed, decadence, and amorality.

Available wherever paperbacks are sold, or order direct from the Publisher. Send cover price plus 50¢ per copy for mailing and handling to Penguin USA, P.O. Box 999, c/o Dept. 17109, Bergenfield, NJ 07621. Residents of New York and Tennessee must include sales tax. DO NOT SEND CASH.

SINS AND SCANDALS!
GO BEHIND THE SCENES WITH PINNACLE

JULIA: THE UNTOLD STORY OF AMERICA'S
PRETTY WOMAN (898, $4.99)
by Eileen Joyce

She lit up the screen in STEEL MAGNOLIAS and PRETTY WOMAN. She's been paired with scores of stunning leading men. And now, here's an explosive unauthorized biography of Julia Roberts that tells all. Read about Julia's recent surprise marriage to Lyle Lovitt—Her controversial two-year disappearance—Her big comeback that has Tinseltown talking—and much, much more!

SEAN CONNERY: FROM 007 TO
HOLLYWOOD ICON (742, $4.50)
by Andrew Rule

After nearly thirty years—and countless films—Sean Connery is still one of the most irresistible and bankable stars in Hollywood. Now, for the first time, go behind the scenes to meet the man behind the suave 007 myth. From his beginnings in a Scotland slum to international stardom, take an intimate look at this most fascinating and exciting superstar.

HOWARD STERN: BIG MOUTH (796, $4.99)
by Jeff Menell

Brilliant, stupid, sexist, racist, obscene, hilarious—and just plain gross! Howard Stern is the man you love to hate. Now you can find out the real story behind morning radio's number one bad boy!

THE "I HATE BRENDA" BOOK (797, $4.50)
By Michael Carr & Darby

From the editors of the official "I HATE BRENDA" newsletter comes everything you ever wanted to know about Shannen Doherty. Here's the dirt on a young woman who seems to be careening through the heady galaxy of Hollywood, a burning asteroid spinning "out of control!"

THE RICHEST GIRL IN THE WORLD (792, $4.99)
by Stephanie Mansfield

At the age of thirteen, Doris Duke inherited a $100 million tobacco fortune. By the time she was thirty, Doris Duke had lavished millions on her lovers and husbands. An eccentric who thumbed her nose at society, Duke's circle of friends included Jackie Onassis, Macolm Forbes, Truman Capote, Andy Warhol and Imelda Marcos. But all the money in the world couldn't buy the love that she searched for!

Available wherever paperbacks are sold, or order direct from the Publisher. Send cover price plus 50¢ per copy for mailing and handling to Penguin USA, P.O. Box 999, c/o Dept. 17109, Bergenfield, NJ 07621. Residents of New York and Tennessee must include sales tax. DO NOT SEND CASH.

INFORMATIVE—
COMPELLING—
SCINTILLATING—
NON-FICTION FROM PINNACLE TELLS THE TRUTH!

BORN TOO SOON (751, $4.50)
by Elizabeth Mehren
This is the poignant story of Elizabeth's daughter Emily's premature birth. As the parents of one of the 275,000 babies born prematurely each year in this country, she and her husband were plunged into the world of the Neonatal Intensive Care unit. With stunning candor, Elizabeth Mehren relates her gripping story of unshakable faith and hope—and of courage that comes in tiny little packages.

THE PROSTATE PROBLEM (745, $4.50)
by Chet Cunningham
An essential, easy-to-use guide to the treatment and prevention of the illness that's in the headlines. This book explains in clear, practical terms all the facts. Complete with a glossary of medical terms, and a comprehensive list of health organizations and support groups, this illustrated handbook will help men combat prostate disorder and lead longer, healthier lives.

THE ACADEMY AWARDS HANDBOOK (887, $4.50)
An interesting and easy-to-use guide for movie fans everywhere, the book features a year-to-year listing of all the Oscar nominations in every category, all the winners, an expert analysis of who wins and why, a complete index to get information quickly, and even a 99% foolproof method to pick this year's winners!

WHAT WAS HOT (894, $4.50)
by Julian Biddle
Journey through 40 years of the trends and fads, famous and infamous figures, and momentous milestones in American history. From hoola hoops to rap music, greasers to yuppies, Elvis to Madonna—it's all here, trivia for all ages. An entertaining and evocative overview of the milestones in America from the 1950's to the 1990's!

Available wherever paperbacks are sold, or order direct from the Publisher. Send cover price plus 50¢ per copy for mailing and handling to Penguin USA, P.O. Box 999, c/o Dept. 17109, Bergenfield, NJ 07621. Residents of New York and Tennessee must include sales tax. DO NOT SEND CASH.

MAKE THE CONNECTION

WITH

Z-TALK
Online

Come talk to your favorite authors and get the inside scoop on everything that's going on in the world of publishing, from the only online service that's designed exclusively for the publishing industry.

With Z-Talk Online Information Service, the most innovative and exciting computer bulletin board around, you can:

- ✓ CHAT "LIVE" WITH AUTHORS, FELLOW READERS, AND OTHER MEMBERS OF THE PUBLISHING COMMUNITY.
- ✓ FIND OUT ABOUT UPCOMING TITLES BEFORE THEY'RE RELEASED.
- ✓ DOWNLOAD THOUSANDS OF FILES AND GAMES.
- ✓ READ REVIEWS OF TITLES.
- ✓ HAVE UNLIMITED USE OF E-MAIL.
- ✓ POST MESSAGES ON OUR DOZENS OF TOPIC BOARDS.

All it takes is a computer and a modem to get online with Z-Talk. Set your modem to 8/N/1, and dial 212-935-0270. If you need help, call the System Operator, at 212-407-1533. There's a two week free trial period. After that, annual membership is only $ 60.00.

See you online!

KENSINGTON PUBLISHING CORP.